VICTORY FIGHTERS:

THE VETERANS' STORY

Winning the Battle for Supremacy in the Skies
Over Western Europe, 1941-1945

STEPHEN DARLOW

GRUB STREET · LONDON

Published by
Grub Street
4 Rainham Close
London
SW11 6SS

British Library Cataloguing in Publication Data
Darlow, Stephen
Victory fighters: the veterans' story: winning the battle for supremacy in the skies over Western Europe, 1941-1945
1. World War, 1939-1945 – Aerial operations, British
2. World War, 1939-1945 – Personal narratives, British
I. Title
940.5′449′41′0922

ISBN 1 904943 11 X

Typeset by Pearl Graphics, Hemel Hempstead

Printed and bound in Great Britain by
Biddles Ltd, King's Lynn

Editor's note: To the best of our ability, all direct extracts from combat reports, letters, diaries, etc., have been reproduced verbatim in the style written at the time.

CONTENTS

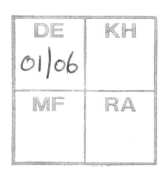

ACKNOWLEDGEMENTS

I would like to extend my appreciation to the following people and institutions for their assistance researching this book.

Marionne Diggles and Jean Hammond of the Toowoomba & Darling Downs Family History Soc. Inc., Peter Maloney, RCAF Museum and Jodi Ann Eskrit, Ann Kidner, James McPartlin, Nina Burls and RAF Museum Hendon, Alan East, Christopher Shores, David Ross, Richard Smith, Mary Stewart, Ian Brodie (New Zealand Fighter Pilots Museum), Stephen Walton and Lucy Farrow (IWM), Carolyn Reaney, Norman Fendall, Michael Kelsey, Jenny Windle, Alison Mackenzie, Rob and Heather Burpee, Chris Bartle, Arthur Collyns, Dave Russell-Smith, Gaye Jameson, Vicky Mitchell, Mary McIntosh, Ed Stevens, John Stocker, Roddy MacGregor, Pip Stowell, Bob Cossey, D. P. F. McCaig, Peter Croft, T. A. J. Stocker, John Annals, Ken Reeves, Grace Seymour, Barbara O'Shannessy, Matthew O'Sullivan, Mark Peapell, Jenny Coffey, Norman Feltwell, Chris Thomas, Jerry Brewer, Countess I. G. Du Monceau de Bergendal, Steve Fraser, Rob Thornley, Tom Jones, and Oliver Clutton-Brock.

Of course, my thanks again to John Davies, Louise Stanley and Luke Norsworthy at Grub Street, for backing the project. I would also particularly like to thank James Jameson for helping with his father's story, Ilona and Peter Alloway for their considerable efforts helping to put together Basil Collyns' story, and Helen Crassweller and Steve Baker for making their father, Wing Commander Reg Baker's, papers available.

I especially extend my gratitude to all the veteran airmen, who were willing to share their stories and put up with all my questions. I am giving their squadrons as at D-Day. *3 Squadron:* Bob Cole DFC, Robert Barcklay DFC, Ron Pottinger; *66 Squadron:* Andrew Deytrikh; *74 Squadron:* John Dalzell, Stephen Brian Harris; *80 Squadron:* Hugh Ross; *137 Squadron:* John Colton, Sam Prince; *151 Squadron:* George Kelsey DFC; *193 Squadron:* Rod Davidge; *197 Squadron:* Derek Lovell, Ken Trott, Derek Tapson and Jimmy Kyle DFM; *219 Squadron:* Jack Meadows DFC AFC AE; *257 Squadron:* Jerry Eaton DFC, Brian Spragg DFC; *263 Squadron:* George Wood; *310 Squadron:* Frank Mares DFM; *312 Squadron:* Tony Liskutin DFC AFC; *403 Squadron:* Hart Finley DFC, Stephen Butte DFC, Andy Mackenzie DFC; *488 Squadron:* A. Norman Crookes DFC and 2 Bars, US DFC; *609 Squadron:* James Stewart DFC, James Earnshaw.

INTRODUCTION

This book tells the story of the RAF fighter pilot experience, primarily through the eyes of six pilots and one navigator/radar operator, from the end of the Battle of Britain through to the final victory for the Allies in Europe. It also includes the experiences of other pilots who took part in the battles and gives their first-hand accounts of the nature of operations. Their actions are set against the background of command decisions, made at the highest levels. The featured airmen's operational careers are outlined in detail, and collectively they cover the entire fighter pilot experience of the struggle in the skies over Western Europe, the night battles over England during the Blitz, the offensive Rhubarbs and Circuses, the night patrols defending against Luftwaffe intruders, the anti-shipping operations, the preparations for and support to the invasion of Normandy, the support to the advancing Allied armies, operation Market Garden, the advance to and crossing of the Rhine, through to the end of the war against Nazism. The featured airmen, flying a whole variety of aircraft – Sunderlands, Mustangs, Tempests, Typhoons, Spitfires, Hurricanes, Whirlwinds and Mosquitoes – take part in ferocious aerial combat, ground attacks, shipping strikes and dive-bombing, and have to deal with fatigue, injury and the loss of fellow pilots. But what these men did through their actions was contribute to the achievement of air superiority over Western Europe in time for the Normandy campaign, and they would reap the reward of this advantage when supporting the land forces in their subsequent struggles. Supreme Commander Dwight Eisenhower would note in the conclusion to his report on action from D-Day to VE-Day: 'The overwhelming Allied superiority in the air was indeed essential to our victory. It at once undermined the basis of the enemy's strength and enabled us to prepare and execute our ground operations in complete security.' In the following pages, the RAF's role in winning victory from the air is charted.

In writing the book I have had the pleasure of meeting and speaking to a number of veteran airmen and they have shared their stories willingly. What impressed me most was that they look back at those times with one particular fond memory – the camaraderie they shared with their fellow men. Of course many of their colleagues would lose their lives, and my book is dedicated to those lost friends in the hope that it will help keep their memory alive.

PROLOGUE

At the beginning of September 1939 Ernest Reginald Baker, second pilot on a Coastal Command 210 Squadron Short Sunderland flying boat, based at Pembroke Dock, Pembrokeshire, South Wales, was carrying out his squadron duties with his crew on escort duty to shipping.

> *Reg Baker:* I had been in the RAF 19 months and was in fact arriving at the stage where I could be considered a reasonably useful flying boat second pilot. A training of 19 months by today's standards may seem long, but in those days after that training one was considered capable of making tea, maintaining the stock of toilet paper, seeing the boat was left clean and in fact doing the countless odd jobs a cabin boy is required to do.

But the cabin boy was about to embark upon a journey that would mature him very quickly. On a starlit morning early in September Reg's pilot taxied their Sunderland flying boat L2165 along the haven, preparing for a take-off in the dark.

> We had received our orders from the operations room, stumbled our way down to the pier and been carried by means of the inevitably greasy dinghy to '65. The crew were all ready on board, the Sunderland was a blaze of light and everything was under control as we climbed on. The two outboard engines were doped and we were ready to start up. The starboard outer lurched into life, then the port outer.
>
> 'Let her go,' shouted Alan. Murphy slipped the buoy and we were away. The two inboard engines were doped and I started them. We taxied out into the channel and proceeded down the haven. As we approached the flare path Alan ran up the engines, which were OK. Once on the flare path the control office gave us a green and we were ready to go. I wound the flaps out one third, checked that the crew were all set, told Alan and stood by to put in the overrides. Alan checked his trimming tabs, grinned, said 'Here we go' and opened up the four engines. At full throttle we passed No.1 flare. I put in the override and at No.2 flare we left the water, smoothly and apparently without effort. We circled the twinkling lights below, picked up St Ann's Head lighthouse and set off on a course of 250 degrees for our convoy.
>
> Dawn found us five hundred miles out to sea, alone in a sky of wispy cloud. Ahead of us about ten miles we could see the straggling convoy, eight ships in a loosely knitted mass; looking rather like toys on crumpled paper as they poured out black smoke and wallowed in the long Atlantic rollers. We spent several uneventful hours looking after these 'children', rather like an indulgent mother, and then set course for base. At 1600 hours we made our landfall and thirty minutes later we came gliding in. As usual we alighted beautifully, finished our run and taxied up to a buoy. I switched off and turned to Alan.
>
> 'There seems to be a hell of a lot of activity here.'

Alan looked out and saw people scurrying backward and forward from the pier; airmen on the pier with machine guns and in fact more activity than we had seen before. By this time a dinghy had come alongside and we climbed in. Alan grinned at the dinghy driver and said, 'Why all the flap?'

The dinghy driver looked at us in blank amazement. 'Flap?! Blimey there's a war on. We declared war on Germany at 11 o'clock this morning.'

It was 3 September 1939.

Reg spent the early years of his life growing up in Doncaster, going to school at Hyde Park and then Doncaster Grammar. He then took a teaching certificate at Chester Training College, and whilst there (unbeknownst to his parents) tried out and fell in love with flying. Reg went on to teach, mainly physical training, at Park Junior Mixed School, Wheatley. His main sporting love was cricket, and he played for Doncaster's first XI.

In December 1937 Reg attempted a career change but was frustrated, just failing to get into the Hendon Police College. Nevertheless, undaunted, and still seeking service life, he obtained a commission with the RAF, becoming an acting pilot officer on 7 May 1938. Reg would describe his life on the squadron prior to the war as:

> A simple life, not exhausting either physically or mentally and yet strangely satisfying. We were not unhappy in our lot, we had all felt for some time that war was at hand, we knew it had to be if the things we believed in were to be preserved. We also knew that when the war started it was about 90 to 1 against our being alive after the first six months. Still, it was our job, and if we managed to keep going until people shook themselves, and trained chaps to take our places, then it was a good show. At the back of our minds too we had a suspicion, or hope if you like, that it was probably 90 to 1 against most chaps but not us, we should be alright.

When he returned to base on that fateful day following his rather ordinary convoy patrol, he knew he quickly had to come to terms with the situation he, his crew and his squadron were in.

> My thoughts were confused but one thing stood out. We had been flying for 5 hours at war with Germany, our only lethal weapon was a Verey pistol and we hadn't been warned. I hoped that it wasn't a portent for the future.
>
> The mess that night was chaotic, everyone stood around clutching pints of beer and taking excitedly. The general feeling was one of relief, at last we knew exactly where we stood. Bets were laid as to how long the war would last, one optimist said it would be over by Xmas. Our CO looked at him and said dryly, 'I seem to remember hearing that said in the last war.'

It wasn't long before Reg began to experience at first hand the harsh realities of war. His first three operations since the start of hostilities involved contact with U-boats, and attacks were made, but there were no visible signs of a success. On the last operation a friendly ship had been sunk by a U-boat and Reg's crew were able to direct a Dutch tanker to the area and the lifeboat containing the survivors. One day at the end of September, Reg and his pilot remained on shore and on station whilst the rest of their normal crew were on an operation in their aircraft, '65. That evening they went to the pub and as Reg's normal crew wasn't due back until midnight he went to bed. The next morning at breakfast Reg noticed a colleague . . .

> looking longer in the face than usual. I ruffled his head and said,
>
> 'Cheer up Ivor, only the good die young.'
>
> He looked at me.
>
> 'What the hell is there to cheer up about,' he answered. '65 crashed last night. Everybody was written off.'
>
> I couldn't believe it . . . all the old crew gone. I sorted out the whole story as far as it could be done. By midnight, when they were due back, the weather was somewhat hazy. W/T fixes had been sent out and 65 had actually flown over the station without seeing it. Ivor was on the flare path and at last he saw 65 coming in, flying over the cliff towards Angle Bay when suddenly her engines spluttered and stopped. She hit the edge of the cliff, crashed into the haven and went down like a stone.

About two weeks later the bodies of the crew began to be washed up and there were 'funerals day after day'.

> Murphy was the last to come up. He lay there on the bare rock, looking more muscular than he had ever done alive; his chest, which was mottled and greeny blue, seemed to be fully expanded, but his face and hands were eaten away. I thought of the fish I had eaten for lunch, turned away and was quietly sick. We rolled the body into a blanket, carried it down to the power boat and with an ensign at half mast headed for the station. Rob and I sat at the stern smoking; the body was lashed forward. My thoughts were chaotic, was this pitiful corpse all that was left of our fitter? What had happened to turn a living man who loved and thought into this? I knew the physical explanation, but was that the end? Were we all just like mechanical toys, capable of running for so long, and then becoming cold and empty? I couldn't quite feel that our life was an end in itself; probably it was wishful thinking. We said little to each other, Rob and I, on that ride home. What could we say, we were in the presence of something which was beyond our understanding?

Reg went to the pub for supper, his spirits low, and later on walked back to camp.

> I passed airmen and soldiers arm in arm with their girlfriends, completely wrapped up in each other. In my mind I said, 'Of course they don't know about my crew, or else they would be bewildered like me.'
>
> But I knew that I was wrong. A fragment of poetry came into my mind and I found myself repeating unconsciously,
>
> 'What is life if full of care
> We have no time to stand and stare.'
>
> To stare. God how those sightless eyes had stared into the heavens. Had they stared in vain? I didn't know.

Reg also had the task of meeting his former crew mate's mother and sister when they came to the station to mourn the loss of their loved one.

> Murphy's mother was slightly built, grey-haired, dressed in black, her fingers curling and uncurling spasmodically. Her face was swollen with crying and her eyes had the dazed hurt look of an animal that had suddenly been cuffed without understanding why. I tried to say that Murphy and I had been in the same crew, but I couldn't. I knew that nothing I could say or do would get through that overwhelming sorrow. My eyes will never forget the dry-eyed sorrow of Murphy's sister and my ears can never banish the sobbing of his mother and the bitterly repeated, 'He was such a good boy.'
>
> That night I went to bed very drunk.

For Christmas 1939 Reg Baker returned to his home in Doncaster, to spend it with his parents. Unsurprisingly they were concerned about the welfare of their son.

> I tried to answer their questions about the war although I probably knew less than they did. Dad startled me by saying, 'How long is it going to last Reg?'
>
> I pondered. Three months had gone and we had done nothing. The last one took four years and the world hadn't been too well developed for dealing out death and destruction.
>
> 'Four and a half years,' I answered. 'Certainly not less.' Mother turned her head away and Dad sighed, 'God as long as that.'
>
> I echoed him, 'Yes as long as that.'

CHAPTER 1

OVER TO THE OFFENSIVE

On 13 May 1940, British Prime Minister Winston Churchill made clear to his parliamentary colleagues, the whole nation, and indeed the British Empire, the task that lay ahead in opposing the Nazi forces, who had in the preceding months torn apart Poland, occupied Denmark and Norway, were overrunning Holland and Belgium, and would soon subjugate France.

> I have nothing to offer but blood, toil, tears and sweat. We have before us an ordeal of the most grievous kind. We have before us many, many long months of struggle and of suffering. You ask, what is our policy? I will say: it is to wage war, by sea, land, and air, with all our might and with all the strength that God can give us: to wage war against a monstrous tyranny, never surpassed in the dark, lamentable catalogue of human crime. That is our policy. You ask, what is our aim? I can answer in one word: it is victory, victory at all costs, victory in spite of all terror, victory, however long and hard the road may be; for without victory, there is no survival. Let that be realized; no survival for the British Empire; no survival for all that the British Empire has stood for, no survival for the urge and impulse of the ages, that mankind will move forward towards its goal. But I take up my task with buoyancy and hope. I feel sure that our cause will not be suffered to fail among men. At this time I feel entitled to claim the aid of all, and I say, come then, let us go forward together with our united strength.

Many young men from all over the world would answer this call.

One such was Basil Collyns who was born in Greymouth, New Zealand on 24 February 1913. Basil grew to be a keen sportsman, excelling at athletics, rugby and fives, and was house prefect in his final year at Nelson College. From here he attended Lincoln Agricultural College for two years, before taking up sheep farming. However Basil had other ambitions and there was obviously a passion for flying in the Collyns' family. Basil's elder brother, Eric, had entered the air force through Cranwell, but terrible news was to reach Basil and his family in 1935, when Eric was killed in an air accident whilst stationed with British Forces in Aden, Egypt. Basil was undaunted, he was determined to be in the air force. Early in 1939 he applied for a short service commission with the Royal New Zealand Air Force but was unsuccessful. Nevertheless he still pursued his ambition, joining the Civil Reserve of pilots and flying at the Marlborough Aero Club. He obtained his flying licence and on 19 November was called up for full-time service, attending Ground Training School at Weraroa. On 20 December 1939 he began his flying training at No.1 EFTS (Elementary Flying Training School) Taieri, initially flying the DH82 Tiger Moth. In Basil's RAF service logbook, the stages of his instruction, which thousands of similar young aspiring RAF pilots would become familiar with, are listed.

Sequence of Instruction

1. Taxying and use of brakes
2. Straight and level flying
3. Stalling, climbing and gliding
4. Medium turns, with and without engine
5. Taking off into wind
6. Approaches and landings
7. Action in event of fire
8. Spinning
9. Solo
10. Side slipping
11. Low flying
12. Steep turns, with and without engine
13. Climbing turns
14. Forced landings
15. Landing with engine
16. Instrument flying
17. Taking off and landing across wind
18. Aerobatics
19. Air navigation
20. Height test
21. Cross country test
22. Formation flying
23. Night flying

On 8 February 1940 Basil transferred to No.2 EFTS New Plymouth to continue his instruction and introduction to a new aircraft, the DH60 Gipsy Moth. On 2 March 1940 he carried out his last flight there; 25 minutes practising steep turns, his logbook now recording 49.10 hours of dual flying and 26.10 hours solo. But before Basil's training continued there was one further development in his life.

Ann Churchward was born in Blenheim New Zealand in 1915, her mother being a descendant of the early settlers, who had waded ashore at New Plymouth. She first met Basil on one of his holidays from agricultural college; later they would meet on and off, destined to become a couple.

> He was very good looking, about 6 feet, a good athlete, good swimmer, great runner. He had a good sense of humour and he definitely became a party type. He liked the girls, quite a flirt he could be, but nothing ever very serious.
>
> We all knew there was probably a war coming. Basil was determined to be in the air force. We were married on 5 March 1940, while he was in the middle of his air force training, he had to get special permission. Basil was then transferred to the local big air station near Blenheim, Woodbourne, where they were training pilots as fast as they could.

It was 14 March when Basil's training resumed at No.2 FTS (Flying Training School) Woodbourne, flying the Vickers Vincent, Vildebeeste and the Moth Minor, and over the next two and a half months he would raise his dual hours to 70.25 hours and solo to 69.05 hours. On 31 May 1940 the Chief Flying Instructor at No.2 FTS would write in Basil's logbook, 'Qualified to wear the Flying Badge… with effect from 20/5/40.'

Throughout June there was further training all on the V.Vincent, e.g., drogue target photography, high level bombing, Lewis gun air to ground, application bombing 10,000 feet, air to ground (firing), air to air (firing). At the end of June Basil completed his training at FTS. His 'Summary of Flying and Assessments for Year Commencing August 1939' detailed his progress to date, pulling no punches.

S. E. [single-engined] Aircraft			**M.E. [multi-engined] Aircraft**		**Total**	**Grand Total**
	Day	Night	Day	Night		
Dual	52.20		4.15		56.35	
Solo	76.20		1.20		77.40	
Passenger	26.30				26.30	160 hrs 45 min.

Assessment of Ability
(to be assessed as:- Exceptional, Above Average, Average or Below Average.)
i) As a L.B. [Light Bomber] Pilot *Below average*
ii) As Pilot-Navigator/Navigator *Below average*
iii) In bombing *Above average*
iv) In air gunnery *Average*

Any points in flying or airmanship which should be watched.
Very erratic and careless. Heavy on controls. Requires constant supervision.

After the Battle of France, and following the evacuation of the British Expeditionary Force from Dunkirk at the end of May and beginning of June 1940, German forces were poised across the English Channel. It looked bleak for the British nation but:

> . . . the British people took little account of the hard facts of their situation. They were instinctively stubborn and strategically ignorant. Churchill's inspiring speeches helped to correct the depression of Dunkirk, and supplied the tonic the islanders wanted. They were exhilarated by his challenging note, and did not pause to ask whether it was strategically warranted.
>
> Deeper than the influence of Churchill was the effect of Hitler. His conquest of France and near approach to their shores aroused them as no earlier evidence of his tyranny and aggressiveness had done. They reacted once again in their long-bred way – intent to keep their teeth in Hitler's skin at any cost.[1]

But before they could set about biting at the flesh of Nazism, the battle for survival had to be won. In the summer skies over England in 1940 the Luftwaffe fought to eliminate the defending air force in preparation for an invasion across the English Channel. The RAF would win the Battle of Britain under the direction of Air Chief Marshal Sir Hugh Dowding, and the enemy were halted. But the battle was close run, and it had certainly cost the Royal Air Force.

Group Captain Sir Hugh Dundas flew with 616 Squadron during the Battle of Britain and would later recall the effect of the attrition on the RAF during those fateful months in 1940.

> The supply of pilots began to dry up. Some were shot down two or three times, but, escaping injury, returned to the battle. Others were killed before they had fired a shot. Most survived a few days before falling in the fury of the fight, either to their death or to a period of convalescence from

[1] Basil Liddell Hart, *History of the Second World War*, (Papermac 1992) p149.

> their wounds. Dowding could not rotate his squadrons fast enough to keep pace with the losses. Squadrons in the south became depleted before others, taken out of the line to re-form, could build-up their strength again. Dowding had to take experienced pilots from the squadrons which were resting and re-forming, in order to plug the gaps in other squadrons, which should really have been taken out of the line. It was a policy of desperation and it could not last for long.[2]

Fortunately it was enough, but it is perhaps indicative of the situation in Western Europe and the nature of the fighting over England in the summer of 1940 that despite the 'qualifications' on Basil Collyns' flying assessment he was dispatched to the battle. Basil obviously still had a lot to learn and the hostile skies over England at that time suggested that it was far from being the best place to improve one's skills. Nevertheless the RAF was all that stood in the way of Germany embarking upon the invasion of England and the RAF needed pilots. Sending such inexperienced men was a risk but a necessary one. And so on 12 July 1940 he began his journey to England, aboard RMS *Rangitane*, expecting to be accompanied by his wife of four months Ann Collyns.

> I was going with Basil, my parents were marvellous – they didn't approve of people just getting married and then the husband going off to war, maybe never to be seen again. So they were in full support that I should go with him. But we were stopped by the British Government the very night before I left home. They said they couldn't cope with looking after any more widows in England. The luggage was all packed, in fact there was a party on at my family's house to say goodbye to us both. All I could do was see Basil off.
>
> Then I started to pester our government and various ministers, and other people became interested and all started doing their best. And Basil's father [Major Guy Collyns MC, of the Royal Engineers] who was living in England and had married a second time, to an English lady, guaranteed that they would look after me in case of the worst happening. Eventually I was allowed to go and I got away in January 1941.

Ann crossed the Pacific accompanied by a friend who was similarly looking to join her husband in England, serving on bombers. Whilst in New York Ann was offered a seat on a Yankee clipper which took her to Lisbon, where she was delayed owing to a storm.

> I had to wait in Lisbon for about a month, but eventually we got out on a flying boat to Poole, Dorset. I was met by a car with a driver. It took me to Basil's father's place in Amesbury, Wiltshire. Basil arrived about an hour after I had got there, in a borrowed car. He was given leave and I then went and lived on his station for a week and met all his squadron people. They were marvellous. They had been following my trip. They were a wonderful mixed squadron of all nationalities.

From the time Ann had left New Zealand until her arrival in England she had heard nothing from Basil.

---

[2] Quoted in *The Battle of Britain*, (Salamander Books, 1997) p164.

He had certainly toughened up with his attitude to life. He was so enjoying meeting all these people from all over the world. In his squadron there were Poles and Czechs, Norwegians, South Africans, the odd Australian and one southern Irishman, who just liked war and came over to fight. And of course a lot of very nice English. His view on the war was still the same. Very definitely it had to be done. It had to be fought. The more they could get at the enemy the better.

On arrival in England Basil awaited his posting at RAF Uxbridge and then began his training at 6 OTU (Operational Training Unit) Sutton Bridge, Lincolnshire on Miles Masters and Hawker Hurricanes, making his first flight on 11 September 1940. But his time preparing himself for the rigours of aerial combat was short. RAF Fighter Command was reeling from the attrition of pilots during the Battle of Britain. Dowding needed men to fly his fighters and the length of training programmes at operational training units had been cut considerably. And so after 16 days at Sutton Bridge, and with just 14.10 hours on Hurricanes, Basil was posted to an operational unit; 238 Squadron at Chilbolton.

When Basil arrived at 238, a significant change in the nature of the Luftwaffe attacks was taking place. The emphasis was now placed on targeting English cities at night, and the large raids by day almost stopped. But clearly, as October progressed, the scale of the Luftwaffe campaign was diminishing. On 21 October Fighter Command had no losses, similarly on 23 and 24 October. But even as October drew to a close small daylight raids continued and Fighter Command maintained a defensive attitude.

Following Basil's arrival at 238 Squadron and for the first three weeks, he honed his skills with the Hurricane, practising aerobatics, formation and dogfighting. Meanwhile his squadron colleagues had engaged the Luftwaffe, intercepting enemy raids on numerous occasions in the early part of the month. The squadron's ORB (Operations Record Book) narrates a typical example of the action on 7 October 1940.

Weather improved becoming bright and sunny in the afternoon with wisps of cloud.

1530-1710 12 sorties comprising the squadron patrolled base at 20,000 ft, subsequently taking a line between Bristol and the South Coast where a raid going to Bristol was intercepted. Battle was joined with a force of about 100 a/c comprising Ju 88, Me 110 and 109. Before the bombers could be reached the enemy launched a surprise attack. Me 109 dived out of the sun. The squadron, however, succeeded in destroying four enemy aircraft for the loss of one Hurricane, which was shot down, but its pilot P/O A. R. Covington, baled out with slight injuries. P/O Doe DFC, P/O Urwin-Mann and Sgt Jeka (Pole) each destroyed a Ju 88 and S/L Fenton destroyed a Me 110.

However as October progressed this type of action died away. One pilot found another way of taking risks:

25.10.40-1800 hrs – P/O J. Wigglesworth indulged in low flying and hit the hedge between the pilots' hut and Orderly Room. The tops of the hedge were cut off as with a hedging hook. He broke the Op. phone line, and smashed a main plane. By remarkable luck he did not crash. On

> landing on the aerodrome he was placed under open arrest [and would subsequently be fined £10 for his actions].[3]

On 25 October Basil Collyns took off on his first sortie, his logbook recording, 'Patrol. No Bandits sighted.' This entry was repeated on 29 October, twice, and on 1 November, 'Patrol Portsmouth, bandits heading for home.' And on 5 November, 'Patrol Bournemouth Me 109s.' On 6 November Basil flew from Chilbolton to Exeter, joining 601 Squadron for a period of training. After four weeks at the squadron developing his skills, during which it should be noted four crashes had occurred and one pilot had lost his life, Basil went back to 238 Squadron.

On 24 November 1940 Air Marshal Sholto Douglas replaced Dowding as Commander-in-Chief Fighter Command and on 18 December, the previous Air Officer Commanding 12 Group, Air Vice-Marshal Trafford L. Leigh-Mallory took over responsibility of 11 Group (south-east England), which had borne the brunt of the Luftwaffe incursions in the summer and early autumn of 1940. With the change in command came a change in the nature of Fighter Command operations, which meant switching over to the offensive. Sweeps of fighters across the Channel and Circuses (joint operations with bombers) were to be conducted to try and engage the Luftwaffe. And with these operations came a general change in the way sorties were flown. Leigh-Mallory, throughout the Battle of Britain had, controversially, advocated the use of big wings engaging the Luftwaffe intrusions in large numbers. Now on the offensive, Fighter Command would develop the theory when sending its fighters across the Channel.

Basil Collyns' logbook entries clearly demonstrate preparations for the general switch in tactics. Throughout December, January and February at 238 Squadron, then part of 10 Group (south-west England), Basil took part in 'Squadron formation practice, flight formation practice, wing formation practice, section formation practice.' In between there was the occasional 'Flap', but there was little action.

His logbook recorded similar exploits through March 1941 and also noted his involvement in patrols, one of which resulted in a forced landing, following a long chase over the Channel, owing to lack of petrol, at East Stoke, Dorset on 20 March. During the middle two weeks of April, with the squadron operating from Pembrey, the patrols were almost daily, over Linney Head, Milford Haven, Lundy Island, and St David's Head. On 16 April 238 returned to Chilbolton and the only excitement Basil could record in his logbook was two scrambles on 25 and 28 April. At this point the squadron was informed it was to move to the Middle East. Basil would not be going with them.

In October 1941 Flight Lieutenant Reg Baker DFC, then stationed at Port Alberta, Ontario, Canada on a specialist navigation course, addressed the joint meeting of Kiwanis and Optimist Clubs of Sarnia (Ontario). He made his audience quite clear on his view of the war.

> My profession, since the war started, is killing and I enjoy it. I don't know anything I like better than when I am killing Nazis. Some people say we

---

[3] 238 Squadron Operations Record Book.

> are fighting for the countries Germany has defeated. We are not only fighting for them. We are fighting for our very existence. If we lose this war there will be no Britain. It will be all over for us. If you keep this in mind you will somewhat understand our cruelty and our feelings. We will fight to the bitter end.
>
> Our job in the RAF is twofold. Any army that tries to operate without the cooperation of an air force is completely lost. This was shown in Greece, in Crete and in France. I saw it myself in Norway. I saw troops go down the sides of mountains and be bombed 24 hours a day. They were completely helpless. Our primary task is to be ready when our army is ready to send out an expeditionary force. Then we will begin to wipe the Germans out of the sky. We look forward to nothing so much as this.
>
> This war is a grim business. I started out with 39 other air force men. Now there are only three left. Only a few of them are prisoners of war. One of the things the Germans can't understand about us is the careless way we speak of our buddies who have been killed. We have to speak that way. If we kept thinking of them, we couldn't keep going.

To date, since the start of the war, Reg Baker's main operational experience had come serving with Coastal Command. He had gained considerable notoriety combating the German U-boat threat to the Atlantic convoys, Britain's lifeline, sending German U-boats and sailors to the bottom of the ocean. Reg's first successful encounter took place on 16 August 1940 when he took Sunderland 'H' of 210 Squadron, 'Queen of the Air', on patrol in very poor weather conditions in support of a five-ship convoy. Owing to the weather he considered aborting, but a call came through informing him that the *Empire Merchant* had been torpedoed and his task was to search for a U-boat. It was five hours later that U-51 was spotted.[4] Reg steeply banked the Sunderland into the attack, throwing members of his crew around.

> *Reg Baker:* My second pilot spotted the U-boat about 300 yards on our port side. It began to submerge at once. As we passed over the swirl we let go a salvo. The bombs apparently got just under the submarine before they went off. It was terrific. The surface of the sea seemed to shudder for yards around then suddenly blow up. In the middle of all the foam the submarine appeared, but sank again.

Reg's rear gunner would receive a painful souvenir of how low the attack had been, when he banged his head on the top of his turret as the explosion buffeted the Sunderland.

> *Reg Baker:* We turned and dropped another salvo plumb in the middle of the patch of foam. Up came the U-boat once more, but this time it rocketed out of the water at such an angle that we could see daylight between it and the sea. It seemed to stay poised for a moment, then slowly went down. I dropped a third salvo just to make sure. If a coup de grâce was needed that supplied it. Huge air bubbles came rushing up – one was a good 30ft across – then masses of oil. The whole thing was over in a minute-and-a-half.

---

[4] *Search Find and Kill, Coastal Command's U-boat Successes*, Franks, N.L.R. (Grub Street).

The Senior Naval Officer with the convoy was informed of the attack and apparent success and a destroyer was sent to investigate further but found nothing. In fact the U-boat had not been sunk, but four days later it would be sent to the bottom by the British submarine HMS *Cachalot*. U-51 had sunk eight ships on four patrols.[5] Reg returned home, landing at 7.30 that evening. Believing a kill had been made, a white star would soon appear on the hull of 'Queen of the Air'.

On 29 August he scored his second success against U-boats, with a third on 17 October 1940, and on 6 January 1941 Reg met a U-boat of a different kind. After flying through miserable weather for hours, with rain and snow, his aircraft suddenly broke into clear skies.

> It was the most amazing thing I have ever seen in my life. We stuck the nose of the aircraft into clear weather while the tail was still enveloped in clouds. As the second pilot and I blinked in the sudden light and looked ahead we both sighted a submarine at the identical moment, turned our faces to each other and howled in unison, 'Sub!'

The U-boat was only a few miles away, on the surface. Reg dived for his enemy, recognising it as an Italian submarine, and men were clearly seen on the conning tower. These men quickly realised they were about to be attacked, and hastily returned inside the sub; the tanks flooded and the submarine began to submerge. But they were too late, and with part of the stern still showing Reg placed his explosives either side. His rear gunner reported the sight, 'There's a sheet of metal about six feet by four, just been hurled out of the sea all torn and twisted.' Fountains of water caused by the release of air gave further evidence of the submarine's demise. One of Reg's crew is known to have remarked, 'If we don't win this war, the crew of this aircraft will be in a devil of a mess.'

Reg's success against the U-boat threat would be rewarded. In March 1941 Reg and his wife of six months Norma Ann went to Buckingham Palace to receive from the King his Distinguished Flying Cross.

In August 1941 Reg flew to Canada to begin his specialist navigation course and whilst there gave numerous talks on the current state of the air war in Europe. At his talk to the Kiwanis and Optimist Clubs of Sarnia, Reg intimated at the change of tactics since the Battle of Britain.

> We are rapidly arriving at numerical equality with the German Air Force. I don't think we have arrived there yet, but we have the superiority in the air. Last year the air battle line was over Britain. Now it is over France, well pushed back. Our boys have to go over there for a fight now.

However, in fact the Luftwaffe was generally not interested in the fight. The fighter sweeps and the Circuses were failing to entice the enemy into decisive daylight combat. But the Luftwaffe was still making its presence felt from the night skies above the UK. Towards the end of the Battle of Britain through to May 1941 German bombers were still setting cities and ports ablaze. At the end of November 1940, 12,696 civilian lives had been lost in London. Consequently, in response to the German night offensive Fighter Command sought to expand and strengthen its night fighter arm. On 14 September a highly influential Night

---

[5] *Search Find and Kill.*

Air Defence Committee was set up. Towards the end of September the committee's findings were translated into recommendations to Dowding. Airborne radar was accepted by all as the way forward, with improvements in ground control. But it was also suggested that single-engine fighters could play their part, although they could not carry such radar. On the latter point Dowding's opinion differed, and he was extremely frustrated when ordered to allocate three Hurricane squadrons to night defence.

On 2 May 1941 Basil Collyns transferred to 1 Squadron, flying Hurricanes, at Redhill. His logbook recorded more practice (including 5.15 hours of night practice), formations, the occasional dusk patrol. On the night of 10/11 May he would not be operational, but 1 Squadron pilots were airborne, trying to repel a large Luftwaffe night attack.

Night Raid on London

Over 500 German bombers were sent to attack London on the night of 10/11 May, in what turned out to be one of the most destructive raids of the war. By the end of the night 1,436 civilians were dead, many important buildings had been destroyed or damaged, and many of the streets were impassable. Above the blazing city the bombers had not had it all their own way however, encountering RAF night fighters including the Hurricanes of 1 Squadron.

1 Squadron sent its pilots out in three sections of four Hurricane IIs. The first section, taking off at 2300 hours, sought the enemy over London. Squadron Leader Richard Brooker, circling fires blazing on the ground, sighted a Heinkel 111 at 15,000 feet. He closed in from behind, let loose his firepower, the enemy aircraft's port engine caught fire and the Heinkel plunged down adding to the inferno below. During the engagement oil splattered Brooker's windscreen, which caused problems, hindering attacks he made on two more enemy aircraft. Over the East India Docks, Frenchman Lieutenant Jean-Francois Demozay closed in on an enemy aircraft, caught by three searchlights at 17,200 feet. From 30 yards astern he fired, sending the aircraft, crewed by men from the nation that had invaded his country, to the ground. Czech Sergeant Josef Dygryn, part of the second section, taking off at 0015 hours, was circling anti-clockwise over London when he sighted a twin-engined enemy aircraft, flying parallel. Dygryn turned and let loose a short burst from 100 yards. An alerted gunner in the German bomber responded. From 50 yards Dygryn opened up again, return fire came back but then abruptly stopped. Dygryn closed further, his Hurricane's machine guns blazing, but he overshot and broke away. He then attacked again having to allow a long deflection, attacking from the beam. The bomber started to dive, Dygryn opened up again and the bomber fell. Czech Sergeant Bedrich Kratkoruky was flying the line of the Thames, when he saw an enemy aircraft over Canvey Island. He climbed into the attack unleashing a one-second burst from the beam. Kratkoruky pressed home further attacks and smoke poured from his enemy's port engine. Kratkoruky, having overshot, had to pull out of his dive at 500 feet, his enemy still appearing to be diving at approximately 2,000 feet. In the third section, which took off at 0130 hours, two further pilots engaged enemy bombers, in inconclusive action. Czech Pilot Officer Behal's Hurricane was hit by enemy fire. He managed to report to control that he was baling out, but he would lose his life.

In this action over London 1 Squadron would claim three He 111 destroyed and one damaged. But some of these men were to see further action and other 1 Squadron pilots would also make claims, all on patrols over their base.

Sergeant Dygryn took off from Redhill at 0135 hours, and over Kenley he spotted a Heinkel 111, slightly above heading south. He turned and attacked from behind to no effect, the Heinkel's gunners returning fire. Dygryn then came in from the beam, and let loose a short burst. The enemy aircraft exploded in flames and spun down. Flight Lieutenant Jackman and Pilot Officer Raymond took off on patrol at 0225 hours. Half an hour later Jackman got onto a Heinkel 111 heading for London. During the pursuit Jackman let off three bursts and his enemy, still firing, went into an almost vertical dive. Raymond too was in action. From 18,000 feet he could see combats below him, then red tracer passed overhead. He turned into an enemy aircraft and opened fire, crossing over to fire another burst from the other side. The enemy aircraft, out of control, disappeared in a steep dive. Flying Officer Robinson, having taken off at 0115 hours, came across an enemy aircraft, whose pilot began to throw it around the night sky trying to evade the attentions of the Hurricane. Robinson fired off five short bursts, and the German gunner returned fire. Robinson lost the diving, smoking German bomber, against the dark of the ground. Sergeant Dygryn was in the air again at 0315 hours, and north-east of Biggin Hill, he sighted what he thought was a Ju 88. Dygryn let fire all his ammunition in the combat, and the smoking bomber eventually fell into the sea, by then on fire, a few miles south of Hastings. An extraordinary night for 1 Squadron, seven enemy aircraft claimed destroyed and two damaged.

Although unknown at the time, the 10/11 May raid was, as Churchill would describe it, 'the enemy's parting fling'. The resources of the Luftwaffe were to head east, to embark upon a new campaign. In the year to June 1941, 43,381 British civilians had been killed, with 50,856 seriously injured.

On 21 May there was a change in the nature of operations for Pilot Officer Basil Collyns, first as an escort to a Lysander (1055-1235 hours) and then on a sweep over France. Basil took off at 1700 hours. 1 Squadron sent 12 of its pilots on an escort of 18 Blenheims on a Circus operation to Béthune, which were detailed to bomb oil refineries and electric power stations. Over Kenley the formation, 1 Squadron, 258 Squadron, 362 Squadron and the Blenheims met up. 1 Squadron were detailed as rear top escort at 15,000 feet. The bombers and fighters crossed the English coast at Dungeness and entered the air space over hostile territory at Le Touquet. Midway to Béthune eight enemy aircraft were noticed in pursuit of the raiding force and when the target was reached they attacked the Blenheims. 1 Squadron's Yellow and White sections broke to engage, but 302 Squadron were already on to the enemy aircraft, so the sections returned. Green section, Pilot Officer Raymond and Basil Collyns, received the order to break and attack two Me 109s, just north of Béthune. They dived starboard, but quickly became the hunted when four Me 109s broke cloud cover in front of them. One Me 109 was quickly on to Basil's tail and he threw his Hurricane around the sky trying to shake him off. Raymond, from dead astern, riddled an Me 109, which began pouring smoke. Then he had to take his own evasive action, when more Me 109s arrived.

Raymond dived, and made for Gravesend, skimming the sea. Basil, having managed to shake off his attacker, joined up with a section from another squadron.

In the mêlée Flying Officer Velebnovsky was attacked by a Me 109 from below; he half rolled, came in behind his attacker, let loose and saw pieces fly off his foe's wings and fuselage. When Sergeant Dygryn saw a Hurricane under attack beneath him he swept down and let off a long burst, bullets riddling the cockpit and fuselage of the Me 109. He climbed and another Me 109 came into his sights. He let off what appeared to be a couple of bursts. He then became aware of danger to his rear, and pulled up the nose of the Hurricane, his enemy overshooting. Dygryn then returned home, seeing a Me 109 dive into the sea 20 miles from Gravelines. Sergeant Nassvetter turned to help a colleague under attack, firing two bursts into the enemy aircraft, pieces coming away. He was then pursued by three Me 109s across the French coast, eventually to receive a Spitfire escort home. Sergeant Kuttelwascher, acting as top weaver, saw four Me 109s attacking two Hurricanes. He selected the rearmost Me 109, fired off two bursts and watched as his burning enemy fell out of control. Sergeant Kratkoruky, weaving below and to the front, saw two Me 109s dive through the squadron, towards the Blenheims, and he fired off a short burst from 50 yards. One Me 109 tail unit fell off and the pilot baled out. Kratkoruky then saw what he thought was Flying Officer Robinson's Hurricane under attack from two enemy aircraft. He turned to assist but was too late. Robinson's Hurricane was in flames as it dived gently towards the sea. Kratkoruky, short of fuel, headed straight for Manston. Robinson would be reported missing.

On 1 June, 1 Squadron moved to Kenley, mainly in connection with moonlight period night fighting, and for the next two weeks Basil took part in three patrols and two bomber escort operations. The first was to Boulogne on 4 June, the second to St Omer on 14 June. On 15 June the squadron returned to Redhill and Basil was soon to learn some more lessons from the school of combat. On 16 June 1941 he would again engage the Luftwaffe, entering in his logbook, 'Battle over Channel'. Twelve 1 Squadron Hurricanes took off from Redhill on the evening of 16 June to give high cover to Lysanders, midway across the Channel. Over Tonbridge reports came in of bandits approaching the Lysanders. Under full boost the Hurricanes swept over the coast, to the south of Folkestone. The Lysanders were under the protection of Spitfires, but further out a Heinkel 59 seaplane was sighted, escorted by two Me 109s. Flight Lieutenant Gray called to his fellow pilots to attack line astern. The Me 109s broke and Gray attacked the Heinkel head on, unleashing a short burst before turning to expend the remainder of his ammunition, resulting in white smoke, changing to black, pouring from the German seaplane. Basil Collyns and other pilots then tore in to finish the kill, the Heinkel finally plunging into the sea. In the general chaos around the Heinkel other 1 Squadron pilots were also engaging Me 109s and would later claim three destroyed and one damaged. But 1 Squadron was to lose one pilot in the action. Sergeant Nassvetter's Hurricane came down into the sea. He was able to get out, was rescued and taken to Dover, but died in hospital the next day. Late on the evening of 16 June Basil was able to record the action and his first score in his logbook, '3 Me 109 by Sqdn + He 59. My Plane shot up. Part share He 59.'

Within a few days he would again engage the enemy. On 21 June

1941, Collyns was one of twelve 1 Squadron pilots who lifted their Hurricanes from Redhill at 1540 hours, to rendezvous with 312 and 258 Squadrons, in support of Blenheims on a Circus operation to Desvres aerodrome. After their mission, between Desvres and the French coast, Me 109s attacked them. Squadron Leader Brooker, seeing an Me 109 on the tail of a Hurricane, intervened, attacking from astern. The enemy aircraft's undercarriage came down, black smoke pouring out, and the pilot baled out shortly after. Lithuanian Pilot Officer Marcinkus came in behind an Me 109 and sent two short bursts the way of his adversary. A fellow pilot would witness the combat and confirm seeing the enemy aircraft break into pieces after Marcinkus' attack. Czech Sergeant Plasil made a stern attack on an Me 109, letting loose one short burst and seeing pieces come off the aircraft, before it went down in flames 'like a falling leaf'. Czech Sergeant Prihoda attacked an Me 109 from quarter astern, which turned over, pouring black smoke, and appearing to be out of control. Prihoda then attacked another which went straight down, with pieces coming off it. Czech Pilot Officer Kopecky attacked an Me 109, firing off a three-second burst at close range. The enemy aircraft began to spin, which Kopecky watched going down. But he wouldn't be able to confirm if it did crash, as bullets then tore through his cockpit, two Me 109s having closed in from the direction of England. Kopecky's throttle controls were taken out, his engine started to smoke and he force-landed in the sea eight miles south of Folkestone. He exited the Hurricane and 45 minutes later was picked up by a rescue launch. American Pilot Officer Maranz would not come back from the operation. Returning pilots would later report a Hurricane diving into the sea three miles south-west of Boulogne, the pilot having baled out.

Pilot Officer Basil Collyns' combat report recorded:

> B Flight 1 Squadron
> Number of enemy Aircraft – 20-30
> Type – Me 109
> Time attack delivered 1645 hours
> About 6 miles W of Boulogne
> Height of enemy – 7,000 feet
> Claim – 1 Me 109 destroyed
>
> Length of burst 540 rounds
>
> I was Green 2. Just after crossing the French coast on the way home I sighted a Me 109 with rounded wingtips at about 7,000 ft, to port and 500 ft below me. I dived down and fired a full deflection burst at him as he came across me; my attack was from close range and the burst 2½ secs. Smoke immediately came from the enemy aircraft and after making a turn I saw enemy aircraft crash into sea 5 or 6 miles West of Boulogne. I was flying a 12 m.g. Hurricane II.

At the end of the action four Me 109s were claimed destroyed by 1 Squadron, four Me 109s probably destroyed and two damaged. 1 Squadron's results this day provide a good example of why it appeared to Sholto Douglas and Leigh-Mallory that, in terms of attrition, the offensive policy and tactics were working. The statistics appeared to provide the evidence. Leigh-Mallory's

11 Group claimed 437 German fighters destroyed and 182 probable between 14 June and 3 September. In fact the actual figure was 128 destroyed and 76 damaged. Fighter Command lost 194 pilots in the same period.[6] There was clearly over-claiming, which would influence policy as the scale of the RAF's offensive action increased.

The day after Basil Collyns' first full combat victory against an enemy fighter, on 22 June 1941, German armed forces began operation Barbarossa, launching into the offensive against Russia. And therein lay one of Hitler's gravest strategic errors. He had made the mistake of leaving an undefeated nation in his rear, a rear he had to guard by manning a sizeable coastal defence line. Britain remained free, in particular the airmen of the British Commonwealth and her Allies were undefeated and their numbers could grow, their weaponry could be developed, the ports could land the vital war supplies and the factories could arm the growing air force. In June 1941 perhaps Hitler could rationalise that the apparent threat from the West to German might was minimal. He also hoped that Britain might even identify with the fight against communism. He had told his generals, 'When Barbarossa begins the world will hold its breath and make no comment.'[7] But Britain was breathing, her lifeblood was still flowing and the Atlantic supply routes would nourish her. And in Churchill there was a man to be reckoned with. On the night of 22 June 1941, he made clear his stance.

> We have but one aim and one single irrevocable purpose. We are resolved to destroy Hitler and every vestige of the Nazi regime. From this nothing will turn us – nothing. We will never parley, we will never negotiate with Hitler or any of his gang . . . Any man or State who fights against Nazidom will have our aid. Any man or State who marches with Hitler is our foe . . . It follows therefore that we shall give whatever help we can to Russia and the Russian people. We shall appeal to all our friends and allies in every part of the world to take this course and pursue it, as we shall, faithfully and steadfastly to the end.[8]

One country already allied to Britain in the pursuit of the defeat of Nazidom was Canada and in the friendly skies over their land young Canadian recruits could gain their wings prior to a posting to the hostile skies over Europe.

Nineteen-year-old Hartland Finley went to McGill University in the autumn of 1939, just as the war was breaking out and he soon signed up for the Canadian Officer Training Corps:

> I don't know why I particularly selected the air force but I was always intrigued with watching pilots up in the air flying aeroplanes and reading about the exploits of some of the WWI pilots. That's what really led me to joining the air force component. We not only had a number of ground lectures in various things like navigation and theory of flight, but we had some field trips. I always remember the most interesting field trip was to

---

[6] Statistics from *The Right of the Line*, Terraine, J. (Hodder and Stoughton, 1985).
[7] *The Struggle for Europe*, Wilmot, C. (Collins, 1952) p78.
[8] *Ibid.*, p78.

> St. Hubert. There was a hangar which had two particular aeroplanes in it, that absolutely staggered my imagination because when I walked in the hangar I expected to see something like a little Taylor Cub or some small type of aircraft that was used for recreational purposes. But here were these two huge aeroplanes, a Lockheed Hudson and a Douglas Digby. And I couldn't believe that I could actually walk underneath the wings of an aeroplane and it was made of metal and that thing would stay up in the air. I just couldn't imagine how it was able to do that. I guess that got the adrenalin flowing and I was highly excited and thought, 'Boy the air force is the place for me.'

In the summer of 1940 Hart took a job at Brownsburg, near Montreal, where Canadian Industries Ltd had an ammunition factory, but a few months later, when his birthday came in August, he decided to join the air force, went to Montreal and signed up. Hart went to Manning depot, Toronto, meeting up with a number of friends, receiving uniforms and equipment and getting shots. But his introduction to service life was far from plain sailing.

> It was incredible the number of people going through. It wasn't the most comfortable place in the world. We were in these upper and lower bunks and the food was absolutely appalling, terrible. There was almost a revolt. I remember it was so awful, so greasy and tasteless. Totally inadequate for healthy young men. We practically went on strike and they finally did something about it.

After about four weeks some of the recruits went off to do guard duty, including Hart, and he was sent to Dartmouth, Nova Scotia. With the Commonwealth Air Training Plan recruiting such large numbers, guard duty was often allocated to buy time for the scheme to adjust. While at Dartmouth Hart had the opportunity to wonder at some of the modern aircraft; a Lysander, a Hurricane.

He was then posted to ITS, Old Hunt Club, Toronto, undergoing lectures, link trainer, 'and the food was much better'. Here Hart's future responsibilities in the air force were to be decided.

> We were all petrified that we were going to end up being bomb aimers or gunners or something like wireless operators. We were all aspiring to be fighter pilots, or pilots anyway.

He obviously did enough to impress, as his future lay in controlling his own aircraft. From ITS Hart then went to EFTS, in December 1940, at Windsor Mills, Quebec. Here he flew the Fleet Finch with civilian instructors, and was certainly appreciative towards his instructor, 'who was probably one of the best pilots at the school'. At the time Hart was there, snow covered the airfield and training was conducted with skis and wheels.

> What most of us were a little apprehensive about in terms of our capability was in cross-country navigation. So much of our training was just around the airport, take-off, go up, do circuits, and do some aerobatics. We didn't have to worry too much on these about getting lost. But cross country was a part of the programme which we were required to do. At least the first time would be with an instructor, so if you did start to stray off course,

pretty soon you'd be brought back by the instructor.

I had attended Bishops College School, Lennoxville, about 30 miles by air. So on one of my solo flights I decided I'd better revisit the place and put on a little show for them. I had a brother who was in the prep school there at the time and when he recounted my escapade it was pretty horrendous. Apparently I went down between the buildings, there was a quadrangle between the skating rink and the main school, not very large, but I touched my wheels on the deck and then went back up again between the buildings. And of course everybody was hanging out the windows and running for cover. When I got back to Windsor Mills I realised what a very foolish thing I had done, not because I necessarily felt it was dangerous, although I guess it was, but more particularly the fact that I could be reported for low flying and if I was reported I probably would have been scrubbed or washed out. I took a lesson from that.

Fortunately for Hart he was not reported. From Windsor Mills he was posted to a depot at Quebec city. 'We thought, "We've been shunted aside here. Are we ever going to get to a service school?"' Finally orders came through and his training continued at Summerside. On arrival Hart, with a friend, couldn't wait to get a look at the aircraft they were to fly, and they made their way immediately to a hangar full of Harvards.

We climbed into one of them, my friend picked the front seat and I, the back seat. We were amazed at the size and comfort of the cockpit, compared to the little Fleet Finch. While I was sitting in the back seat I was looking around at the various controls and instruments and then I looked down and I saw this tube with a kind of a megaphone-like cup on it. I thought that must be the way to talk to the guy in front. So I pulled up the tube and I started to talk, asking my friend if he could hear me. He said, 'Well yeah I can hear you, you're just behind.' I said, 'Well I'm talking into the microphone.' He said, 'That's not a microphone. That's for urinating in.' I very quickly set it aside.

Hart was certainly impressed by the size of the Harvard and felt, 'if you flew it well you could fly almost anything. Anybody that trains on a Harvard can get into any plane and fly it.' But the Harvard could also sort out those who did or did not have the ability for a career as a pilot. 'I suppose everybody has their limitations. Some people just couldn't hack the high speeds and more complicated aircraft. We did have a few wash outs.'

On receiving his wings he automatically became a sergeant pilot, but was frustrated when some on his course were commissioned. As he had finished near the top of his course he couldn't understand why he hadn't received the same recognition, and was disappointed when told that he was going to Trenton to be an instructor.

Of the 21 people that were on Hart's course only one was posted overseas, the remaining men, including Hart, designated for instruction duties. This was not met favourably by the young aspiring airmen.

I guess they were really short of instructors at the time. There were more and more service schools opening up across the country. That was our fate.

It was a disappointment in two ways. Firstly that I didn't get a commission and secondly that I didn't get a posting overseas. However I learned later that the reason I didn't get a commission was that they felt that I was just a little bit too young and a little bit too immature at that point in time and being an NCO for a time would do me a lot of good.

Hart would later understand that the experience he gained as an instructor would benefit him long term.

When I was going through service school I thought, particularly when I got my Wings, that I was an ace. I thought I knew all there was to know about flying. I would do some rather ridiculous things but I guess being a young fellow I was full of beans. I did a lot of low aerobatics, rolls and loops close to the ground and got a great thrill out of how close you could come to the ground without hitting it. When I got to Trenton and started to learn something about instructing I understood what really made an aeroplane fly and how you had to control the plane. I realised all of a sudden how little I knew about flying. From Trenton on, all through my instructing period I felt that I was probably one of the luckiest guys in this world and I realised that if I had gone overseas after graduating from service school I probably would not have survived. I would almost certainly have got myself into trouble in an accident of some sort rather than enemy action. I think most of the instructors I knew felt the same way.

By the time we went overseas, most of us had anywhere from 1,500 to 2,000 hours of flying – a lot of flying in those days.

Hart Finley completed his instructor's training at Trenton, flying Ansons, Tiger Moths and the Lockheed 10 and then was posted back to Summerside. From here he then went to Uplands Ottawa, the main reason being that he had a reputation as a pretty good footballer. That autumn Hart's team won their league and went on to the Eastern Canadian final, which they lost. Despite appreciating the opportunity to play football, Hart remained keen to get overseas and he couldn't wait until the season finished. But when it came time for postings Hart was overlooked, despite the fact that one of his friends, who had trained at the same time and played football, did receive a posting. Hart challenged his squadron commander but was told that he was near the bottom of the list, as he had only been at Ottawa for three months, although, as he protested, he had been instructing for 15 months.

I was very upset and when we played the Eastern final in Toronto, the morning after the game, Group Captain Sammie Sampson, who was the Commanding Officer at Uplands during that period, came into my room at the Royal York Hotel in Toronto and asked if I had a comb he could borrow. So I said, 'Sir, while I've got you here using my comb, I'd like to twist your arm a little bit.' He said, 'Oh what's that about', and I told him the story about why I wasn't being posted overseas. 'Finley,' he said, 'leave it with me.' Within a week I was posted overseas, arriving in England in February 1943.

Whilst the RAF was expanding and developing its fighting capabilities, there were still front-line duties to perform, in particular fulfilling the obligation to

Russia to maintain an aerial threat from the UK and hence force the Luftwaffe into maintaining a presence in the West.

Following Basil Collyns' first aerial victory he remained active on offensive operations for the rest of June 1941, a further convoy patrol, Channel sweep, fighter sweeps and a scramble, and on 28 June he was also promoted to Flying Officer.

On 1 July the squadron moved to Tangmere, again for night fighter patrolling, and Basil spent the first nine days concentrating mainly on night-flying tests. On the 10th it was back to convoy patrols but then no activity until the 22nd when he flew a reconnaissance to Cherbourg, to look for the German battle cruiser *Scharnhorst* but without success. The next day 1 Squadron aircraft again flew a fruitless reconnaissance looking for the cruiser. Basil saw the month out with a dawn patrol, and a 'co-op with Havocs' (bombers). It was much of the same in the first half of August, further night-flying tests and the odd Havoc co-op but then on 18 August was the first of 14 Havoc co-ops over nine days, five at night. This was a clear response to Fighter Command's belief in the strategic value of their offensive operations, forcing a Luftwaffe presence over France and therefore assisting the Russians.

In September, October and the first two weeks of November, Basil's logbook records similar activity including 15 further Havoc co-ops, and a lot of night fighter training, but he was seeing little action. The 1 Squadron ORB recorded the lack of aerial opposition: 'In the nature of things pilots prefer operational activity. They realise however, lack of this is unavoidable, since the Luftwaffe fight shy of giving them the opportunities they long for.' The Luftwaffe was busy elsewhere. In November however, it was time again for Basil to move on. His last flight with 1 Squadron was on 15 November 1941, an aircraft test of 45 minutes. On 20 November he arrived at 60 OTU East Fortune, Scotland, flying a Master on 23 November for 30 minutes on a local reconnaissance to familiarise himself with the area. He would spend the next seven months imparting his knowledge to less experienced men, flying Blenheims, Masters, Defiants, Oxfords, Dominies and Bisleys.

CHAPTER 2

NIGHT DEFENDERS

On the night of 27/28 July 1942, New Zealander George 'Bill' Jameson opened the throttles of his Bristol Beaufighter II. The twin-engined night fighter began to rumble along the runway at Fairwood Common near Swansea, Wales. With Bill was his navigator/radar operator A. Norman Crookes. Shortly after the two men were airborne contact was established with the ground controller at Ripperston, whose job was to locate any enemy intrusion and direct this particular 125 Squadron aircraft in to intercept.

The basic rule for successful night fighting was firstly to find any suspect aircraft, then get close enough to identify it, preferably without being seen, and then get into a position to shoot it down. It had been a shallow learning curve for the night fighting air crews of the RAF, and various methods were considered and tried out in order to locate and illuminate a suspect aircraft. Ground radar could give advance notice of an aerial intruder and ground controllers could speak directly to the men in the aircraft. But at night, the key was for the night fighter aircraft to be placed in the best position relative to the intruder, going in the same direction and at the same speed. There had been considerable tactical and technical development since the end of the Blitz in May 1941. Over England the control of patrolling night fighter crews from the ground had become more efficient, and in particular, in mid 1942 new variants of the Beaufighter were becoming available, equipped with the latest AI (airborne radar), and there was also now a specialist crew member to operate the new electronic weapons.

Norman Crookes was born in the mining village of New Tupton near Chesterfield on 23 December 1920. He won a minor scholarship to the local county secondary grammar school, leaving at 18 to do a degree in History at King's College London. When war broke out the whole college moved to the University of Bristol.

> We were in Bristol for two years before I joined the RAF. During that time Bristol was heavily bombed. The college lost most of its books when the library went up in flames during one heavy raid in December 1940. I left university with a promise that I could go back to King's to finish my degree course at the end of the war. The Board, which interviewed students about to enlist in the armed forces, recommended me for training as an infantry officer. I wished to join the Royal Air Force. So in June 1941 I left Bristol, and went to the RAF recruiting agency in Sheffield to volunteer for flying duties. Three weeks later, after an interview at Cardington I was recruited for training as an Observer (on special duties). The specific nature of the flying job was to be explained later. Subsequently, I learnt the urgency was to train crews to fly the new night fighters which were equipped with AI.
>
> I joined a number of other people who had similarly enlisted, at Lord's cricket ground, where we were medically assessed and so on, before going on to ITW at Aberystwyth. There were about fifty of us in this

particular flight. After two months of being knocked into shape physically, we went on a short navigation course at Staverton, near Cheltenham, before going to do an AI training course at Prestwick, near Glasgow. Flying at Prestwick was very difficult because of the weather and in January 1942 a number of us from the original entry were posted to 125 Squadron which was then being reformed from a Defiant night fighting unit to a Beaufighter unit at Colerne in Wiltshire. As the squadron was not quite ready to receive us, some of us were sent to join 604 Squadron, a very active unit at Middle Wallop. There I spent almost three months learning the trade. Initially I flew as third man in a Beaufighter and eventually I was regarded as being competent as a night fighter navigator. I rejoined 125 Squadron at Colerne and teamed up with Bill Jameson, a young New Zealand fighter pilot. He was very keen and anxious to learn. So was I. We became very firm friends as well as a crew. Bill wanted to succeed and demanded efficiency. We were of a similar inclination and soon became adept at the job.

George 'Bill' Jameson was born on 20 November 1921, in Rotherham, New Zealand. He joined the RNZAF in February 1941 and later that year, via Canada, arrived in England. On 12 September 1941 he wrote home.

East Lothian
'Somewhere in Scotland'

Dear Family
It seems ages and ages since I last wrote to you though actually it's only about two weeks or so. Now that I'm over here I'm afraid you'll just have to guess at everything as I can't tell you a thing – they're so strict on the censorship racket. Worse still I shan't be able to tell you much about my job as it is especially secret – in fact it's unfortunately the most secret and the youngest branch of the RAF 'Night Fighters'. Believe me I'm absolutely thrilled with it and wouldn't go onto any other job for anything as this is so jolly interesting – and believe it or not it's a remarkably safe business too.

They picked us for the job by giving us an eye test – 'Night Vision Test' – as soon as we got over here in England, and as I got an assessment of exceptional I expect that's what put me here. First time I knew my eyes were any good at night. I certainly pity the rest of the boys as I'm dashed if I can find my way around in the black out. Anyway it's got me into an awfully interesting job and so far I'm having a marvellous time. It's a jolly nice little station here and being an officer is beautiful. I'm woken up every morning by my batman with a nice cup of hot tea and then for a shave while he cleans my buttons and polishes my shoes etc. The meals are great, you really wouldn't realise there was a war on it's so good. Sugar in our tea (and no tea shortages either), a little butter and plenty to eat always of really good food. Of course being a night fighter we get extra good food as we have to be fed well and have a fairly careful diet so that we won't lack the essential vitamins and so on and so on. However if Hitler thinks he's starving Britain he's miles out as far as I've seen. They're even telling of increasing some rations during winter. And as far as invasion goes well I just don't think it's possible for any country to invade Britain and every minute their chances are getting worse.

Well to start from where I left Canada. We eventually got onto the same boat as the rest of the NZ boys . . . and as we officers had all the first class cabins and so on – including sole rights to the drawing rooms and lounges etc – we had a marvellous trip over here in a very short time too. No occurrences of any note on the way either. Old Hitler is wrong again in thinking he'll stop British shipping. I was amazed at what we saw on the way and at present can't help feeling what is maybe a bit too optimistic about things . . . We didn't come straight to our various OTUs as there was of course a lot of arrangements to be made etc, and so we were stationed in a beautiful seaside resort. A really grand town and gosh we had a great time. England is absolutely beautiful isn't it – and seeing these old buildings and farmhouses etc, with the vivid green fields and little hedges is just like the views on the postcards . . . We've seen everything here now almost, Spitfires and Hurricanes (which incidentally came out and shot up the boat as we arrived), looked just like a thin sliver of silver hurtling along and sounded just like a powerful motor car. They fly so effortlessly and make no noise at all. Some of the bomb damage was noticeable as we came through in the train, but I really can't see how they ever hope to bomb us out, it's useless to try.

Bill wrote about his tailored uniforms and new kit – 'wonderful stuff' – and his experiences of getting lost during the black out in London, before getting the Flying Scotsman to Scotland. Three months later he would again write home. Perhaps he was beginning to feel a little homesick, but he was certainly relishing his flying experiences.

Officers' Mess
RAF Fairwood Common
Swansea
Sunday 14 Dec

Dear Mother
Well an awful lot seems to have happened out at home recently hasn't it and I'm now keeping a close look out for any signs of the forming of a NZ Squadron on our job to go out to the Pacific but unfortunately there doesn't seem to be any hope as we'll be quite busy in our job. However I'd much rather be out there – it would seem like fighting for something and not just doing a job remotely connected with looking after NZ. Not that we get a lot to do though. I've honestly never done so little before in all my life – partly because it's winter and winter here is quite different from home.

I expect you've read all the articles in the papers and magazines about 'Britain's Carrot Eaters' – 'the boys who see in the dark' etc – and the usual long and ridiculous accounts of daring in the dark and so on. Well that's your little Willie's job and it's the best job in the war, even if it's not quite as fantastic as the magazines describe it. You can't imagine the sense of independence and power it gives you, sitting snugly in your nice warm cockpit with all the cold dials gleaming – cruising along quietly at 200 odd and singing at the top of your voice through the 'intercom' in duet with your gunner and the feel of the old kite with 1,000 h.p. or so at your control. The sight of a sunset above the clouds or the moon shining on top of a cumulus layer, all silver and pink, is just like flying off the cloudy and dark earth way up to heaven – it's absolutely superb.

I expect you'll get no petrol at all at home now or any fuel oil either – God it's going to be quite a blow to the country in that way unless the States hurry up and wake themselves and clear off these little yellow pests. I'll bet my old kite would be deadly in amongst those lumbering old Jap bombers. I only wish I could get a crack at them.

On the night of 27/28 July 1942, he *would* get a crack at a German bomber. In the very early hours of the morning Bill and Norman were working with their ground controller trying to find and engage a hostile intruder.

Norman Crookes: The procedure on a night patrol was that you flew to a designated area and contacted a ground control unit, which had its own radar. It swept the area and they could inform you if there were any aircraft, which were likely to be enemy aircraft. They would tell us if there was a 'bogie' in the area. If they were absolutely certain it was an enemy aircraft it would be a 'bandit'. They would tell us to fly in a certain direction and how far away the bogie or bandit was. We flew in that direction until we had contact on our own screen. We then informed the ground unit that we had contact and once we had a good contact we would line up and follow the aircraft. We then went in to establish its identity. In the early stages the range of the radar that we had in the aircraft was limited to the height that we had above the ground, so if we were flying at 10,000 feet we had 10,000 feet of range ahead of us otherwise the radar gave up ground returns that swamped anything else. There were two scopes, one azimuth and one elevation, so we could tell where the target aircraft was in relation to us. My job was to tell the pilot to turn to port or starboard or go down or go up or increase speed. We literally had to tell the pilot what speed, what altitude, and what attitude to fly the aircraft when we were on a chase. If the pilot had faith in what you were telling him he would do what you were asking him. That was the secret in a competent crew.

In the Beaufighter I sat halfway back in the fuselage in the blister, facing backwards to look into the radar set. Once Bill had got a visual and was about to decide whether or not he should shoot if it was an enemy aircraft, I would swing round on the swivel seat, looking to confirm the assessment if it was enemy or otherwise. Then Bill did the rest. He was an excellent shot, in fact he became much better as we went on.

The classical approach if we could do it was to come in underneath the aircraft and fire at it before it knew we were there. It did happen sometimes on a very dark night. On a moonlit night it was a very different matter altogether. If the enemy aircraft was keeping a decent lookout he could probably see the following fighter up to half a mile away or maybe more and then there was a bit of a chase as the aircraft tried to get away.

You would aim at the engines in the main because they were the vital part. And having fired you then tried to establish whether the aircraft had been shot down or just damaged. Obviously there was a bit of a combat sometimes if the enemy realised you were on his tail, but normally if you were taking him by surprise it was a bit murderous.

Bill and Norman achieved their first kill early on the night of 27/28 July 1942.

Combat Report: I was ordered to scramble on an interception patrol, and shortly after being airborne was taken over by Ripperston. After 5 or 6 contacts on various enemy aircraft I obtained a visual of a bogey showing no IFF [Identification Friend or Foe]. I suspected this to be a Ju 88 and it passed over and behind me and was lost.

At 0208 hrs I obtained a visual of an enemy aircraft at 11,000 ft height, 15 miles to sea from Cardigan. Enemy aircraft was below and probably saw me first. It immediately took evasive action in the form of deep spirals, but I followed it down, identifying it as a He 111 by the clear silhouette and large exhausts. Contacts after the visual were intermittent, but I opened fire during the dive and continued to fire until my guns stopped. There was fairly accurate return fire from enemy aircraft's dorsal turret, about 9 strikes registering on my aircraft, one of which passed through the cockpit, severing the electric lead of the m/g control, while another lodged in the mainspar of the wing.

This return fire ceased after a short while, and as I closed to point blank range I observed a large glow on the starboard engine of the enemy aircraft, which then went into a dive and continued to go down until it hit the sea. To avoid doing the same, I was obliged to pull out and pass over the top of the enemy aircraft.

Destruction of enemy aircraft was confirmed by three separate sources.

I claim 1 He 111 destroyed – Pilot Officer G. E. Jameson.

On the night of 4/5 August, Bill and Norman claimed their second enemy aircraft destroyed, another Heinkel 111 off Milford Haven. Then came a change in the nature of operations:

Norman Crookes: For a time after August 1942 we were concerned in flying at daytime over towards southern Ireland to try and combat the Ju 88 weather reconnaissance aircraft the Germans sent out from France. As a squadron we had a number of initial sightings but very few combats because we were equipped with Beaufighter II aircraft. Beaufighter IIs had Merlin engines and the Ju 88s were too fast for us. So we were equipped then with Bristol engines, given Beaufighter VIs and that enabled us to catch up with the Ju 88s and the squadron had one or two successes. We were then sent as a detachment up to the Shetlands to combat the weather reconnaissance aircraft that flew over the North Sea from Norway. Bill had a scrap with one without me as navigator because at that time I was a sergeant, he was commissioned and we were in quarters that were quite a long distance away from each other. It was a sudden call so he took a commissioned navigator with him) much to my disgust.

Combat Report:
27 October 1942
125 Squadron
Beaufighter VI
1742 hrs
48 miles N of Sumburgh
Cloudy, 10/10 in patches 1,500-8,000 feet, vis poor, rain, failing light

I took off from Sumburgh at 1706 hrs on 27 Oct 42 and was given vector 045 degrees, angels 15 [15,000 feet], ASI 220. After reaching 15,000 ft flying in NNE direction was told to orbit and controller warned me that bandit was approaching from the west, angels 11 about ten miles away. Obtained visual of enemy aircraft at extreme visual range flying along the top of cloud layer some ten miles to the NW. I dived very steeply down on it turning slightly so as to approach from the sun and opened fire with quarter deflection from about 300 yards to 100 yards closing rapidly to minimum range ASI 330. Just before passing under enemy aircraft I observed about five brilliant white flashes along the starboard fuselage and wing root. In diving under enemy aircraft I passed into cloud and my windscreen became immediately obscured with ice. Turning back and keeping AI contact I obtained another visual of enemy aircraft in cloud by looking through side panels. Enemy aircraft opened very inaccurate fire from dorsal position apparently with twin guns, brilliant red tracer being used. I then throttled back and followed enemy aircraft with AI while attempting to clear windscreen with de-icer pump. It was then that I lost contact at about 6,000 ft, enemy aircraft diving away very fast. After continuing search with control's help for some time in the failing light I returned to base and pancaked at 1827 hrs.

I claim 1 Ju 88 as damaged.

Bill and Norman, flying together again, went out a few days later to try and intercept the enemy's weather reconnaissance aircraft. About 150 miles out over the North Sea the prop seized up on one engine.

Norman Crookes: Instead of being able to feather it, it stayed in a flying state and so there was a tremendous drag. We decided to abort the combat and head for home. We were at 16,000 feet at that time and rapidly lost height to about 2,000 feet and it seemed as though we were heading for a ditching in the North Sea which was not at all comfortable. Fortunately Bill managed to maintain height, ground control at Peterhead sent out aircraft, and we subsequently learnt that they had despatched boats too, but the weather was such that we reached Peterhead without any assistance. That was the nearest we thought we had come to the end.

Shortly after Bill and Norman returned to Fairwood Common; a lean period followed. It wasn't until February 1943 that they next engaged the enemy...

Norman Crookes: ... when a number of aircraft attacked Swansea which was our base. There were a number of us scrambled that night and we had only one contact, one visual, and we got behind a Dornier 217.

Combat report:
16 Feb 1943
Beaufighter VI Mk IV AI
2225 hrs
South of Gower peninsula
8/10 9,000 ft Moon, vis excellent

Flight Lieutenant Jameson and Pilot Officer Crookes flying Beau VI Mark IV AI took off Fairwood 2156 landed base 2324, were flying on a vector 030 degrees at 10,000 ft when they got a beam contact at 2221. Jersey 27 brought this contact to a visual at 2,000 ft range at 9,000 ft just below cloud. The enemy aircraft was identified probably Do 217 by three exhausts on each motor. The pilot opened fire with a 2 sec burst from dead astern at 200 yards and the port motor exploded. The enemy aircraft began to lose height with port motor blazing. As our aircraft came in for a second burst – 1 sec – the Navigator warned the pilot of contact from starboard – closing in to minimum range astern – showing no cockerell [IFF] and immediately the Navigator told the pilot the aircraft was hit. Pilot observed strikes on his own aircraft and broke off combat with steep starboard turn. After breaking away the burning wreckage of enemy aircraft was observed in the sea and another fire was seen some distance away.

Norman Crookes: When we landed we discovered there were a number of bullet holes in our aircraft and I had a bleeding finger. We thought we had been shot up by an enemy aircraft, having discovered a .303 bullet.

As Norman would describe it, 'That was the end of our adventures with the enemy in 125 Squadron.' The two men were sent to Exeter with the intention that they should start on Intruder operations. However it was not to be as they went on rest for six months.

Bill, by then sporting a DFC ribbon, and Norman then separated for a while and began to impart their knowledge to trainee night fighter crew. During this period Bill would also receive sad news. His 27-year-old brother, Lance Corporal John Jameson MM, serving with the 26th Battalion of the New Zealand Infantry in North Africa, lost his life on 28 April 1943. Bill wrote home on 16 June 1943.

Mother Dear
I have just got back from leave and there were two lovely letters from you, March and April's. I am sure that I get nearly all you write and they are an enormous comfort. I thought the words of the cable you sent me about poor old John were marvellous. I know you must have taken it marvellously for you are the most sensible and understanding mother in the world. It was very, very hard though; John has always been my hero and he was the finest brother in the world. It always seems so unfair that all the finest ones are the ones to go.

War must be very much harder on the people who stay at home and do all the work and have to live an ordinary life and wait. But you mustn't worry at all – it's all going to be over very soon now. In fact maybe even as you get this…

That of course was not to be. As it was, only a few months after Bill and Norman separated they were back together again.

> *Norman Crookes:* After three months I rejoined Bill who was then commanding a night fighter shooting flight at Chedworth, Gloucestershire. But there was precious little for me to do there. It just so happened that my girlfriend who became my first wife was in the Land Army quite close to Chedworth. It was a happy posting.

On 27 June 1942 Basil Collyns had arrived at 243 Squadron Ouston, for temporary duty as a flight commander, given the rank of Flight Lieutenant, and the next day experienced his first flight handling a Spitfire. But there was not a lot happening. The squadron ORB recorded on 3 July, 'Pilots have now started leave as it is the only satisfactory way of dealing with the abundance of unemployable flying personnel.' For Basil the next two and a half months was taken up with formation flying, air to air, air to ground, air firing and five scrambles. On 11 September 1942 he was posted to 222 Squadron, Drem and his logbook entries continue in a similar vein with the odd sea sweep and convoy patrol.

Then another transfer came, and Basil was sent to 485 NZ Squadron in November for a brief three-week spell, the first week in December involving two bomber co-op sorties, the second on 6 December, rear support to a light bomber attack on the Phillips works at Eindhoven. The squadron ORB noted, 'The Squadron patrolled over the sea off the north Belgian [coast] and Walcheren and attracted AA fire but were not hit. On the way back several dinghies were orbited and aircraft were seen in the sea.' By this time Basil had spent just over a year at operational squadrons during which he had completed 240 hours of flying. Although undoubtedly reluctant he was now to be rested.

On 12 December 1942 he again found himself at a new unit; AFDU Duxford. To the end of January 1943 action involved 14 bomber co-ops, 12 more in February, 11 in March, the only incident of note being a force landing at Top Ladder Farm, Friday Bridge, owing to the Spitfire's engine cutting, and five co-ops in April.

On 4 May Basil left Duxford and transferred to No. 25 Course Central Gunnery School, Sutton Bridge, and over the next four weeks he would post 41.20 hours of air training. His 'Summary of Flying and Assessment for Front Gun Marksmanship' reported his performance.

Assessment of Ability

(To be assessed as:- Exceptional, Above the Average, Good Average, Average, or Below the Average).

i) As a Marksman	Air to Ground	*N/A*
	On Drogue	*Average*
ii) As a Marksman in	Fighter Combat	*Average*
	Bomber Combat	*Good Average*
iii) As an Instructor		*Average*

Degree of Pass/~~Fail~~ 'B'

To be assessed as: Pass A – Above Average Instructor & Marksman
Pass B – Pass on both

Fail C – Fail as Instructor
Fail D – Fail as Marksman
Fail E – Fail on both

> This Officer completed a good average course. His sighting has remained rather erratic, but this may improve with further practice. He has, however, benefited considerably from the course and has a good grasp of theory of sighting. He lectures well and should prove an average Instructor.

On 6 June 1943 Basil took up position as CO of 1493 Flight, Eastchurch, gunnery instruction, and here he would languish for the next six months only managing 32 hours in the air, and only in Masters and Martinets at that. His wife Ann would recall the effect it was having on her husband, 'He was instructing and he hated that. He got very scared. Young pilots!' But Basil was doing a most important job. He was training the newer generation of pilots, many of whom would take part in the escalations of the air offensive in the run up to, and during, the decisive land and air battle in Western Europe.

In the spring of 1942 the Allied planning for a return to the continent had begun in earnest. Recommendations were made that under the auspices of a supreme commander, British commanders were to be appointed to make plans. As soon as possible, training of suitable ground and air forces was to be started and at the same time there was to be a serious rethinking of the organisation of the Royal Air Force commands in the UK, to cater for offensive operations. In particular a British Air Commander-in-Chief was suggested to control an Air Striking Command, and Assistant Chief of Air Staff (Policy) Air Vice-Marshal Slessor put forward proposals on the nature of this force, the command structure and the force composition, drawing on the experiences of the opposition.

> They were modelled to a large extent on the organisation of the German Air Force for the reason that the problem facing the Allies, i.e. land invasion of their neighbours supported by air power, was similar to that which had confronted Germany.[9]

The initial plans for the force required that it was to be:

> ...flexible so that the air effort whether for direct support, reconnaissance, cover or more distant bombing, could be rapidly switched from one part of the battlefield to another. It must be able to carry out close support tasks at very short notice. The Army Commander fighting the battle on the ground was to select objectives for supporting aircraft and was to determine the proportion of available striking power to each objective. One air commander was to be appointed who would see the air situation as a whole and co-ordinate support and reconnaissance operations (the latter to be controlled by the army) with fighter operations and thus maintain supremacy in the air.[10]

Slessor suggested (and it was later ratified by the Chief of the Air Staff) that an Air Officer Commanding-in-Chief would control British and US Air Forces

[9] Public Record Office AIR 41/66.
[10] *Ibid.*

designated for the support of an invasion. He also suggested that a specific British air force be responsible for the airspace over the British army, and a US air force the skies above the US army. It was also envisaged that the Air C-in-C would control US and British heavy bomber forces, although this idea would be seriously challenged.

> The principle, which governed the proposed plan, was that the existing RAF organisation would, once it had been adapted as above, project itself over the continent and the necessity would not arise to form a new and cumbrous command overseas as happened in France in 1940. In the initial stages, as aerodromes in France were captured, they would be used as advanced landing grounds for squadrons based in England. The aircraft would be serviced by servicing commandos, each commando being capable of servicing fighters, light bombers, or reconnaissance aircraft, and would be operationally controlled by an advanced headquarters (Sector and/or Army Support wing). The Group areas would then be extended into France. When the Army had occupied sufficient ground in France to enable squadrons to be based there, stations, each organised to maintain up to three squadrons, would cross the Channel with an advanced Group headquarters and the necessary supply echelons.[11]

But concerns remained over the nature of air support to the army, so the plan needed further development and a Special Planning Staff suggested that:

> . . . the first requirement of such a plan was the immediate formation on a fully mobile field force basis of a Composite Group of fighter, light bomber and reconnaissance squadrons which should include not less than twelve ground/air support squadrons. The Composite Group would become a model for the formation of other Composite Groups and would be responsible for developing the technique of ground/air support, the command and training of squadrons allocated for this task, and it would carry out exercises in conjunction with the Army. The Group would be a separate entity and would not share any of the operational commitments of RAF Fighter Command.[12]

However, attention then shifted to the Allied invasion in North Africa and operation Torch, November 1942, which involved the redeployment of 17 day fighter squadrons from the UK. In light of this Slessor put forward new temporary proposals, but when emphasis again came back to invasion on the coast of Western Europe, his original reorganisation plans were seen as the way forward. By then the Allied planners would also be able to draw on the lessons learnt from the assault on Dieppe.

On 19 August 1942 the UK-based air forces gave their support to one particular operation, which would provide considerable experience of working in conjunction with a seaborne assault. As something of a rehearsal for a full blown invasion across the Channel, operation Jubilee was mounted. The French port of

---

[11] Public Record Office AIR 41/66.
[12] *Ibid.*

Dieppe was approached from the sea by an Anglo-Canadian force, but they would pay a terrible price. The Canadian 2nd Division suffered 882 killed, and 597 wounded from the 4,963 men that took part. The British No. 3 and No. 4 Commandos lost 275 men. In the skies above the battle on the beaches AVM Leigh-Mallory, commanding the sizeable air force assembled to support the assault, ordered over 2,471 sorties flown, seeking to test out the Luftwaffe's reaction, and hopefully engage the enemy aircrews in a decisive battle. On the day there was initially little response from the Luftwaffe. But as the morning went on more German fighter pilots and bomber crews became airborne and engaged the RAF flyers. When the RAF pilots returned, combat reports were collated and it appeared that they had indeed achieved a notable victory. Claims totalled 43 enemy bombers and 49 fighters destroyed, 10 bombers and 29 fighters probably destroyed, 56 bombers and 84 fighters damaged. Compared to the RAF losses of 106 aircraft (88 of which were fighters), it is clear why the air element of the operation was deemed a success. In fact the Germans lost only 25 bombers and 23 fighters destroyed, and 16 bombers and 8 fighters damaged. Over-claiming, as in previous years, was still a problem.

But the true value of the failure of the Dieppe landings was the tactical lessons that were learnt. Notably, in terms of air power, there were obvious improvements needed in co-ordinating the ground support by bombers and fighter bombers, In general, operation Jubilee also highlighted the serious shortfalls in Allied equipment and tactics, with regard to a seaborne invasion. Allied planning for a full-scale decisive assault, wherever that may fall on the Atlantic coast of Europe, clearly needed a lot more careful consideration.

Sholto Douglas, in considering Slessor's reorganisation plans in July 1942, suggested Leigh-Mallory as tactical commander for the major cross-Channel invasion, stating that, 'there is literally no officer with his qualifications for the job.' Discussions with the Combined Chiefs of Staff ensued and on 11 March 1943 Leigh-Mallory was informed by the Chief of the Air Staff, Sir Charles Portal, that he had been selected as Allied Air Commander-in-Chief (Designate), the appointment being approved by the British Chiefs of Staff but only agreed in principle by the Combined Chiefs of Staff.

Leigh-Mallory felt he could not fulfil his responsibilities without the proper and official status being approved. He needed a definitive directive from the Combined Chiefs of Staff. But COSSAC (Chief of Staff to the Supreme Allied Commander), tasked with the outline planning for Overlord, was having a similar problem. Lieutenant General Frederick Morgan had taken up the role of COSSAC in 1943, and it wasn't until September 1943 that he would receive proper executive authority. So until Leigh-Mallory received the same, his main responsibility would remain planning. Meantime, he could learn from the experience of the Dieppe raid, and draw on the lessons of the North African campaign. He also looked to instigate his own experiment.

On 8 December 1942 Leigh-Mallory wrote to the Air Ministry recommending that units of Fighter Command should be put on a mobile basis well in advance of any contemplated move to the continent and that trials (to be known as Exercise Spartan) should be carried out early in 1943 to determine how mobility could best be achieved. And on 22 February 1943 he again wrote to the

Air Ministry proposing the formation of a Mobile Group Headquarters with the object of testing the organisation and control of air forces in mobile operations and training personnel. In addition, it would provide a nucleus on which to form the mobile air contingent for the invasion.

Spartan pitted two forces against each other, Eastland representing a German force and Southland an Allied one. Eastland was presumed to have overrun Allied territory, an area within Cambridge, Coventry and Gloucester. Southland was to regain the occupied territory, from a staring point of Swindon to Maidenhead. Eastland had an air force called X Group; Southland's was named Z Group. With respect to preparing for and examining plans for the cross-Channel invasion 12 of Z Group's squadrons were mobile, and could move between airfields, unlike any of the X Group squadrons. Spartan ran from 1 to 12 March 1943, and although there had been difficulties the basic concepts appeared workable and would be adopted. Notably fighter squadrons, reconnaissance aircraft and light bombers were to be established in respective 'Airfields' (the nomenclature later changed to 'Wings') and a number of these would constitute a 'Group'. The exercise had certainly been of value to the high command and invasion planners. Spartan also gave many of the squadron personnel involved a taste of what might come later.

One of the squadrons operating as part of Southland Z Group was 182 Squadron. 182 was formed in September 1942 and for the following two months the squadron's aircraft, Hawker Typhoons 1A and 1B, started to arrive. There then began a period of training, with the first operational sorties carried out on 3 January 1943, with two Typhoons attacking installations at Bruges. From then on training focussed on army support and practice for shipping attacks. In the middle of February 1943 one notable and experienced pilot joined the squadron, Flight Lieutenant Reg Baker DFC.

Reg had returned to the UK and 210 Squadron in December 1941, in May 1942 transferring to 240 Squadron and in July 1942 being posted to Malta, returning a few months later. The nature of Reg's operational flying was now to change markedly. In November 1942 he attended 59 OTU, then in February 1943 fighter pilot Reg Baker arrived at 182 Squadron. When he arrived the squadron was already planning for Spartan. On 20 February though a different kind of exercise was conducted.

> *182 Squadron ORB:* In the afternoon all pilots took part in an exercise, the object being to get into the aerodrome without being caught. Police, Home Guards and the RAF regiment were their opponents. Four of our Squadron managed to get in. Everyone agreed that it was grand fun.

During the last week of February preparations for Spartan continued, the squadron ORB recording on 23 February, 'Spartan hangs over our heads and we shall all be glad when it starts.' On 1 March the squadron established itself at Middle Wallop. Fascinating excerpts from the squadron ORB record some of the conditions the personnel experienced trying out the 'mobile' system.

> 1 March – Aircraft arrived at 1420 hrs in perfect formation. After much difficulty located site of camp. Only 4 tents up out of 8. The dispersal field so small that only 15 yards between each of 14 aircraft, also narrow

bottleneck entrance. Tents up by 1700 hours and everyone packed in. Lorries unloaded and returned to Cambridge, squadron now without transport. Airfield transport arrangements poor. Mess extremely poor, most food cold, and not sufficient staff.

2 March – Ground personnel of AHQ have little idea of jobs: orders given to them but many different people with resulting confusion. An urgent priority such as u/s aircraft tackled after comparatively unimportant servicing. Suggested that Eng O's should contact squadron COs and be informed of jobs to be done so that priority list may be arranged. Intelligence set up not arranged yet. Weather bitterly cold, food continues poor, but this due to a mistake in issue in rations.

3 March – Food infinitely better on new scale of rations. Air Marshal Leigh-Mallory, General Paget and Air Marshal Barrett and staff visited squadron in afternoon. Discussed inadequate briefing arrangements. Lack of adjutant felt as amount of paperwork enormous. IO [Intelligence Officer] unable to cope with and give proper attention to Intelligence. Battle dress would be advantage for ground crews. More tent accommodation is required for aircrews, office accommodation totally inadequate.

4 March – Squadron detailed for 60 minutes availability from 0635 hours. Placed on readiness at 1155 hrs and kept until 1535 hrs, too long a period at readiness. Practice Air Raid at 1122 hrs. An attack by 16 Typhoons at 1205 – 8 high level – 8 low – no result awarded. One flight allowed on to 60 mins, available at 1535 hrs to get DIs completed. Other flight at readiness until 1950. Too long for pilots' nerves. An order of the day received from AOC i/c Z Group at 1745 'Enemy making for line Gloucester – Cirencester – Swindon – Hungerford – Newbury – Reading. Our aim to reach river on this line and hold. Air forces to delay enemy.'

5 March – The squadron ordered to readiness at 0645 hrs. Morning very foggy and flying impossible. There was no breakfast at 0715 hrs. CO met with insolence from cooks when complaining. Little or no news of military situation comes through; anything that does is hours behind. CO suggests an officer detailed to supervise mess as feeding remains very badly organised. Telephone communications hopeless – continual delays, cutting of lines. No flying whole day. Squadron released at 1945. IO visited Z Group (Haslemere). Arrived to find everyone at tea. Little or no information when staff did arrive. No appearance of control at all. Staff in permanent buildings in considerable comfort. Whole set up somewhat sickening. Our forces crossed Thames, and established bridgeheads at Clacton – Aldeburgh – Southwold or E.Coast on Thursday 4.3.43.

6 March – Squadron ordered to readiness at 0900 hrs. Weather thick. Order to scramble came through 1055 hrs. Target MT (300 Vs) concentration in wood. Squadron took off on course 028 degrees to Newbury. Above Newbury squadron given new target sector 110 degrees, 9 m from Oxford believed Woodston Church (this is 017 degrees from Oxford 4m). Visibility less than 1 mile owing to fog. CO orbited Oxford then headed towards Bicester – returned base, before reaching. Note impracticability of giving new targets in air, and briefing over R/T. CO

pointed this out to Controller on return to base. Squadron cover by 1 Flight of No. 247 Squadron. Squadron up 1115 down 1200 hours. Second scramble at 1653 hours. Airborne 1705 down 1746. Attacked a column of Tanks (Canadian) and MT in Heyford area with bombs and cannon, two Mustangs destroyed, Squadron Leader Pugh and Flight Lieutenant Manak. Excellent results. Eight aircraft took part. Briefing very quick with new method – CO gets gen on his map, then calls Squadron. Flying Officer Snowdon force-landed in morning's show near M.W. engine cut – Snowdon safe.

7 March – Squadron put on readiness at 0630 hours and instructed to carry out bombing on Newmarket airfield at first light. Squadron up 0727 down 0845. Target not located owing to heavy mist 10/10 at 2,000 ft. CO collided with aircraft on take-off. Squadron given three target areas in afternoon. But no operation materialised. At 1610 hours the squadron was ordered to scramble to attack enemy MT and armoured concentration. The 4 aircraft detailed were unable to take off owing to weather conditions and the show was called off... remain entirely in the dark as to the Military situation, and Air Force activity, as no communiqués are broadcast... The latest Military communiqué reports our troops beyond Thames on a line Swindon – Wantage – Wallingford – Henley.

8 March – Our forces on line Banbury – Oxford and sweeping round. Squadron took off to attack enemy HQ at 1145 hours. Attack success with bombs and cannon from low level... Cranfield airfield attacked on return with cannon. 6 Typhoons, 5 Mustangs, 1 Hurricane damaged on ground. 3 Mustangs destroyed in circuit above Airfield. More impending Airfield preliminary movement orders received. More tomorrow? Squadron scrambled again 1642 down 1730 to attack Tanks. Tanks attacked also 100+ MT 2 Mustangs destroyed. 2 Typhoons damaged... 3 Aircraft took off at 1826 down 1914 to bomb panzer concentration. Target not located, at 1840 Flying Officer Payne bombed four 25lb guns in Thame Main street. C-in-C visited squadron in late afternoon.

9 March – Advance party left Middle Wallop at 1120 hours. Journey took nearly 2 hours. Main party started to arrive at 1630 hours and continued arriving until 2300 hrs. Cookhouse staff did marvellous jobs. Cookhouse arrangements do not seem good as squadron will have a long way to walk to either mess. Squadron scrambled at 1355 to attack MT. Task successfully accomplished. Squadron again scrambled at 1651 to attack armoured column. Bren carriers and armoured cars cannoned. Others... bombed and cannoned. 2 Spits were destroyed and one damaged by Flying Officer Richards and Sgt Houghton on return from target.

10 March – Air party arrived at 1115 hrs. Aircraft were refuelled by hand pumps as no bowsers available. The small mess hopelessly crammed with arrival of pilots – queues. The idea is to have an Air Crew mess. There are 69 aircrew and the mess holds 16. The whole set up is ridiculous and highly demoralising. Recommended one large marquee to hold all aircrew at once. The Intelligence set up changed. Squadron IOs take turns at main office and squadron have to come up to office to be briefed, then return to squadron to take off. Complete waste of time in view of the efficiency of

> old method. This must be squashed at 11 Grp. Tents were all up at 1600. Spin PBX phone out all day – RT communication only with ops – and that very faint as cows had knocked over aerials at 'Linle'. Most people have now had enough of 'Spartan'.
> 11 March – Squadron put on readiness at 0800 hours (message 0630) ordered to attack concentration of MT and armour Northampton – Olney – Wellingborough. Squadron up 0826 down 0900. Weather N of Oxford V P muddled order on R/T not understood by CO. Squadron were taxying out to attack same target at 0955 hrs when Airfield strafed by enemy Spitfires. 3 Typhoons destroyed on the ground and Squadron Leader T. P. Pugh DFC, Flying Officer Richards, Flying Officer Vize 'Killed'. Other 3 aircraft took off on 2nd runway and claimed 6 Spits destroyed. 2 Spits awarded to Squadron by umpires. 3 aircraft scrambled at 1140 hours to attack MT and armour but were ordered to return to base, as weather conditions u/s. There is no parachute packer or facilities for packing on the Airfield. Feeding at the aircrew mess continues to be very bad as arrangements totally inadequate.
> 12 March – Squadron notified that we would have to give 1st Canadian Corps first priority for air support at 0745. The following message received at 0931 'Spartan ceasefire, all troops standfast' from 1st Canadian Army. HQ Z Group sent 'Spartan standfast Spartan' at same time. Much confusion caused by this wording as should mean exercise concluded prematurely. Normal terminal signal followed at 1048. Squadron to standfast for further orders. Order to return to MW came through at 1300 hours. This cancelled during afternoon. Whole Airfield and squadrons to move to Zeals (1700 hrs). Finally decided late at night that the Airfield should move back to Middle Wallop. No gen on the future.

Clearly a lot of the detail for the working of a mobile air force still had to be sorted out, and therein of course lay some of the value of the exercise. But such was the usefulness of Spartan, that Z Group HQ and some of the ground units were retained for the formation of 83 Group, which would eventually be at the forefront of Allied air striking when the invasion began.

On 29 April 1943 Chief of Air Staff Sir Charles Portal proposed the reorganisation of the UK-based air forces in preparation for cross-Channel invasion. He proposed abolishing Army Co-operation Command, and Headquarters Expeditionary Air Force was to form within, and subordinate to, Fighter Command until such time as the Allied Air Commander-in-Chief was confirmed, when it would transfer to the control of Allied Air Headquarters. The Chiefs of Staff Committee endorsed the proposals and gave further clarity on the forces the Allied Air Commander-in-Chief was to control:

> The latter will also control through appropriate channels the strategic bombing forces allotted to the operation, the formations concerned with the Air Defence of Great Britain, the air element of the Airborne forces, all transport aircraft and such photographic reconnaissance units and Coastal Command squadrons as may be allocated to him for the purpose of the operations.[13]

[13] Public Record Office AIR 41/66.

As such with effect from 1 June 1943 the Tactical Air Force (the new name given to the aforementioned Expeditionary Air Force) was to form within Fighter Command. This Tactical Air Force was to be made up of:

No. 2 Group
No. 83 (Composite Group)
No. 38 Wing
No. 140 Squadron

But in discussing the formation of this new force, Sir Alan Brooke (Chief of the Imperial General Staff) asked for consideration to be given to the formation of a second Composite Group to operate with the First Canadian Army. Leigh-Mallory had already been contemplating such a formation, but the demands of North Africa coupled with the formation of 83 Group, meant there were just not the resources available at that time. It was therefore proposed that until 84 Group could be established, the Second British Army and First Canadian Army who were keen to start training, had to work just with 83 Group.

But the Canadians were not satisfied and it was decided on 29 May 1943 that 83 Group should be working with the First Canadian Army and the new Group, 84 Group, should align its operations with the Second British Army. In fact this would be reversed once the plans for Overlord had been further developed, in January 1944. With the Second British Army to be first in assaulting the Normandy beaches it was allocated the support of 83 Group, with 84 Group then supporting the First Canadian Army following up the initial assault. The formation of 84 Group was formally authorised by the Air Ministry on 22 July 1943.

On 12 June 1943 Leigh-Mallory issued his first directive to the 2nd TAF outlining its primary function . . .

> was to plan and prepare for continual operations in close collaboration with Army Group Headquarters. This would entail exercises in combined operations, the study of airborne operations and the subsequent training of the RAF component (No. 38 Wing) with the airborne forces allotted to the Army Group. The Tactical Air Force would also be responsible for the training and exercise on active operations of the Composite Groups and light bomber squadrons. Finally it was to fulfil immediately all requirements for strategical reconnaissance in connection with continental operations.[14]

In the following months 2nd TAF would steadily grow and evolve as the nature and demands of the cross-Channel operation became more apparent. In that time RAF fighter squadrons kept up their offensive action over north-west France.

Immediately after Spartan there was still uncertainty at 182 Squadron about the future, although the food did improve somewhat.

> *182 Squadron ORB:* 19 March – A decided browned offness is setting in with everyone, even though life is much softened in comparison with the exercise days.

At the end of March training resumed and on 5 April the squadron moved to

---

[14] *Ibid.*

Fairlop to begin operations. Reg Baker made his contribution; 13 April a Ramrod in the St Omer/Fort Range area, 18 April dive bombing Courtrai airfield. On 25 April 182 Squadron conducted three Rhubarbs, on one of which: ‘Flight Lieutenant Baker and Flying Officer McMane, Blue section, [airborne] from Fairlop 1115, down 1220 hrs crossed coast at Rye and made landfall at Berck sur Mer. The target being railway at Doullens. The section followed the course of the River Authie to the main arterial road at Le Boissot. The weather became extremely bad with heavy rain and section turned 5 miles beyond Le Boissot to return to base. Out over Fort Mahon where bombs jettisoned on the beach, and made landfall at Hastings – nought feet throughout.’

Rhubarbs

Rhubarbs were short-range low level attacks, in poor weather conditions, by small formations of two or possibly four fighters, on targets of opportunity. Ken Trott flew Typhoons with 195 and 197 Squadrons and recalls how such operations could be testing.

> From my point of view it was always what we called bad weather flying. They liked to send you across when the weather was a bit duff. So you could go in low level, in most cases, find the target and come out again. The idea being that you were sort of avoiding the flak. That was alright if you avoided the towns and cities, or some of the railway lines.
>
> I have a Rhubarb in my logbook for January 1944. It was a rather bad weather day. We took off from Fairlop, flew down over the Channel and over the coast. As we were going in, the chappy who was with me called up and said, ‘I’ve lost you. What shall I do?’ So I said, ‘Either proceed to the target or if you’re not sure where the target is then you’d better return to base.’ He returned to base. I went on and found the target, then turned to come home. By that time it was raining hard and the weather was really closing in. I happened to find myself over a railway junction. I wanted to get out of there quick, because at junctions you could expect flak. So I just pulled straight up and went on to instruments. I suppose I climbed through about 10,000 feet of cloud on instruments and when I came out of the top it was a lovely day, beautiful sunshine, cloud everywhere however, no breaks. I called up Control and asked for a homing. They just gave me a course to steer, and from then on kept me under control until told to come down through the cloud. As I was coming down they said when you break cloud you’ll be at about 800 feet, which sure enough I was. Control said, ‘I want you to land at Lympne.’ I landed, stayed for lunch and then got permission to fly to Manston in the afternoon. But the weather didn’t clear for some time. I finally got back to Fairlop in the evening. That one Rhubarb had taken all day.

On 28 April 182 Squadron conducted six Rhubarbs. Reg and his wingman attacked a goods train, one locomotive and 15 open and covered trucks in the station at Daunes, bombing at low level. Reg scored a direct hit on the centre of the train with his two 500lb bombs.

On 29 April the squadron moved to Lasham and in early May carried out numerous exercises. On 13 May 182 detailed some of its pilots to cross the Channel and attack an enemy airfield. The squadron ORB recorded the details:

> 13 May – In the afternoon Flight Lieutenant Baker [and 6 others] flew down to Ford where bombing up and briefing took place for the dive bombing attack on Abbeville Drucat Aerodrome, with 8 aircraft from 181 Squadron. The aircraft took off from Ford at 1440 hours and set course direct for Abbeville. The escort joined 181, 182 Squadrons over Ford, while still orbiting, causing Squadron Leader Crowley-Milling to set course immediately, leaving 182 well in the rear. The escort took up position to the rear and to the other side of 181. 182 Squadron were thus forced to fly through starboard escort in order to take up position in line abreast, and to starboard of 181 Squadron. The squadron crossed the French coast at 6,000 ft north of Ault, then climbed to 10,000 ft. The formation leader Squadron Leader Crowley-Milling gave his squadron the order line astern and attacked the target in a steep dive 10,000 ft to 5,000 ft followed by his second flight, the last two aircraft of which were some considerable distance behind the rest of the squadron. This caused 182 leader Flight Lieutenant Baker to delay his attack for some 30 seconds. Squadron dived 70 degrees 10,000 ft to 5,000 ft dropping 14 x 500 lbs GP on target. Hits were observed on or near bowsers and aircraft in both NW and SE dispersals. No enemy aircraft were seen in the air. Intense light and medium flak was experienced both over the target and from Crécy forest for some 10 miles. Squadron received no orders from formation leader and Flight Lieutenant Ireson ordered them into formation. Out over coast S of Berck where squadron dived to 0 feet and made cannon attacks on machine-gun posts. Landfall Worthing/Littlehampton. Landed Ford 1610 hrs. Flight Lieutenant Baker, the squadron leader, was hit by flak OT at the end of his dive. Flak burst in his cockpit blowing the top off and wounding him in the thigh, elbow and head. All instruments except rev counter and compass were u/s. The aircraft dived out of control to 100 ft where Flight Lieutenant Baker regained control. He gained height to 2,500 ft and headed back to Ford making landfall at Beachyhead. Attempted a crash landing on side of runways at the airdrome, but found himself heading towards Littlehampton village at 50 ft. He swerved and successfully crash landed near the railway line. This fine performance was a truly magnificent one and an example which has filled the rest of the squadron with pride and awe. There were large holes in the airplane, aileron, and cockpit of the aircraft and only first class ability could have brought it home, as F/Lt Baker succeeded in doing. The crowning incident was that, when his wounds had been bandaged, he insisted on being flown back to Lasham the same evening, refusing to remain in Ford sick quarters, as he was acting CO at this time. Amusement was caused by a small box of sundry objects extracted from Flight Lieutenant Baker. This included a screw!

On 16 May squadron personnel visited Reg in hospital, but it wasn't too long before he was back with a view to getting on ops as soon as possible, on 30 May taking part in a dive-bombing attack on steel works at Caen. But his time at 182 Squadron was about to run out, and the squadron ORB paid tribute to his leadership qualities.

> *182 Squadron ORB:* 14 June. Flight Lieutenant Baker DFC was posted to No. 263 Squadron, Warmwell as CO. This appointment was very popular and well deserved, but he will be very much missed.

CHAPTER 3

SHIPPING STRIKES

On 9 September 1943 the Allies enacted a threatened amphibious landing, operation Starkey, a rehearsal for the forthcoming invasion, attempting to fool the Germans into believing the invasion was underway, draw up the Luftwaffe and engage and shoot down as many enemy aircraft as possible. There were three main phases to the air side of the plan. Firstly to reinforce 11 Group and escalate the scale of offensive operations in the Pas de Calais from 16 to 24 August. Secondly reconnoitre and bomb enemy airfields and military targets in the Pas de Calais from 25 August to 7 September. Thirdly to bomb coastal guns north and south of Boulogne on the nights of 6/7 and 7/8 September and again on the morning of 8 September, carry out attacks on enemy airfields and communication lines on 8 September, and shield the naval force and escort the bombers. The first two phases went pretty much according to plan. The third phase was delayed owing to poor weather, so it wasn't until the morning of 9 September that a seaborne force of 355 ships headed for Boulogne. The assault force then turned back a few miles short of the enemy coastline. 263 Squadron's Squadron Leader Reg Baker would be involved in the operation. So also would Typhoon pilot Bob Cole.

Bob Cole was born in Gloucestershire on 8 August 1922. When he was 18 he volunteered for the air force. At the interview he said he wanted to be a pilot, but was told he would be an air gunner, which he wouldn't accept at all. Bob persisted and was finally granted his wish of training to be a pilot, gaining his wings flying on Stearmans and Harvards in California. On return to the UK he was eventually posted to 56 OTU Tealing, near Dundee, flying Hurricanes and then to Kinnel, near Arbroath.

> *Bob Cole:* Then of all things they posted eight of us to an Air Sea Rescue squadron, and we had just done a fighter OTU. We went to see the CO and found that there were people on rest and someone had buggered up. They then sent us in pairs to Typhoon squadrons. Potty [Ron Pottinger] and I went to 3 Squadron, joining in May 43.

On 26 May 1943 Bob took up a Hurricane IIC on a 50-minute sector recce. Five days later he would have his first experience of the Typhoon IB:

> It's a big jump a Typhoon from a Hurricane, much bigger and faster. The Typhoon is like flying a tank. It vibrates like hell, a hellish noise.

The 'Ladylike' Typhoon

Ken Trott flew Typhoons with 197 Squadron and recalls his feelings of the aircraft.

> Rather a large aircraft shall we say, for a single-engine fighter. Terrific power. Quite something to control. I liked flying it from the point of view of speed and being a very stable gun platform. You could come in on a target at 400 mph and the thing was as steady as a rock. With the Hurricane I could throw it all over the sky and do any aerobatics I liked. I always felt I could never take liberties with the Typhoon. You'd got to know what you were doing. They warned you in the pilots' notes not to undertake anything under 8,000 feet – that was to give you a little bit of leeway.
>
> I recall once when we were at Coltishall in Norfolk. They had a captured FW 190 and they said one evening to all the pilots, 'We are going to have a 190 come over and a Typhoon.' I thought it was the worst possible thing they could do because the 190 came over right across the sky, flicking, rolling, looping, so quick. Then the Typhoon came over almost ladylike. To me it so showed up, in my opinion, how much better the 190 was. But at the same time the Typhoon was a very solid aircraft. I recall one or two that came back after being shot up with flak, I don't suppose the 190 would have got back. But they were ideal in the end for what they turned out to be.

On 1 June, Bob Cole prepared to land his Typhoon following an hour of local flying. At this point his hydraulics failed, Bob's logbook recording: 'Flaps and radiator shutter unusable. Crash on landing, aircraft swings to left + undercarriage collapses.'

Bob Cole: Chiefy said, 'I just put that engine in that morning!'

During June and most of July Bob gained further experience of the Typhoon, conducting five low level bombing practice flights, with reasonable results, recording in his logbook average errors of (14 June) 119 yards, (26 June) 66 yards, (13 July) 175¾ yards, (15 July) 41 yards and (25 July) 51 yards (dive bombing), 59 yards (low level bombing). On 29 July Bob conducted his first operational sortie and recorded in his logbook, 'Ops. Close support escort to Hurricanes. Shipping strike. Fail to rendezvous with Hurri's off Zeebrugge, nothing seen. Return to base. Ack ack from one gun N. of Zeebrugge.'

> *Bob Cole:* We were supposed to support Hurricanes and took off in the dark at about four in the morning. We circled around the enemy coast waiting for the others to come but every time we got in the circle the enemy unloaded their 88s. The op had been called off. We were just target practice.

For the next few weeks Bob had more time familiarising himself with the aircraft, conducting air and cannon tests, night flying tests and one dive and low level bombing practice, average errors of 66 and 55 yards respectively. Then it was back to ops, in particular Roadsteads, low level attacks on shipping and coastal targets.

> *Bob Cole's logbook:*
> 24 August: Ops nothing seen.
> 26 August: Ops. Roadstead. N/S. Light + Heavy A.A. from French coast. Very accurate. Lots of Tracer.
> 2 September: Ops Fighter support to Hurricanes. Heavy Flak from Flushing.
> 5 September: Ops Roadstead. Dutch Islands. Near miss with 250s on 500 ton ship. Cannon attacks on four boats. Little Flak. Make seven attacks.

Bob Cole recalls the operation of 26 August, which would go some way to forming his opinion of the CO Squadron Leader S. R. Thomas DFC AFC.

> *Bob Cole:* Thomas was crackers. He took us to two ships. We hit the coast somewhere south of Dieppe. We turned up in three lines of four aircraft, I was on the one on the inside, on the back. I had just joined the squadron and I was useless. We kept going up the coast and every time we came to something that had a house on it, the 40 mil tracer, bloody stuff, we would watch it coming out. If it was high, dive underneath it, if it was low, climb like hell. It would splash in the sea around us. We were fired at about fifteen times – they'd opened up with any and everything – never hit anybody. When we got back, I said to the chap who was in front of me, 'What were you doing?' and he was doing the same as me. Thomas said, 'Well we didn't see any ships to have a go at, but it cost them more for flak than it cost us for petrol.' So he reckoned on that rate that we had come out on top. Bloody peculiar.

But what was becoming apparent to Bob at the time was the danger of conducting bombing operations. On the 5 September mission Squadron Leader Thomas came down in enemy territory and was captured.

> *Bob Cole:* It was the only low level I did. We did some shipping in the Dutch Islands. I got credited with a small boat. I was about the third in, with 250s. Neither of the others had hit it. When I turned in they had strafed it so much all the flak had stopped. We went on round strafing other things, and Thomas went over a small harbour and something blew up. He crashed on a beach and was heard to speak on the radio.

Meanwhile, another of our featured pilots had been seeking out enemy shipping. On 15 June 1943 the 263 Squadron ORB recorded:

> Squadron Leader E. R. Baker DFC comes to the squadron [as CO] in his third tour of operations. He has fought and flown aircraft of many designations in almost every theatre of the war, other than the Far East. It is felt that the squadron has again been most fortunate in his appointment.

George Wood, who had joined 263 Squadron in February 1943, recalled the impression he developed of the new CO.

> He was larger than life and a wonderful person. He would brief a dicey-do op and your eyes would come out like organ stops, expecting all that flak. He'd say, 'Well you've got to die some time', and then carry on. He

was hard in that respect.

On 19 June 263 moved to Zeals, Wiltshire, where a period of intensive training began, owing to the fact that there were a lot of new pilots on staff. On 20 June one pilot is recorded as having made 'a successful landing on his first Whirlwind solo', but then selected wheels up instead of flaps up. On 12 July the squadron moved back to Warmwell, Dorset, and Reg Baker would lead four shipping recces on 13, 18, 20, and 23 July without any real incident except the threat of flak. Although George Wood had become aware of an enemy presence on the 18 July mission.

> *George Wood:* On this particular op I had sighted a Focke-Wulf stalking the squadron and I reported this to Reg. Then unknown to me, my RT failed and I didn't pick up that Reg had called up two of the escorting Spitfires to go and investigate. When I suddenly saw another aircraft crossing my bow I gave it a squirt before realising it was a Spitfire. I wrote this in my logbook, adding, 'Missed him'. Reg wrote underneath, 'Rotten shooting'.

The 263 Squadron ORB recorded the lack of real action against the enemy.

> Thus July ended without any contact with the enemy other than four reviews of the Channel Islands and rocks and the occasional and not inaccurate bursts of flak which are a commonplace of these reconnaissance operations.
>
> It seemed that the enemy now very seldom moves any shipping by day between Brest and Le Havre. 164 Squadron of Hurricane IVs have been at Warmwell since the squadron moved to Zeals in June, and have not yet had even one strike.
>
> Moreover the presence of a new squadron of Typhoon bombers in the Portreath Sector removes the possibility of a good deal of offensive work in the far south-west which formerly fell to the detachments of this squadron. The work of the squadron has therefore tended to become a kind of anti-convoy patrol whose success is measurable by the absence of enemy shipping in the Channel Islands and off the coasts of the Cotentin.

But in August, matters were about to change and 263 Squadron would see plenty of action. On 11 August 1943 Reg Baker led his Whirlwind pilots, escorted by Spitfires, to an area off the Brittany coast. In a small bay where the Abervach river flowed into the sea, enemy boats were sighted, seven E-boats and a trawler. The aircraft too were soon spotted and the boat crews scrambled about removing the tarpaulin from their guns, but the Whirlwinds were on to them too quickly. Reg Baker took the first flight of Whirlwinds in, and with his No. 2 they homed in on two E-boats. Reg's No. 2 would later report that. 'We just couldn't miss them. The CO scored a direct hit on one with a bomb and I managed to do the same with the other.' George Wood also took part in the operation.

> I was in the second wave going in, and all around E-boats were blowing up. We went for those that hadn't yet been hit, dropping bombs from low level. Sadly I still have a vivid picture in my mind of a German mariner who was diving overboard, looking up at me, horrified, and I just dropped a bomb on him. It's been in my mind ever since. Not a happy thought.

Eventually four E-boats were claimed blown-up by the squadron, another set on fire and a sixth, either an E-boat or an armed trawler, was destroyed. The Squadron ORB recorded the 11 August operation as 'The Massacre at the Aber Vrach [*sic*] River'. The day after, Leigh-Mallory and the Secretary of State for Air sent congratulatory messages. The mission was also reported in the cinemas, on Pathe news, and when Reg Baker was asked what had happened he had simply replied, twirling his wizard prang moustache, 'We caught Jerry with his pants down.' George Wood also recalled that there was one other notable person taking an interest in the operation.

> At the time Queen Mary was in the ops room listening to the raid. Now when on operations a deaf ear is turned to all the language that's used on the air. A Polish squadron happened to be escorting us, so when the swearing started the group captain accompanying Queen Mary, in order to spare her blushes, remarked that they were speaking in Polish. The reply that is alleged to have come from the Queen is, 'Not bloody likely.'

Three days later Reg Baker further inflicted his wrath upon the enemy. On the night of 14 August 1943 moonlight helped in the sighting of an E-boat between Jersey and Guernsey. Reg swooped from up moon, dropped his bombs and the ship was struck, causing an explosion midships. He then watched as two men struggled in the sea amongst the debris. Reg Baker would later recall, 'I think the E-boat was taken by surprise because though it opened up with one gun, it did not put up as much flak as these boats usually do.' And then just off Guernsey Reg, flying at 300 feet, caught sight of a Heinkel 111 silhouetted against the full moon, 200 feet above. He rose slowly and from 200 yards let loose, and his enemy's port engine caught fire. Then as the Heinkel turned Reg opened up again and his foe plunged into the sea.

On 18 August he took off at 0015 hrs on a night recce. He was 'flying down moon along the north coast of the Cotentin when he saw flak coming from port and astern. He turned to investigate and saw a trawler lying about a mile off Cherbourg and firing vigorously. He turned inside Cherbourg harbour positioning for attack, meeting two searchlights and flak from shore batteries. Then he bombed the trawler up moon from 50 feet, and saw a large explosion on the stern of the ship. After orbiting he saw the ship well down by the stern and apparently sinking. Its guns were silenced. Flight Lieutenant Ross found no trace of the ship an hour later. This armed trawler was claimed Cat 2, probably sunk.'

The rest of the month was taken up with convoy escort duties and then on 7 September the unit moved to Manston, Kent, as a detachment to 11 Group, to take part in operation Starkey.

On 8 September Reg led 12 aircraft on a dive-bombing operation to the naval and flak positions at Hardelot, an attack which was designed to assist in the protection of the ships of the amphibious exercise, detailed to make the feint on Boulogne the next day. Reg and four others had to return early, but seven aircraft did attack the positions. The next day Reg again led 12 aircraft to the Hardelot gun positions, taking off at 0800 hours, the Squadron ORB recording, 'It went well from the start to finish. Dives were from 14,000 to 3,500 feet and bombing results were good – all bursts were in the target area, within a circle of 150 yards radius. In both operations the coast was crossed at Hastings at 4,000 feet, after which the squadron climbed to 14,000 feet, dive bombed in echelon starboard and returned in formation at 1,000 feet.'

3 Squadron and Bob Cole would also take part in Starkey. Bob recorded in his logbook: '9 September: Ops Ramrod. Dive bomb gun positions + strong points on French coast 500 x 2. One bomb would not release. Fell off on approach leg.'

Despite all the effort, 11 Group having despatched its aircraft on over 2,000 sorties on 9 September, there was little sign of the Luftwaffe, and only 12 enemy aircraft destroyed. Possibly the threat went unnoticed. Or perhaps the Luftwaffe didn't want to engage in a fight against such overwhelming numbers. However, the exercise did provide valuable lessons with regard to fighter control and bombing policy. Lessons that could be translated into the plans for the real invasion.

On 10 September 263 Squadron returned to Warmwell. A week later a special operation was laid on. Operation Chatternooga Choochoo was devised by Reg Baker in co-operation with 10 Group Intelligence, the aim being to sever the main Rennes-Brest railway line if possible in nine places between Lamballe and Morlaix.

> *263 Squadron ORB:...* so that (a) trains should be bottled up [for] 'ranging' on that night (b) trains should be diverted to the southern loop line single track and become targets for Mosquitoes on the following night. Pilots were carefully and extensively briefed at Warmwell during the previous days. They were to make landfall at 2,500 feet at the point nearest to their targets where no flak was to be expected and to bomb their allotted targets as an absolute priority. Eleven aircraft were to be on target at approximately the same time. These orders were nicely carried out. Our aircraft met neither S/Ls or flak, tho' these were seen out of range at Morlaix. Bombing was carried out between 0205 and 0215 from 2,000 to 700 feet. No pilot 'lost his way'.

Reg contributed as one of four aircraft detailed to attack the Ponthou viaduct. One pilot bombed the line SW of Morlaix. Reg and the other two attacked the viaduct but think they hit the cuttings to the side.

Shot down in the CO's Whirlwind

On 23 September 1943 George Wood took part in a 263 Squadron operation to Morlaix airfield. Reg Baker didn't take part in the raid; he was on leave. George Wood was flying Reg's Whirlwind.

> When we came in over Morlaix there was lots of ack-ack. I dived from about 14,000, and when I got to 4,000 feet I was hit. I had pressed the tit to off-load the bombs and then everything blew up. I think some flak must have hit my bomb. The escorting aircraft all said it was like a flower opening, and a chap looking through binoculars down below later told me it looked like two aircraft had collided, as there was so much debris falling. I couldn't get out of the aircraft. I tried everything

> but nothing happened. So I just shouted, 'Oh God help me.' Suddenly I found myself outside the aircraft, don't know how, and I pulled the ripcord. As I was decending the Germans started shooting at me. There were bullets whistling past my lughole. I was just hoping they wouldn't hit the parachute or me. Fortunately I wasn't suspended for too long and I landed on the aerodrome. I ran like hell and reached some barbed wire. I walked along until I came to a tree that had a convenient branch. I shinned up and dropped over to the other side and then kept running.

George, as he was to find out later, had actually run across a minefield. It was, however, believed to have contained anti-tank mines.

> They probably would not have exploded if I had trodden on one. At least it dissuaded the Germans from giving chase. I later learned that about 900 men had been mobilised to look for me.

George believed this was because he had been flying Reg Baker's aircraft, and a piece of wreckage had been found carrying Reg's call sign, 'Lochinvar'. Reg was known to the enemy. In fact on some operations the Germans had tried impersonating him, using his call sign, over the radio. George recalled: 'The Germans therefore believed they were looking for a VIP, who should be captured at all costs.'

George hid his Mae West in a hedge. He started walking south and eventually climbed a tree to survey his surroundings. From his vantage point he became aware of numerous German patrols keen to capture the 'VIP'. One stopped beneath his tree, for a smoke and a chat. George recalled: 'I remained still hardly daring to breathe, but not one man glanced up.' For the remainder of the day George managed to evade the patrols, eventually making his way to a farmhouse where he received help. For the next month George's fate was controlled by French civilians and members of the Resistance. Eventually passage back to England by boat was arranged.

> When I got back one of my first things was to phone up Reggie and apologise for pranging his aircraft. His typical flamboyant response was, 'That's alright old chap. I'd only have done it myself later on.' He said, 'Come down, let's have a party.'

For the three weeks following operation Chatternooga Choochoo Reg flew on night shipping recces and armed recces. That would change on 8 October. Taking off at 1900 hrs Reg bombed an E-boat off Varriville but was prevented by searchlights from investigating further. He landed at 2025 hrs. Then at 2215 two pilots returned from a night recce in which one aircraft was shot up by a 2,500-ton flak ship and damaged. Five minutes later Reg led seven aircraft out and found the aforementioned ship off Cap de la Hague:

> *263 Squadron ORB:* … and bombed it from mast height without seeing more than indistinct explosions. He was forced to orbit in accurate heavy flak from Alderney and Cap de la Hague, as well as much light flak from the ship … As the visibility was very poor in sea haze the CO decided that this ship should not be further attacked in this land-defended area and

ordered the six aircraft which were following him to return to base. Meanwhile fog had come in rapidly at Warmwell and all aircraft were ordered to return to Tangmere. It seems that Pilot Officer Simpson who was next to Squadron Leader Baker, the squadron's most experienced pilot, had engine failure not due to enemy action and that his other engine failed during his run in at Tangmere. He crashed into an anti-landing post a hundred yards from the runway and was killed instantly.

263 Squadron's offensive continued on the night of 17/18 October.

263 Squadron ORB: This operation, locally devised, planned and briefed as Chuffa Prang was designed to disorganise railway communications in and near the Cherbourg Peninsula and thereafter to take advantage of the tactical situation. It was a great success. Each pilot arrived at his target after a route which had correctly avoided the intense flak, which is to be met with by the unwary and Squadron Leader Baker blew up an ammunition train SE of Valognes, then probably damaged a loco near Bricquebec.

Over the next few days some of the squadron pilots carried out Rhubarbs, attacking trains with some success. Then on the afternoon of 24 October a series of raids began against one particular target in Cherbourg harbour, a blockade-running merchant ship called the *Münsterland.*

263 Squadron ORB: This was the squadron's first (and perhaps the first of the war) low level attack upon shipping in Cherbourg harbour. Our aircraft flew at just above sea level on a course which brought them between the outer moles and straight to the *Münsterland.* Four aircraft bombed the *Münsterland* and two of these attacked with cannons, leaving her on fire in two places – she was well ablaze 11 minutes later but the fire had been extinguished 90 minutes later. The other four aircraft bombed two ships aft of the *Münsterland* and saw cannon strikes on one of them. Two pilots then scored strikes on two of six M Class minesweepers in the transatlantic dock. Flak was fired at our aircraft from more than a hundred guns within range from harbour and ships: 'It was like a horizontal hail storm, painted red', (Flight Sergeant Beaumont). All our aircraft were hit more or less seriously. The formation broke half to port ESE over the peninsula. Flight Sergeant Gray's starboard engine was smoking and he glided down to port from 150 feet, about three miles ESE of Cherbourg just in the manner of a controlled forced landing. The country here is fairly open and it is hoped that he may still be alive. Flying Officer Mercer's aircraft was hit over the target and it may have been for this reason that he was flying considerably above the formation when they recrossed the coast three miles S of St Vaast. Here his aircraft received a direct hit from a coastal flak battery and dived into the sea, disintegrating on impact. It is not thought that he could have survived. Flight Lieutenant Ross's aircraft was severely hit in the starboard wing, juddered and stalled at 180 mph as well as the wing root. He made a perfect belly landing at Warmwell at this speed. Flight Sergeant Cooper's undercarriage, damaged by flak, collapsed on landing. Squadron Leader Baker was bruised on the

> shoulder by perspex dislodged by bullets. Ninety minutes later 183 Squadron Typhoons attacked the *Münsterland* and lost Squadron Leader Gowers DFC, a veteran of the Battle of Britain, and two other pilots.

On 28 October Reg led eight aircraft on a dive-bombing attack, again against the *Münsterland*, all bombs reported within 500 yards of the target, warehouses hit and an oil fire started. Two days later *Münsterland* was the target yet again.

> *263 Squadron ORB:* The CO started the dives rather too early and pulled back again to 12,000 feet, then almost vertically. A cluster of bursts hit warehouses W of the target, two bursts were in the dry dock area. The Hun now has dive bombing weighed up. His heavy flak was intense and accurate at 12,000 feet and during the dive from 9,000 to 7,000. The CO therefore led on down to 5,000. This and the change of the early dive seems to have led to only one Whirlwind being slightly damaged by flak. The six aircraft returned over Warmwell in excellent formation, close two vics, vics line astern.

During November 263 Squadron would continue attacking shipping targets, including revisits to the *Münsterland*, although poor weather would disrupt operations. At the beginning of December 263 Squadron would start to receive Typhoons. But Reg Baker, having now added a Bar to his DFC, was to leave to take on more senior responsibilities.

Fighting a Condor

On 28 July 1943 James Stewart DFC, serving with the Merchant Shipping Fighting Unit, found himself aboard the *Empire Darwin*, having left Gibraltar on 23 July. On the evening of the 28th it became clear that the convoy had unwanted company.

> *James Stewart:* It was one of the most amazing things I can think of. The Condors (FW 200s) had been shadowing the convoy and reporting our position. We could see them on the horizon. I was on readiness in the cockpit of my Hurricane I and just before I was launched off, from the starboard side about 150 feet above the water came a FW 200 side by side with a US Liberator, guns firing. I'd never seen anything like that before – never will again. Sure enough the Condor's inner engine caught fire and down he went into the water. The Liberator took off and I guess there was a mayday heard, but from what I understand I don't think he ever got back, he also suffered damage.
>
> Then I was launched off. It was just a case of getting up there and attacking.

> *James Stewart's combat report:* I recognised it as an FW 200, flying at 1,000 feet, and gave chase. He was flying north, but turned and flew south for a minute, then proceeded eastward, reducing height to about 200 feet. I had no difficulty overtaking at about 6¼ boost, 2,600 revs and at approximately 250 mph and made my attack from the port quarter out of the sun. My attack was delivered from 40 degs

> to 15 degs, opening fire at 300 yards and closing to almost point blank. I aimed at the cockpit, giving it $1^1/_2$ to 1 ring deflection and gave a five-second burst. I could see strikes in the sea around the nose, then a vivid white flash from near the turret. Return fire was very heavy and uncomfortably close, but I could not see any strikes on my aircraft. Having broke away to port, I repeated the attack, but my guns ceased firing after about a $^1/_2$ second burst. However, I continued making dummy attacks, but gave up when I saw I was drawing well away from the convoy, and returned.

James Stewart then chased off another two aircraft and having done his bit to protect the convoy had to get himself back on board ship. He had two choices. He could either bale out or ditch.

> *James Stewart:* It was always recommended that you bale out. Because I guess that the Hurricane would be about 40 feet under before the hatch opened. I signalled to the senior officer escort HMS *Leith*, that I was going to bale out and did so. It was a beautiful evening and the sun was shining. I got into the dinghy, ate up my rations and fired off the rockets. They came rowing up and picked me out of the water.

James then enjoyed the hospitality of HMS *Leith*, with a hot bath and a glass of whisky.

CHAPTER 4

RANGERS AND RAMRODS

On 13 November 1943 authority was given for the formation of the AEAF (Allied Expeditionary Air Force), with Leigh-Mallory confirmed in command. The title ADGB (Air Defence of Great Britain) was also authorised with 'Fighter Command' temporarily becoming a thing of the past. Leigh-Mallory's directive of 16 November 1943 read:

> You have been designated by the Combined Chiefs of Staff as 'Air Commander-in-Chief, Allied Expeditionary Air Force' under the Supreme Allied Commander to exercise operational command over the British and American Tactical Air Forces, supporting the invasion of North-West Europe, from the United Kingdom. A United States Air Officer has been appointed as 'Deputy Air Commander-in-Chief, Allied Expeditionary Air Force'.
>
> The Allied Expeditionary Air Force will comprise the Royal Air Force Tactical Air Force and its administrative units, the United States IXth Air Force and, initially, such forces as may be allotted to the Air Defence of Great Britain. Other units may be assigned to the Allied Expeditionary Air Force at a later date.[15]

Command of the RAF 2nd TAF and ADGB passed over at once, with that of the United States IXth Air Force due to pass on 15 December 1943.

> You will be directly responsible to the British Chiefs of Staff for the Air Defence of Great Britain, until such time as your Headquarters moves overseas, when separate arrangements for the Air Defence of Great Britain will be made.
>
> Directives as to the control of the strategic air forces will follow at a later date [actually came through on 17 April 1944]. In the meantime, subject to the satisfactory progress of preparations for the invasion you should, during the preparatory period, exercise operational control of the airforces under your command in such a manner as to lend maximum support to the Strategic Air Force offensive.[16]

During the autumn of 1943, Leigh-Mallory had already been working on the requirements of the ADGB and 2nd TAF, initially within the constraint that the Air Ministry had allocated 85 squadrons (excluding night fighters). Leigh-Mallory's weaponry consisted of Typhoons for fighter/bomber roles, Mustangs for fighter reconnaissance and Spitfires and Typhoons (and later Tempests) in the fighter role. Leigh-Mallory would later seek a further allocation of four photographic squadrons – his force now made up thus:

---

[15] Public Record Office AIR 41/66.

[16] *Ibid.*

ADGB	**Day Fighter Squadrons**	**Fighter Bomber Squadrons**
10 Group	3	1
11 Group	7	1
12 Group	4	
13 Group	3	

Overseas Base Group (85 Group)

Day Fighter Squadrons	6

TAF Headquarters

Photographic Squadrons	2

Reserve

Fighter/Recce Squadrons	3

83 Group

Fighter Squadrons	18
Fighter/Bomber Squadrons	8
Fighter/Recce Squadrons	2
Photographic Squadrons	1

84 Group

Fighter Squadrons	18
Fighter/Bomber Squadrons	8
Fighter/Recce Squadrons	3
Photographic Squadrons	1

Totals

Fighter Squadrons	59
Fighter/Bomber Squadrons	18
Fighter/Recce Squadrons	8
Photographic Squadrons	4

Directives were sent to 2nd TAF on 17 November 1943 and 6 December 1943, the latter making clear the objective of operation Overlord, 'to secure a lodgement area on the continent from which further offensive operations can be developed', and a date of 1 May 1944 was given for action. In January 1944 the vastly experienced Air Marshal 'Mary' Coningham took over from Air Marshal D'Albiac and by 2 February 2nd TAF had established itself at tactical headquarters Uxbridge. But what of the detailed plan for Overlord? In the summer of 1943 planners at COSSAC worked on designing the means of assault.

> The outline of the plan which was evolved by 2 July 1943 was that during the initial assault the Allies would capture Caen and the hinterland to the south-west while it was anticipated that the port of Cherbourg would be occupied by about D plus 14. In the next phase the left flank of the Allies would rest on the Seine while the right went forward to cut off the Brest peninsula and occupy the ports of St. Nazaire and Nantes. When sufficient troops had been landed the Allies would expand into the area beyond the Seine and the Loire.
>
> The principal reasons for the choice of the Caen sector were that it was lightly defended, once a breakthrough had been achieved; the terrain was suitable for mobile warfare and except for an area between Caen and Bayeux the ground was unfavourable for a counter-attack by panzer divisions. On the other hand the distance from the shores of southern England would make a great fighter effort necessary to provide adequate cover. It was for this reason that a special effort should be made by the ground forces to gain territory for the construction of airfields.[17]

[17] *Ibid.*

This element was key to ensure that the best use could be made of air superiority.

> Even if our short range aircraft were deployed close to the south-east coast, our fighters would be operating at extreme range, and could maintain effective defensive patrols for relatively few minutes at a time, and hence must be constantly replaced. To maintain simple equality with the German Air Force, the Allies would need to have available many times as many aircraft as their opponents. Increase of the distance from the fighter bases to the assault beaches would correspondingly increase the number of fighter aircraft required.
>
> Superior skill and morale of pilots (which the Allies undoubtedly possess) will tend to minimise and sometimes outweigh weaknesses in other directions. But it was clear, that in an operation such as that contemplated the Allied fighters would be at a serious disadvantage. Pilots of damaged aircraft would be faced with a long sea crossing, with obvious dangers, whereas enemy fighters would be operating over or close to their own territory. In combat the Allies would be restricted by the need to retain sufficient petrol for the return journey, while the enemy, hampered by no such considerations, would be able to disengage from combat or re-enter a fight with comparative freedom.
>
> The scale of effort at which the Allies would be able to operate their fighters would decline rapidly through having to operate at extreme range. This factor made it essential for the Allies to establish fighter units on the continent at an early date. Thus, the acquisition and development of suitable airfields was of primary importance in the selection of assault areas. Though the Pas de Calais was suitable in this respect, so also was the Caen area. To the south-east of Caen potential sites became increasingly abundant, particularly in the area between the Seine and the Loire immediately west of Paris. On the other hand, the area southward and westward of Caen, excluding the coastal strip as far as Isigny, was generally unsuitable. Particularly the Cotentin peninsula where potential sites were few and far between.[18]

Initial plans were for a three-division assault, but this was considered under strength and the area of assault was extended. The influence of North African veteran commander General Sir Bernard Montgomery, who was to command 21st Army Group, was key in expanding the area of operation, although there were concerns within RAF circles that this would stretch their resources even further. In the original plan COSSAC had intended that by D plus 90, 75 percent of the airfields constructed would be within 60 miles of the Seine and the rest within 90 miles. Montgomery's interventions meant that the capture of Cherbourg and Nantes became more of a priority than the expansion of airfield sites, and it was felt by the air planners that without the area to the south-east of Caen it would not be possible to provide sufficient air cover over the beachheads.

> Whilst there was very little difference between the two plans up to about D plus 74, there was a very grave difference from this time onwards. The 21st Army Group plan provided for a long pause near the coast

[18] *Ibid.*

> after D plus 25 up to D plus 60, and again up to D plus 90, and almost as great a pause farther south from D plus 35 to D plus 60 and then to D plus 90.[19]

There were also concerns that the area around the beachheads would be congested as the armies and the tactical air forces sought space for facilities and storage of supplies, making them better targets for enemy air action. Herein, as we shall see later, lay the seeds for considerable tension and argument between the air commanders and Montgomery as the invasion progressed.

As it was the Combined Chiefs of Staff approved the revised plan and on 10 March 1944 Eisenhower issued a directive to his air, sea and land commander-in-chiefs with the objective of operation Overlord being:

> To secure a lodgement area on the continent from which further offensive operations could be developed. The lodgement area must contain sufficient port facilities to maintain a force of some 26 to 30 divisions, and enable that force to be augmented by follow-up shipments from the U.S. and elsewhere of additional divisions and supporting units at the rate of three to five divisions a month.
>
> The operation was to be carried out in two phases. Phase I was an assault landing between the limits of Quineville in the west and Cabourg les Bains in the east, to be followed by the early capture and development of airfield sites and the capture of the port of Cherbourg. Phase II was the enlargement of the area captured in the first phase so as to secure the whole of the Cherbourg, Loire and Brittany group of ports. The target date for the operation was to be 31 May 1944.[20]

Detailed planning was now underway. The objectives of the air plan for Overlord being:

> a) To attain and maintain air superiority.
> b) To assist the Allied Armies ashore.
> c) To impose delay on enemy reinforcement of the bridgehead and, in particular, to prevent German panzer formations from massing for a counter-attack during the first critical period immediately after the assault.[21]

Each of these requirements was to be met in phases. Reference was made to the Pointblank directive. In February 1943 the American and RAF heavy bomber commands, engaged in the strategic bombing offensive against Germany, had been directed: 'Your primary objective will be the progressive destruction and dislocation of the German military, industrial and economic system, and the undermining of the morale of the German people to a point where their capacity for armed resistance is fatally weakened.' In June 1943 Pointblank changed the emphasis of this particular directive, still under the same broad guidelines, but with a focus on depleting German fighter strength, attacking industry, airfields, and destroying the Luftwaffe in the air.

---

19 *Ibid.*
20 *Ibid.*
21 *Ibid.*

The phases of the Overlord air plan were:

a) Preliminary, which in 1943 was already in progress in the form of Pointblank, and which included strategical and tactical air reconnaissance.

b) Preparatory, which comprised the continuation of Pointblank and attacks on strategical rail centres, selected enemy coast defence batteries, Crossbow [enemy secret weapon] targets, naval installations and selected airfields and their installations, particularly those within 130 miles of Caen and in the Brest-Nantes area, also intensified strategical and tactical reconnaissance.

c) The Assault and Follow-Up, which can be summarised as follows:

i) Protection of the cross-channel movement from enemy air attack and assistance to the Navy in protection from surface attack.

ii) Neutralisation of coast and beach defences.

iii) Protection of the landing beaches from enemy air attack.

iv) Interference with the enemy's ability to mount effective counter-attacks.

v) Support of the land forces in their advance from the beachhead.

d) Air Operations Subsequent to the Assault – which included generally a continuation of the following tasks as events might demand.

i) Continued attrition of the G.A.F. in the air and on the ground and maintenance of bombing pressure on Germany.

ii) Delay of the arrival of enemy reserves into and movement of reinforcement towards the lodgement area.

iii) Direct support of the ground forces in the development of the lodgement area.

iv) Providing airlift for further airborne operations.

v) Providing air transport when necessary and practicable.[22]

In the early planning stages it had also become clear that the most critical factor in the success of the invasion was not the actual assault on the beaches, but the battle against enemy reinforcement, notably the panzers. The outcome of the battle rested upon whether or not the Allied build-up was sufficient to counter the German reinforcement of the area, and the ability of the Allies to seriously hamper the German redeployments.

Leigh-Mallory during the planning for Overlord always considered:

> ...the most significant feature in the situation of the GAF in western Europe is the steady increase in its fighter strength which, unless checked and reduced, may reach such formidable proportions as to render an amphibious assault out of the question. Above all, therefore . . . an overall reduction in the strength of the German fighter force between now and the time for the surface assault is essential.[23]

It was further felt by the AEAF commander and his staff that this could not be achieved in the short period leading up to the invasion by the prosecution of Pointblank, as they believed the Luftwaffe would only be drawn into battle in the defence of 'vital centres' or if they could achieve local superiority. It was considered that the vital centres were out of range of the Allied fighters. A

---

22 *Ibid.*

23 *Ibid.*

solution was then put forward of executing a considerable feint to draw the Luftwaffe into a battle on favourable terms to the Allied airmen. But their opinion was not shared, in the main, by the Chiefs of Staff who put faith in the attrition resulting from the prosecution of Pointblank. On 16 November 1943, Leigh-Mallory wrote to d'Albiac (then commanding 2nd TAF).

> There is no doubt in my mind that we shall not have fought our main battle for air superiority before the Overlord battle begins. In fact it will be the Overlord battle which will give us the opportunity for bringing the German Air Force into action and destroying it. I would not, however, be prepared to recommend commencement of Overlord unless I was certain of the favourable outcome of the air battle.

Leigh-Mallory acknowledged the success to date of Pointblank, and the battles in the Mediterranean, assessing from this that the Germans held little in reserve behind the front lines.

> Taking these factors into consideration, I can say quite definitely that if the allotted build-up is completed satisfactorily, and provided no fresh factors arise favourable to the operation of the German fighters, and provided our operations between now and the launching of Overlord are as successful as our operations during the past six months have been, there is no reason why the air situation should not be sufficiently favourable to undertake Operation Overlord.[24]

But the emphasis of the attacks carried out by the Allied heavy bomber commands was to be realigned in an attempt to deplete the enemy airforce. The aircraft industry was to be targeted, notably by the American daylight bomber forces escorted by long-range fighters. The defence of the sky over the Reich became a priority to the German High Command and the Luftwaffe would throw its airmen into battle over Germany. Both sides suffered considerable losses. The Allies could afford the losses, the Germans couldn't, and because of this air superiority was steadily being secured. A new directive was issued on 29 January to the RAF and American strategic bomber forces, defining their role as:

> The progressive destruction and dislocation of the German military, industrial and economic system, the disruption of vital elements of lines of communication and the material reduction of German air combat strength by the successful prosecution of the combined bomber offensive from all convenient bases . . .

Certainly the scale of the offensive against the target system mentioned above would escalate. In addition the Luftwaffe would enter battle against the daylight American bomber formations. Thus the opportunities for Allied fighter pilots to engage in combat grew and consequently their success in chipping away at the Luftwaffe fighter strength. One such fighter pilot was Hart Finley, who would get his chance to score.

When Hart Finley arrived in England, in February 1943, he was first sent to Bournemouth where he was able to enjoy some leave.

---

[24] *Ibid.*

> *Hart Finley:* They would look down a list for places available, of people who opened their homes to us Canadians. My buddy and I were in the New Forest, the family name was Faber and he was president of Strong's Ale. So needless to say we had lots of fine beer and a tour of his brewery. We did some cycling and played some golf and tennis. We had a great time.

Hart was then posted to 14 (P)AFU ((Pilot) Advanced Flying Unit) and then 5(P)AFU, to fly Miles Masters, for about a month, learning principally to navigate the British countryside, 'which was very different to our wide open spaces and railway tracks and network of highways you could follow home. In England it is so close knit, the geography much different.'

In April 1943, Hart was posted to 59 OTU at Milfield, initially training on Hurricanes and then doing a conversion onto Typhoons. 'Very powerful and a rather unforgiving aircraft and one I would not like to have flown operations in, but I guess you would get used to it, all its subtleties.' On completion of the conversion course, in July, Hart was posted to 1 Squadron at Lympne, close to Dover. His task was to be to counter and intercept the German hit and run raiders, however he didn't even manage a flight. 'Before I knew it I had another piece of paper in my hand which said report to Digby, up on the Wash, to 416 Squadron, a Canadian Spitfire squadron.' On arrival there was a familiar face in one pilot who had transferred overseas with him, and had done the Typhoon conversion too but been posted straight to 416 Squadron. 'So when I got to 416 I was very happy to be there, to fly the Spitfire, which I always had a desire to do, and I was getting back with some of my buddies.'

Before Hart had the chance to make an operational flight, 416 was posted to Merston, a satellite of Tangmere. Two squadrons were there, 402 and 416. Within a week he was detailed for his first operational flight, 12 August 1943.

> I was given the job of flying as Red 4. We took off and rendezvoused with 96 Marauders who were going over to drop bombs on one of the airfields near Paris that was being used by the Germans. It was rather a nice day, although there was an overcast. I remember climbing up from our base and we must have hit the cloudbase at 6,000 feet. We climbed through the cloud and came through at about 10,000 feet, and continued to 17,000 feet where we met the bombers. We crossed the Channel and into France, and headed for the target. There was a lot of opposition from anti-aircraft fire. Our particular role in this mission was to fly close escort to the bombers, so that if any Germans tried to attack the bombers from high above, we would be the last to protect them. Hopefully the squadrons who were high cover would be engaging the Hun there. But the flak was very heavy around us and around the bombers. I wasn't that aware of it, I didn't have the sense that I had been hit at all but I could smell the Cordite of the bursting flak and you could almost hear the thunder. Then as we completed the bombing run and headed out, the bombers went in one direction, because they no longer needed our escort, and we started into a closer formation and headed back for the Channel. The cloud more or less stopped at the French coast, so as we were flying out we could see the ground, but once we hit the Channel it was solid cloud. Flying at 17,000

feet I wasn't concerned about anything and I thought 'this is a piece of cake, this is wonderful'. I suddenly looked down at my gas tank and noticed that I was getting in to the bottom tank (we had an upper and a lower). I was using the fuel in the lower tank, and it seemed to be at quite a rate. We were supposed to maintain radio silence, not say anything unless we thought it was absolutely necessary. I thought it was absolutely necessary, because I was concerned about whether I would get home or not. So I called up the squadron commander, using his codeword, and asked him what his fuel state was. He said, 'Fine. Why?' I said, 'Well I'm into my bottom tank.' And all I heard him say was 'You're what!' I said, 'I'm into my bottom tank.' He ordered one of the other pilots to slip underneath me and have a look, see what was going on, and the report from the other pilot was that the fuel was just gushing out of my wing. I was told to open up my throttle and get as far out across the Channel as I possibly could. I had the alternative of course of turning round and going back and baling out over France. I opted to go across the Channel, as I thought it was only 20 miles wide and I was conscious of our position. I could glide if necessary. Well it turned out that we were over the widest part of the Channel, some 60 odd miles across, because we had come down on a different route. So I went down through the cloud, once the engine had stopped and there was that deathly silence, and I started to glide. One of my wing men came with me, through the cloud. When I broke out of the cloud it was at about 3,000 feet, not 6,000 which I expected. I looked around for land and no matter which direction I looked there was no sight of land. I thought, 'This is it.' I prepared to bale out, I had very little time. I got the coop top open, got my harness off, took off my helmet, which I had to get rid of, and got ready to go out. When I got down to about 2,000 feet I thought, I'd better not go much lower, so I pulled the nose up, reduced the speed to about 110 and then I bunted by pushing the control column forward very rapidly, which had the effect of literally blowing me out of the cockpit – it was almost like an ejector seat, it was a delightful feeling. When I was well clear of the aircraft I pulled the ripcord and then just dangled under the chute until I hit the water.

Funny things happen to you when you bale out like this, especially when you are not fully prepared for it. When we were at Bournemouth we had certain activities that we were supposed to do, and one of them was to go to the local swimming pool and learn how to use a dinghy and a Mae West. Well I happened to avoid going to the pool with my buddy, and instead we decided we would go down to the local dance hall to have an afternoon dance with a few girls. Little did I know then that I was going to end up in the water and have to use that dinghy. So when I got in the water I actually had to read the instructions on the dinghy in order to understand how to get it out of its pack, how to inflate it and how to get into it. And of course all this time I was in the water with my Mae West on. It was in August so fortunately the weather was reasonable. There was quite a swell but the water wasn't as cold as at other times of the year.

I sat in the dinghy for about three hours. Suddenly an aircraft came out, circled around but didn't land or give any signal but I had the feeling they saw me. He disappeared and I thought, 'Well that's a fine how do you do.' I guess he was reporting to an Air Sea Rescue launch, which was on its way. One of the times when I rose up on a fairly high swell I looked around and in the distance I could see a boat. I would then go down into the pit of the swell then I would rise up again and I would see the boat again. Finally when I thought it was close enough to signal I got my little signal flares – and had to read the instructions, again, on how to use them. Little did I realise what sort of a reaction you get from firing off a flare. I held it with my bare hands and waited for the ball of fire to go off, and as it went off the tube went down and ended up in the dinghy right between my legs. Fortunately it was aimed towards the end of the dinghy where my feet were. The second ball went shooting off right over the top of the dinghy. That taught me a lesson. The next time I used a flare I curled my little finger round underneath to use as a backstop.

Eventually the boat came and hauled me out. They got me down below and stripped off all my clothes and rubbed me down with huge towels, and got me warmed up. Then the leading man there said to me, 'Would you have a tot of rum.' I said, 'No, that's the last thing I could tolerate right now.' 'Oh come on sir, have a tot of rum. It will warm you up.' I said, 'No, I think it will make me sick.' Not really sea sickness, just reaction, shock. 'Oh come sir,' he said. 'You know, if you say yes then we can open the bottle and then we can finish it.' So I said, 'Give me a drink.' I can tell you it burned all the way down to the pit of my stomach.

Hart returned to base later that afternoon and he was straight back on to ops the very next day. 'I was glad of that. I didn't want to sit around and think too much about what had happened.'

Hart was only with 416 Squadron a few more weeks and then a very good friend who was the CO of 403 Squadron sought his services, along with his friend Bob Pentland. 403 Squadron was with 127 Airfield (later changed to Wing) at the time. 'We were absolutely ecstatic about the idea of going to 403.' But between the time that Hart received his notice to transfer and arrival at the squadron, it had suffered a setback, with the loss and death of CO Bitsy Grant on 4 September 1943. 403 Squadron was heavily involved in the run up to Starkey, but Hart, newly arrived, would only do local flying on the day of the operation itself.

Hart Finley: With 416 Squadron we had been flying the Spit V, with the clipped wing. When I got to 403 Squadron we were flying the Spit IX, and they were more for high altitude. Our role was different to that previous. Instead of close escort to bombers we became high escort, where all the action was. I was elated about that. When we joined 403 Squadron there were just two squadrons forming the Airfield, 403 and 421. It wasn't until later when we moved from Headcorn to Kenley in the winter of 43/44 that we had our third squadron, 416.

If you got into some sort of dogfight you would break up. You couldn't fight in a tight formation. You'd break up into smaller easier-to-manoeuvre components. We would try to keep as four aircraft as much as possible, which is what we call finger four. The leader, his number 2, the number 3 and number 4. And the idea was that if for any reason this

> formation had to split up in a dogfight you would still be 1 and 2, 3 and 4. You would give some protection to each other. It got down to almost every two men for themselves.

Throughout October 403 Squadron took part in numerous Ramrods (attacks on ground targets) and Rodeos (fighter sweeps) and sections were placed on daily readiness. In November it was the same. On 8 November on a Ramrod, 403 Squadron pilots patrolled the Boulogne – Griz Nez area, then swept in over Fruges and St Omer. Near Lumbres a section broke and went down to attack locomotives. Hart and Flying Officer Lecoq shot-up and damaged one train. Pilot Officer Weaver damaged two locomotives and also shot-up an 'enemy formation in a field'. Again in December it was Ramrods and Rodeos with the occasional Rhubarb.

Immediate DFC

On 20 December 1943, 421 Squadron's Andy Mackenzie took part in a Ramrod over France. His actions would earn him the award of an immediate DFC.

> I was flying No. 2 to Wing Commander Hugh Godefroy and we were over France, heading west. Some Huns were reported. I spotted them first, and told the Wing Commander. The enemy were below us and there were a lot.

It then appeared to Andy that the Wing had 'overshot the bounce'. Andy broke off, on his own, and went into attack.

> I shouldn't have done that really, but I managed to get three of the Huns. The commanders from the other squadrons verified the claims. When it was all finished I gained height and found myself alone in the sky. I spotted a Spitfire up high and I climbed up beside him. It was Hugh Godefroy, who I should really have stayed with.
>
> We got back to the base and reported to Intelligence, and I told the Group Captain about shooting the three enemy aircraft down. He said, 'Hughie. What were you doing in the meantime?' He replied, 'Oh, I was giving top cover.'

On 30 December 1943, 24 Spitfire IXs of 17 (Fighter) Wing (126 Airfield and 127 Airfield) led by Squadron Leader R. A. Buckham, DFC and DFC (US), flying with 403 Squadron, were detailed to act as withdrawal cover to American Flying Fortresses returning from bombing targets in Germany. At 1303 hrs the Wing was airborne crossing the French coast at Le Treport and was vectored onto the bombers who were flying north of the original rendezvous point. The Wing, at 24,000 feet in the Albert area, was approaching the new rendezvous point when Hart Finley sighted and reported four enemy aircraft flying line abreast at about 10,000 feet, and directly below. Squadron Leader Buckham gave permission for Yellow section, which included Hart, to go down and attack. In the ensuing combat two Me 109s were destroyed.

Flying Officer Hart Finley's combat report: I was flying Yellow 4 with

403 Squadron when just prior to our rendezvous with our returning bombers I sighted and reported four aircraft flying line abreast at 10,000 ft and directly below our section. I asked Darkwood leader for permission to go down and investigate. He gave me permission.

Hart Finley: I sat there fat, dumb and happy for a minute and then thought, 'Gee. He's telling me to go down.' So I peeled off with Claude Weaver, who had come up from Malta and had a DFM and had a score of about seven aircraft at this time. I hadn't engaged with a Hun at this point.

Flying Officer Hart Finley's combat report: I dived from approximately 24,000 feet to roughly 10,000 and closed very fast on them.

Hart Finley: Unfortunately I closed on these aircraft so fast that I had great difficulty in trying to stay behind them. We almost overran them because we were coming so fast from high altitude and they were in normal cruise. The next thing I knew I just looked over and there beside me was this Messerschmitt with a great big black cross on it. And I thought, 'Oh my God.' By this time I was slowing down very rapidly and I was able to just pull in behind. The German formation had broken, two to the left and two to the right.

Flying Officer Hart Finley's combat report: I gave a snap burst at one of the ones turning starboard, at about 30 degrees to 45 degrees deflection; I didn't see any strikes. I then followed the two which broke port and they dived away in a slow turn to port. I was closing in on them rather quickly and they seemed to be diving for cloud cover. As I opened fire on the port aircraft the starboard one broke hard to starboard and so I stuck with the port one and continued firing as I closed from approximately 450 yards, to 200 yards. The glare from the sun made it very hard to see the bead and bars in my sight, but as I was by this time dead astern I more or less hosed the air around him. At approximately 200 yards, the enemy aircraft blew up and trailed heavy smoke. This was at about 2,000 ft. He rolled slowly onto his back and went straight down into a large wooded area.

Hart Finley: By the time I got rid of him I couldn't find the second one. Suddenly I realised I couldn't see Weaver. But he was alone and neither one of us could see the other, we were miles apart. So I just got into a very steep climb, spiralled up, and I climbed, and I climbed, and I climbed. Suddenly I looked at my altimeter and thought, 'Oh my God, I don't believe it.' I was at 27,000 feet. I just headed back across the Channel and for base.

Pilot Officer Weaver would also later be able to claim a success. He had followed Hart down.

Pilot Officer Weaver's combat report: I attacked the one on the starboard side, firing a short burst from dead astern at 200 yards, and seeing a cannon strike below the cockpit, white smoke started pouring out but soon stopped. I chased him down through the cloud firing about seven more one-second bursts again from dead astern and from 200 to 50 yards and seeing a cannon strike in the port wing root. As I came out of the cloud I saw the enemy aircraft level out and crash into the trees.

For 403 Squadron, the first three weeks of January were spent searching for the enemy, conducting occasional sweeps and Rangers (large formation freelance actions over enemy territory). And on numerous occasions sections were on readiness for any intrusions by the enemy. But the Luftwaffe was rarely seen, usually not at all. Weather conditions were often not favourable, but on 21 January a break in the weather allowed 403 Squadron another chance.

On this day 403 (Wolf) and 421 Squadrons supported a Marauder attack on targets in northern France. Airborne at 1149 hours the Spitfires crossed in at Cayeux at 20,000 feet and were directed first west to the Dieppe area and then south of Amiens and down to 9,000 feet. At approximately 1230 hours bandits were reported at 23,000 ft due north of Lens flying south. The Spitfires climbed rapidly to 21,000 ft and ran into four enemy aircraft coming head-on slightly above. Yellow section and Red 3 and 4 were detailed to take out a section of two enemy aircraft respectively while Red 1 and 2 gave cover. Fifteen plus enemy aircraft were sighted further above just ready to bounce the 403 Squadron pilots. They dived through, more in an effort to shoot as they went down than to engage individually. Yellow section of 403 continued their attack down to 4,000 ft and lower.

Pilot Officer Weaver's (Yellow 1) combat report:... we attacked two FW 190 just north and west of Lens coming from below and ahead. They half rolled at 20,000 ft and I chased one of them down to about 4,000 ft, firing a total of 5 or 6 seconds, from about 250 to 150 yds, and 20 degree to 0 degree deflection. Saw considerable number of strikes on enemy aircraft's wings and fuselage, and at one time enemy aircraft seemed to be out of control. We were doing about 460 mph when we pulled out of dive and I blacked out for a few seconds. Yellow 2 said that enemy aircraft flicked and went straight down, he gave it a one-second burst and followed the enemy aircraft to 2,500 ft where he thought it was unsafe to continue chase. He pulled out of dive at about 600 mph levelling out at about 1,000 ft but the enemy aircraft HAD NOT started to pull out. When I regained sight I saw an aircraft burning on the ground below us about half a mile west of Lens and another about three miles south. The other is believed to be a FW 190 attacked by Yellow 3. Yellow 2 did not think he hit enemy aircraft so I claim one FW 190 destroyed.

403 Squadron combat report: Yellow 2 (F/L Hill) followed Yellow 1 throughout the attack from 18,000 ft and continued the chase after Pilot Officer Weaver broke off at 4,000 ft – unfortunately he broke in front of his No. 1 and crossed through his arc of fire receiving cannon and machine-gun fire through his starboard wing but was unhurt himself. Yellow 2 pulled out of his dive at 2,500 ft only with the utmost difficulty and left the FW 190 going straight down in aileron turns to its ultimate crash.

Flying Officer Hart Finley's (Yellow 3) combat report: Red 3 sighted and reported a gaggle of enemy aircraft at twelve o'clock and slightly above as we approached Lille, flying in a northerly direction. I saw one aircraft break from the gaggle and come straight at me in a head-on attack. I was preparing to engage him when he suddenly broke away to my port and I noticed him to be a Spitfire. I noticed two others break away in a half roll and dive towards Lens. I identified them as FW 190s and immediately half rolled after them and went right down to ground level over Lens. They were out of range but I gave a short burst hoping to split them up. They did, but I could not catch either of them. As I was about to pull up I noticed on my port side a FW 190 doing turns on top of the trees south-west of Lens. I immediately jumped him and with my excessive speed closed very rapidly. I opened fire between 100 and 150 yds about 5 degree deflection and closed to 0 yards. I saw strikes or rather bits fly off his port side. As I did not see him blow up I shoved the nose down at the last moment and fired point blank from almost dead line astern at 0 yds. I was so close that I almost took off his tail with my starboard wing as I pulled up. We were right on top of the trees and as I pulled up I almost hit a tree and he was under me. I swung round at about 1,500 ft and could not spot him anywhere. I didn't waste much time looking for him though as I thought I was alone and knew other Huns were about. I climbed up rapidly and at approx 4,500 ft I noticed two aircraft breaking into me from my port side. I broke into them and they turned out to be two Spitfires. I joined up immediately with them and they turned out to be Yellow 1 and his No. 2 (Pilot Officer Weaver and F/L Hill respectively).

403 Squadron combat report: Yellow 4 (Pilot Officer Myers) because of his initial diving speed closed easily on the FW 190 Yellow 3 broke away from. He positioned himself beautifully for the 'Kill' but his guns jammed at the critical moment. He pulled over beside the FW 190, flew in line abreast long enough to give the Hun pilot the sign of the digit, then peeled off and returned home.

Red 3 and 4 unable to close on their enemy aircraft broke starboard to engage some of the bouncing Huns. Red 3 of 403 (F/L Browne) about one mile west of Lens, at 21,000 ft closed to 400 yds on a Me 109 and gave a two-second burst from 10 degrees, the enemy aircraft's tail kicked up, wavered, allowing another good burst from below, at which time black smoke poured out and it skidded off and down. F/L Browne is not claiming a damaged until confirmation by cine – he was unable to finish this enemy aircraft off because of other Huns at 6 o'clock to him.

Blue section of 403 also broke off to starboard to attack some of these bounders but could not close to effective range, except Blue 4 (Flying Officer Denison) who closed from 200 to 50 yds firing cannon and machine guns – he awaits cine assessment before making any definite claims.

421 Squadron remained above as top cover and have no claims.

The Wing was split up on their return but all landed safely at base with the exception of Yellow section who refuelled at Hawkinge before returning.

The following week saw numerous 403 Squadron pilots complete uneventful sweeps, but on 28 January four pilots were detailed for a Ranger, one pilot having to remain at Manston when his aircraft became unserviceable. The three remaining pilots were bounced by 12 + FW 190s and in the ensuing combat one pilot would later claim a 190 damaged, although his aircraft, as that of another pilot, was badly damaged. One pilot failed to return; Pilot Officer Claude Weaver who lost his life.

The Luftwaffe and 403 Squadron did not meet for the remainder of January. Indeed the first three weeks of February were uneventful, although the squadron lost one pilot on a 20 February Ramrod, his failing engine forcing him to bale out over enemy territory. For the last week of February 403 Squadron moved to Hutton Cranswick to undergo training, bombing and gunnery practice, although poor weather hampered flying opportunities. At the beginning of March it was back to ops, with Flight Lieutenant Finley now OC B Flight, although as the Squadron ORB recorded, 'Jerry seems to be conserving his fighter strength for something big.' On 8 March the squadron lost two pilots to flak whilst on a Ranger, one man losing his life, and on 15 March during a sweep 403 Squadron airmen were spectators as 401 Squadron saw action. Tragedy struck on 18 March, during a sector recce by three pilots, when Flying Officer Denison lost his life attempting a crash landing after an engine failure. Denison was buried at Brookwood cemetery four days later, with most of 403 Squadron pilots in attendance and at the end of the ceremony all the pilots present led by the CO stepped up to the grave and 'saluted Flying Officer Denison for the last time'. There would be one further loss to the squadron on 24 March when one pilot crashed on the edge of the aerodrome during a dive-bombing practice.

But what is noticeable during March is that 403 Squadron began to spend more time on Army co-operation exercises. The Squadron ORB recorded, 'Our squadron has been getting plenty of practice with the Army lately and the pilots are getting anxious to do some more operational flying.' But the 403 Squadron airmen were seeing little action against the enemy, the Squadron ORB again recording some frustration on 20 March – 'as usual no enemy aircraft seen'. Poor weather curtailed any action for the first week of April but on the 8th a morale-boosting operation was laid on.

> *403 Squadron ORB:* At last the sun came out today and the Wingco came over to the dispersal and advised us he had requested permission to send the squadron on a dive-bombing mission. Spirits soared when the OK came through and at 1500 hrs the squadron led by 'Brownie' took off with five hundred pounders to prang a 'Noball' [German secret weapon target]. Near Le Treport, our squadron had the distinction of being the first Spit Group to commence the bombing of Europe. A huge success, so much so that everybody is eager to have a another go just as soon as possible, and a party is planned for tonight to honour the occasion.

Allied Intelligence, acting upon agent reports, POW interrogations and evidence from aerial reconnaissance, had been closely monitoring possible German secret weapon developments for some time. The German research establishment at Peenemünde had been scrutinised from the air and when photographs of strange constructions in northern France revealed they were similar to some of those at Peenemünde, it became clear that the Germans were planning an offensive, to be launched across the Channel. These distinctive constructions, 'ski' shaped storage buildings and launch ramps, were being built to fire V1s (flying bombs). The Allies were watching closely as the number of constructions grew and eventually the decision was made to bombard these Noball sites, as they were called. The Allied commanders looked to the heavy bombers of the USAAF 8th Air Force and RAF's Bomber Command, but targeting was also allocated to fighter/bomber and medium-bomber squadrons to seek out and bomb these small targets, often camouflaged and well hidden. Such duties were given to 403 Squadron.

> *Hart Finley:* In the lead up to the invasion of Normandy we got involved in a lot of dive bombing, which was something that hadn't been done before. The targets we had to attack were Noball targets, the launching ramps for the V1. The idea was to attack and destroy them. We had a lot of intelligence coming out of France as to where these were constructed. They were very well camouflaged and very difficult to see from the air. But with the intelligence we were able to attack a number of these targets and we did this for quite a period leading up to the invasion and I think we had a fair degree of success. We lost quite a few boys in these missions, often because of flak. These launching ramps were in the Pas de Calais, all along the coast and that was just a heavy flak belt.

Throughout the early months of 1944, the attacks on the Noball targets required a significant contribution from the fighter/bomber squadrons. The Allies actually thought they were getting on top of the perceived threat. Whether or not they had would become clear shortly after the invasion. On 10 April 403 Squadron once more saw action of a sort, as target cover for Mitchells and Marauders 'which plastered the marshalling yards at Charleroi. Yellow section received a dose of "Green" flak over Lille.' On 13 April the squadron began preparing for another move, to Tangmere, but there was a delay, owing to poor weather, and the aircraft didn't arrive until 18 April. The men then started to accustom themselves to being part of a mobile unit, the squadron ORB noting on 18 April, 'arriving… at about 0930 hours, ready to commence a healthy?? outdoor life, the rest of the day was spent in erecting tents and getting settled.' 403 Squadron saw plenty of operational activity for the rest of April, escorting bombing raids, carrying out their own bombing operations on bridges in the planned invasion area, a Ranger to Brest, and numerous attacks on Noball targets. May continued in the same vein, 403 Squadron being involved in numerous operations, attacking Noball targets, acting as escorts, going on Rangers and sweeps. Barges and trains were shot-up, trucks and staff cars were 'pranged in good fashion'. And there was the occasional clash with the Luftwaffe, which resulted in losses to both sides. But as the date for the invasion approached Hart Finley was posted away, on 22 May. Nevertheless when the assault came he would not miss out.

In the Drink

403 Squadron ORB
3 May 1944: At 1350 hrs the squadron took off on an escort job, this time for Mosquitoes, bombing in the region of Abancourt, no flak, just another dead

beat trip. At 2005 hrs the squadron set off with bombs to prang a Noball in the vicinity of SW Abbeville. All hell was let loose by the Hun and Mac Hume was the unfortunate one this time. He had to bale out over the Channel and spent an uncomfortable hour in the [water], just five miles off the French coast, when he was picked up by a Sea Otter of the Air Sea Rescue, which in landing damaged a float, which meant taxiing as it couldn't take off in the heavy sea that was running. A launch finally took all aboard and the Sea Otter joined the Spit at the bottom of the drink.

But Hart Finley wasn't the only one of our featured airmen to have success against the enemy in the months leading up to the invasion. In January 1944 Reg Baker took up his responsibilities as Wing Commander, Harrowbeer Wing. On 8 February 1944, Flight Lieutenant Beake accompanied Reg on an attack on Gael airfield in Brittany and would report, 'we were right down on the deck and were actually slightly below the level of the airfield itself, which is on a hillside. We saw two FWs about to land and four more further south. One was just going down but the other was going round again. I was lucky enough to go in first and get one which was making another circuit. He rolled over, burst into flames and spread himself over the field nearby.' Reg would also lay claim to one FW 190 destroyed. The next day the Harrowbeer Wing would add to its score, an Me 109 and Do 24 claimed on a Ranger. On 10 February, Reg led eight Typhoons of 193 and 266 Squadrons on 10 Group Rodeo 80. By the end of the operation nine enemy aircraft were claimed destroyed and two damaged. On the approach to Etampes Mondesir aerodrome Reg reported enemy aircraft on the ground. The Typhoons swept into the attack.

Flight Lieutenant Deall's combat report: I attacked a Ju 88 firing a short burst from 300-200 yards, hitting the enemy aircraft on the fuselage between the main planes. The enemy aircraft burst into flames. Looking back after the attack I saw [it] burning fiercely, flames nearly ten feet high. I claim the enemy aircraft as destroyed.

Flying Officer McGibbon's combat report: My R.T. at first was working alright but faded just before we reached Chartres. I did not hear the order to attack Etampes Mondesir aerodrome, but after I saw my No. 1 attack a Ju 88 on the ground I managed to get a quick attack in on an He 111. It was dispersed outside the 'drome'. I think there were about 10 aircraft on the airfield and 10 round near the airfield. My burst hit the starboard engine and the nose. It started to burn. I turned back and saw both engines and fuselage to be well on fire. I consider this aircraft to be destroyed. There was no flak from this airfield until we were leaving.

Warrant Officer Richardson's combat report: I was flying as Lochinvar 2 to W/Cdr Baker. On the instruction to attack Etampes Mondesir a/f I turned to starboard and flew directly across the middle of the field at 0 feet. At the opposite end of the field was an Me 110 facing south. At 700-800 yds I opened fire but only one gun was in working order. As I got really close I saw a small crowd of men under the starboard wing. Some of these were hit by my fire. I saw strikes down the length of the fuselage. After firing 25-30 rounds approx my one cannon ceased firing and I passed very close over the aircraft.

Flying Officer Haworth's combat report: On seeing Etampes Mondesir, I turned starboard and attacked an Me 110 on the ground simultaneously with Warrant Officer Richardson. Ground crews were standing round the aircraft and I observed several strikes near engine and fuselage. On looking back I saw an aircraft burning furiously on the starboard side of the aerodrome. [Ju 88 attacked by Flight Lieutenant Deall], and the Me 110 was also burning well.

The Typhoons then reformed and headed toward Brétigny aerodrome and more aircraft were sighted.

Flight Lieutenant Deall's combat report: I attacked a large enemy aircraft which had landed on its belly, a Do 217 I think. [It] was being worked on by a working party, a vehicle of sorts was standing next to this enemy aircraft. My first shells fell a little short but eventually I got strikes on the enemy aircraft, scattering the working party left and right and probably killing a few. After this attack I saw a Ju 88 flying west at 1,000 ft. Calling up W/Cdr Baker I went in to attack firing a 2 secs burst from 350 yds to 150 yds, angle of attack 20 degrees–10 degrees, getting large strikes all over the enemy aircraft which went up in flames, broke in half, the tail and part of the fuselage hitting the deck after the main part of the enemy aircraft.

At this point Reg Baker and his No. 2 Warrant Officer Richardson became separated from the other Typhoons, which were about to engage further enemy aircraft.

Flight Lieutenant Deall's combat report: I set course westwards. After about three minutes on this course my No. 2 Flying Officer McGibbon reported enemy aircraft to starboard so we turned towards the enemy aircraft, which were trainer (Harvard) types going into land. I was unable to get in an attack.

Flying Officer McGibbon's combat report: There were about seven of these aircraft, in appearance similar to a Harvard, with wheels and flaps down. The first one I did a 10 degree attack on & firing a short burst closed from 300 to 250 yds. I saw strikes on the fuselage behind the wings. It caught fire and dived into some trees where it blew up. I went to attack another but this already had two Typhoons attacking it. The second one I attacked was at about 200 feet, 400 yards from the edge of the aerodrome. I did a 20 degree attack from 300 yds closing to 200 yds, firing a short burst. I saw hits on the fuselage and cockpit, and it dived straight into the ground where it blew up. The third one I attacked was just crossing the perimeter track at about 200 ft. I did a 45 degree attack closing from 250 to 150 yds, firing a short burst. I saw strikes all over the tail plane. It did a steep diving turn to the right, straight into the ground where it blew up. I claim these three aircraft destroyed. Their speed I estimated to be between 120 mph and 100 mph. On reforming there was slight light flak from the aerodrome defences.

Flying Officer Haworth was also able to get behind one of the training aircraft.

Flying Officer Haworth's combat report: I had a short burst at one that was about to touch down, but did not get strikes on him; and immediately had another squirt at a similar aircraft that was landing at 90 degrees to the first one, saw strikes under fuselage, damaged.

With no more enemy aircraft around Deall ordered the section to reform and head for home.

Flight Lieutenant Deall's combat report: On course for home the weather deteriorated so I climbed the section through cloud breaking at 8,000 ft. Later descending again breaking cloud cover over the inner estuary of the Seine at 4,000. We crossed out of France five miles S of C. d'Antifer. Landing back at Tangmere 2.25 hours after take-off.

Meanwhile Reg and Warrant Officer Richardson were also in action, although unable to stay together.

Warrant Officer Richardson's combat report: I lost my leader in cloud so climbed straight ahead and broke cloud at 10,000 feet. After flying on a vector at this height for a few minutes I turned starboard and dived through an opening to 0 ft and continued on a 340 degree, 10 minutes later I hit a storm and seeing no way around it climbed through it and broke cloud at 20,000 ft. Severe icing conditions experienced. I was getting short of fuel so called for homing and carried on at 20,000 crossing coast about 6 miles S of Le Touquet and English coast at Dungeness. Landed at Lympne to refuel.

Wing Commander Reg Baker's combat report: After losing touch with my No. 2 in cloud I found my aircraft icing up and broke cloud at 700 ft, going down. After having sorted out the cockpit I suddenly saw a Do 217 flying east at 600 feet/200 yards ahead. I closed to about 70 yards dead astern and below, and tried one short burst. The enemy aircraft burst into flames and I saw it hit the ground. I then discovered that I was steering east, so I changed my course to WNW flying at low level through snow flurries. I emerged from one of these and saw one FW 190 flying NNW at 600 feet 500 yards ahead. I closed to 50 yards astern and slightly underneath enemy aircraft, and carried out the same attack as on the Do 217. Enemy aircraft's engine caught fire, aircraft rolled over and I saw it hit the deck in flames. Still steering WNW in bad snowstorm I suddenly found myself over Paris at roof-top level, and immediately changed course to NNW. I saw the Arc de Triomphe from close range, also a game of football going on in a large stadium. There was no flak at all from Paris. I recrossed coast at 0 ft 8 miles SW of Le Treport, and eventually landed at Newchurch very short of petrol, although Shellpink had given me several vectors around 190 degrees as homing course for English coast.

An extraordinary few days for the Wing. Reg was certainly working his airmen hard to meet their objective of depleting the strength of the German Air Force.

Following operation Starkey, in September 1943, Bob Cole had been transferred to No. 1 SLAIS (Special Low Attack Instructors' School) Milfield, Northumberland to undergo intense ground-attack training, flying a Hurricane IV, as his logbook testifies: low level bombing practice; dive-bombing practice; low attacks on a tank using cine camera; 40mm firing on wreck; 40mm firing on screen target; low flying + dive on ground target using cine camera; 40mm + machine-gun attacks on ground target; 40mm machine-gun attacks on tank; low flying; formation flying; cine-camera attacks on tank concentration; RP (Rocket Projectile) firing 4 prs + cine-camera attack; RP firing at beach target 4 singles; RP firing at beach target 4 pairs; RP firing at beach target 2 prs per attack, 8 RPs; RP firing at beach target section attacks; RP firing at beach target 4 prs night.

Whilst Bob had undergone his training 3 Squadron had kept up the offensive, but at a cost. In the month that Bob had been away it had suffered the following losses:

13 September Flight Sergeant C. Chrisford (POW), crashed near Dordrecht.
13 September Flying Officer J. M. Downs (POW) hit by flak and baled out.
13 September Sergeant G. A. Whitman ditched on an Air Sea Rescue operation.
17 September Flight Lieutenant G. L. Sinclair, aircraft damaged/destroyed on landing at Manston.
25 September Pilot Officer J. de Callatay (killed) shot down by flak.
4 October Flight Lieutenant G. L. Sinclair (POW) hit by flak and force-landed.
5 October Flying Officer J. L. Foster (killed) shot down by FW 190s.
5 October Squadron Leader Hawkins (killed) shot down by flak.
5 October Warrant Officer J. A. La Roque (killed) shot down by flak.

> *Bob Cole:* The strangest thing. The losses didn't affect morale. You just accepted it. You didn't expect to live yourself. Potty and I discussed it and he said, 'The only way would be if you were shot down and not killed.' Then we got Squadron Leader Alan Dredge.

Dredge had served in the Battle of Britain and also in Malta.

> *Bob Cole:* He was the dependable type. He stopped low level as our casualties were very high. He took us dive bombing. Two fingers of four. One would fly up sun. We'd link up and go into echelon and when we got over the target the CO would dive. You'd roll on your back, pull down and as the target disappeared under your nose, drop your bombs. And then get the hell out of it as fast as you could.

In the second week of October Bob returned to 3 Squadron at Manston and for the rest of that month saw little flying, only 4 hours 40 minutes. On 31 October the squadron practiced dive bombing and the next day ops were on. For the next few months Bob would take part in numerous operations against shipping targets, aerodromes, and other enemy positions. Quite often poor weather conditions and cloud cover would prevent operations being carried out. Bob's logbook recorded his operational experience in the last two months of 1943.

> 1 Nov: Ops Dive bomb convoy in Dutch Islands with two 500 pounders. Little flak.

7 Nov: Ops Ramrod on St. Moer. Cloud 10/10 drop bombs safe in the sea and return to base.
7 Nov: Ops Attempt Ramrod on Abbeville. Cloud 10/10 drop bombs safe in sea.
10 Nov: Ops Ramrod. Cloud 10/10. Return to base with bombs. Some heavy AA from Griz Nez.
11 Nov: Ops Ramrod. Dive bomb village near Cape Griz Nez. Little flak. Two 500 pounders.
19 Nov: Ops Dive bomb village near Cape Griz Nez with two 500 pounders. Some light flak.
20 Nov: Ops Dive bomb village of Audinghem on Cape Griz Nez with two 500 pounders. Lots of light flak.
26 Nov: Ops Fighter escort to Marauders to Audinghem. Lots of flak aimed at Marauders. Bombing poor.
29 Nov: Ops Dive bomb Moorslede aerodrome Belgium. Two 500 pounders. Fire at balloon on French coast.
4 Dec: Ops Ramrod attempted on Moorslede Belgium. Fail to find target. Dive bomb road with 500 pounders.
11 Dec: Ops Attempt Ramrod. Weather 10/10. Drop bombs in sea and return to base.

But just like Hart Finley and Reg Baker, Bob was soon to experience some real action in the preliminary phase of the Overlord air campaign. During early 1944 his main activities had been on dive bombing and fighter escort.

Bob Cole's logbook:
6 Jan: Ops Holland. Vis poor drop bombs in sea.
21 Jan: Ops Dive bomb steel works at Ijmuiden Holland with 2 x 500s. Bombing good some flak.
24 Jan: Ops Fighter escort to Beaufighters north of Emden + off Borkum. See no ships or enemy aircraft.
30 Jan: Ops Fighter escort to dive bombers attacking shipping at Brouwershaven in Dutch Islands.
8 Feb: Ops Dive bombing shipping off Den Helder Holland. Results not seen. Lots of heavy + light flak. Get hit in tail + near radiator with heavy.
11 Feb: Ops Fighter escort to Den Helder Holland.
12 Feb: Ops Fighter escort to Den Helder Holland. Some heavy flak.
24 Feb: Ops supporting sweep 15,000′ into France. See nothing.

Later that day however Bob *would* see something when 3 Squadron detailed some of its Typhoons as the first fighter sweep of a Ramrod. Seven Typhoons took off from Manston at 1520 hrs, with Typhoons of 198 Squadron, but two had to return early. The remaining Typhoons set course for Domburg at sea level and began climbing when 30 miles off the Dutch coast, crossing in at Domburg at 9,000 feet. Here they split up. 3 Squadron lost height and flew at deck level in line abreast past Woensdrecht, east of Antwerp, and Pilot Officer Dryland gave a short burst at some barges without seeing strikes.

Bob Cole: I saw a car with two people standing by it. I didn't shoot it and when I got by it I saw two German soldiers. I didn't turn back or I would have lost everybody.

The formation then swept on past Louvain to a position 10 miles east of Mons where a Lioré et Oliver 45 was sighted three miles ahead flying in a south-easterly direction at 500 to 800 feet.

Bob Cole: This Leo 45 went right across our nose, a few hundred feet at the most, slightly above us. We dropped our long-range tanks.

Pilot Officer Dryland's combat report: I immediately jettisoned my tanks and turned towards it passing underneath and noticing the yellow belly, black crosses and underslung fins and rudders. Breaking port I made a full beam attack on its starboard side allowing $2^1/_2$ rings deflection at 300 yards, no strikes observed. I came in again from the port but was unable to fire owing to other Typhoons attacking.

Flight Sergeant Bob Cole's combat report: I dropped my jettisonable tanks and did a sharp left turn and overtook the enemy aircraft. I attacked from starboard at an angle of 30 degs allowing 1 ring deflection opening fire at 300 yards. As I closed I came round into line astern firing, whenever my sight was on, and finally broke and ceased fire at 50 yards dead astern. I saw strikes on the port engine and all along the fuselage. The port engine started to smoke badly and as I broke I noticed the starboard engine on fire.

Flight Sergeant Pottinger's combat report: I did a climbing turn to starboard and made an attack from 10 degs port astern. Opened fire at approx 400 yards and got a two-second burst in before having to break off to port to avoid Yellow 2 and 3. As I broke I saw strikes on the fuselage and inboard section of the starboard mainplane.

Pilot Officer Dryland's combat report: I then made a 40 degs attack from the starboard giving $1^1/_2$ rings at about 300 yards. Strikes were seen on the fuselage and engine. When last seen aircraft was attempting to force land with starboard engine dead and port engine smoking. Apart from a shallow dive no evasive action was taken at all!

Bob Cole: We had riddled the damn thing and it went down into a field on fire. It was like a lot of mad dogs. Potty and I went round and put a burst into the burning wreckage. I didn't know what aircraft it was, I thought it was a bomber and I thought it now won't drop a bomb on us. It was twin-engined and not one of ours. Young men are callous. I take the intelligent view now. But when you are young and your country is at war and you're taking part, the enemy is nothing. That's the trouble. You can talk young men into doing anything.

Following the rather one-sided combat the Typhoons reformed and landed at Manston at 1700 hours. Each of the three pilots would be credited with a share of the kill. The next one of our featured airmen to engage in combat with enemy aircraft was Basil Collyns.

A Belgian at War

Count du Monceau de Bergendal DFC and Bar commanded Belgian 349 Squadron in the run up to D-Day. In a letter to his godfather on 27 March 1944 he comments on the morale of his fighter pilots and their willingness to expand the offensive.

> ... we are no longer at Friston but with the Tactical Air Force and you can imagine how glad we all are. It gives us the assurance of taking part directly in the Invasion of the continent & my squadron should be the first Belgian unit to land on the other side.
>
> After months of hard fighting I finally managed to get what I wanted: new aircraft and our transfer to Tactical AF. You cannot imagine the difficulties we had to overcome. Being in command of a national squadron is no picnic & one has to struggle with one's own authorities more than one has to fight against the Huns. One has also to fight against one's own discouragement and lassitude. I may now tell you that between November and mid-February I lost over twelve pounds in weight through sheer worry – I have caught up with my normal weight now but I felt pretty rotten at that time... [in previous letters he wrote of problems between RAF and Belgian authorities, getting aircraft and the like and he was also ill.]
>
> Now everything is simply grand. The boys who shared my worries are putting up a grand show as they don't want to spoil their chance. Can you imagine the first to land on the continent? If father and mother knew that how worried but how proud they would be...
>
> The news from the Ukraine is too wonderful for words. It certainly will strain the Nazi armies, which will help on the western front. Meanwhile I would not like to be in any German's boots just now. It seems that no German town can escape the RAF Bomber Command or the 8th USAAF and raids which are fifty times more concentrated than anything London has known up to now.[25]

Letter of 14 May:

> Just a few words to let you know that I am still kicking. I have been fairly busy lately taking part in operations over the 'Other Side' beyond Paris or Brussels. What is exasperating is that the Nazis won't come up and fight. I suppose they are storing up reserves. Such inactivity on their part is unbelievable.
>
> In any case life in Tactical Air Force is grand. I enjoy every minute of it.[26]

On 1 January 1944 Flight Lieutenant Basil Collyns became operational once more, joining 2nd Tactical Air Force, 83 Group, 122 Airfield's 65 Squadron, but in his first week he would manage just 2.20 hours familiarising himself with the Mustang III. Then January was taken up with formation flying and a couple of Army co-ops. Indeed it wasn't until 15 February that Basil took his Mustang over

---

25 Papers of Major General Count du Monceau de Bergendal DFC and Bar, IWM Con Shelf and 02/35/1.

26 *Ibid.*

enemy territory on a two-hour fighter sweep over Holland, the squadron now giving its support to the bomber offensive over Germany. On 20 February cover to Flying Fortresses was given south-east of Liège, 22 February 'Fighter sweep over Holland', 24 February 'Withdrawal cover Libs St Vitch', 25 February 'Escort cover Marauders to Venlo'. The next action was on 6 March supporting the USAAF 8th Air Force assault on Germany, 65 Squadron providing withdrawal cover. Then two days later Basil and 65 Squadron again defended their 8th Air Force allies on the flight back from bombarding German targets.

He wasn't then back on ops until 9 April, a 4.05-hour flight acting as cover on yet another 8th Air Force mission, Basil having a close call when hit by flak over Bremen. On 10 April, 3.35 hours escorting Beaufighters on a shipping strike; 12 April, 3.40 hours escorting Fortresses to Schweinfurt, 18 April, Fortress withdrawal cover, although he had to return early. But during all this he was having little contact with the Luftwaffe, a situation that would change on 19 April when 65 Squadron prepared for a Ranger south-west of Bordeaux. The Mustangs took off at 1440 hours, under instructions to concentrate on aircraft either in the air or on the ground. Over enemy territory all the aircraft dropped to 100 feet and sections flew individually. Basil's section swept low over an aerodrome, Cognac, Chateau/Bernard, strafing and damaging an Me 109 and Junkers 52.

On 22 April he flew 2.05 hours on a fighter sweep to Nancy/Strasbourg. Me 109s were met and a combat ensued, the squadron claiming three destroyed and one damaged. Wing Commander Johnston would claim one Me 109 destroyed and one damaged. The 65 Squadron ORB recorded, 'the Wing Commander had struck a telegraph wire while chasing his Hun. Luckily it had struck the spinner.' On 24 April, 2.40 hours, 'Fortress escort SW Stuttgart'. Then on 27 April it was time once again for Basil to be part of a Ranger; to Metz. At 1010 hours Red and Yellow sections (including Collyns), four aircraft in each, took off. Yellow section would see action, later claiming an Me 109 on the ground and an FW 190 just airborne.

Basil's logbook records a continuation of intense operations for the first two weeks of May: 1 May, 'Fighter sweep Paris-Rheims, Metz, Liège'; 2 May, 'Dive bombing Nantes marshalling yards'; 5 May, 'Fighter sweep Juvincourt area'; 8 May, two operations 'Dive bombing 6m SE Lierre' and 'Dive bombing marshalling yards St Quentin'; 11 May, 'Dive bombing Charleroi Monceau'; 13 May, a 4.10-hour 'Fighter sweep Koblenz-Giessen-Kassel-Osnabrück'; 15 May, 'Dive bombing railway Clermont'.

It was certainly a busy time. During all this operational activity, however, the young pilots managed to relax in the traditional fashion. The squadron ORB recorded their exploits. Obviously morale was fairly good.

> *65 Squadron ORB:*
> 13-5-44 The F/S pilots took a few of the ground crews out in the evening and ended up in walking approx 6 miles along the railway in a very inebriated state.
> 14-5-44 The day for the move to another airfield. It looked rather grim but the rain kept away until the evening and then only a few spots. The Wing held a party in the pub nearby nicknamed most appropriately 'Shaky-Do'. By lunchtime we were quite happy and this feeling remained until late in

> the afternoon. We were unable to take off until 1955 hours owing to the runways at Funtington airfield being under repair. We landed there at 2015 hours to find things fairly well under control... of course one or two tents were missing, but that a mere detail. No one pranged.
> 15-5-44 We all went into Chichester to find a shortage of beer.
> 16-5-44 Chichester being a dead loss as regards beer it was decided that a liberty run to Portsmouth would be the form and sure enough we enjoyed ourselves although we had to return fairly early.

It is likely that a call was made to return early as the next day (17 May), briefing was at 0500 hours. It was time for another Ranger, this time to the north, Denmark and Aalborg. As the squadron ORB recorded, 'The "Y" service reported a movement of airfields in that area and suggested that we might find bags of Hun there.' Find them they did.

After the briefing, Wing Commander George 'Robin' Johnston took off from Funtington with five other aircraft from 65 Squadron and two more from 122 Squadron, to fly to Coltishall to refuel and eat breakfast. Johnston then led the force of eight Mustangs over the English coast and kept the formation low over the North Sea, flying through numerous thick rain squalls. The eight Mustangs made landfall at Klitmoller and turned for Aalborg. As the formation approached the target area, just before noon, Johnston sent Blue section (Lt Nyerrod, Flying Officer Pinches, Flight Sergeants Kelly and Williams) to the south of the town. Johnston took his 'Gander' section, which also included Squadron Leader Westenra, Basil Collyns and Flight Lieutenant Barrett, to the north. Immediately the enemy was sighted and the Mustang pilots seized their chance to attack.

Johnston closed on a Ju 88 from slightly below and fired, ripping into the port engine. Westenra followed firing a short burst and then Collyns came in. The stricken Ju 88 turned for the airfield NW of the town, and intense light flak saw off any further attack from the Mustangs. Nevertheless the Allied pilots witnessed it crashing on the far side of the aerodrome. There was no time to feel satisfied as more trade came Gander section's way, in the form of three more Ju 88s. At this point Barrett broke off in pursuit of a FW 190 and the three remaining pilots lined up on the Ju 88s, Johnston took out the centre aircraft, Westenra the port aircraft and Collyns fired a long burst from 300 yards range at the starboard Ju 88. All three enemy aircraft fell, and although some German airmen lost their lives, three parachutes were seen coming from one aircraft.

Gander section, less Barrett, reformed and set course for Hobro. Then Johnston spotted another Ju 88, low, but having no ammunition made a dummy attack. Westenra followed up, managing to get off a long burst, most of which went wide although a few strikes were seen. Collyns was then able to get onto a Ju 188, but only his starboard gun would fire, from 200 yards, so he broke off the attack, the enemy aircraft heading east with one engine streaming smoke.

Meanwhile Blue section was also seeing action. On the approach to Aalborg, Nyerrod heard enemy aircraft reported at 11 o'clock to Gander section. He called Johnston, asking if help was needed. He didn't receive a reply and so broke to port, pulling up towards the formation. He then saw Gander section preparing for the attack so he broke starboard, at which point he observed two Ju 34s in the circuit of Aalborg East aerodrome: 'I attacked the first one from 30 degs port and gave a short burst from 400 yds, but saw no strikes. I closed to 200 yds, and gave a long burst from 10 deg port closing rapidly, and saw strikes all over the engine and cockpit, flames and black smoke came pouring out and pieces fell off enemy aircraft. When I overshot it banked steeply, I broke to port and saw it burning on the ground.' Nyerrod then broke north towards three Ju 88s flying north-west in tight formation, but he then had to react quickly as he sighted an FW 190 at 3,000 ft preparing to attack him. Nyerrod let off a long-range burst at a Ju 88, not seeing any strikes. Three of his guns then stopped. He broke towards the FW 190 and managed to get on his tail. The FW 190 started turning, but Nyerrod pulled inside him and let off two short bursts with his remaining gun, although he wasn't able to see any strikes. He climbed to attack again but the FW 190 turned on its back and went into cloud.

Flying Officer Pinches, on approaching the target, spotted two aircraft at 12 o'clock. He closed in, identifying one as a Ju 34. Closing further to about 100 yards he let off several bursts from directly behind, and saw strikes on the starboard side of the fuselage and wing root. As he broke he saw smoke and flames and several pieces come off the aircraft. Flight Sergeant Kelly then followed up, getting in a burst of about three seconds. Kelly witnessed strikes on the port wing and an explosion on top of the hood. The Ju 34 appeared to shudder and then dived steeply, flames streaming behind. Kelly was then about to attack one Me 109 when he saw strikes registering on it (possibly from Barrett), so he latched on to another and from 300 yards line astern 10 deg port closing, he let off a three-second burst, seeing his fire slam into his enemy's wing root. The Me 109 pulled up steeply, inverted and then plunged into the ground, bursting into flames. It wasn't over for Kelly though. He then managed to get in position on an FW 190 and saw strikes register on his opponent's wing. He turned and then saw a formation of three Do 217s heading in a westerly direction, climbing fast. Kelly seized his opportunity, closed on his prey and fired from about 400 yards but saw no strikes. He fired again; this time hits registered along the port wing, engine and on the glass house 'which blew to pieces'. Kelly then had to turn steeply as a Ju 88 came in to attack, but he was able to see the Do 217 dive steeply and a parachute open behind it. Kelly dived his Mustang down to the deck, the Ju 88 attempting to follow but having to break off the pursuit after a minute.

Following his attack on the Ju 34, Pinches then saw two seaplanes on a lake at 5 o'clock, identifying them as Arado 196s. He swept his Mustang down to the deck and tore into the attack, pouring his fire into the aircraft on two passes. He then saw an He 177 flying low across the water and immediately turned into attack, getting behind his enemy, opening fire from 500 yards, closing to 150 yards. The Mustang's munitions ripped into the fuselage and starboard engine, which caught fire. Pinches then hit his enemy's slipstream, which almost inverted him, but he pulled up and was able to see the Heinkel slam into some buildings on the SE coast of the lake, and explode. But this wasn't the end of the action for Pinches. As he flew south he saw an Ju 88 to his port, but at some distance. He then saw Gander section approaching from the north. Pinches reported an enemy aircraft to their starboard but as they had now no ammunition and 'did not wish to play', he turned into attack and pursued his foe back towards Aalborg, recognising it as a Ju 188. At full throttle and revs, he managed to get in range, opening fire with short bursts from 500 yards astern closing to 200 yards, at which point he ran out of ammunition. However, the enemy aircraft's starboard engine was smoking and as Pinches pulled over it, its engine cut, it turned onto its back, and disintegrated in a field below.

Johnston, Westenra, Collyns, Nyerrod, Pinches and Kelly all left the carnage behind and made their way back to England, able to tell their tale. Barrett and Williams were initially posted as missing. It had been an extraordinarily successful operation, nine enemy aircraft claimed destroyed, one probable and four damaged. But there would be further good news, when Flight Sergeant Williams returned to give his side of the story and add to the claims. He had managed to get behind a Ju 34 and claimed it as damaged. He then latched on to three He 177s opening fire on one before a Mustang (likely to be that piloted by Pinches, but possibly Barrett) cut in front and he had to break off. He then came across three Ju 34s approaching Aalborg airfield, and sent two to the ground. Turning, he came into contact with and attacked what he thought was an He 177, although he subsequently learnt it was a Ju 88. He would later recall:

> The Ju 88 I was attacking at low level was on fire and the pilot gave the order for the crew to bale out. He pulled the aircraft up in front of me, as I was making a rear attack with 20 degrees flap down to avoid overshooting. In order to bale out the lower turret gunner had to jettison a piece of armour plating . . . this lodged in my air scoop causing the engine to seize and the Mustang to stall, leaving me no height to bale out, hence the forced landing. Having crashed near Hjallerup in the north of Jutland, I hid in a water-filled irrigation ditch about three quarters of a mile from the crash site. When the Germans had thoroughly searched a nearby barn, within my view, I hid there after daylight.[27]

However it seems that actually whilst attacking the Ju 88, an enemy aircraft had got onto Williams' tail, his Mustang being the 53rd victory of Hauptmann Siegfried Simsch of 10./JG 11.[28] Williams avoided capture and with the help of the Danish Resistance he returned to England via Sweden. Williams was also able to report that all flying was suspended for a few days after the attack and from then on FW 190s protected the skies over the training unit.

Without a doubt the conduct of the operation and the reports of claims boosted morale, and unsurprisingly the celebrations followed the tried and tested format.

> *65 Squadron ORB*
> 18-5-44 The W/Cdr and Squadron returned from Coltishall with all the details of yesterday's operation and very interesting they were too. The Squadron was released in the afternoon and every man wended his way to his favourite Haunts. The beer is still rotten around these parts.

It appeared that Flight Lieutenant Barrett had been able to achieve some success, possibly shooting down two, maybe even three Me 109s. But the action cost Barrett his life. Shot down, his aircraft crashed into the north bank of Lim Fjord. The Mustang's tail could be seen from the shore and Barrett's body was recovered to be buried at Frederikshavn cemetery next to the airmen of the

---

27 Quoted in Shores, C. and Thomas, C. *2nd Tactical Air Force* (Classic Publications 2004) p109.
28 *Ibid.*

Luftwaffe killed the same day.[29]

Low Level Flying

Stephen Brian Harris was a Spitfire IX pilot with 74 Squadron and recalls that on 22 May 1944 he experienced at first hand one of the many problems associated with low level flying.

> On recce sweeps and ground attacks, the ground ack-ack was a bit hot. We were doing a low flying job and I hit a tree – one of those poplar trees. We were flying in between the trees, down one of the main roads and I went straight through the top. The old man went over and I went straight through.
>
> When I hit the tree I bent my prop and I had to go down with a dead engine. I was lucky because I saw a field that I could go down in with my wheels up. But just as I was heading for it I realised I was going straight into some high tension cables. Well I went underneath them, I had no power, I couldn't go over them. They were pretty high and the Spits pretty small so I just managed to skid underneath. I went through about two hedges and then stopped.
>
> The next thing to do was get away as quickly as possible. Luckily the Spit caught fire straight away, so I didn't have to bother about anything. I just scarpered.

Harris spent some time in hiding but eventually his luck ran out and he was picked up by the Gestapo and imprisoned in Brussels. Whilst there he heard of the Allied land advances and witnessed first hand how, 'it spooked the Germans.' From here Harris was to be transferred to Germany. But whilst in transit:

> I met a young American on the train and we decided to go over the side. So we did. I was a fairly good French speaker in those days and we got back to Brussels. Then we just waited for the Guards Armoured Division to come in. When things settled I reported back to the British HQ. And it was quite incredible. Walking along one of the streets in Brussels, whilst waiting to be repatriated, I recognised the Gestapo interrogator. By another chance there was an SP sergeant nearby. I whistled him over and got the man arrested.

---

[29] Information from an article by Paul Sortehaug published in *NZ Wings*, July 1997.

CHAPTER 5

D-DAY AIR POWER

Deputy Supreme Commander Sir Arthur Tedder, in his post-war memoir, summarised his view on Army/Air co-operation in battle, following the North African campaign.

> I claimed, with confidence, that these events proved co-operation with, but not subordination to, the Army, to be the right way of employing the Air Force in support of land power. This method had secured for us air superiority in the Libyan and Tunisian battles. As a result we were not only able to concentrate the main air effort to give direct assistance to the Army, but our land forces were also given a freedom of movement otherwise impossible.
>
> ...The four years of the Mediterranean campaign provided us with a clear step-by-step demonstration of the development of air-power and its relationship to land and sea forces, and introduced in rather brutal terms the new factor of air superiority and its effect on the operations of the land and sea forces. To attain that position air forces must be adequately equipped, trained for battle and securely based.
>
> ...It was there in Africa that first the British and then the Americans learnt how to fight a war in which action by land, air, and sea was closely integrated, and but for the lessons learnt their victory in Europe would not have been gained so speedily or at such little cost.[30]

One of the key air commanders in North Africa and the Mediterranean theatre of operations was 'Mary' Coningham who had attained the position of Air Officer Commanding (AOC) AHQ Western Desert in October 1941 and AOC North African Tactical Air Force in March 1943. With his considerable experience in tactical air command he was brought back to the UK to lead 2nd TAF. Coningham was also keen to bolster his new command with men who had experienced at first hand the campaigns in the desert, in Malta and in Sicily.

In a letter from Air Marshal Sir Bertine E. Sutton KBE, CB, DSO, MC to Coningham on 2 February 1944, the 2nd TAF commander learnt of some ways to strengthen his command with experienced airmen.

> CAS [Portal] has just received a letter from Slessor [with the Mediterranean Allied Air Forces at the time] in which he suggests that the TAF here might be able to make good use of a few officers from his Command who have had considerable experience of fighter bomber operations in close support of the Army. If you wished, from them he would be prepared to send home a few experienced squadron commanders (or flight lieutenants for promotion).

Coningham replied a few days later:

---

[30] Tedder, *With Prejudice*, p687-688.

> I should be most grateful if Jack Slessor's offer could be accepted and up to half a dozen squadron commanders or flight lieutenants for promotion could be sent.

But there was also one person in particular that he was after.

> ...One thing... is absolutely necessary and I have written to Jack Slessor to this effect. We must have Broadhurst available for the assault for a period of approximately one month from D-7... *If he cannot be posted, and there is no valid reason against it as his command is now, and in the future, in a comparative backwater in Italy, then I urgently request that he be given a month's attachment on temporary duty. The hard fact in England is that we have no commander with experience of the 'hurly burly' that happens during and after an opposed landing. I must, therefore, leave it to you and to Jack Slessor to decide whether it is to be posting or loan but I must continue to ask for Broadhurst's presence at that time.[31]

Coningham's wishes were granted and he would have Broadhurst for the invasion, in command of 83 Group. But of course, not only the most senior positions were to be filled by men of experience. Throughout the command airmen who had fought and learnt their lessons in previous campaigns, took on roles of responsibility and leadership. To illustrate this, below are details of some of those in command positions at a selection of our featured men's squadrons.

In January 1944 South African George Johnston took command of Basil Collyns' 65 Squadron and in March was promoted to lead 122 Wing, comprising 19, 65 and 122 Squadrons. Johnston had commanded 73 Squadron in the Desert, where he had gained a DFC, credited with four aerial victories and two probables.

By the end of the Battle of Britain, Alan Dredge, serving with 253 Squadron, had four victories to his name. In April 1941 he became one of the 261 Squadron airmen operating in the defence of Malta. On 6 May 1941 four Hurricanes fell to German fighters, Dredge being one, his aircraft crash-landing and he was severely burnt. Sent back to England Dredge's recovery came under the supervision of Sir Archie McIndoe, who was developing his plastic surgery technique, reconstructing the physical appearance of airmen disfigured by burns. Such was Dredge's improvement that he went on to join 183 Squadron flying Typhoons, earning a DFC. Then in October 1943 he took command of Bob Cole's 3 Squadron. And 3 Squadron would come within 150 Wing under the command of Wing Commander Roland Beamont, by then sporting a DSO, DFC and Bar.

Denys Gillam was 616 Squadron's leading scorer during the Battle of Britain, seven and one shared destroyed, four damaged and three probables. He then became a flight commander with 312 (Czech) Squadron, took command of 306 (Polish) Squadron, went on to Headquarters 9 Group, and then to command 615 Squadron. On 23 November 1941 he received wounds to an arm and his legs from flak, baling out and having the Air Sea Rescue services to thank for his recovery. After a spell lecturing in the United States, Gillam, by then recipient of a DSO, DFC and Bar, arrived at Duxford to pass on his experience to the first

---

[31] Public Record Office AIR 37 1237.

* Air Vice-Marshal Harry Broadhurst had considerable experience in the Mediterranean theatre of operations, becoming AOC Desert Air Force.

Typhoon Wing. From October 1942 to December 1943, his leadership and command skills were developed at RAF Staff College, Headquarters 12 Group and the Command and General Staff School at Fort Leavenworth. Gillam's next duty was to command, as Wing Leader, 146 Wing, then going on to 20 Sector 2nd TAF in April 1944. The position of wing commander flying was taken up by another pilot of considerable operational experience, Reg Baker. One pilot, Jimmy Kyle DFM, would recall 84 Group, 146 Wing's new commander.

> Wing Commander Baker was a tall fair-haired handsome character with a typical flowing RAF wartime moustache and the appropriate call sign of 'Lochinvar'. He had a happy-go-lucky personality, full of animated anecdotes and generous use of clichés with a plethora of words for ostentation to give splendour to his and our commonplace line shoots. Wholly extrovert and always talking shop like most of us, his passion for words cared more for the expression for its own sake rather than substance. It made great and easy, enjoyable listening.
>
> We nicknamed him 'Young Lochinvar', a brave and glamorous knight amongst us. We all loved his flamboyant personal force and delightful character. His influence inspired laughter, enthusiasm and confidence and did much to facilitate a very high standard of morale throughout the whole of the operational unit, for both air and ground personnel.[32]

A Ranger to Rennes

On 6 April Reg Baker led a Ranger to Rennes. The following combat reports describe the action.

> Sqn 266
> Typhoon IB
> 1153-1355 hours
> Time of attack – approx 1300 hours
> 1 Ju 88 shared – Flight Sergeant J O Hulley and Pilot Officer M R Eastwood
>
> Pilot Officer Eastwood – I was on a Ranger Rennes/Gael area flying as Blue 2 at zero feet. We were flying south of Rennes on a westerly course when I sighted an aircraft, 4 miles away at 2,000 feet on my starboard. I reported same and was ordered by W/Cdr Baker to attack it.
>
> The aircraft which I recognised as a Ju 88 was flying head on but started turning starboard allowing me to turn port onto it. During the turn enemy aircraft was approx 200 yds and I fired my first burst at 70 degrees decreasing to a stern attack and saw strikes on port main plane and engine which appeared to catch fire. I then broke underneath enemy aircraft, pulled up, made another attack and fired a burst but overshot. My No. 2, Blue 3, went in and attacked aircraft from astern. He fired one long burst and broke away, I then managed to drop back and fire a final burst at 100 yds closing in rapidly. Aircraft was burning furiously during this last attack, especially starboard engine.
>
> I then watched enemy aircraft and saw one of the crew bale out. The

32 *A Typhoon Tale*, Kyle, J. p146-7.

enemy aircraft then crashed after losing height slowly, a column of smoke rising to 1,000 feet, where enemy aircraft was seen to crash. During attack on the Ju 88, flak heavy and light appeared to be coming from Rennes airfield. The enemy aircraft put his undercart down during first attack. I then joined up with the Squadron and returned to base.
One gun used.
20 rounds, 20mm per cannon, no stops.
Total 40 rounds HE/I 40 round SAP/I – Total 80 rounds.

Flight Sergeant Hulley – I was Blue 3 to W/Cdr Baker on the 6/4/44. We were on a Ranger and had just arrived south of Rennes when Blue 2 (Pilot Officer Eastwood) reported an aircraft at 3 o'clock. The enemy aircraft was at about 2,000 feet and we were on the deck. Blue 1 told B2 to chase it, and B2 and myself broke away, dropped tanks and climbed to meet the enemy aircraft, which was flying towards us. B2 did a $^1/_4$ attack onto the Ju 88's (identified) port, closing right up to it. He then broke away, and I came in and attacked. I saw strikes on his tail, and allowed a bit more deflection, and got better results, seeing strikes up forward and on the engines. It had been badly hit by Blue 2, and as I broke away I noticed the starboard engine blazing, and the port engine smoking well. Blue 2 then attacked again, and the Ju 88 sailed down eventually and flipped into the deck, where it sent up a very thick column of smoke.

The Ju 88 had lowered his u/cart just as B2 made his first attack. One of the crew baled out after my attack. His parachute opened. There was a lot of heavy flak from Rennes aerodrome, and I think from Rennes itself. The CO Squadron Leader Holmes silenced an AA post, which was firing in the direction of Blue 2 and myself when we were attacking. The Ju 88 did not return fire, and only carried out diving and slight evasive action.
Cine gun used.
50 rounds, 20mm per cannon. No stops.
Total 25 He/I 25 SAP/I Total 200 rounds.

In the run-up to the invasion the squadrons of 84 Group escalated the offensive against enemy targets in north-west France:

5 to 11 April	32 missions	257 sorties
12 to 18 April	56 missions	351 sorties
19 to 25 April	101 missions	1,239 sorties
26 April to 2 May	136 missions	1,507 sorties

As part of 84 Group, 146 Wing made its contribution with the odd Ranger and attacks on rail marshalling yards, and also played a key part in the attacks on Noball targets.

A Leo 45 Goes Down

On 29 April 257 Squadron's Brian Spragg would get a part share in the shooting down of a Leo 45. Similar to Bob Cole's experience attacking the same kind of aircraft a few months earlier, there was no opposition. The twin-engined enemy aircraft, once seen, had no chance.

> It was a fairly long trip, two hours, we were carrying tanks. We were looking for trouble. There were six of us and we were right on the deck, absolutely low level. We saw this aeroplane on the horizon also at low level. And it really was very low down, about 50 feet or so. It was who was first in, gets to fire at it. I was one of the first and fired. I gave it a little bit of deflection, and I know I hit it. It couldn't take much evasive action being a lumbering little transport aeroplane and it went down, very close to a farm.

Into May 1944 the 2nd TAF Typhoon squadrons began a campaign of attack against enemy radar installations, in an effort to blind the Germans to the approach of the invasion force. The campaign would prove a success. But these installations were well defended and the Typhoon squadrons lost many pilots. Part of 146 Wing, 257 Squadron's Brian Spragg recalls attacking the sites.

> We used to go in low level, line astern, north or south of the radar site, 90 degrees to the coastline. We'd go behind the site inland and all turn together so we came in in a four-line abreast, attacking the various aspects of the radar sites, with 11-second delay bombs. Then on out to sea. We sometimes went back round again and gave them a bit of cannon fire as well. I didn't think they were too bad. We were going out to sea always as we came out of the attack. [With regard R/P squadrons] They were having to run in on a steady track all the time without deviating.

> *Derek Tapson, 197 Squadron:* Before D-Day there was an attack on one of the radar stations on the French coast, east of Normandy. Our job was to go in as the final squadron, and drop delayed-action bombs, after the target had been damaged by the rocket squadrons. I always remember sitting up there, circling over the target, watching the other aircraft attack with their rockets. I remember seeing three of them come down the coast, getting ready to line up to fire, and going straight into the drink, 1, 2, 3, one after the other got shot down as they were approaching the target. It was one of the reasons why we didn't want to fire rockets actually.

James Stewart DFC flew with 123 Wing's 609 Squadron and recalls his attacks on radar sites.

> It was on 11 May that we had two casualties, attacking a radar station at Cap d'Antifer. We came in at 2-3,000 feet, pretty well in twos, and then came down one behind the other and let go of the rockets hoping they'd hit. [Flying Officer P. L.] Soesman was ahead of me and he got hit by the flak. I could see the glycol pouring out from underneath his fuselage. We peeled away and it wasn't too long after that that we were back on the coast again. Soesman went up and baled out.

Two Typhoons circled Soesman's position until he was forced to return owing to low fuel. However an ASR Walrus with escorting Spitfires was due but on arrival nothing was found. 609 Squadron also lost Flight Lieutenant R. L. Wood who was killed when his aircraft was shot down. Wood's aircraft also collided with, and took 30 inches off the wing of, Flight Sergeant Adams' Typhoon, although he was still able to fly back to England.

Bang!

A couple of days after James Stewart's operation against the radar site at Cap d'Antifer he was on operations again.

> It was a Saturday morning, we were sent out on a target of opportunity. Some Spits had seen some tanks and soft-skinned vehicles moving along a highway towards Rouen. So we were scrambled off to see what we could do. Well we flew awfully close to Rouen and some of the fellows there, I guess, had some pretty good training. There were a bunch of 88s, I think, and they started peppering all around us, big black bursts, and bingo, bang! The prop stopped. I was at about 4-5,000 feet and had to glide down and call up and tell the CO I was going to bale out.
>
> I went to get out and my foot stuck in the rudder bar, so I came back in again and then went out over the side. I was only a couple of thousand feet up and as I was drifting down I could see people milling around. I made a good landing right in the middle of a field in the middle of a copse. I just dumped the parachute and made hell for leather for the woods, then just dashed down, laying right low. After I had finished up the few cigarettes I had I moved along to the edge of the woods and that was the first time I ever saw a big pair of jackboots and a bicycle going by. I waited for a while and eventually stood up. There was a great big smoking hole, which was obviously where my aircraft had crashed, with a whole bunch of Germans all standing around, having fun looking into the hole. They went one way and I naturally went the other.

Stewart eventually came to a farmhouse, and hid in hay for the night. In the morning he approached an old woman, and asked for help in his Scottish accent, telling her he was a British airman. She gave him an old black coat, some cheese and wine and suggested he head south. In the next village he met a Frenchman and again told him he was a British airman. He took him to see the graves of some British soldiers killed in 1940. James was led to a farmhouse and put in a barn, where he managed to get a shave. A few days later he was taken to Rouen and met some Resistance members in a café, although they weren't too endearing towards him, Rouen having been bombed by the RAF a few days previously. James returned to the farm and then a few days later went to Paris on the train, where he stayed with a French brother and sister and 'had a great time'. However this particular evasion line had been infiltrated by a Gestapo agent and on 8 July James was captured. He was taken on the last train out of Paris before its liberation and after five days of travelling ended up at Buchenwald.

James Stewart: ... and learned to our dismay what had been going on.

> We had a fine senior officer who kept us all together and we insisted we were military personnel. It was run internally by prisoners, externally by the SS. We just acted as military people and refused to work. There was a big arms factory right outside the camp and big stone quarries.

After 2½ months at Buchenwald James was transferred to Stalag Luft III, and saw the rest of the war out as a regular POW, returning to England on 13 May 1945, the anniversary of his shooting down.

In the week prior to D-Day, 146 Wing maintained attacks on German radar sites. They were trips that would give the pilots a clear view of the Allied build-up.

> *Ken Trott, 197 Squadron:* When we flew along the coast, as we were doing everyday virtually, you could see the enormous motor transport dumps. I remember flying over one area and seeing about 20 engines lined up. It was all so obvious that something was happening, and the Americans were all around us, near Needs Oar Point. When we used to go on a Liberty run to Bournemouth, we would be virtually going through Americans until we reached Ringwood, all the way through the New Forest. One sensed that something was going on… [On eve of D-Day] The Channel was covered with boats of various kinds, a fantastic sight and it seemed impossible that the Germans did not know what we were up to. There was so much going on you couldn't understand why there was no retaliation.

Blinded

One other key achievement resulting from the air superiority was the successful screening of the invasion build-up from prying eyes. On 21 May 1944, German Army Group B's Field Marshal Erwin Rommel reported his concerns to C-in-C West Field Marshal Gerd von Rundstedt: 'There are no results of air reconnaissance of the island for the entire period.' This situation barely improved the next week as the Luftwaffe was only able to reconnoitre three of the seventeen harbours in which the invasion force was gathering. It was also unable to penetrate far enough to see the main concentration around the Isle of Wight, yet could report that there were 'only a small number of landing craft at Folkestone and Dover'. On 5 June Rommel's weekly situation report was sent to von Rundstedt who learnt that, 'Air reconnaissance showed no great increase of landing-craft in Dover area. Other harbours of England's south coast NOT visited by reconnaissance aircraft… Survey urgently needed of harbour moorings on the entire English south coast.'[33]

The general feeling amongst the Germans was that invasion was not imminent. Their weather reports suggested conditions adverse to a Channel crossing. And although a massive invasion force was assembling, the Germans were blind to the fact, in part due to the RAF's air screen over southern England.

---

[33] *The Struggle for Europe*, Wilmot, C., (Collins, 1952) p217, 229.

On the eve of the Normandy invasion Reg Baker led an attack on the radar installations at St. Valéry. Results were later reported as moderate, with near misses on the aerials, the whole area being sprayed with 8,700 cannon shells. Squadron Leader Ross of 193 Squadron was seen to bale out of his Typhoon and then try and climb into his dinghy. Fixes were transmitted and patrols were later sent out to search. A mist came down hampering the hunt and Ross was never found.

Flying Officer Jerry Eaton flew with 257 Squadron as part of 146 Wing. He took part in ops on 5 June 1944:

> We came back from a dive-bombing trip and later went out again from Tangmere where we'd landed to search for Squadron Leader Ross of 193 Squadron who had baled out over the Channel just south of the Isle of Wight. We couldn't find him but we were flying across in a long line, searching the sea, when we suddenly became aware of all these boats, hundreds and hundreds of boats, as far as the eye could see. It was an incredible picture and our Wing leader, Reg Baker, called up and ordered R/T silence '... not another word until you land.' So when we got back he said, 'Well, obviously you know tomorrow's D-Day' – and that was it.[34]

Flight Sergeant A. Shannon, 257 Squadron, commented on the scene set by Reg on the eve of D-Day.

> Wing Commander Baker... got us all together on the evening of the 5th and said the possibility is that I won't be with you here tomorrow and many of you may not be here tomorrow – but it's going to be a great day for all of us. Circumstances rather overtook us and we were quiet rather than thrilled or emotionally affected by it, more or less reflective.[35]

'My Longest Night'

WAAF Mary Stewart (née Coote) was a plotter at Biggin Hill.

> A night to remember, which I think I can say was 'My Longest Night' was June 6 1944. We walked on duty as usual [from a house off station], it was dark and unusually silent. No aircraft about. We remarked on this. Only searchlights. Anyway when we got on duty about 2300 hours there was a fuss of excitement. We were greeted by the watch going off duty – who said that all leave was stopped and we were in for a very exciting long night. How right they were. When we had plugged in and adjusted our head sets, we were given the news that we had been waiting for for a while – that the invasion was on, and looking at the table not only were there aircraft plaques but also plaques in the shape of boats. You will have gathered I plotted the boats across the Channel in the invasion of D-Day. The night seemed endless – boats of course are slower to plot than aircraft and as they got nearer their target, the beaches, our thoughts were for those men, their families sending them to 'what'? Of course we all know now

34 *Typhoon Attack*, Franks, N. (Grub Street, 2003).
35 *Ibid.*

'what' that was. One felt a feeling of helplessness. The watch coming on duty were quite envious and realised why all leave had been stopped. The walk back that morning was silent. All our thoughts were for those men on the other side. We usually went to the village for breakfast but we weren't allowed to talk to civilians or contact our families.[36]

The build-up of transport and shipping could clearly be seen from the air. A further clue of impending action had come when the distinctive black and white invasion stripes were painted on the undersides of aircraft, a few days into June.

Hart Finley: D-Day didn't come as a surprise. We sensed at the time that it was fairly imminent, with the build-up that we were seeing along the coast. However two weeks before the invasion itself I got instructions to report back to Milfield to take the Fighter Leaders course. I guess that was a sign to me that I was being considered for command of a squadron. I was taking this course when suddenly I got an urgent signal to return immediately to Tangmere (having moved from Kenley). That was another sign that things were imminent. I couldn't believe my eyes as when I got to Tangmere the aerodrome was absolutely plastered with aeroplanes. There were five times as many on the ground as when I had left and not only that they were all marked up with the invasion markings.

I got back the evening of the briefing for the next morning. We went into the briefing and got all our instructions, that we were to take off at the crack of dawn on our first mission across and we were to go over and cover the American beachheads.

403 Squadron ORB: 5-6-44-... We certainly feel that great happenings are in the offing, as tonight we are all confined to camp, and sure enough we all attend a 'Gen' session with all the pilots of 126 and 127 Airfields in the Mess at 126. The long-awaited big day is here at last.

Through the Normandy beaches codenamed Gold, Juno, Sword, Omaha and Utah, Montgomery's 21st Army Group (Lieutenant General Sir Miles Dempsey's British 2nd Army on the left, Lieutenant General Omar Bradley's US 1st Army on the right) was to fight for the beachhead. The flanks were to be protected to the east by one British airborne division and to the west by two American airborne divisions. The key objective was to break the German defensive crust, and secure and expand the beachhead, enabling further troops and supplies ashore. The sea lanes to the beaches were under naval protection, with naval gunfire pounding the German positions on the beaches and inland. In addition, during the hours before the assault, Allied heavy bombers carried out an aerial bombardment on enemy gun emplacements. Spitfires and USAAF P47s protected the skies over the beaches. P38 Lightnings patrolled the Channel approaches. Allied fighters escorted the transports of the airborne troops. Mustangs and Spitfires assisted in directing the naval bombardment. Some

---

36 Papers of Mary Stewart (née Coote) held at the RAF Museum, Hendon.

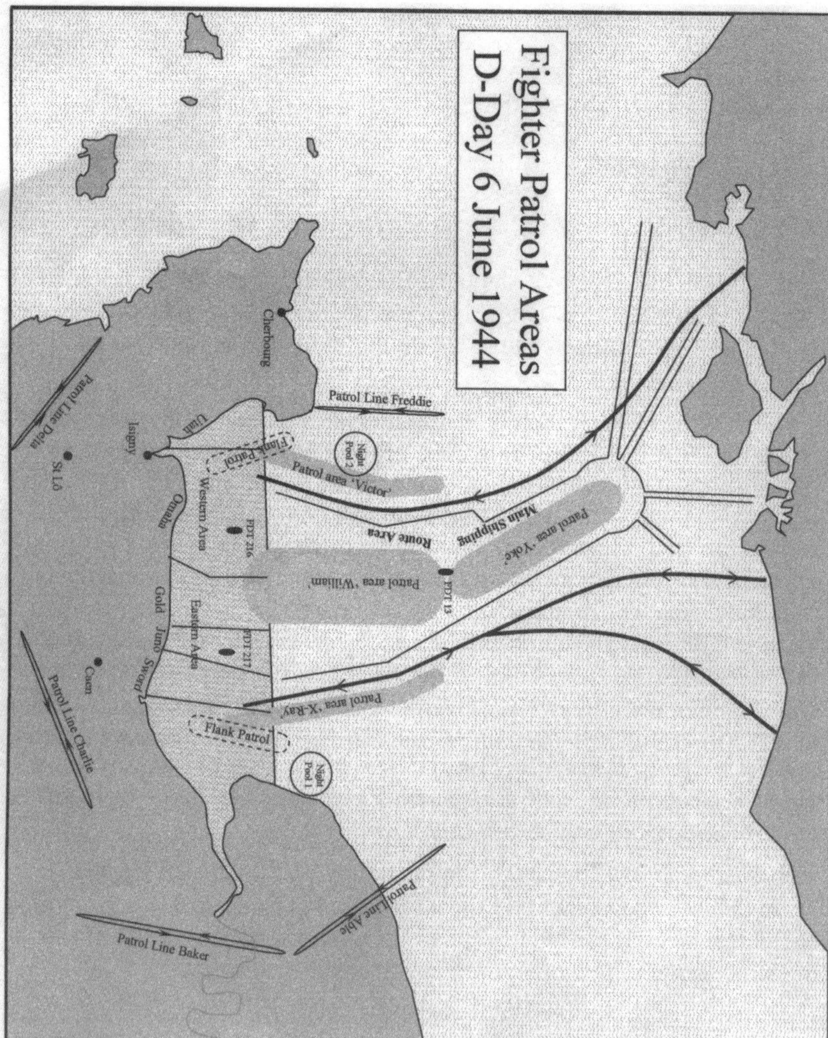

Typhoon squadrons attacked their prescribed targets, others awaited calls from the beachhead to attack targets as and when they became apparent. In addition a Pool of Readiness was maintained, six fighter squadrons from a reserve of thirty, to enter any battle that may arise. On the perimeter of the battle zone American VIIIth Air Force fighters and some ADGB squadrons provided a fighter screen.

Command Structure

The vast Allied air power was co-ordinated centrally at the Headquarters Allied Expeditionary Air Force, Stanmore, under Leigh-Mallory. This was also home to the HQ of ADGB. Advanced HQ AEAF, under Coningham, was at Hillingdon.

Control of all the air forces under Advanced HQ AEAF was carried out through the Combined Operations Room at Hillingdon and the Combined Control Centre next to it in the operations room at HQ 11 Group, Uxbridge. From here Coningham and Major General Lewis Brereton (commanding the American IXth TAF) could control 2nd TAF and the IXth TAF as a single air force. 11 Group's existing structure, with some additions, could be used to control the air situation in the early stages until control centres could be set up in captured territory, although there were some control capabilities aboard ships near the beaches. Also present at Coningham's HQ was a representative of 21st Army Group. Montgomery and Admiral Ramsay had their HQ at Portsmouth, Eisenhower at Forward SHAEF, Southwick Park, Portsmouth.

At 0630 hrs on the morning of 6 June 1944, 403 Squadron pilots took off to patrol the skies over the invasion fleet, the ORB recording, 'and what a show, it was almost beyond description, boats of all shapes and sizes, destroyers standing off from shore and pounding away at the Hun positions, giving covering fire for the landings.'

> *Hart Finley:* We went across as a wing, Lloyd Chadburn leading, a great wing leader. And as we approached the weather was poor, the cloud base not much higher than a thousand feet. We were just under the cloud and came across all these US ships, battleships, destroyers, you name it they had it. And I think these people had probably just come across the Atlantic right into operations because they were so trigger happy, they couldn't identify us, they thought we were Germans coming into attack them. They let loose with all their anti-aircraft fire at us. We just broke up into the cloud immediately and climbed up on top and called back to our control centre in England and said, 'Look, just tell these boys to lay off. If they want any protection they better not shoot at us.' So we went out over the Channel, circled around and went back down under and came in a second time and we got the same treatment, obviously the word hadn't got to them yet.

When 403 Squadron returned to base they were quickly turned around and airborne again at 1200 hrs, the patrol being uneventful, but the returning pilots could report that there appeared to be progress on the beaches. 403 put up two more patrols that day 'without a Hun being sighted'.

> *Hart Finley:* We didn't get any Hun reaction at all. Lots of activity on the surface though, the American ships, some of them were being sunk by shore batteries, others were being hit and exploding and they in turn were doing a lot of damage inland. We could see the people landing on the beaches and all the activity, it really was an incredible sight. It was hard to believe that the landing was succeeding, but it was.

The Luftwaffe response on D-Day had very little effect; indeed on the day of the assault only 319 sorties were flown over France. Frank Mares DFM flew with 310 Squadron and recalls one brief engagement with the enemy.

> At dawn on D-Day, myself flying with A Flight... a course was set,

climbing towards the heavily moisture-laden grey clouds. It did not take long to reach a level of just under the cloud bank as down below us was a mass of sea-going craft of every shape and size, including warships on the widely spread flanks, nursing the potent invasion fleet towards its destination, which was a section of the Normandy beach where they were to land, scale the cliffs and engage the enemy. With one eye firmly fixed on the epoch-making event going on below me, the other spotted a Junkers 88 piercing the clouds only 500 yards ahead of me. My gun button was at the ready. I fired my four cannons, at which salvo the plane very quickly climbed into the clouds. From then onwards, during three more sorties that I flew on the never-to-be-forgotten day, I did not see any other enemy plane polluting the sky above the allied armies and navies making their historic incursion onto the continent of Europe. Even now as I write this over 50 years after the event I can still recall the feeling of pride that engulfed me as I viewed the soul-stirring scene from on high, flying in relative safety protected by the thick layer of cloud above. What enemy flak there was, was ineffective, with myself anxious to be down low to fire my cannons at the opposing German forces.

I was flying over the beaches of Sword, Juno and Omaha, witness to the shells, mortars and bombs exploding among the very brave men swarming inland. Casualties were unavoidable and I considered myself somewhat impotent. Individual deeds were being heroically performed by soldiers and sailors of the great armada made up of British, Canadian and American forces, creating the most potent force for liberation that had ever been welded together specifically with the aim of fighting, with united determination, the enemies of peace and liberty and driving them to permanent extinction.

It was a scene that became etched in my memory bank, one that I have often recalled realising just what a privileged position I was in to take an 'eagle-eyed' panoramic view of the D-Day operation. It was history in the making and I was part of that process – it was exciting to be involved and to this day I can still feel that 'tingling of the spine' which remains with much pride.[37]

Controlling the Fighters

To assist with control of aircraft over the assault area, three Fighter Direction Tenders (FDTs), on ships and two Ground Control Interception (GCI) units were to be ready for operations on the evening of 6 June. The FDTs arrived in their positions as planned and began operating. The GCI in the British assault area was set up near Arromanches on D-Day, but the other became a victim of the carnage at Omaha beach, a replacement not being put in place until 11 June.

Flight Lieutenant R. J. Unstead, a controller in FDT 13 (the other two being FDT 216 and FDT 217), kept a diary of their role during the invasion, which was to act as forward control of layers of fighter cover over the invasion

[37] Papers of Frank Mares DFM, held at RAF Museum Hendon.

beaches by day and to accept night fighters reporting to the ship by night.

Monday June 5: Preparations continued. Despite high wind and choppy sea, we and the great company of ships left anchorage at Cowes for Yarmouth, to turn south-east at the Needles and proceed to point Z.

The Captain read General Eisenhower's message at 1130 to the ship's company.

A mine exploded some 600 yards from us when off the Needles.

Full watches manned from noon.

From point Z the vast procession of shipping heavily escorted by Naval units proceeded south.

Tuesday June 6 'D' Day: Throughout the night there was nothing for us to do but to wait, the enemy was inactive and Y service unable to report any realisation on his part of the vast approaching fleet.

Our role commenced at 0430 hours: we had reached our position (WV 4040 approx) and the four Lightning squadrons were on patrol punctually. From the bridge were seen lines of shipping and overhead at 0500 hundreds of Liberators going in to bomb.

The wind was so strong that it carried away all sound of the Navy's bombardment and the sea was rougher than anyone had imagined it could be for an invasion.

H-hour 0730 passed without incident, as far as we were concerned, save for a mine or depth charges exploding not far off. There appeared to be no enemy air reaction whatsoever.

[During the day] Slight enemy activity was plotted over the beaches but although our Lightnings arrived, patrolled and departed with astonishing accuracy, there were no clients for them.

June 7: During the night 6/7 there was little enemy activity. We were given three N/Fighters by 217, for the GCIs did not appear to be operational although contact had been made with one. Our three N/Fighters had no joy.

Our Lightnings patrolled uneventfully, chasing every bogey with enthusiasm, but bogeys were always friendly.[38]

By the end of the first day the beachheads had been secured, although the cost to the Americans at Omaha had been heavy. But what of the defensive response? The assault area fell within the boundary of the German 7th Army, part of Field Marshal Erwin Rommel's Army Group B (Rommel was subordinate to Commander-in-Chief West Field Marshal Gerd von Runstedt). Rommel knew his coastal defences were weak. He also knew that the key lay in deploying mobile reserves quickly to the battle area, predominantly the panzers, in an attempt to counter the invasion before the beachhead had been secured and extended. He did have some panzer divisions close at hand but they would not prove enough. Reinforcement was needed, but a complicated command structure would seriously delay the transferral of further German armour.

[38] The papers of Flight Lieutenant R. J. Unstead held at the Imperial War Museum file p270.

Major General Günther Blumentritt was Chief of Staff to the German Commander-in-Chief West and in a post-war interview told of the problems of moving reserves to the battle area.

> Time was vital. The nearest available part of the general reserve was the 1st S.S. Panzer Corps, which lay north-west of Paris. But we could not move it without permission from Hitler's headquarters. As early as 4 a.m. I telephoned them on behalf of Field Marshal von Rundstedt and asked for the release of this Corps – to strengthen Rommel's punch. But Jodl, speaking for Hitler, refused to do so. He doubted whether the landings in Normandy were more than a feint, and was sure another landing was coming east of the Seine. The 'battle' of argument went on all day until 4 p.m., when this Corps was at last released for our use.
>
> Then further difficulties interfered with its move. The Corps artillery had been kept on the east bank of the Seine – and the Allied Air Forces had destroyed the bridges. The Field Marshal and I had seen some of them being smashed. The artillery thus had to make a long circuit southward by way of Paris before they could get across the Seine, and was repeatedly bombed on the march, which caused more delays. As a result two days passed before this reserve was on the scene ready to strike.[39]

In the meantime Rommel attempted to contain the expansion of the beachhead, but with the Allies dominating the skies, enemy movements were continually harassed from the air. The German land forces needed some kind of intervention from the Luftwaffe. And now that the invasion was underway it attempted to move units from Germany to bolster and reinforce its presence over northern France. In doing so, the GAF had to penetrate the Allied air umbrella.

Fighter Control over the Beaches

Lieutenant (A) C. F. (Freddie) Corpes, RNVR assisted in the control of Allied fighter aircraft over Normandy.

> In March 1944 I received instructions to report to London, from where I and a number of other Naval officers (all air crew, though not for flying duties for this appointment) were sent to the headquarters of the Air Defence of Great Britain. For about three weeks we understudied the Naval Liaison Officers stationed there, and got to know the workings of those manning the 'Plot' deep underground. Then we were all dispersed to various RAF units. Some went to RAF stations in the UK, but we more senior ones were primed ready to go to the 'Far Shore' with the forthcoming 'Second Front', the Allied invasion of Northern Europe. A couple were attached to an HQ in the American sector.
>
> Lieutenant Commander (A) Gerald Arnold RNVR and I were appointed to the Staff of the Flag Officer, British Assault Area, Rear Admiral Rivett-Carnac, and attached to the mobile HQ of the 24 Base Defence Sector, RAF as Naval Air Liaison Officers. Our party

39 *The Other Side of the Hill*, Liddell Hart, B.H., (Pan Books, 1999) p405.

included eight Naval Ratings, (telegraphists, etc.) and two Royal Marine drivers for our two vehicles.

While awaiting events, camping out in the south of England, Gerald and I attended two or three conferences in London, dealing with planning for Neptune, the seaborne part of Overlord. We had been bigoted, bigot being a higher degree of secrecy than top secret for the planning and preparations for Overlord! We were issued with maps of the whole of the north coast of France in one scale, and in a larger scale, the invasion area from the Seine Estuary and Le Havre Peninsula to the Cherbourg Peninsula! We carried these around with us as necessary, and slept with them under our pillows! Being under canvas we had nowhere to lock them up!

On D-Day our landing ship anchored off the beach at Graye-sur-Mer at about 1000 hours. We were under fire for a time, but were not hit, though several shells landed uncomfortably close. The earlier smaller assault craft went right into the beaches, but, to prevent the larger landing ships being damaged or stranded on beaching, the early ones across (including ours) each towed over a rhino raft, built from many watertight sections joined together, with a ramp forward, and two large outboard engines aft. The ship unloaded on to the rhino raft, which then ferried the vehicles and men the short distance to shore. It took three trips to unload our ship. We (our naval party and others) were on the second trip. On the third trip the rhino raft ran into underwater explosives, suffered casualties and damage to vehicles and the raft itself.

By the afternoon, when our raft-load went ashore, bulldozers were already at work making roadways up from the beaches. Signposts to the casualty stations, ammunition dumps, fuel dumps, etc., were already being erected, and groups of German prisoners were on the beaches ready to be shipped to the UK. Some of the landing ships would carry prisoners on their return trips to the UK, others (including the one which we went in) had medical staff and equipment for transporting wounded. Most vessels (the larger ones) flew two barrage balloons on D-Day, one to be retained for its own protection, the other to be put ashore to protect the beaches from low flying aircraft. The air was full of Allied aircraft, but I only saw one German aircraft in daylight on D-Day, a fighter bomber, FW 190, which dropped a couple of bombs on the beach, but as soon as it was dark the German bombers came.

Having got ashore, we, (the sector HQ) were held at up at Graye-sur-Mer for the night, as the Germans were holding out in a wood nearby, barring the way to our setting-up point at Meuvaines. They were dislodged next morning when our infantry went in after a Naval bombardment. We then proceeded to Meuvaines, where we set up our HQ. The HQ operations room was formed by three large vehicles fitted out with a phone and radio links etc., forming three sides of a square, with the plot in the middle. The inner sides of the vehicles were opened up for the CO, controllers, Naval and Army Liaison Officers etc., to have a clear view of the plot, which showed the movements of the aircraft, hostile and friendly.

The 24 Bass defence sector HQ, with its outlying Ground Control Interception and other radar units, was responsible for controlling the RAF night fighter Mosquito aircraft, based in the UK to start with, patrolling the assault area. We Naval Air Liaison Officers had radio contact (and in due course, land-line contact) with the Naval HQ at Courseulles-sur-Mer, and we directly controlled the ships' AA gunnery when necessary, to safeguard our own aircraft flying over the anchorages. We also carried out general liaison duties between the three Armed Services, and one of us attended the Admiral's daily conference at Courseulles-sur-Mer. The RAF Air Sea Rescue launches were based at Courseulles-sur-Mer, and when required to be sent out, we gave instructions via the Naval HQ.

In the first few months from D-Day, most of the German air activity was concentrated on laying mines in the approaches to the anchorages. Thus, even when ships were not sunk or damaged, they were held up from bringing in reinforcements and supplies until the mines had been located and cleared. In the 11 weeks that I was in Normandy, our night fighter aircraft shot down more than 100 German bombers operating in the area.[40]

On 7 June 403 Squadron covered the skies above Omaha beach, cloud base at 2,000 feet, but despite being sent after a reported 20 plus FW 190s on one patrol, nothing was seen. The next day 403 carried out further 'quite uneventful' patrols, the weather deteriorating later in the day. Indeed on 9 June the ORB recorded 'even the birds are walking today – dirty weather'. But late in the day 403 got the chance to cross the Channel, where considerable opposition was met.

403 Squadron ORB

9-6-44–... As we came in over Omaha beach our Navy let everything they had go at us. We immediately got out of the way and called 'Research' who told us to come in again as it would be alright this time. So in we went again, this time flying line astern and with our navigation lights on, but still those trigger twitchy guys of the Navy let us have it a second time, those guys must really be blind because of all the aircraft that have been seen most in this show, the Spit most certainly has, so away we go again, giving 'Research' hell, and prepare for a third go, and sure enough the Navy cut loose with everything they have a third time, hitting four of our Kites, causing F/L Williams' aircraft to disappear, nothing more being seen of him. [Although wounded he would survive.] Flying Officer Kelly was slightly wounded but landed his aircraft safely at Tangmere and taxied over to the ambulance at flying control.

Indeed two other aircraft were damaged, with the pilots uninjured.

The next day 403 carried out further patrols, and ran into flak 'and red tennis balls', one aircraft hit, the pilot having to return to base. But there was little other

---

40 Correspondence with Lieutenant (A) C. F. (Freddie) Corpes, RNVR.

activity, although the pilots could see landing strips under construction inland from the beaches.

Belly Landing

On 11 June 1944, 403 Squadron's Andy Mackenzie DFC was forced to try out one of the new landing strips.

> We were on patrol over Utah beach, flying fluid sixes – twelve aircraft in two flights of six. I was leading one flight about 3,000 feet over the beachhead. The American flak seemed to think we were Huns and they put one in my rad, and in about 30 seconds my prop had stopped. When it's short of glycol the old Merlin doesn't go very far. I looked around and saw a field they were bulldozing, preparing an airfield. I managed a dead-stick landing, which was quite easy as it was a sizeable area. Despite coming down with my wheels up it was soft enough not to jar the aeroplane too much. So I still had use of the radio. I told the guys in the air to not report me as missing. I was OK and I'd get back on my own.
>
> Anyway the cockpit had filled with dust and I was covered in it, all brown. I wasn't hurt and I stepped out of the aircraft and looked around. Then a Jeep came roaring up the strip and this chap, carrying pearl-handle pistols, jumped out. He said, 'You've had it for the rest of the war.' He was pointing the pistols directly at me. I said, 'Who are you?' He replied, 'I'm the commanding officer of the ack-ack unit that just shot you down.' I patted my shoulder which shook the dust off, and I said, 'Look that's a Canadian badge, that's a Spitfire and you're an asshole.' We ended up quite good friends and went back to his tent where we polished off a bottle of scotch.

The squadron ORBs of Reg Baker's 146 Wing describe their action:

> *193 Squadron:* Greatest day in our lives – Invasion Day. All the boys in readiness at 0430 roaring to go but nothing doing for us in the morning and we waited round for a show, listening to all the news broadcasts etc. In the afternoon the first show was laid on and the boys clobbered some tanks – nice work. Another 'op' was laid on but there was no joy in this as no targets were found. Packed up about 2200 hours everyone feeling pretty tired and ready for bed.

> *197 Squadron:* At last the day for which we have all been waiting has arrived. All last night our aircraft were over France in great numbers. At first light we had the honour to share with 266 Squadron two bombing shows on territory later to be occupied by our own troops. Both shows were successful. Our show was led by S/Ldr Taylor leading one section and W/C Baker the other. We all waited hopefully for the return of the aircraft to find out how the big show was going on. Our hopes were raised when we were told of how everything appeared to be going smoothly the other side. Squadrons from the Wing attacked targets for our forces all

today. Later in the day our squadron once again started sorties against ground targets. Good results were seen in all cases. Tanks, MT and dumps were attacked along with anything else which may have been of use to the enemy. We finished our work late in the evening just as the night bombers were again going out.

257 Squadron: Der Tag – but ours. Not such a heavy programme as anticipated, but almost all our pilots ranged over the beachhead once, and to the south seeking and attacking enemy transport. Shelling from our warships was visible as spasmodic flashes, no Hun aircraft were seen by any of our chaps, but Spits and Thunderbolts, patrolling over the massed shipping in the Bay du Seine approached our formations enquiringly several times, but sheared off as recognition dawned. A fairly successful bag of assorted transport including tanks, trucks and staff cars were 'britched up' and a tented Hun camp was strafed. The occupants of one staff car tumbled out and sought shelter in a chateau. This was promptly demolished by a direct hit with a 500 lb bomb. There was little flak opposition in all these prangs.

266 Squadron: D-Day, everybody tense. Boys over the beaches when first landings were made, a wonderful sight. Sgt Mitchell crash-landed on the beachhead. No activity during the afternoon.

After D-Day 146 Wing Typhoons roamed inland of the beachheads attacking gun positions and MT, bombing troop concentrations in woods and villages, bombing enemy HQs, and carrying out armed recces. 193 Squadron's ORB 11 June, 'Plenty of Hun transports found and attacked.' 197 Squadron's ORB 10 June, 'Several vehicles and a gun and trailer "bought it" while other transport were left smoking. Strikes were obtained on about 12 transports in all. Very good show!' 197 Squadron's Ken Trott describes what a typical armed recce was like.

It was usually four or eight of us being led over France, from this country in the early stages. Over France what sort of height we would fly at depended on who was leading. We would be looking for targets, usually MT or tanks. When a target had been selected, whoever was leading would give an indication of what it was and we would then go in line astern or spread out a bit depending on what it was.

If it was a road convoy then obviously there were several vehicles. You would be in battle formation anyway, which would be four aircraft spread out, and the other four would come in behind. You would go in and attack the target and hopefully blow up the transport. We usually carried a couple of bombs and of course we had our 20 mm cannon, using either depending on what the target was.

You could be told of the target in the air. Whoever was leading could be called up on the radio and given a map reference. But generally after D-Day an armed recce was going round an area, Caen generally, looking for anything that was likely to move.

But of course despite operating virtually free of Luftwaffe intervention, there was still considerable danger to the low flying fighter-bomber pilots of the tactical air forces. Flak was the main opposition; some pilots force-landed, some used the emergency landing strips, some had to bale out and others were seen to go down in their aircraft. Losses would rise.

122 Wing's Mustangs were held on D-Day in the Pool of Readiness, but with the Luftwaffe generally absent its squadrons were somewhat frustrated.

> *65 Squadron ORB*
> 6-6-44 – At 0330 hours this morning we were dragged out of bed. We were to be on immediate readiness at 0400, but lunchtime came, then teatime and still nothing doing. Periodical reports came in to give us information about the invasion. The landing had been carried out successfully except in the American Sector where one small stretch of coast was causing some difficulty. The most remarkable feature was the amazing lack of air opposition.
>
> It was not until late in the day that we got our chance to help in any way. We were briefed to escort a great number of gliders [and] their towing Halifaxes, rendezvousing six miles SW of our base. At 2015 hours the first lot of airborne troops passed overhead, mile after mile of them. Eventually as the first of our particular lot came over, we took off. The squadron split up into sections, each taking individual action, and so we escorted them over the beachhead at 2,000 feet when but a few miles north of Caen, the gliders were released and the paratroops left the Halifaxes and Lancasters. Later it was learned that none of these aircraft was lost due to enemy action, for which we were congratulated. We landed at 2215 hours and so ended D-Day – for us anyway.

Basil Collyns didn't see any of the action on 6 June but over the next two days he would fly four operational sorties, contributing to 65 Squadron's support to the land forces. Early on 7 June Air Vice-Marshal Groom SASO (Senior Air Staff Officer) 2nd TAF met with a representative of the enemy 21st Army Group to discuss the movement of 21st Panzer Division from around Argentan and of 12th SS Panzer Division from Dreux and Évreux. A decision to increase the number of armed recces in the area was made, in particular to throw in the six Mustang squadrons from the Pool of Readiness. 65 Squadron went on the offensive. The day had started early again for the squadron, the airmen being woken at 0320 hrs and by 0640 hrs the pilots were lifting their Mustangs from the runway detailed for an armed recce in the Argentan area. But the poor weather curtailed any chance of getting at the enemy and 'they gave up in disgust and brought those beautiful bombs all the way back again.' The squadron was airborne again at 1130 hrs, but again the weather was poor, although convoys were found and bombed and strafed. At 1745 hours 65 Squadron sent airmen across the Channel again, and at 2110 hours 65 Squadron once again added its weight to the aerial onslaught, in the Dreux area, although the weather was getting very bad again. Flight Lieutenant Stillwell, who was to lead, had to return immediately after take-off with engine trouble and the operation was described as 'a complete shambles'.

On 8 June, 'at the unearthly hour of 0505' 65 Squadron pilots were again airborne. As the formation approached the French coast the cloud thinned and they found a convoy parked on a road lined with trees. Squadron Leader Westenra ordered his men in to bomb in sections, each section to become top cover on completion of bombing. As Red section went in, Westenra sighted an FW 190 which he pursued. Red section bombed and then on the return unloaded their munitions into a train, managing to escape any damage from flak. After the squadrons returned to base Westenra, Flight Lieutenant Milton and Flight Lieutenant Sutherland were able to post their claims for an FW 190 each, the ORB recording, 'Some people get all the luck.' Ops were on again later in the morning and 65 Squadron attacked marshalling yards and some trucks but, 'we got no satisfaction out of it.'

On 9 June the weather at Funtington really took a turn for the worse with rain all day. 'The dispersal leaked, the tents leaked and we positively soaked in every drop that ******* well dropped.' 65 Squadron weren't the only ones grounded and there was frustration all the way up the chain of command. On 9 June Air Vice-Marshal S. C. Strafford, Chief of Ops & Plans Advanced HQ AEAF noted in his diary his concerns over gaining airfield space in France.

> The expected improvement in the weather later in the day has not materialised, and although it is actually better on the other side of the channel, it is quite impossible over bases in the UK. These conditions reinforce the necessity to establish airfields on the other side at the earliest possible moment.[41]

So where was the Luftwaffe? Much of its strength had been depleted in the battle against the American bombers and escorts over Germany in the months leading up to the invasion. On 31 December 1943 the Luftwaffe had a strength of 2,395 single-engined fighters at operational units. By the end of May 2,262 single-engined fighter pilots had been lost, just short of 100%. Such attrition rates were not sustainable in terms of pilot ability and experience. The area of operations over the invasion was covered by Luftflotte 3. Its strength had declined as Luftflotte Reich, defending the skies over Germany against the American bombers and fighters, was reinforced. The Allies estimated only 100 GAF day sorties on 6 June and 175 that night, over the battle area. When the invasion came the Germans had planned to send reinforcements to Luftflotte 3 from Luftflotte Reich. In the first instance this would be seriously disrupted owing to the Allied campaign of bombing airfields and the transportation system on the approaches to Normandy. Secondly, Allied fighters were patrolling the approach routes. Nevertheless reinforcements did arrive.

Strength and Serviceability of the GAF in France, Belgium and Holland

	31 May		**10 June**	
Type	**Strength**	**Serviceable**	**Strength**	**Serviceable**
Reconnaissance	123	58	102	48
Singe-engine fighters	313	152	430	266
Night fighters	92	47	170	96
Twin-engine fighters	66	43	57	30
Ground attack	40	36	16	9
Bombers	555	263	521	307
Transport	64	31	140	100
Others	86	70	94	78
Total aircraft	**1,339**	**700**	**1,530**	**934**

[41] PRO AIR 37/574, diary of AVM S. C. Strafford CB, CBE, DFC.

The Value of Enigma

When the Germans started to bring in air reinforcements to the invasion area, the Allies were often aware of their deployments. German signals, intercepted and decrypted by the code breakers at Bletchley Park, could give the names and locations of the units. The following 8 June 1944 decrypt gives a clear example of such movements (which includes in brackets comments arising from previous intelligence). Gruppe refers to the basic Luftwaffe operational flying units, approximately 30 aircraft, three, four or sometimes five of which usually made up a Geschwader. JIG refers to Jagdgeschwader (a fighter Geschwader). NAN JIG refers to Nachtjagdgeschwader (a night fighter Geschwader) and Zebra refers to Zerstörergeschwader (twin-engined 'destroyers').

> Arrangements evening sixth, Second Gruppe JIG one arriving Flers. Third Gruppe JIG two seven arriving Romilly. Fourth Gruppe JIG two seven arriving Champfleury (comment, this gruppe at Szombathely on 31st). Second Gruppe NAN JIG two arriving Coulommiers (comment, gruppe at Koeln Butzweilerhof on 18th). Stab and one NAG thirteen arriving Dinard (comment, other elements already there). Zebra one with two gruppen arriving Lorient (comment first and third gruppen hitherto in west and second gruppe in Austria). Second gruppe JIG five three arriving Vannes (comment, this gruppe at Oettingen – Noerd – Lingen on 28th). Three issues (comment, on fuel, ammunition etcetera, one issue for one operation) to be made to each unit. Special orders (comment, no details) regarding issue of two one cm Mortar shells.[42]

The Allies were also able to intercept numerous signals detailing the location and strength of the Luftwaffe units, the results of air attacks on enemy airfields, and the progress of repairs. Such information was obviously invaluable in conducting the campaign against the Luftwaffe over Normandy.

Leigh-Mallory kept a diary throughout the Normandy campaign. The entry for 8 June demonstrates part of his response to the Luftwaffe redeployment. It also gives an indication of the frustration caused by the poor weather over Normandy.

> The German air force is beginning to thicken up and about half the fighters in Germany are now, I think, moving against us. I have put the American 8th Army Air Force on to the bombing of enemy airfields. Now is the moment to mess them up, for equipment for the Luftwaffe is beginning to reach them. I am, therefore, going to do an Aunaye attack [by this phrase the AOC-in-C means 'a heavy attack' – the airfield at Aunaye had been almost totally destroyed a few days before] on Flers, Laval, Le Mans and Rennes, and for that purpose I am going to use my heavies. I want to catch the German air force while they are moving in. At the moment they are very fluid. When they begin to take the air seriously against us they will need dumps, and it is my intention to blow these to hell. The situation is evolving but it is a terrible thing to me to feel all these troop movements going on while I am not able to stop them because of bad weather and low cloud.[43]

---

[42] Public Record Office DEFE 3/166.

[43] Public Record Office AIR 37 784.

On 10 June 1944, 65 Squadron saw combat action over Normandy, against some pilots of the reinforced Luftflotte 3. On the first operation of the day, Wing Commander Johnston led a small formation of six on an armed recce, taking off at 0550 hrs, with two Mustangs operating as top cover. When the formation attacked a convoy of enemy transport the top cover became separated. They then came down and attacked some more transport, but one pilot (Flight Lieutenant Anderson) failed to pull out on the dive and he was seen to go straight into the ground, losing his life. At 0920 hrs 65 Squadron sent another six Mustangs, one of which was piloted by Basil Collyns, on an armed recce of the same area. Shortly after crossing the French coast Me 109s pounced.

Flight Lieutenant Stillwell (acting as Presto Leader) had just finished his bombing and was orbiting above Presto 3 and 4 (Flight Sergeant Dinsdale and Flying Officer Driscoll) and Presto 5 and 6 (Basil Collyns and Flight Sergeant Boon). At about 1045 hours:

> *Flight Lieutenant Stillwell's combat report:*... I saw four aircraft coming in from port which I took to be Mustangs, as they had black and white stripes on the mainplanes and red, white and blue roundels on the fuselage and upper ring surface. I think one had a yellow outline around the roundel on the fuselage. The wing tips were painted to give a square appearance and the remainder of the camouflage was a dark green and brown. As Tonic section (19 Squadron) were operating nearby and had just turned in that direction, I assumed them to be Tonic aircraft. The leading aircraft opened fire from 150 yds in a 1/4 attack. I immediately saw they were Me 109s... I broke hard to port and up, and reported them on the R/T. Presto 2 (Flight Lieutenant Milton) broke starboard and half-rolled – I saw no more of him. By that time 12+ enemy aircraft had arrived and were carrying out determined attacks in pairs. I finally got behind one and gave several bursts from about 300 yds, 1/4 to astern, but observed no strikes. He pulled straight up and rolled on his back. I followed and rolled with him, firing whilst inverted. As he dived down his u/c dropped and he continued straight on down. I then saw tracer passing over me, and observed four Me 109s behind. I pulled up hard to the left, blacking out. I saw no enemy aircraft after that. Throughout the combat my gunsight was u/s due to oil from the defroster. I claim one Me 109 damaged.

Basil Collyns and Flight Sergeant Boon heard Stillwell...

> *Flight Lieutenant Basil Collyns' combat report:*... say he was being attacked by Me 109s with British markings. With my No. 2 F/S Boon, I opened up and flew to Caen. As we arrived SE of Caen I saw an aircraft approach head on and at first by the markings presumed it was another Mustang joining up. As the aircraft came into line astern I noticed that he was laying off deflection and suddenly realised that it was an Me 109. I pulled round immediately and yelled at No. 2 to attack.

> *Flight Sergeant Boon's combat report:* Arriving south of Caen an aircraft which I identified as an Me 109 got on to Presto 5's tail, and he immediately broke hard to port while I tried to close the range to under 200 yds, and saw white and black stripes and RAF roundels, but had

trouble with the new gunsight and did not fire. The enemy aircraft then broke hard to port and I followed.

Flight Lieutenant Basil Collyns' combat report: No. 2 did not fire and the 109 flicked to the right, so I dived and fired from 20 degrees to line astern. The aircraft started to catch fire, turned on its back, and dived into the ground close to the SE corner of Caen a/d. I saw the pilot bale out and his parachute open. My No. 2 confirms this as destroyed. The markings on this aircraft were RAF roundels, and black and white stripes on wings and fuselage, also the wing tips were shaded to make them look square. The parachute was definitely German type, in outline being of a more circular shape than the flat British kind.

Flight Sergeant Boon's combat report: I chased two other Me 109s but one disappeared in cloud and the range was too great to open fire. The other aircraft was being chased by nine Allied aircraft so I turned round and returned to base.

Presto 3 and 4 were also in the action.

Flight Sergeant Dinsdale's combat report: I had just bombed two MT and was strafing and set one on fire when Presto Leader, who was acting as cover, reported Me 109s. I opened up and climbed, my No. 2 Flying Officer Driscoll lagging behind. I did not see him again. As I climbed up I saw the rest of our flight engaging 109s. Three more were about 7,000 ft acting as cover to the others. I engaged one Me 109 who began turning tightly. I was turning with him and fired two or three short bursts when he either spun down or did a complete aileron turn. I could not follow him down as two more Me 109s were coming up behind me. I did not notice any roundels on the 109s, but there were some white and possibly black stripes on the wings. The fuselage was a yellow brown colour.

The first enemy aircraft I saw was 300 yds away, 9 o'clock slightly below and going in the same direction. I had a very good view of it and had no doubt that the aircraft was a 109, especially recognising the slender fuselage and the downward curve of the top side of the nose. There was black smoke behind the aircraft.

Flight Lieutenant Milton would survive, having been shot down by flak, and then evading capture, later credited with one Me 109 destroyed and one damaged. Flying Officer Driscoll lost his life. So was this an incident of friendly fire? It is unlikely that we will ever know. However, friendly fire was a factor in the air battle over Normandy, hardly surprising considering the concentration of aircraft. The Allied High Command were obviously aware of the problem. On 11 June AVM Strafford's diary recorded that at the morning's Allied Air Commanders meeting . . .

> Reference was made to the continuance of AA fire against friendly aircraft. Three Spitfires had been shot down the previous day by friendly flak and this morning's air cover had again been greeted by heavy AA barrage.[44]

[44] PRO AIR 37/574, diary of AVM S. C. Strafford CB, CBE, DFC.

And he would also record on the same day:

> Reports yesterday of enemy using RAF markings would appear to have been accounted for by an instance in which the Eighth Air Force fighters encountered tactical air force fighters in low cloud conditions. AEAF were asked to prevent publication of these incidents in official summaries before they had been fully investigated.[45]

The Air Historical Branch narrative of the Normandy campaign gives a summary of the friendly fire problem over Normandy.

> One unwelcome but not unexpected feature was to show itself early in the campaign as soon as bad weather and enemy attacks had affected the nerves of the AA gunners ashore and afloat. This was concerned with the difficulty of recognising which aircraft were friendly and which were hostile when cloudy conditions prevailed. General Montgomery was worried when RAF fighters had to be withdrawn from over the beaches. Admiral Vian, on the other hand, complained bitterly if friendly aircraft appeared over our ships. Despite the agreements reached at Inter Service conferences that no AA gunner on HM Ships . . . should be allowed to fire at aircraft unless he was fully trained and qualified to recognise all types of aircraft.
>
> For some weeks this tendency was to cause much ill feeling because despite great efforts the problem was never entirely solved. It was at all times made more difficult by reports of German aircraft with Allied markings or the use of captured Allied aircraft by the Germans. The Air C-in-C deprecated these reports because their acceptance justified the AA gunners and in fact no proof has ever been found that the enemy made a habit of these practices. The fact was that aircraft often had to fly low in bad weather, in combat or when damaged. On the other hand, the greatest hazard to shipping was from low flying enemy aircraft which could not be quickly recognised and which sometimes appeared when friendly aircraft were also in the vicinity.

The Non-Combatants

A. J. May was a GCI fighter controller and once he was ashore with his unit he recalled learning of the difficulties some of his colleagues had trying to get their GCI unit on land and set up on D-Day:

> We the officers of our unit, (minus the adjutant, somebody had to mind the shop) reported to 21 Sector HQ as ordered and found the CO Wing Commander Anderson with his arm in a sling. He had been wounded on D-Day during the landing and had not yet gone home.
>
> Our headquarters and the D-Day unit 15082 were in the same field and we were pleased to be reunited with those of our colleagues who had been loaned to them for the big day and also to find that they had not been injured and could rejoin us now.

[45] *Ibid.*

We learned the story of D-Day from them and it told of a considerable ordeal. In fact they had lived through a very frightening experience, especially so as they were a non-combative unit. 15082 were ordered to land on D-Day with the Americans on Omaha beach, get ashore, find a site, set up their GCI station and be operational on their first night ashore. This order should have offered few problems if all had gone well, but there was a serious hitch. The Germans were shelling the beach along its entire length. They were putting up very strong resistance and holding up the Army. The Americans were temporarily pinned down and making no progress in getting off the beach.

This was no place for a GCI and the decision was taken to withdraw from the beach until conditions improved. What came to pass aboard the ship carrying 15082 I have no way of knowing but it came back to the beach at about five p.m. and still the Americans were pinned down on the beach. In spite of this the GCI was put ashore. It would have been too late in the day to set up and be working that day even in good conditions but in those prevailing it was hopeless.

Five men of the unit were killed and others wounded. Some vehicles were completely smashed and much technical gear destroyed. Their medical orderly was overwhelmed and the padre who went with them told of his 'complete helplessness and despair' when faced with such gaping wounds. All that men could do was take cover behind what was left of their vehicles and hope that the bombardment would soon stop.

The Americans gradually gained the upper hand and began moving off the beach. What was left of the GCI which could travel under its own power joined in the exodus, found a suitable site a little way inland and awaited replacements for lost equipment. 15082 were operational in two days. I was not there but that is the story of this brave unit as told to me.

Losses and Morale

Now that the number of sorties carried out by the Allied fighter forces had grown considerably, there was unsurprisingly an increase in casualty rates.

George Kelsey DFC, 151 Squadron: We started to lose crews of course. We lost one on 10 June. Our losses got very heavy. But the morale on the squadron was absolutely superb. When you were losing one out of two you knew your time was going to come sooner or later – 'Is it my bloody turn today?' Before we went off on these trips, down at Predannick, we had an air crew restaurant where they fed us a good meal before we went off. And the padre always used to come and sit with us and we used to call it the Last Supper. It was the Last Supper for some of us. You just waited for the end and that was it.

CHAPTER 6

ATTACK AND DEFENCE

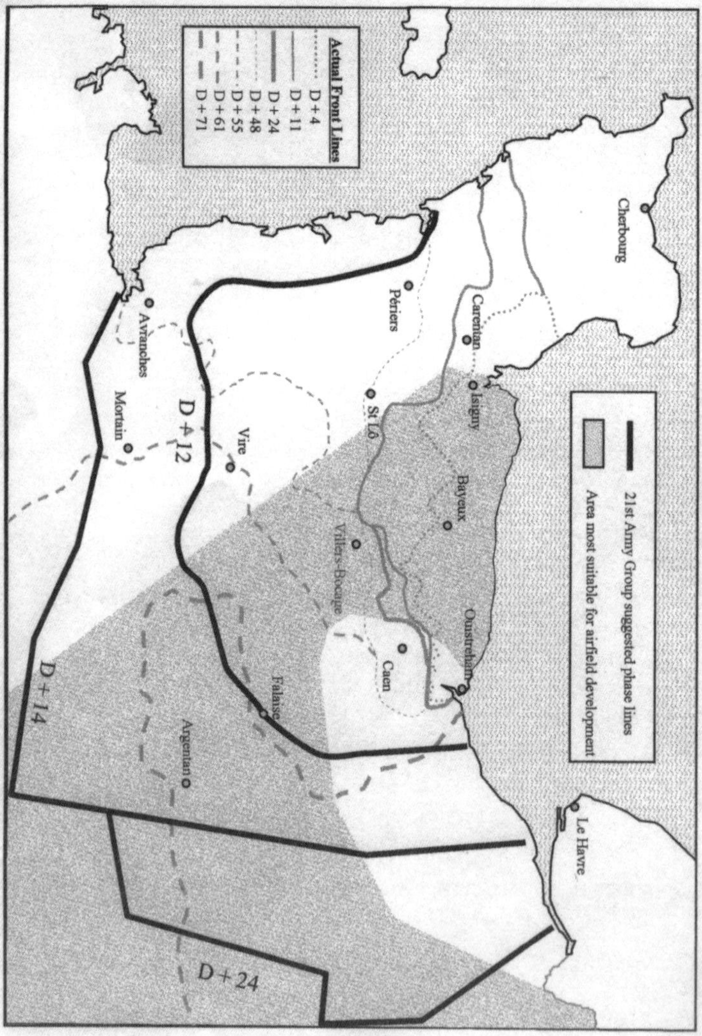

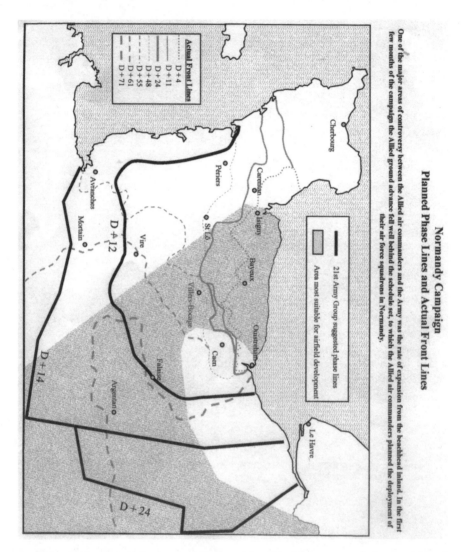

Normandy Campaign
Planned Phase Lines and Actual Front Lines

One of the major areas of controversy between the Allied air commanders and the Army was the rate of expansion from the beachhead inland. In the first few months of the campaign the Allied ground advance fell well behind the schedule set, to which the Allied air commanders planned the deployment of their air force squadrons in Normandy.

By the middle of June the Normandy beachhead had been extended to a width of approximately 50 miles and a depth of 10 miles. Caen remained in German hands, but Bayeux, Carentan and Isigny were in Allied hands. Six landing strips were available for Allied fighters acting operationally.

> Allied strength was such as to be able to guarantee a virtual immunity from direct enemy air attacks by day to both shipping and the ground forces, although the complete answer had not at that stage been found to the night raider and particularly to the mine-laying aircraft. Until the

> lodgement area was greatly extended there was little chance of organising night air defences that could secure a high degree of protection.[46]

The priority now was to secure port facilities and for the Americans to take Cherbourg, the British to overrun Caen. When it became apparent that a frontal assault on Caen was not practicable, considerable German force being the barrier, the British looked to swing round with armour in the Tilly – Villers-Bocage area, and with the 51st Highland Division on the east bank of the Orne River. In fact the Germans were preparing their own armoured push but a highly successful 2nd TAF attack on HQ Panzer Group West on 10 June completely disrupted their plans.

The British push, despite initial success on the right around Villers-Bocage, also stalled, indeed the 7th Armoured Division was forced to withdraw. For the time being the 2nd British Army acted defensively, fearful of a German armour offensive, although the Germans were not capable, owing to disorganisation and the impact of the Allied air attacks. However the Allied command feared a serious threat on the eastern flank and the commanders looked to Allied air power to intervene. A plan to use heavy bombers in direct support of the Army around Caen was abandoned, for the time being. It would fall upon the medium and fighter-bombers to support any Army moves. But Montgomery would face considerable criticism from the air commanders, notably Coningham, who was expecting at this stage to have more space in which to construct airfields, move his squadrons over and hence of course lessen considerably the range at which they had to operate.

With the air battle over Normandy escalating and the flak, engine failures and crashes taking their toll, a steady flow of new pilots was required. One such airman was Derek Lovell:

> I first thought about joining the air force during the summer of 1940. I lived in Essex, not far from Hornchurch and we used to watch all the action going on above our heads. Late 1940 I went down to the recruiting office at Romford, and was sent to Uxbridge for assessment. I passed everything except eyesight. They said you can't be a pilot you can be a navigator or air gunner. I didn't want that so I went home. I applied again in the beginning of 1941, was sent to Uxbridge again, and by the time it came to the eye test I knew what the form was. A red line was supposed to be through a white light, and when I could see it off to one side I said, 'it's through the white light'. They said, 'You've passed.'
>
> I was then sent home and told to present myself at Babbacombe in June 1941, where we were kitted out and inoculated and that sort of thing. Then we went to Stratford on Avon, ITW, and from there to the Canadian prairies, to a place called Swift Current where I did my EFTS. When we arrived the wing commander flying said, 'You're three weeks too early, so you had better do ground duties until we are ready for you.'

Soon Derek was flying, but he was having problems.

[46] AHB Narrative, Public Record Office AIR 41/67.

Derek Lovell: I was lucky to have the flight commander as my instructor. I couldn't land the thing. I couldn't get the height right, but he was determined to get me through. He took me to a satellite and when I suddenly realised the grass stopped being a green mass and became blades of grass, I'd got it and I was alright from then on.

We went from there to Bowden near Calgary, Boxing Day. We should have gone Christmas Day but the trucks to take us there had frozen solid. And from there I went to Medicine Hat, which was half Harvards and half Oxfords. I did my SFTS on Oxfords and got my Wings in April. At the end of the course, to my disgust at the time, I was sent to Trenton, to be an instructor. We all wanted to go home and go on ops. I did the instructors' course and then went to Kingston, Ontario, 31 SFTS, with Fleet Air Arm pupils. It gave me a lot of experience and by the time I left Kingston, I reckoned I could fly! I was there for about a year and then came home on the *Queen Elizabeth* in a first class cabin, with 23 others, and went to Harrogate where I had the interview to decide where I should go.

At the interview board they said, 'What did you do your SFTS on?' I said, 'Oxfords'. They said, 'Right. Bomber Command.' I suppose rather cheekily I said, 'Hang on a minute. I've haven't flown twins for over a year. I've got over 500 hours on Harvards, and on top of that we always understood that if you had been an instructor you could pick your command.' Much muttering went on. The next day I was posted to a Master AFU at Watton in Norfolk. So I gathered up my kit, and went from Harrogate to Leeds, Leeds to Peterborough, Peterborough to March, March to Thetford, Thetford to Watton, called for transport, reported to the adjutant and he said, 'Sit down. I've got bad news for you. Your unit moved yesterday.' 'Where to?' 'Wrexham, North Wales.' So the next morning it was a transport to Watton, Watton to Thetford, Thetford to March, March to Peterborough, Peterborough to Leeds, Leeds to Crewe, Crewe to Wrexham, transport to the airfield, report to the adjutant. He said, 'Where the hell have you been?'

I finished off on Masters there and then on to OTU at Milfield, Northumberland, on Hurricanes. It was then that I was posted to Coningsby, working with Lancaster pilots on fighter evasion. I did three months on fighter affiliation and then I got posted to 84 GSU, which meant nothing to anybody at the time, but which turned out of course to be 84 Group Support Unit 2nd TAF, at Aston Down. Here we lived in tents in a ditch.

On 6 June at Aston Down, I got into this beast called a Typhoon. I was shown around the cockpit by an experienced Typhoon pilot. Having read the handling notes he warned me about it swinging right on take-off, and then said off you go. I remember going down the runway. There's this sledgehammer hits you in the back when you open the throttle, and then she started to swing to the right. But I got her off the deck alright. I think it was about 1,500 feet before I sorted out where the undercarriage was. I had two flights that day, one of 15 minutes and one of an hour. And then two days later I was posted to an operational squadron, and after four

> hours flying round there and being accepted into the squadron, I found myself bombing a bridge. That was my initiation into ops.

Derek had arrived at Needs Oar Point on 9 June, becoming part of 146 Wing's 197 Squadron.

> It was an air strip in the New Forest, two sommerfeld matting strips, cut through the forest, and tents. I met the chaps who were very nice and friendly. It was mixed nationality, New Zealanders, Canadians, Australians, Scots, Irish and English. Morale was pretty good. We had a very tough squadron commander, Squadron Leader Taylor, known as Butch Taylor. Initially I used to fly as his number 2, which is not a good thing to do as the CO's number 2 tends to get shot down more than anybody else. When we used to come back across the Channel he used to put us in line astern. I'd fly behind him and if he could see me he'd scream his head off. I was very tightly tucked under his tail wheel, and 500 hours on a Harvard paid off at that point.

On 11 June Derek managed an hour of local flying, and 30 minutes formation flying. Then on 14 June, having a little over 7½ hours on Typhoons, he was detailed for his first operational sortie, to bomb bridges at Groucourt, and on reaching the enemy coast he had his first taste of hostile opposition:

> I remember seeing these big black puffs appearing in front of us and thinking A – it was flak, and B they were firing at me. It was a grand awakening, although the amount of flak, thinking back, on that first trip was nothing like what we got later.

Despite the flak Derek described the sortie in his logbook, 'Uneventful – Near misses. Bridge not hit.' But the Wing was suffering losses. In the period from D-Day to 14 June, 146 Wing lost 12 Typhoons in action, six of the pilots killed, including Squadron Leader Ronnie Fokes DFC, DFM, commanding officer of 257 Squadron. The airmen would have little time to reflect on the losses, the level of activity was so intense. But there were rare opportunities to escape from the battle.

A few days into the invasion Reg Baker wrote to his wife Ann from Needs Oar Point.

> 146 Wing
> Royal Air Force
> Army Post Office
> London
>
> Ann, my darling
> I received a very newsy letter from you this morning, it was like a breath of spring, no war, nobody being killed, just a picture of quiet home life.
>
> I had hoped to see you before this assault on Europe started, but it couldn't be so; nor shall I be able to see you before going to the other side. Try not to worry, I am doing the job I have always wanted to do and I am very happy about it.

This is very short because I have so much to do. I will let you know as often as I can that I am alright – always remember no news is good news.

God bless you and keep you safe and the children.

All my love
Reg

On 16 June 1944 the Army put in an urgent call for assistance. It was thought that the Germans were reinforcing the front opposite the British from the south through the village of Thury Harcourt, south of Caen. The RAF were thus called upon to blast three road-over-river bridges, and so seriously impede this reinforcement. It was feared that this was going to be a very dangerous operation with low cloud over the target and considerable flak defences. But as Flight Lieutenant Neville Thomas recorded (the Intelligence Officer at Needs Oar Point), 'despite all this, realising the urgency of the mission, Wing Commander Baker decided to make an attempt.'[47]

Reg briefed pilots of 197 and 257 Squadron late that afternoon. The flight took them over the French coast near Point de la Percée, flying south at 4/5,000 feet, just below the cloud base. Soon they ran into trouble a few miles to the west of Caen, as German flak batteries opened up. The pilots of both squadrons lost sight of their wing commander as the formation was disrupted by bursting shells. Then a voice was heard over the radio: 'Hello Carefree and Vampire aircraft, Port 180 – Lochinvar – out.' Nothing more was heard from Reg Baker. One pilot would later report that just before the last order was received he caught sight, through the cloud, of a Typhoon, out of control, in an almost vertical dive. It was believed that this was Reg and whilst plummeting to earth he had ordered his Wing to fly away from the danger. Flight Lieutenant Neville Thomas recorded, 'Later we learned, to our sorrow, that he had crashed near St Manvieu[48], where he was buried by our front-line troops. So the Wing lost a fine leader, to whom it owes much, and I – a great friend.' Four and a half years earlier Reg had spent Christmas with his parents, his father asking him how long the war was to last. 'Four and a half years,' Reg had replied.

John G. (Jack) Brown was a pilot with 193 Squadron, and recalled Reg's loss.

He was considered by many of us to be invincible, to be one who would survive the war. Most of us would have accompanied him on any difficult operation, we had such confidence in his leadership. It was a great shock when he did not return from the operation on 16 June and a pall of gloom and sadness fell over the Wing for some time.

On 3 July 1944, Denys Gillam wrote to Reg's wife.

20(F) Sector
RAF, APO
England

Dear Mrs Baker
May I add my sympathy to you for your recent great bereavement. Your

---

[47] *The Odyssey of No. 146 Wing* compiled by Senior Intelligence Officer Flight Lieutenant H. Neville Thomas. September 1945.
[48] Actually Saint-Manvieu-Norry.

husband was second in command of this unit and actually took over my Wing when I was promoted to this Sector. Of all Wing Leaders that I have met I do not think that I have ever met one who was so keen, popular and efficient. It was a very hard and tragic blow to all of us when we lost him.

I have just received some further news. His aircraft crashed near a small place named St Manvieu, which is approximately three miles west of Caen. It was found by Capt J. B. Lynd of HQ 3rd Canadian Division with our forward troops and your husband was buried beside his aircraft right in the battle area, beside 30″ Gun position.

May I once again extend my sympathy and say that it was a great personal blow to me also, to lose such a great friend & leader.

Yours sincerely
Denys Gillam G/C

On 21 November 1944, but with effect from 15 June, Reg Baker was awarded the DSO to go with his DFC and Bar. He was finally buried at Beny-sur-Mer Canadian War Cemetery.

Tribute to a Pilot

News of Reg Baker's loss soon reached his home town. Claude Enfield would write in *The Doncaster Free Press* later in June 1944:

> **Great Doncastrian** – Wing Commander E. R. Baker, Doncaster's air ace, a freeman of the Borough, is missing. Those of us who had followed his career with such deep and proud interest were clinging to the hope that he who had so brilliantly avoided misfortune would continue to baffle the odds, so to speak, and come through the war unscathed, but it was not to be.
>
> Yet what a brilliant record. How many planes he shot down, how many submarines and E-boats he sank, I do not know, but I should say his bag put him among the greatest air aces of the war. It seemed as if nothing could go wrong for him. That he should have flown day after day and week after week for the best part of four and a half years getting the better of Jerry every time is a record bordering on the miraculous. And this great gladiator of the skies was once a school teacher. If he has been lost to us we shall treasure his memory as a great Doncastrian and a personification and embodiment of our great race of young men who, devoted to peace, enemies of no man, have shown that when the life of the old country is at stake they can rise to immortal heights.

A Change of Clothing

A. J. May GCI fighter controller: We now cursed the decision to send us on the invasion in blue RAF uniforms. A lot of American servicemen taking part had come direct from the United States, had not landed in England, and had been told that German Air Force men wore blue uniforms. Two of our men were shot at and one arrested. We had to put a stop to this.

'Go down to the beach, see if you can find a clothing store and get some clothes to cover us up,' the CO said to me. I took a motor cycle, wandered about for a while and eventually in an old farm barn I came upon the very place – a clothing depot.

In charge was just one man, a younger man eager to please and after listening to my story he said, 'How about these?' and held up a pair of working overalls, green in colour. You stepped into the legs, pulled the top half up, pushed your arms through the sleeves, buttoned up the garment to your chin and finished off with a belt. There were pockets everywhere. They were just the job. 'How many?' the man enquired and I said 74 and he started counting off.

In the meantime I had been looking around. There were some very nice jackets, brown in colour with a zipper up the front. 'We have five officers, do you think I could have one each of these for them?' 'Sure pal,' he said. I explained that we were still in transit and hadn't unpacked our marquee and tents and asked if I could have five of the one-man tents. He agreed and put them with the others. When I enquired what I had to sign for this lot, he said, 'Nothing to sign.'

A quick rush back to our camping site to pick up a 15 cwt, the goods were packed aboard and I thanked the storeman very much. We parted on splendid terms. Incidentally it took years to wear out these two items of clothing in the garden after the war and the children had many hours of pleasure playing in the one-man tent.

The CO and the men were very pleased with my visit to the clothing store. They put on the overalls and there were no more shootings or arrests. The irony of it was that a week or so later the RAF issued us with khaki uniforms. I think they must have heard me swearing.

As the Allied land forces fought to push the front line inland, Rommel, especially against the British front around Caen, had to throw reinforcements in piecemeal to plug the gaps. Allied air might, the fighters and the fighter-bombers, kept the Luftwaffe at bay and plagued such enemy deployments. 65 Squadron had been busy on armed recces and escorting medium bombers, Basil Collyns making his contribution on an armed recce of 12 June. Two days later, on the second operation of the day, 65 Squadron despatched six pilots, including Basil on an armed recce in the Argentan area. However with no targets seen it was decided to bring the bombs back, but then someone reported, 'Huns SW of Rouen'. Yellow 1, 2, 3 and 4 engaged. Although Basil saw strikes on one Me 109 he would make no claim. Flying Officer Ashworth claimed one destroyed and Flight Lieutenant Stillwell claimed a damaged FW 190. Meanwhile the two remaining Mustangs (Yellow 5 and 6) had found some of their own trade and would claim two Me 109s. The Squadron ORB recorded the score as, 'Pretty good eh?'

On 15 June 65 Squadron didn't get into action until the afternoon. Eight Mustangs including that of Basil Collyns, led by Wing Commander Johnston, set out to attack a bridge at Cabourg on the coast east of Caen. When all the bombs had been released, hits registering on the road to the target, the Mustangs 'continued further into enemy territory in an endeavour to raise the squadron's score. Much to everyone's disgust the hated Hun refused to be enticed within range of the dreaded 65th. On return to base we were told to gather up our kit and proceed to Ford, following which, all being well, we should immediately proceed to France.' And this wouldn't be the only move for Basil Collyns as, staying within 122 Wing, he was posted to command B Flight in 19 Squadron. That very evening, taking off at 2120 hours he would take part in an armed recce to attack a reported enemy MT move south-east of Falaise. On arrival at the target area nothing was found, and rail bridges were attacked as an alternative.

Hart Finley and 403 Squadron would also see plenty of operational activity. On 11 June the squadron pilots, according to the ORB, 'went to brief and a coin was tossed to see which squadron would remain here on readiness. We won, went on the show and made the first landing for the squadron on 126's [Wing's] landing strip in France, after patrolling for 2 hours and 20 minutes. We all returned with plenty of French soil on us as the landing strip was like a dust storm.'

That afternoon 403 was again operational, a patrol during which Flight Lieutenant Andy MacKenzie had made his belly landing on a landing strip in the Utah beach area. There were further patrols, which were uneventful, the next day and on 13 June poor weather kept the pilots grounded. 416 and 421 Squadrons managed to get up in the air, but on return the airmen of 403 Squadron learnt of a tragic incident during the patrol. Wing Commander Chadburn's Spitfire collided with that of Flight Lieutenant Clark's and both men lost their lives. Chadburn's loss hit the Wing hard: 'We have indeed lost a great leader and also a grand friend.' On 14 June 403 Squadron carried out sweeps, but no contact was made with the Luftwaffe, and the next morning there was still no sign of the German pilots. In the evening 403 Squadron would again miss out on contacting the enemy, but to the east of their patrol 421 Squadron 'had a real fight' and would claim nine destroyed, one probable and two damaged 'which was an excellent job well done… We all joined with 421 in celebrating their victory.'

However with 403 Squadron carrying out most of its patrols over the western sector of the battle area, it was unlikely to see as much action as the squadrons operating on the east flank. The Luftwaffe would have had to penetrate the eastern patrols first and there were just not the numbers to do so in strength.

A Journalist's View

Reporter Richard Dimbleby flew over the invasion area early in the campaign and recorded the sights.

> This is Richard Dimbleby calling you from over the English Channel, flying between England and France. We are on our way out south from the coast crossing over towards Normandy with a wing of Spitfires on its way to take over the patrol and the protection of the Allied armies on the beaches and inland. A very lovely sight the Spitfires are on our port side ranged in their ranks of three. And now we are going in over the cliffs and the green fields of France and over there to starboard are

the big warships firing inshore towards the Cherbourg peninsula where the Americans are. A flash of their guns just gone now. Another flash from a ship further down the line. And now we are winging in behind the Spitfires, they're spreading out now right and left searching for German aircraft as we follow them inland. Right ahead of us there are great fires burning on the ground and clouds of white smoke coming up from the battle front. There's the great pattern of France, cratered and re-cratered where our bombs have fallen in the past. Here is the new landing strip lying out, looking for all the world like an old established and magnificently prepared aerodrome. We're diving down and coming in over it, right now, flying straight over the top. And there in the distance and all round us inside a great semi-circle is the battle front. I can see the whole of it from east to west. Fires are burning in every direction, there's smoke going up in clouds. We've seen the guns firing and the ships firing inshore. And we are flying so low now that I can see individual people on the ground. There are anti-aircraft guns. There are some cows, sitting in a field. More guns. And at that road junction, just below us is a military policeman waving them on. I can even see his red cap from here. He's wearing that and not his tin hat. The roads are full of our transport. All our chaps driving on the right hand side in the continental style.[49]

The experiences of the featured airmen indicate clearly that the Allies held air superiority over Normandy. The fighter-bombers could range over the battle with little fear of an aerial enemy, flak being the most serious risk. And if the Luftwaffe did try and invade the air space over the expanding beachheads, the Allied fighters could counter with superior force. The air situation appeared most favourable for the Allies, but now a new threat materialised, one which would divert attention and resource from the beachhead.

On 1 March 1944 Bob Cole had had his first opportunity to fly a Hawker Tempest, with 25 minutes of local flying, and soon he began to appreciate the new weapon he was to fly.

> *Bob Cole:* The Tempest was a much better aircraft to fly than a Typhoon – much like a Rolls-Royce after a tank. The first time I taxied out I thought, 'Christ there isn't enough noise,' and I questioned if it would take off.

But the next day and the day after it was back on ops in a Typhoon, escorting Marauders to targets in France. On 6 March Bob flew from Manston to Bradwell Bay, Essex, and the rest of the month was spent training, notably 5 hours 20 minutes night flying a Typhoon and 4 hours 20 minutes familiarisation with the Tempest.

> *Bob Cole:* They wouldn't let Tempests go over the continent. They didn't want to let them know we had the things. It's just as much fun flying around doing nothing, as being on ops.

[49] Reproduced with the kind permission of the BBC.

Throughout April there was further experience gained on the Tempest, at Ayr in Scotland, including firing at drogues, ground targets and cine-camera attacks. Then in May it was back to operations flying from Newchurch, near Folkestone in Kent. Bob's logbook recorded his activity.

> 9 May: Ops. Night Intruder. Shoot up six barges in Dunkirk area. Fire at RDF mast near Courtrai. Get strikes on all barges.
> 10 May: Scramble. ASR escort Walrus back from off Gravelines.
> 20 May: Ops sweep into France 10,000' see nothing.
> 24 May: Ranger to Marle. Shoot at two trains + a car. See strikes on one train.
> 28 May: Weather recco. Gravelines, St. Pol. Engine rough. Cut trip slightly.
> 29 May: Ops sweep to St. Pol. Land back at Thorney Island.
> 30 May: Shipping recce. Ostend – Dieppe.

Bob would then not be operational again for a week, missing out on the great day.

> *Bob Cole:* We were aware D-Day was going to happen and the night before we were confined to camp but all I did on D-Day was absolutely nothing.

On D-Day itself 150 Wing had carried out escorting and shipping reconnaissance tasks protecting the Allied sea lanes. On 7 June Bob did manage to get airborne, his logbook recording the operation, '7 June: Scramble. Patrol off coast Griz Nez to Gravelines. No luck.' It went on:

> 10 June: Sweep Dieppe – Rouen – Le Havre + around beachhead. Nothing doing.
> 12 June: Convoy Patrol. North Foreland.
> 14 June: Sweep Rouen – Le Havre – Évreux area. No enemy aircraft or flak.

For Bob and 3 Squadron acting mainly on the periphery of the battle, there had been little action. That was about to change, when 3 Squadron was detailed to fight the menace of the flying bomb.

On 15 June 1944 the German V1 offensive opened in earnest. Deputy Supreme Commander Sir Arthur Tedder recalled when the first reports began to come in:

> ...we were inclined at SHAEF to treat them with some detachment, refusing to allow the new threat to overshadow 'Overlord'. The enemy had chosen his moment well, for the main sites in the Pas de Calais were cloud-covered. On the evening of 16 June, I attended a meeting which the Prime Minister had summoned to consider the 'Crossbow' operations. Churchill refused to allow these developments to upset our concentration on the battle in Normandy. Our attitude could not be maintained for long, however. By the morning of Sunday 18 June the situation was more serious. Eisenhower ruled that the air force's first priority must now be 'Crossbow'. He minuted to me later that day: 'These targets are to take first priority over everything except the urgent requirements of the battle; this priority to obtain until we can be certain that we have definitely gotten

the upper hand of this particular menace.'[50]

The first flying bomb had actually fallen at Gravesend at 0418 hrs on the morning of 13 June, with only three more reaching England that day. ADGB's Air Marshal Hill held back, awaiting any further developments before he put in place his defensive measures. He had available ten squadrons of day fighters and seven squadrons of night fighters in ADGB, 250 heavy AA guns, 400 light AA and 2,000 balloons. But at the Allied Air Commanders' Stanmore meeting on 16 June reports came in that 160 flying bombs had been launched and the next day 245 were reported launched. Defensive and counter-offensive measures now became a priority. Heavy bombers went after the identified supply sites and launch sites. Also Coningham directed some of his 2nd TAF squadrons to attack launch sites, and from 13 to 20 June 213 tons were dropped by fighter-bombers, 165 tons by medium and light bombers. But attacks by the fighter-bombers were producing little result, and were costly in terms of aircraft and pilots lost. Therefore, for the rest of June and first few days of July the scale of attack by fighter-bombers was considerably reduced, that by medium and light bombers increasing, and there was significant input from the heavy bombers. Tactically measures against the flying bomb were a significant diversion to the support of Overlord. But with 735 civilians killed and 5,435 injured in the first week, it was a menace that had to be met.

> *Ron Pottinger, 3 Squadron:* D-Day had come and gone. We had done our stint of patrols over the beachheads, without incident as far as I was concerned. In addition to the patrols and sweeps we were maintaining a state of readiness from dawn to dusk. Two in the cockpits, engines warmed, two kitted up in dispersal, another pair on five minutes readiness.
>
> On 13 June I was among those on the first shift. A truck picked us up from our tents, probably at about 3.00 a.m and ran us down to dispersal. As we were alighting from the back of the truck there was a strange continuous burping sound and a small dark object flew across, quite low and fast, one tubular shadow on top of another and a long fiery tail behind the upper one. I'm afraid that on that first sighting we all stood and gaped. Then someone shouted, 'Flying bomb! What are we standing waiting for? Get up and after them!' That ended any chance of No. 3 Squadron joining the Normandy invasion.

On 16 June 1944 Bob Cole got his first chance to make his contribution to opposing the German V1 offensive. His logbook recorded, 'Ops scramble after jet propelled wireless controlled bombs. Intercept one off Dover. Shoot it down near Faversham. Blew up in orchard. Shared.' And Bob was able to draw a half swastika in his logbook.

> The first one I shot down I shared with Beamont. We were flying up the Channel and this thing crossed our nose and we turned after it. I was on the inside so I had a lead on him. We went straight over Dover and they fired at it and we caught it up at Faversham. I hit it and put the jet out. It slowed and I had to break or I would have run into the damn thing.

[50] Tedder, *With Prejudice*, p580.

> I turned round and Beamont fired at it. He told me his gunsight was u/s and he didn't hit it. I went in and had another go at it and knocked it down.

Later that same day Bob again went on patrol but this time recorded in his logbook, 'No excitement'. The first patrol the next day gets a 'No luck' in Bob's logbook but the excitement was back later in the day, and the following day, as his entries show:

> 17 June: Patrol anti diver [i.e. anti flying bomb]. Intercept one at Dunge. Chase it with F/S Rose. Fire from 600 feet. It crashed + blew up. Our A.A. continued to fire throughout chase.
> 18 June: Patrol at Dungeness. Shoot down a diver at Ivychurch. Intercept it off Dymchurch. Fly through wreckage. Blazing petrol burnt half my rudder, scorched aircraft.

> *Bob Cole:* I was closing on it and I didn't hit it the first time, I hit it a bit late on. But when I did it blew up and I went straight through. It burnt the dope off the aircraft. Burnt the rudder. But the aircraft still flew. I went back on patrol and it seemed to be flying alright. But then Bob Moore flew alongside me and told me to return to base. I didn't know what the hell was the matter with the aircraft. All he would say is return to base. He wouldn't say anything else. I didn't know there was a hole in the rudder. I took it up to about 12,000 and put the wheels down, flaps down and threw it around. I thought if it breaks up I can get out up here. But if it breaks up low down I won't. I was a bit apprehensive coming into land, thinking what the hell is the matter with the damn thing, but it flew just as well on half a rudder as the whole rudder.

A few days into the V1 offensive the squadrons detailed to reduce the threat quickly began to adjust to the tactics required to give their pilots the best chance of shooting down the pilotless bombs.

> *Bob Cole:* We thought originally that they would be too fast to catch. But actually they weren't. They cruised at 370, well a Tempest would get about 440 flat out. Of course you couldn't fly flat out all the time – you would use all your fuel up. You would cruise at about 300, but you could push it up to 440.
>
> Tactics were haphazard to start with and then we had standing patrols. You couldn't scramble and catch them. You had to have standing patrols. You would be told where they were crossing and if the weather was good enough you would aim to get a thousand feet and cruise at 300 and when you saw it you'd shove the nose down and open up. You could overhaul it then.
>
> When it went down I used to turn the aircraft on its side as there was quite a kick from the explosion. There was a ton of bomb blowing up and you were only about a thousand yards away. It's a fair way but it's quite a thump. And if it comes up and your aircraft is plan [i.e full on] to it, it really bangs. Rolling to the side took off some of the shock.
>
> We would have a patrol up and then another two in the cockpit, they sat in the cockpit for an hour and if something happened, and there was too much activity, they would be sent up. Then two more at fifteen

minutes readiness and two at an hour. And as one lot went off you moved up. It was quite a reasonable system. Normally we had patrols from Eastbourne to Hastings, Hastings to Rye and Rye up to Folkestone.

On Bob Cole's next four patrols, he would record, 'No Luck'. Then on 21 June he would get the chance to draw two full swastikas into his logbook: 'Patrol anti diver. Shoot down one NW of Hastings + one off Bexhill. Both explode on hitting ground + sea.' Five further patrols met with no success then on 23 June: 'Air + Cannon test. Get a third share in both of two divers. One N. of Hastings + one 2 mls N. of Newchurch.' Three further patrols recording, 'No Luck'. Then on 25 June: 'Scramble. Destroy a diver 7 mls N. of Hastings. Blew up in open country.' Next patrol was a 'No Luck' and on the next Bob had to return to base shortly after take-off: 'Wheel farings wouldn't retract.'

Then a chance on 28 June: 'Patrol. Intercept diver off Eastbourne. Get a piece off. It escaped into cloud.' The next two patrols recorded, 'Nothing over', 'Nothing doing'. Then 29 June: 'Patrol. Destroy a diver 3 mls SW of Maidstone.' Next patrol, 'No luck' and at the end of the day on 30 June Bob was to add two full swastikas in his logbook: 'Patrol. Destroy one diver 1 ml W of Rye + one in Tonbridge area. Strikes on another. It goes into balloons. Land at Friston for fuel.'

Bob Cole: I chased this damn thing and I suddenly saw the cables. I pulled vertically to get the hell out of there. If the cable hit your wing it would cut it off and it would kill you. You would not have time to get out at 3,000 feet.

The month of June had certainly been a busy time for Bob Cole and 3 Squadron. He had notched up 38.45 flying hours and been involved in the shooting down of 11 V1s. From the middle of the month and the opening of the V1 offensive in earnest (16 June 1944) Bob had conducted 27 patrols. The intensity of operations certainly taxed the airmen's powers of concentration.

Bob Cole: Physically it was tiring. At the time we were sleeping on a bag of straw in a tent. And of course these damn things were going over and there was a fair bit of flak. We'd get to bed about midnight and then you were up at half past three and then the first aircraft off before four, just before light.

I've been asleep flying actually. I was doing Hastings to Eastbourne. I remember turning over Eastbourne and coming to. I had been out for a couple of minutes. I used to fly on trimming tabs – to give myself something to do, occupy the mind. If you fly up and down the coast on a hot day, and nothing happens, and you have had damn all sleep anyway, I think it's quite easy to drop off.

And of course even when not on operations the chance of encountering a V1 was still ever present. Bob Cole again:

We had one come down near our tent. We wandered out of the tent and walked across to the mess and we heard the engine stop – there was cloud down to about 300 feet and everybody was looking where the hell it was. It came out of the cloud and it was just teetering on the stall. Another 20 yards and it would have hit our tent. Everybody was running like hell

> across this field to get away from it. It tipped in, just in a stream with a bank, the blast went up and it blew the latrines down but otherwise nobody was hurt.

Whilst Bob and 3 Squadron had enjoyed considerable success against the V1s, and lessened the sufferings of Londoners somewhat, V1s were still getting through. There were numerous civilian casualties. By 27 June 1,769 people had lost their lives. The balloon, anti-aircraft and fighter patrol tactics were consequently kept under scrutiny, but one major problem, as far as the pilots were concerned, was areas of exclusivity. Bob Cole recalled, 'There were guns all over Kent and fighters all over Kent and anyone who saw something fired at it.' Bob had certainly experienced the problems of trying to engage the pilotless bombs when under friendly fire:

> I had a couple of close calls. I chased one flying bomb and the damned ack-ack kept firing and that's the only time I broke away. I didn't do it again as it affects your morale actually. I was closing in and had got to about 300 yards. The flak was being pumped up right between me and the thing. So I got out of the way. I could have shot the bloody thing down easily.
>
> One night there were two of us up on patrol. It was pitch black. This damned flying bomb, we were on its tail and there was tracer coming up like a wall. We were flying through a V of tracer, with the flying bomb stuck in the middle of it. And you couldn't turn out of it or you would have turned straight into the flak. I kept flying and in the end it went down, so the guns did stop. I claimed half of it with whoever I was with. We were both firing at it, though we couldn't see one another of course.

And there wasn't just competition from the ground to shoot down the V1s. In the air too, pilots were keen to get themselves a diver.

> *Bob Cole:* There wasn't supposed to be any competition but anybody who was doing an air test would tend to come down, they weren't supposed to, and see what they could see. I know one night, it was a lovely night, I was chasing this damn flying bomb and so were about eight others, including a Meteor. I passed that.

'Angelic' Guidance

310 Squadron's Frank Mares DFM describes the assistance given from the ground during an encounter with a V1.

> Having already flown a sortie on 9 July, an escort to 57 Lancasters bombing the Noball site at L'Hey had me landing at dusk after flying through some very dense and lethal flak. Some of our planes had been hit, never to return to their base, others were badly damaged and required nursing back in order to force land at the nearest airfield in England. Although tired from the long day's flying, my loathing for the continued use of the flying bombs spilled over when we were encouraged to volunteer to lay in wait for these devices. After

refuelling I took off with the intention of venting my feelings by shooting down one of these Hitler-inspired monsters.

I took off in the dark of night with the full and encouraging co-operation of Flying Control who I informed over the R/T that I was airborne. I was passed over to the operations room from where an 'angelic' voice took over. She gave me a vector to steer and a height to level off at, giving course alterations as necessary. After some 20 minutes of precise guidance, the voice calm and firm announced – 'I have a "witch-craft" for you at 11 o'clock below.' No sooner had I received the message, than I discerned the flame of a flying bomb racing towards me. While shouting 'Tally Ho', I stood the aircraft on its nose, spiralled through 180 degrees, the throttle opened to its fullest extent, lined the flame in the gunsight and pressed the button. While the cannons loudly responded, the roar of the Spitfire engine began to cough, then gave up in silent protest.

For a Spitfire B to catch up with a 'Doodle Bug' as they were commonly known by the never-to-be-forgotten Londoners, the pilots had to have a good advantage of height, be in the correct position and react speedily. Thanks to the expert guidance given by the operations room, such perfect conditions prevailed but having exploited them a shade too energetically I had disorientated my aircraft's Merlin engine management, thus losing its obedience which meant that I was powerless to blast the thing out of the sky. Just as I began to despair the engine regained it senses, roared into life and I was able to continue with the pursuit of the, by then, more distant 'witch-craft' flame. Both man and machine revitalised, the cannons spitting out their venomous message, I was willing the shells towards their target. Just as I was declaring my mission a failure there was a blinding flash and a terrific explosion, which preceded some very severe turbulence. My feeling was one of gleeful satisfaction as I reported my success to Flying Control. The ever gentle voice then guided me through the darkness to a safe landing and a night of dreams about the body and soul that was attached to the angelic voice – I slept really well.[51]

But despite the best efforts of airmen like Bob Cole and 3 Squadron, and the AA and the balloons, and despite the bombardment of V1 targets in northern France, the V1 offensive did not diminish in its scale. It was a serious diversion from Overlord, as was hoped for by the Germans, and Bob Cole would have plenty more to do fighting the defensive battle against the V1. Meanwhile his RAF colleagues still had their work cut out fighting the offensive battle over and around Normandy.

---

[51] Papers of Frank Mares DFM, held at RAF Museum Hendon.

CHAPTER 7

OPERATING FROM FRANCE

A Nervy Landing

Tony Liskutin DFC, AFC took part in patrols over Normandy after D-Day.

During one of these patrols over Normandy our squadron was subjected to a heavy bout of anti-aircraft fire from the German lines near Caen. An explosion somewhere under my aircraft tossed me up and it felt as if my controls were damaged. I could not see any damage but the feel of the controls was not normal. It appeared to be serious but certainly not a case for baling out. However, the thought of crossing the Channel in this state seemed unattractive. There was an unknown risk-potential, which had to be assessed, so I told my number two to stay with the squadron while my problem was sorted out.

From previous briefings I remembered that the Royal Engineers were completing some landing strips in Normandy, about halfway between the front line and the coast. Most of them were to be regarded as safe for emergency landings, even though they were within range of the enemy guns. Mine was a kind of strange emergency just for such a try out. The squadron was nearly over the B.2 landing strip when I reached the conclusion that I had to land. The field below did look quite serviceable and seemed to be definitely a much better choice than flying across the water.

From the moment I decided to leave formation and go for landing in France I tried all I could to establish the facts about the controllability of my aircraft, without much success. The elevator control on my Spitfire certainly felt most peculiar, regardless of changes in airspeed. I even started wondering if the attempted landing was such a good idea, because there could occur a loss of control on final approach with unpleasant consequences. But after a re-appraisal of my options I assured myself that the chances were good and I should try. With my mind made-up, I carried out a very cautious approach and landed safely in France.

It was immediately clear to me how close I was to the fighting line. The shooting war was going on less than three miles away, with the B.2 landing ground well covered by German guns. As soon as I switched off the engine I became aware of a myriad of strange noises. Thumping explosions and whistling bullets were creating strange sensations and particularly the artillery shells exploding nearby at irregular intervals sounded rather disconcerting.

The Royal Engineers, including their specialist technical personnel, came to meet me and to see what could be done! To my great relief the damage was insignificant. The real cause of my problem was the radio, which had fallen off its shelf onto the control cables. This problem was quickly rectified and I rejoined the squadron on the patrol line a few minutes later.

It was obvious that the radio man was at fault, not having secured the VHF radio on its shelf after the last maintenance check. Under different circumstances I may have felt nettled but due to my extraordinary experience on the ground in Normandy I did not like to say anything at all. This brief incident gave me a glimpse of the war on the ground. It made me feel full of admiration for the Army chaps; the way they went calmly about their jobs, ignoring the hellfire which was blazing so near to them. I felt thankful to Providence for allowing me to see the picture down below, without having to stay there any longer.[52]

As the beachhead expanded, work went ahead preparing the landing strips for fighters and fighter-bombers. The first Emergency Landing Strip (ELS) to be available was at Asnelles and a Spitfire came in for an emergency landing at 1300 hrs on 8 June. A Refuelling and Rearming Strip (RRS) was constructed at St. Croix-sur-Mer. Three ELSs were built in the American sector ready for operations by 10 June. But of course there had to be ground personnel to service any aircraft that came in. Ed Stevens served as an armourer with 3209 Servicing Commando Unit and recalls the morning of the 6 June 1944 and his subsequent trip across the Channel.

We didn't know where in France we were going. Reveille was at 0230 in the morning and we got into the backs of our vehicles and ended up at Gosport in a side street, near the hards. It was about 0730/0830 in the morning, breakfast time for the rest of civilisation. A woman came out of a house and said, 'It's just been on the news that paratroops have landed in Normandy.' That's when we knew definitely where we were going. We had four flights and a headquarters flight. The headquarters flight went on a tank landing craft and the rest of us went on an American ship. The landing craft was torpedoed and some of our blokes were picked up and taken back to England. We never saw them again. Some were picked up and were actually waiting for us in France. There was a very limited amount of accommodation, in the form of bunks, and not enough for all of us, you just slept anywhere you could. We started out on the 6th and landed on the morning of the 7th.

Everyone was raring to go. This was what we had been training for. We were all volunteers for Normandy. We landed near Courseulles – there were dozens of ships. The cruiser *Mauritius* was firing broadsides. It was an amazing sight, the whole thing would rock back with a belch of yellow flame and black smoke, then it would settle down and then the next broadside would go, firing inland.

I remember seeing a motorboat with two men in it with one standing at the back with a loud hailer. He must have been some sort of marshal. They hit a mine. There was only one man swimming. There was no sign of the other. We had an assembly area in a field just off the beach and from

[52] The papers of Tony Liskutin DFC, AFC. IWM 88/45/1.

there we went off in convoy. I think we had about 12 three-ton Bedfords, each flight had two or three. I was an armourer and we had an armament truck with all our gear in. As an armourer I got the Bren gun and I stood on the petrol tank. We started off on a road and then the engine spluttered and we conked out. The rest went on and we were left. All the trucks had been waterproofed and the waterproofing on our truck's exhaust had not been taken off properly and the engine packed up. We soon realised what had happened and were off. We then got lost. Getting lost in Normandy just after you have arrived is not a very good idea. At one point we saw tanks firing into a wood and the next second an MP suddenly sprung out in front of us in the road. He told us if we went any further down there we'd be in the front line. We turned round and eventually found the rest of the unit. It was too late to have a hot meal, it was getting dark, we daren't light our 'tommy' cookers.

We were camped in a field next to wheat fields – and a company of the Durham Light Infantry came through the middle of it going up to the front, about three miles or so away.

They began construction of the airfield straight way, and it was operational within four days of the landings. We were not involved in the construction. We were getting fuel and ammunition up from the beach. It would come up in Ducks. We would unload it and establish dumps. I was standing on a Duck loaded with petrol, one evening, as it was getting dark, and the Germans were dropping incendiary bombs. It was a bit uncomfortable but fortunately nothing was hit. Another time they dropped a shower of butterfly bombs all over the airfield.

A squadron of German aircraft came directly over the airfield one day and all these things started to drop out. I thought, 'God that's it.' We had dug slit trenches and everyone was scattering into these. However they had dropped empty overload petrol tanks. I have always maintained that it must have been a German squadron leader with a sense of humour, because he waited until he was right over the airfield. All that happened was a plop, although it wouldn't have done you much good if it had hit you.

In the early days individual flights would come in. We just saw the aircraft coming in. The flying control was a jeep on the far side from the runway. One day there was a scramble when the Germans were coming over, and one of the Spits took off one way and another took off the other way. They met halfway and there was a bloody great explosion. With regard the refuelling, we were just tipping it in. I was an armourer although you did do anything, whatever was needed. As an armourer my main job was rockets. There were 60 lb warheads, and the fins and the body of the rocket. We would screw these things together and the R/P Typhoons took eight.

Eventually the squadron groundcrews appeared, and as soon as they were there the squadrons moved in and stayed there. We became redundant and came back in time for August bank holiday. We thought we were going to move from one airfield to another. But it didn't work out that way – they withdrew us and other units came in.

We weren't being attacked – it was the Typhoons who were doing all the attacking. We would re-arm them, they would take off and go out towards the sea. You could see them come back and could actually see them start the dive down in the early days, just two or three miles away. They would be back in no time and you would be re-arming them again twenty minutes or so later. I never worked so hard before that or since, those 60 lb warheads were damn hard work. The refuelling wasn't very easy either, you didn't have big bowsers.

Feverish Activity

A. J. May GCI fighter controller: The road which runs out of the Cherbourg Peninsula and then through Carentan and east to Caen had always been the main artery. The part of this road in the American area was the piece best known to us and we watched with great admiration the enormous build-up of war-winning resources. Nothing seemed beyond them. On the day before we left to go back to the peninsula we watched as an airstrip was built in one day. Work began at six o'clock in the morning in a field opposite the side of the road from us with the arrival of fifty or so bulldozers. The machines stripped off the grass and two inches of soil on a width of approximately thirty yards. Having completed 200 yards of the runway some of the bulldozers were fitted with rakes and ran up and down levelling off the surface, while the remainder continued to lengthen the runway. Rollers followed next to make a good flat surface and then very large lorries arrived carrying sommerfeld tracking which they began laying soon after midday. After all this tremendous activity men and machines departed and Thunderbolts were landing by five p.m.

...Thunderbolt fighters were here in great numbers and many took off at dawn every morning. They were looking for trouble, I think, but didn't find much in the air. They had to run the gauntlet of their own Ack Ack gunners who started firing as soon as any engine made itself heard. They were very trigger happy.

On the Normandy beaches supplies and equipment were streaming ashore, the Allies striving to win the battle of the build-up. The Germans were trying to get reinforcements to the area, although some commanders still held the belief that there may be a second Allied invasion in the Pas de Calais. In the main this was owing to Fortitude, the Allied deception plan, whereby much of the operational air activity leading up to D-Day suggested that the beaches of the Pas de Calais would be the Allies main assault area. Nevertheless German reinforcements were now on the roads and railways on the approaches to Normandy, which the Allied air force was trying to delay and destroy.

On 17 June the new CO of B Flight 19 Squadron, Flight Lieutenant Basil Collyns, completed a two-hour flight bombing rail targets at Vimoutiers, and the next day took off on a bombing operation, which was aborted owing to the weather. 19 Squadron was non operational on 19 June, again owing to the weather. On 20 June following an armed recce in the morning, the squadron despatched its pilots, including Basil Collyns, who were tasked to bomb marshalling yards at Rambouillet. As the Mustangs approached Dreux aerodrome FW 190s were

Top left: Reg Baker's wife, Norma, wrote on the back of the photograph, 'Collecting Reg's DFC from the King, 30 June 1941, my 21st birthday.' *(H. Crasswelle/S. Baker)*

Top right: Sunderland pilot Reg Baker. *(H. Crasswelle/S. Baker)*

Middle: Sunderland DA-H at Oban, from where Reg Baker, and other 210 Squadron aircrew, flew in defence of the Atlantic supply routes in the latter half of 1940 and early 1941. *(H. Crasswelle/S. Baker)*

Left: A Sunderland taking off. *(H. Crasswelle/S. Baker)*

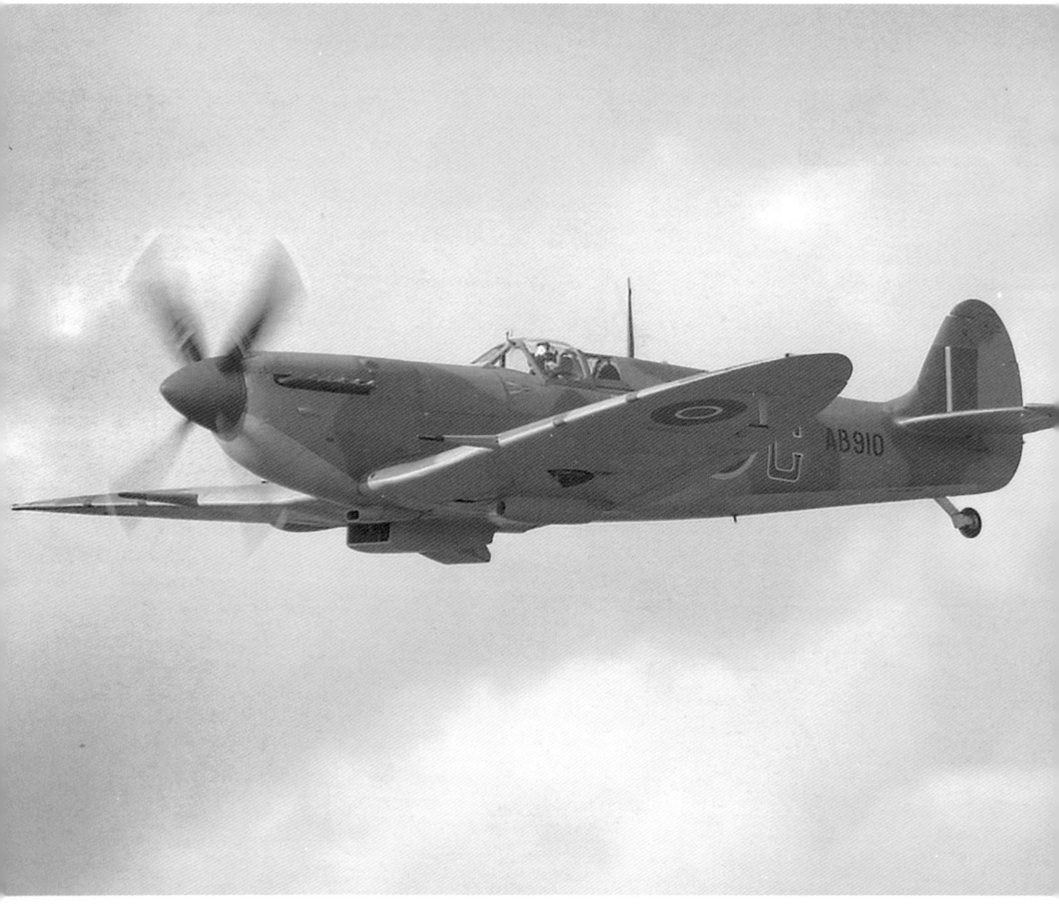

Top left: A portrait of New Zealand fighter ace Basil Collyns. *(A. Kidner)*

Top right: No. 25 Course Central Gunnery School, Sutton Bridge, May 1943. Flight Lieutenant Basil Collyns front row, second from left. *(A. Kidner)*

Bottom: Modern photograph of the Battle of Britain Memorial Flight's Spitfire Vb AB910, which, notably, flew in support of the Dieppe Raid (19 August 1942) and over the Normandy beaches in June 1944. *(Jenny Coffey)*

Top: Squadron Leader Reg Baker, CO of 263 Squadron in the second half of 1943, sits amongst the rest of the squadron personnel, holding a placard recording the squadron's operational record. *(H. Crassweller/S. Baker)*

Middle left: 182 Squadron's Flight Commander Flight Lieutenant Reg Baker, 1943. *(H. Crassweller/S. Baker)*

Middle right: 263 Squadron's Westland Whirlwind P7113. Standing in front, third from right, is Squadron Leader Geoff Warnes DSO, DFC, who was replaced as CO by Reg Baker when he joined the squadron. Reg normally flew this aircraft, but on 23 September 1943, George Wood, inset photo, took the aircraft on an operation to Morlaix airfield and was shot down, managing to evade capture. *(G. Wood)*

Left: 263 Squadron Whirlwind. *(G. Wood)*

Top: Wing Commander Reg Baker stands proud amidst his Harrowbeer Wing, early 1944 (without cap and hands in pocket, directly behind the airman sitting on left). *(H. Crassweller/S. Baker)*

Bottom: Picture taken on 10 February 1944 of the Harrowbeer Wing pilots, who had achieved considerable success against the enemy tha day. From left to right: Flying Officer Richardson, Flight Lieutenant Cassie, Wing Commander Reg Baker, Flight Lieutenant Deall, Flyin Officer Haworth, Flying Officer McGibbon. *(H. Crassweller/S. Bake*

Top left: New Zealand night fighter ace George Jameson. *(James Jameson)*

Top right: Flying Officer A. Norman Crookes, 488 Squadron, February 1944. *(N. Crookes)*

Middle left: August 1944 photo of one of the most successful RAF night fighter teams of the war – Flight Lieutenant G. E. 'Bill' Jameson and Flying Officer A. Norman Crookes. Bill had earned a DSO and DFC by the end of the war; Norman a DFC and 2 Bars, and a US DFC. *(A. N. Crookes)*

Middle right: 488 Squadron's Squadron Leader J. Gard'ner, far right, hears and sees how one of his pilots managed a kill, early 1944. *(Royal New Zealand Air Force Museum)*

Bottom: The last parade of 488 Squadron at Gilze-Rijen, at the end of 1945. The CO of 149 Wing Group, Captain Moon, addresses the personnel (out of shot) from the bonnet of the jeep. Next to the Mosquito's propeller is the CO of 488 Squadron, Wing Commander Ron Watts, and in front of the jeep is A Flight Commander Squadron Leader J. Gard'ner. *(NZ Fighter Pilots Museum)*

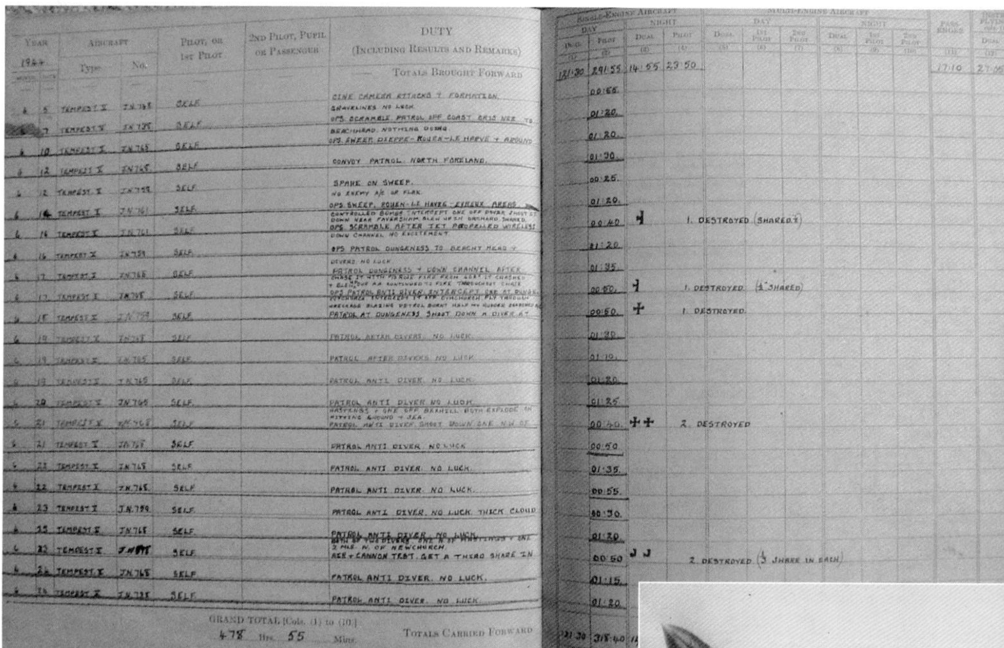

Year 1944 Month	Date	Aircraft Type	Aircraft No.	Pilot, or 1st Pilot	2nd Pilot, Pupil or Passenger	Duty (Including Results and Remarks)	Single-Engine Day Dual (1)	Single-Engine Day Pilot (2)	Single-Engine Night Dual (3)	Single-Engine Night Pilot (4)	Passenger (11)	Instr. Flying Dual (12)
						Totals Brought Forward	181:30	291:55	14:55	23:50	17:10	27:05
6	5	TEMPEST V	JN 768	SELF		CINE CAMERA ATTACKS + FORMATION. GRAVELINES NO LUCK.		00:55				
6	7	TEMPEST V	JN 735	SELF		OPS SCRAMBLE PATROL OFF COAST [illegible] TO BEACHHEAD. NOTHING DOING		01:20				
6	10	TEMPEST V	JN 765	SELF		OPS SWEEP DIEPPE-ROUEN-LE HAVRE + AROUND		01:20				
6	12	TEMPEST V	JN 765	SELF		CONVOY PATROL. NORTH FORELAND.		01:30				
6	12	TEMPEST V	JN 759	SELF		SPARE ON SWEEP. NO ENEMY A/C OR FLAK.		00:25				
6	14	TEMPEST V	JN 761	SELF		OPS SWEEP. ROUEN-LE HAVRE-EVREUX AREAS.		01:20				
6	16	TEMPEST V	JN 761	SELF		CONTROLLED BOMBS INTERCEPT ONE OFF DOVER SHOOT IT DOWN NEAR FAVERSHAM. BLEW UP IN ORCHARD. SHARED.		00:40	1. DESTROYED (SHARED ½)			
6	16	TEMPEST V	JN 761	SELF		OPS SCRAMBLE AFTER JET PROPELLED WIRELESS DOWN CHANNEL NO EXCITEMENT.		01:20				
6	16	TEMPEST V	JN 759	SELF		OPS PATROL DUNGENESS TO BEACHY HEAD + DIVERS. NO LUCK		01:35				
6	17	TEMPEST V	JN 768	SELF		PATROL DUNGENESS + DOWN CHANNEL AFTER [illegible] CHASE IT WITH [illegible] FIRE FROM [illegible] IT CRASHED + BLEW UP [illegible] CONTINUED TO FIRE THROUGHOUT CHASE		00:50	1. DESTROYED (½ SHARED)			
6	17	TEMPEST V	JN 735	SELF		OPS PATROL ANTI DIVER. INTERCEPT ONE AT DUNGENESS [illegible] DYMCHURCH. FLY THROUGH WRECKAGE BLAZING PETROL BURNT HALF MY RUDDER [illegible]		00:50	1. DESTROYED.			
6	18	TEMPEST V	JN 759	SELF		PATROL AT DUNGENESS SHOOT DOWN A DIVER AT		01:30				
6	19	TEMPEST V	JN 765	SELF		PATROL AFTER DIVERS. NO LUCK.		01:10				
6	19	TEMPEST V	JN 765	SELF		PATROL AFTER DIVERS NO LUCK.		01:20				
6	19	TEMPEST V	JN 765	SELF		PATROL ANTI DIVER. NO LUCK.		01:25				
6	20	TEMPEST V	JN 765	SELF		PATROL ANTI DIVER NO LUCK. HASTINGS + ONE OFF BEXHILL BOTH EXPLODE ON HITTING GROUND + SEA.		00:40	2. DESTROYED			
6	21	TEMPEST V	JN 768	SELF		PATROL ANTI DIVER. SHOOT DOWN ONE N.W. OF		00:50				
6	21	TEMPEST V	JN 765	SELF		PATROL ANTI DIVER NO LUCK		01:35				
6	22	TEMPEST V	JN 765	SELF		PATROL ANTI DIVER. NO LUCK.		00:55				
6	22	TEMPEST V	JN 765	SELF		PATROL ANTI DIVER. NO LUCK.		00:30				
6	23	TEMPEST V	JN 759	SELF		PATROL ANTI DIVER. NO LUCK. THICK CLOUD		01:20				
6	23	TEMPEST V	JN 765	SELF		PATROL ANTI DIVER. NO LUCK. [illegible] 2 MLS. N. OF NEWCHURCH.		00:50	2. DESTROYED (⅓ SHARE IN EACH)			
6	23	TEMPEST V	[illegible]	SELF		AIR + CANNON TEST. GET A THIRD SHARE IN		01:15				
6	24	TEMPEST V	JN 765	SELF		PATROL ANTI DIVER. NO LUCK.		01:20				
6	24	TEMPEST V	JN 735	SELF		PATROL ANTI DIVER. NO LUCK.						
						GRAND TOTAL [Cols. (1) to (10)] 478 Hrs. 55 Mins. Totals Carried Forward	181:30	318:40				

Top left: Bob Cole stands beside his 3 Squadron Tempest, damaged after flying through the explosion of the V1 he shot down on 18 June 1944. *(Bob Cole)*

Top right: 3 Squadron Tempest V with identity stripes. *(Bob Cole)*

Middle: Bob Cole's logbook entries, recording his first successes against V1s. *(Bob Cole)*

Right: The V1 or flying bomb. In the summer of 1944, pilots like 3 Squadron's Bob Cole were tasked with pursuing and shooting down these pilotless aircraft, to prevent them reaching London. *(Martin Ford Jones Collection)*

Top left: Hart Finley stands next to his 403 (Wolf) Squadron Spitfire IX, at Kenley, early in 1944. *(H. Finley)*

Top right: Ken Trott in the cockpit of his 195 Squadron Typhoon at Ludham, Norfolk, 1943. *(Ken Trott)*

Left: Ken Trott in front of his 195 Squadron Typhoon, 1943. *(Ken Trott)*

Below: An example of a Spitfire IX of 403 Squadron. This particular aircraft, LZ997 KH-A, was lost on operations on 17 August 1943 in a mid-air collision. The pilot, Flight Lieutenant Wally Conrad, survived and evaded capture. The other 403 Squadron pilot involved, Flight Sergeant Shouldice, was killed. *(Chris Thomas)*

Top left: Air Chief Marshal Sir Arthur Tedder, Deputy Supreme Commander. *(RAF Museum Hendon)*

Top right: Air Chief Marshal Sir Trafford Leigh-Mallory, Commander-in-Chief of the Allied Expeditionary Air Force. *(RAF Museum Hendon)*

Above: Air Marshal Sir Arthur 'Mary' Coningham, who would command the 2nd TAF in the run-up to D-Day and during the liberation of Western Europe.

Right: General Dwight D. Eisenhower, Supreme Allied Commander Allied Expeditionary Force. *(RAF Museum Hendon)*

Above: 146 Wing's Wing Commander Reg Baker at Needs Oar Point, shortly before D-Day. Notably absent is his familiar moustache, half of which had been shaved off in a mess party. *(H. Crassweller/S. Baker)*

Left: 197 Squadron pilots at Tangmere, early in 1944. At the base of the pyramid from right to left: Derek Tapson (POW 10 February 1945), Toby Harding, Bob Jones (killed 31 December 1944), Gerry Mahaffy, Johnny Rook, Bruce Gilbert, 'Dumbo' Taylor (killed 27 June 1944). Top triangle right to left: 'Tunna' Coles (killed 24 May 1944), Jack Watson (killed 17 June 1944), 'Fibber' McFee (POW 24 December 1944). *(D. Tapson)*

Below left: 197 Squadron Typhoon OV-Z MN925 with invasion markings and a 500lb bomb under the wing. *(D. Tapson)*

Below right: 164 Squadron Rocket Projectile Typhoon MN304 at Thorney Island, just prior to D-Day. *(D. Lovell)*

Top left: Instructor Derek Lovell in a Harvard, at 31 SFTS Kingston, Ontario, summer 1942. *(D. Lovell)*

Top right: A close-up of Lovell in the seat of a Harvard, at 31 SFTS Kingston, Ontario, summer 1942. *(D. Lovell)*

Middle left: Trainee pilot Derek Lovell in the back of a DH 82c, Dec 1941, 32 EFTS, Swift Current. *(D. Lovell)*

Middle right: Lovell following his last flight as a trainee pilot, 4 April 1942, Medicine Hat. The next day he received his wings. *(D. Lovell)*

Right: A Tiger Moth pranged at 32 EFTS, Swift Current, autumn 1941, highlighting the perils of mistakes whilst undergoing flying training. *(D. Lovell)*

Above: 65 Squadron, Mustang III, Funtington, May 1944. Basil Collyns fifth from right. *(A. Kidner)*

Left: 65 Squadron's Mustang III YT-J, flown on a couple of occasions, non-operationally, by Basil Collyns. *(A. Kidner)*

Below: Basil Collyns' logbook entries for August 1944. *(A. Kidner)*

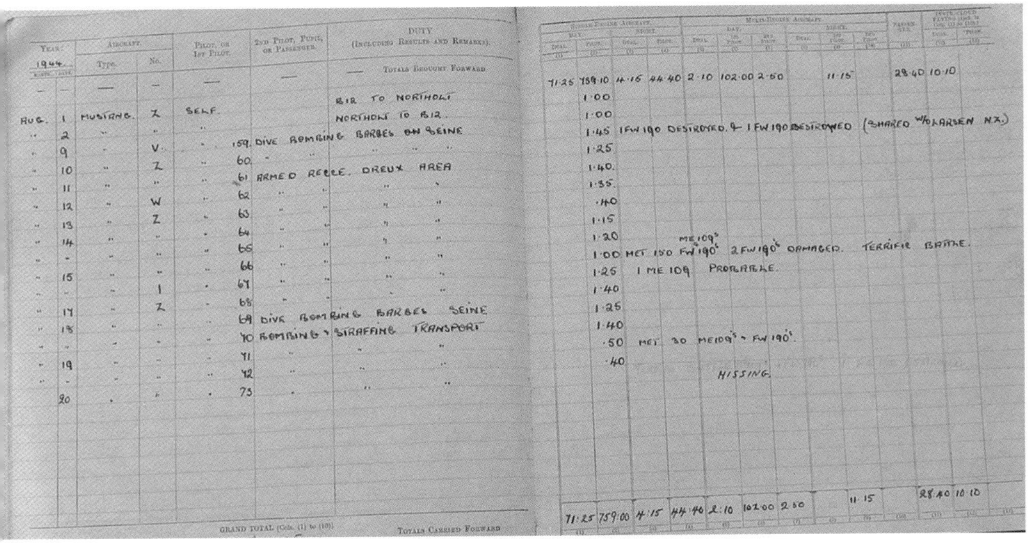

Totals Brought Forward: 71.25 759.10 4.15 44.40 2.10 102.00 2.50 11.15 28.40 10.10

Year 1944 Month	Date	Aircraft Type	No.	Pilot, or 1st Pilot	2nd Pilot, Pupil, or Passenger	Duty (Including Results and Remarks)	Day Pilot	Remarks
—	—	—	—	—	—	B12 TO NORTHOLT	1.00	
AUG.	1	MUSTANG.	Z	SELF.		NORTHOLT TO B12.	1.00	
"	2	"	"	"	159.	DIVE BOMBING BARGES ON SEINE	1.45	1 FW 190 DESTROYED. & 1 FW 190 DESTROYED (SHARED W/O LARSEN N.Z.)
"	9	"	V.	"	60.	" " "	1.25	
"	10	"	Z	"	61	ARMED RECCE. DREUX AREA	1.40.	
"	11	"	"	"	62	" " "	1.35.	
"	12	"	W	"	63	" " "	.40	
"	13	"	Z	"	64	" " "	1.15	
"	14	"	"	"	65	" " "	1.20	
"	"	"	"	"	66	" " "	1.00	MET 150 FW 190s ME 109s 2 FW 190s DAMAGED. TERRIFIC BATTLE.
"	15	"	"	"	67	" " "	1.25	1 ME 109 PROBABLE.
"	"	"	I	"	68	" " "	1.40	
"	17	"	Z	"	69	DIVE BOMBING BARGES SEINE	1.25	
"	18	"	"	"	70	BOMBING & STRAFFING TRANSPORT	1.40	
"	"	"	"	"	71	" "	.50	MET 30 ME 109s & FW 190s.
"	19	"	"	"	72	" "	.40	
"	"	"	"	"	73	" "		MISSING.
	20	"	"	"				

Grand Total (Cols. (1) to (10))

Totals Carried Forward: 71.25 759.00 4.15 44.40 2.10 102.00 2.50 11.15 28.40 10.10

Charges to pay
s. d.
RECEIVED

POST OFFICE
TELEGRAM

No.
OFFICE STAMP

Prefix. Time handed in. Office of Origin and Service Instructions. Words.

61

11.54 10.7 BH/T OHMS . 47

1292

~~CPD BHT 879~~
From ~~ISC~~

PRIORITY CC MRS. TROTT 65 WEST WAY BOURNEMOUTH =

14 JULY REGRET TO INFORM YOU THAT YOUR SON F/O K A J TROTT IS MISSING AS THE RESULT OF AIR OPERATIONS ON 13 TH JULY 1944 STOP ANY FURTHER INFORMATION RECEIVED WILL BE IMMEDIATELY COMMUNICATED TO YOU =

OC RAF HURN +

For free repetition of doubtful words telephone "TELEGRAMS ENQUIRY" or call, at office of delivery. Other enquiries should be accompanied by this form, and, if possible

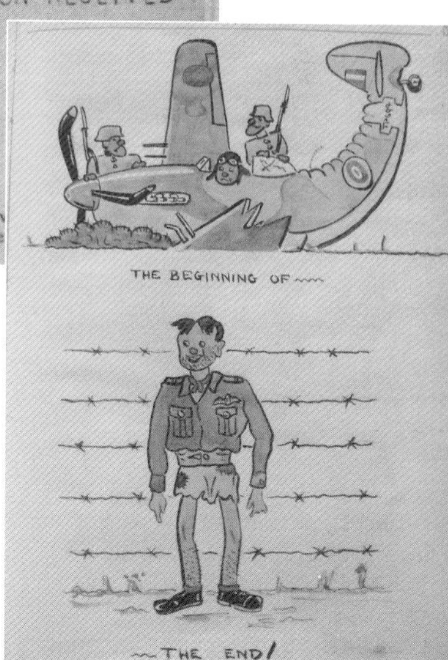

Top: A drawing in Ken Trott's POW logbook, depicting his collision with an enemy aircraft on 13 July 1944. *(Ken Trott)*

Middle: The telegram sent to Ken Trott's parents informing them that he was missing, 13 July 1944. *(Ken Trott)*

Right: Based on an original of a downed Spitfire, 197 Squadron Typhoon pilot Ken Trott depicts his version of 'The Beginning of the End', in his POW logbook. *(Ken Trott)*

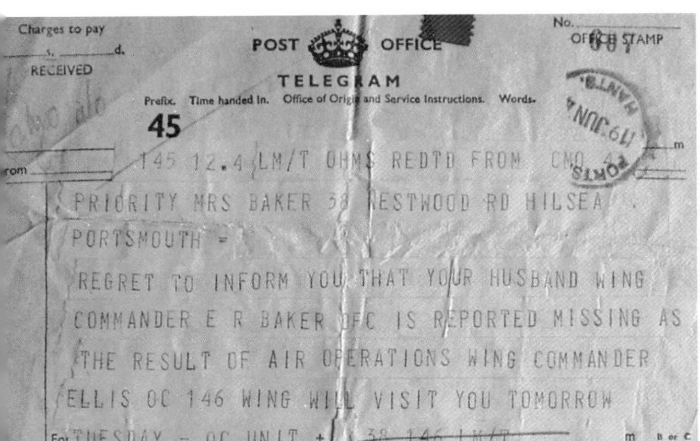

Charges to pay
s. d.
RECEIVED
POST OFFICE
TELEGRAM
No.
OFFICE STAMP
Prefix. Time handed in. Office of Origin and Service Instructions. Words.
45
145 12.4 LM/T OHMS REDTD FROM CMQ 4
PRIORITY MRS BAKER 38 WESTWOOD RD HILSEA
PORTSMOUTH =
REGRET TO INFORM YOU THAT YOUR HUSBAND WING
COMMANDER E R BAKER DFC IS REPORTED MISSING AS
THE RESULT OF AIR OPERATIONS WING COMMANDER
ELLIS OC 146 WING WILL VISIT YOU TOMORROW
TUESDAY = OC UNIT + ~~38 146 LM/T~~

op left: A portrait of Reg Baker.
H. Crassweller/S. Baker)

op centre: Reg Baker's grave, 13 March 1947.
le was buried three times following his death in June
944. First by his aircraft and then, in September 1944,
y the side of a temporary airfield near Bény-sur-Mer.
le was finally laid to rest in March 1947, at the
'anadian War Cemetery at Bény-sur-Mer.
H. Crassweller/S. Baker)

Top right: Reg Baker's original grave, next to the wreckage of his Typhoon, St. Manvieu. *(H. Crassweller/S. Baker)*

Middle: The medals of Wing Commander Reg Baker DSO, DFC and Bar. *(H. Crassweller/S. Baker)*

Bottom left: The telegram sent to Reg's family following his loss in action. *(H. Crassweller/S. Baker)*

Bottom right: 3 Squadron's Pilot Officer Bob Cole, Volkel, Holland, November 1944. *(Bob Cole)*

Top left: Squadron Leader Allan Smith addresses 197 Squadron pilots amidst the tented accommodation at Lille, September 1944. *(D. Tapson)*

Top right: 197 Squadron's CO, Squadron Leader Allan Smith, at B.3 airfield, Normandy. *(D. Tapson)*

Middle left: Prime Minister Winston Churchill meets 146 Wing personnel at B.3 Airfield. 23 July 1944.

Middle right – both photographs: 197 Squadron accommodation at B.3 Airfield, Normandy, July 1944. *(D. Tapson)*

Bottom left and right: Spirits obviously running high, with 197 Squadron's doc Ken Horn and the Adj Vic Whitear debagged at B.3 Normandy. *(D. Tapson)*

Top left: 151 Squadron navigator George Kelsey. *(G. Kelsey)*

Top right: Barry Kneath and George Kelsey, by then both sporting DFCs, stand by their 29 Squadron Mosquito, April 1945. *(G. Kelsey)*

Middle: 151 Squadron's George Kelsey and Barry Kneath, just after they had returned from the eventful operation of 22 July 1944. Damage to the wing is clear and a hole can be seen in the starboard engine. *(G. Kelsey)*

Below left: The Mosquito carried out many varied duties during the war – photo reconnaissance, night fighter, bomber and fighter-bomber. Depicted here is a Mark VI fighter-bomber of 151 Squadron, 1944. *(G. Kelsey)*

Below right: 151 Squadron night fighter Mosquito, early 1944. *(G. Kelsey)*

Right: 197 Squadron Typhoon OV-Z MN925, early September 1944, with invasion markings and long-range tanks. *(D. Tapson)*

Middle: 197 Squadron Typhoon OV-F, with a 1,000 lb bomb under the wing, late 1944. *(D. Tapson)*

Bottom: 80 Squadron, in front of a Spitfire IX at West Malling, July 1944. Hugh Ross leaning against the trailing edge of the wing, second from left. Bill Maloney crouching, third from right. *(Peter Maloney)*

Left: Flying Officer Derek Lovell sits in the cockpit of a 197 Squadron Typhoon Ib, at Mill, March 1945. *(D. Lovell)*

Middle: 197 and 193 Squadron pilots outside the ops tent at one of Group Captain Denys Gillam's operational briefings for the attack on the one man submarine factory at Utrecht, 4 November 1944. Derek Lovell stands to Gillam's left with his back to the camera. *(197 Squadron Association)*

Bottom: 197 Squadron Typhoon Ib OV-S, flown on numerous occasions by Derek Lovell, Mill airfield, Jan/Feb 1945. *(D. Lovell)*

Top left: Aerial photo of an MT workshop attacked by 146 Wing on 19 March 1945, near Doetinchem. *(D. Lovell)*

Top right: 19 March 1945. Low-level photo of the aftermath of the 146 Wing attack on an enemy MT workshop, near Doetinchem. *(D. Lovell)*

Bottom left: Low-level photo showing the destruction caused by the 146 Wing Typhoon attack on army store at Oldenburg, 17 April 1945. *(D. Lovell)*

Bottom right: The result of the 146 Wing Typhoon attack on the HQ of an enemy Para regiment, 17 April 1945. *(D. Lovell)*

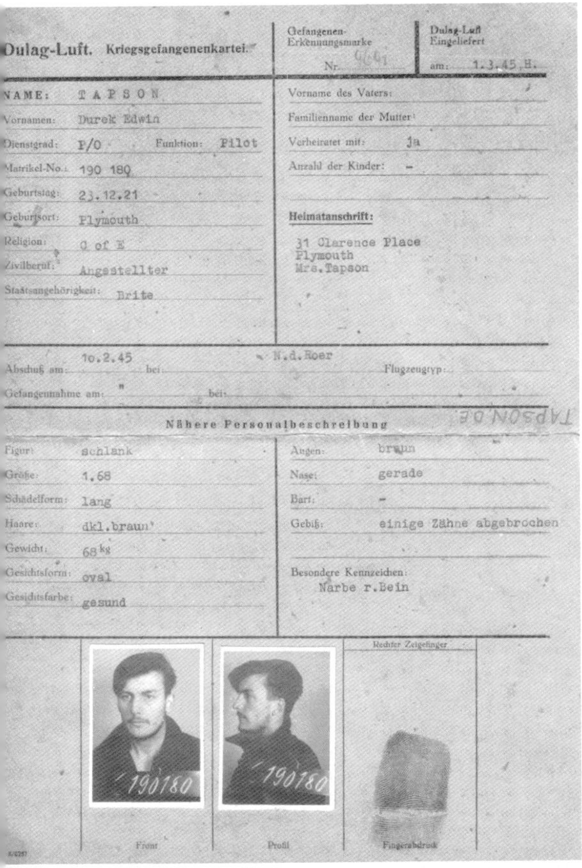

Dulag-Luft. Kriegsgefangenenkartei.

Gefangenen-Erkennungsmarke Nr. 9641

Dulag-Luft Eingeliefert am: 1.3.45 H.

NAME: TAPSON

Vornamen: Durek Edwin

Dienstgrad: P/O Funktion: Pilot

Matrikel-No.: 190 180

Geburtstag: 23.12.21

Geburtsort: Plymouth

Religion: C of E

Zivilberuf: Angestellter

Staatsangehörigkeit: Brite

Vorname des Vaters:

Familienname der Mutter:

Verheiratet mit: ja

Anzahl der Kinder: –

Heimatanschrift:
31 Clarence Place
Plymouth
Mrs. Tapson

Abschuß am: 10.2.45 bei: N.d.Roer Flugzeugtyp:

Gefangennahme am: " bei:

TAPSON D.E.

Nähere Personalbeschreibung

Figur: schlank

Größe: 1,68

Schädelform: lang

Haare: dkl.braun

Gewicht: 68 kg

Gesichtsform: oval

Gesichtsfarbe: gesund

Augen: braun

Nase: gerade

Bart: –

Gebiß: einige Zähne abgebrochen

Besondere Kennzeichen: Narbe r.Bein

190180 190180

Front Profil

Rechter Zeigefinger

Fingerabdruck

Top left: Modern photograph of the Battle of Britain Memorial Flight's Spitfire LF IXe MK356, which was flown operationally, and with some success, by 443 Squadron in the run-up to, and during, the D-Day campaign. *(Jenny Coffey)*

Top right: 403 Squadron's Flying Officer Stephen Butte at Petit Brogel, Holland in March 1945. On 1 January 1945 he had earned a DFC, shooting down three enemy aircraft. *(S. Butte)*

Middle left: Derek Tapson's POW identity card. Derek was shot down and captured on 10 February 1945. *(D. Tapson)*

Middle right: 197 Squadron's Warrant Officer Derek Tapson (standing), at Antwerp, December 1944. *(D. Tapson)*

Left: 443 Squadron Spitfire XVI 2I-W (in the foreground), B.90 Petit Brogel, March 1945. *(Chris Thomas)*

Top: General Dwight D. Eisenhower and Air Chief Marshal Sir Arthur Tedder celebrate VE-Day at Reims, May 1945. *(RAF Museum Hendon)*

Bottom: The memorial at Noyers Bocage, France, 'To the Glorious Memory of the 151 Typhoon Pilots Who Gave Their Lives During the Liberation of Normandy May – August 1944.' The name of Wing Commander E. R. Baker DSO, DFC and Bar appears third down on the left. *(Ken Trott)*

sighted slightly above. Squadron Leader Gilmour's combat report would note, 'Bombs were jettisoned smartly and a merry battle ensued.' It went on:

> I got behind a FW 190 and started firing from about 300 yards 10 degrees deflection. I saw strikes. The FW 190 started for cloud and I followed closing to astern still firing. I hit him squarely just before entering cloud. I came through to see a FW spinning down to crash in a pall of flame near some woods behind a small village. I climbed again and closed on a 190 starboard firing. I had to break smartly after this attack but my No. 2, Pilot Officer Staples, saw strikes on this aircraft and saw it going down.
>
> I claim 1 FW 190 destroyed, 1 FW 190 damaged.

> *Flight Sergeant Carson's combat report:* I was flying Tonic IV. Four FWs came at us from 5 o'clock below; I immediately broke and my number one spun off his trim and I lost sight of him. There was a big mix-up and I attacked four or five aircraft. I saw strikes on one but he broke down and I lost him. I got strikes on another and saw smoke from him. I had to break but he appeared to be hit pretty badly and was going down smoking. I lost sight of him, then I attacked some other aircraft until my ammunition ran out and then rejoined Tonic section and came home.
>
> I claim 2 FW 190s damaged.

> *Flight Lieutenant Lamb's combat report:* I was leading Green section of 19 Squadron… and was flying at 'Readiness' 2,000 feet above the squadron. When over Dreux I saw eleven 190s come up through clouds to 11 o'clock to the squadron and climb through it. I ordered 'Jettison Bombs' and engaged. The Hun showed considerable inclination to stay and dogfight but was obviously inexperienced as it was quite easy to outfight him, though at first we were outnumbered by three to one. I engaged two 190s with short bursts and saw one spin with pieces chipped off him. Later I bounced another and closed in seeing many strikes, a bright explosion from the fuselage, and large pieces drop off. I saw him spin in and explode on the ground. Unknown to me Green 2 also had a squirt and saw the same results.
>
> I claim 1 FW 190 damaged, $1/2$ FW 190 destroyed with Green 2 Pilot Officer Davies.

> *Pilot Officer Davies' combat report:* I was flying Green 2 to Flight Lieutenant Lamb and saw eleven 190s climbing up at 10 o'clock. I jettisoned my bombs when ordered. I kept with Green 1 to guard his tail during the dogfight. We were on the tail of a 190 and I had an opportunity to have a squirt from 200 yards from slightly below and dead astern. I saw a bright flash and strikes all over the fuselage with pieces falling off. Green 1 did most of the shooting while I watched his tail. The 190 dived through cloud and crashed.
>
> I claim $1/2$ FW 190 destroyed with Flight Lieutenant Lamb.

> *Flying Officer Plumridge's combat report:* I was flying No. 3 in Green section… When over Dreux 12+ 190s were reported and Green section jettisoned bombs and prepared for attack. My No. 2 was unable to get rid of his bombs and spun off a turn and failed to join up again. I stuck with

Green 1 and 2 and saw a 190 about to attack Green 2. I opened up from a range of 300-400 yards about 45 degrees off, fired 2 bursts; no strikes, closed to less than 200 yards about 10 degrees off, 1 burst and saw strikes on fuselage and starboard wing. On looking over my shoulder I saw a 190 about to attack me so I had to break off my own attack. Both enemy aircraft then disappeared into cloud.

I claim 1 FW 190 damaged.

Flight Lieutenant Basil Collyns' combat report: I was leading White section flying at 10,000 feet over Dreux when Green leader called up and reported 12+ 190s behind and above. I immediately called White section to jettison bombs and turned to attack. I attacked an FW 190 from 200 yards and fired just as he started to zoom and turn. The first burst missed, so I altered deflection to $^1/_2$ ring and saw numerous strikes on and around the cockpit and pieces falling off. Just at this moment I was struck in the starboard wing by a cannon shell and had to break off combat as the FW 190 I was firing at started to roll away. I was attacked by another FW 190 but shook him off and then set course for base.

Two destroyed and six damaged. 19 Squadron was keeping up the attrition of the Luftwaffe, but it had cost them a pilot, Pilot Officer Schofield, who would survive.

Between 19 and 21 June the 'Great Gale' hit the Normandy beaches. The artificial Mulberry harbours, towed across the Channel from England, particularly the one at St. Laurent, along with shipping and beach facilities, were destroyed or seriously damaged. This seriously hindered the build-up of supplies and of course therefore Allied offensive operations. The need to capture Cherbourg's port facilities quickly became crucial, to keep up with the expansion plans.

On 16 June US divisions had pushed to the west coast of the Cotentin peninsula and reached it within two days. The corridor was widened and secured to the south. The American VIIth Corps then began a push north to take Cherbourg. On 20 June Valognes fell and the Americans closed in, but Hitler had ordered that Cherbourg be held at all costs. The Germans withdrew within its defences, awaiting the siege. The ground assault on the crucial port was fixed for 1400 hours on 22 June, with American and RAF fighter-bombers to attack German positions south of Cherbourg. Midday on the 22nd the American ground forces withdrew 1,000 yards and an artillery barrage was laid to suppress German flak. Four R/P Typhoon squadrons and six Mustang squadrons, including 19 Squadron, tore in between 1240 and 1300, then IXth AF Thunderbolts for the next hour added their fury. Then at H-hour Marauders bombed the defences. The results in terms of damage would later prove variable but the effect on the morale of the defenders was considerable. Lieutenant Colonel Hoffmann, of the Schlieben Group defending Cherbourg, reported to HQ Seventh Army on 24 June that his troops, 'were worn down by the incessant bombardment by enemy naval artillery and by air attacks.' But the German defenders still fought hard as the Americans advanced and it wasn't until 24 June that considerable ground was gained. On 26 June the port was surrendered, although some pockets still held out until 29 June. The peninsula was finally secured on 1 July. The Allies then set about preparing to repair the sabotaged port facilities.

Basil Collyns hadn't taken part in any operations on the day before the assault on Cherbourg, although 19 Squadron would conduct an armed recce, during which a combat with Me 109s took place and 'by good shooting and team work four 109s were shot down without loss', although one pilot was injured.

Then on 22 June Basil, with his 19 Squadron colleagues, took off from Ford at 1210 hours tasked to strafe, as part of a wing attack, enemy troops, positions and transport in the Cherbourg peninsula. The formation of Mustangs approached the target area, and from 15,000 feet, the pilots dived their aircraft, gaining considerable speed as they approached the deck, and then strafed, line abreast, anything deemed of worth to the enemy. Basil held his Mustang 30 feet above the ground, hurtling along at 420 miles per hour, his cannon firing into a gun position. Then there was a bang and a jolt. He reacted sharply by taking his damaged Mustang to 3,000 feet. If the damage was serious he hoped to be able to cross American lines, but when flames from the engine began to lick the sides of his aircraft, Basil realised he had to act fast, baling out and landing heavily by a hedge in a small field near Montebourg, to the east of Valognes. He looked around and caught sight of enemy soldiers in the village gathering up rifles and starting to run in his direction. But there was also another hostile-looking group of people approaching him, clearly French civilians. Still dazed from his fall, he placed his hand on his revolver, then called out, 'Je suis Anglais.' The expressions changed on their faces. They took his hand, slapped his back, some kissed him and he was quickly swept away to a farmhouse. And here his rescuers took the opportunity of properly welcoming Basil to their country, opening a bottle of cognac, which had been set aside for when the Americans would liberate the area. The celebration continued and eventually Basil departed, when some Americans arrived in a jeep to collect him. He felt somewhat embarrassed as the villagers cheered him off and threw flowers at him.

Basil ended up at St Mère Eglise and was soon flown back to England, accompanied by a group of men who had experienced a similar fate, some of them Thunderbolt and Spitfire pilots, and an entire Havoc crew.

Of course while all this was going on, Ann Collyns, who was working for the New Zealand Air Force in London, feared for the welfare of her husband, having heard news that Basil hadn't returned from the operation and then receiving a telegram, the morning after he was shot down, informing her that her husband was missing.

> *Ann Collyns:* One was expecting something like that all the time, but even so I was pretty shaken. I couldn't just sit in the flat so I went back to the office. I thought if there was any news it would come through to them. They were all marvellous to me. Then in the late afternoon the telephone rang. It was Basil having just slept off all this carry on, the party in France and everything else. He was in an American mess. It was absolutely incredible and went through the whole of our office, several floors of it, very quickly. Basil then came to London and he had a 48-hour leave before going back to Caen.
>
> I didn't go to the office for those two days. We just enjoyed ourselves,

> we went to the Kimmul club. And dear old Bobbie Page had a permanent table at the Savoy Grill, and he always used to take any of the chaps who were about for dinner. So one of the nights we had dinner there.

While Basil was enjoying his days off 19 Squadron kept active on armed recces. On 24 June, 'a good fight ensued during which the squadron shot down four and one damaged without loss.' The pilots landed at B.7 Martragny and were able to conduct another operation that afternoon before returning to Ford that evening. On 25 June Basil joined them, along with the Wing, as they moved to B.7. 'The remainder of the day was spent putting up tents and digging slit trenches etc. Everyone got "organised" and felt completely at home. As we are only some five or six miles from the front the guns can be heard quite plainly.' The next day the weather put paid to any flying and the day was spent sitting in leaky tents and playing cards.

Although many squadrons were now established in Normandy there were not as many as hoped for, the number constrained by the availability of airfields. This matter was causing a certain amount of friction between the services. As far as the air commanders were concerned the stalemate around Caen had to be broken.

To take Caen Montgomery planned operation Epsom to secure the high open terrain south and south-east of Caen, which was good tank country and also good ground for airfields, critical to the expansion and deployment of 2nd TAF squadrons. In conjunction with 2nd British Army, Broadhurst made his 83 Group aircraft available for this critical push, although hampered by the weather. The ground offensive began on 25 June, east of Tilly-sur-Seulles, and a few miles west of Caen, but stiff opposition was encountered. At 0730 hours on 26 June fighter-bombers had been given the task of attacking enemy gun positions and strong points, but bad weather over England intervened to keep home-based squadrons from the battle. Nevertheless 83 Group squadrons managed to conduct 524 sorties on 53 missions, but not all on land-based attacks, as the Luftwaffe put in an appearance.

The troops advanced and by 27 June had managed to cross two bridges over the Odon, but the fighting had been fierce. With squadrons in England still grounded for most of the day 83 Group had to provide the air might, flying 349 sorties. On 28 June some Spitfires from England were able to join the battle, with 575 sorties from 83 Group. Again the Luftwaffe would seize their chance, sending fighters to the battle area. AVM Strafford's diary entry of 28 June summed up the day.

> Fighter operations from this side of the Channel were also hampered by bad weather and the value of the airfields on the other side was well illustrated by the effort 83 Group were able to put out in close support of the Second Army. Enemy fighters and fighter/bombers were taking full advantage of the bad weather to operate under conditions favourable to them on the Second British Army front. A total of 240 enemy aircraft were actually sited by our aircraft operating in formations of 40 to 60. Second TAF had a very successful day and claim 26:10:3. Ninth Tactical Air Command destroyed the only enemy aircraft seen on their front, where the

situation was very quiet. Arrangements are being made to ensure that the two tactical Air Commands on the continent give one another mutual assistance when one is having a busy time with fighter/bombers and with enemy fighter opposition.[53]

On 29 June 83 Group carried out 650 sorties and 84 Group would weigh in with 600. Certainly Coningham's men were doing all they could in support of the offensive. They were also, fortunately, frustrating German counter-attack plans.

At 0955 hours on 29 June the Chief of Staff, Panzer Group West told the Operations Staff, Seventh Army that the counter offensive by the 2nd SS Panzer Corps could not begin before the afternoon because concentrations were under continuous artillery and air bombardment. At 1340 hours, a further message logged by the Seventh Army referred to the 'heavy losses by fighter-bomber attacks' and ten minutes later a very urgent request was sent to Luftflotte 3 for air support because 'Allied strafing from the air has increased our losses by knocking out several tanks and a large number of vehicles.' It is worth noting the influence of this on the ground battle. Army Group B issued instructions that concentrations were to be ordered only at night for the time being. Thus, Allied air superiority also imposed definite limitations upon the tactics that could be employed by the enemy ground forces.[54]

But the Germans had managed to muster enough armour for a counter attack. Allied air power was readied to intervene.

29 June, 2000 hours, AVM Strafford's diary: 2 TAF informed AVM that he had a warning request from 83 Group by telephone that things were not going so well with the Second Army and that they would probably ask for all possible air assistance both during the night and from as early as possible after first light tomorrow morning. 83 Group had promised to let 2 TAF have full details of these requests by 2130 hours. AVM therefore called a Meeting of the Reps. of 2 TAF and Ninth Air Force in Advanced AEAF War Room at 2130 hours and also arranged for the Commander to join the meeting by 2145 hours. Details of the Second Army requests were not received until approximately 2150 hours and consisted mainly of request to stop enemy movements through 15 pin-points (in small towns or villages) and in the Villers-Bocage, Thury Harcourt area, south-west of the Second Army's bulge. No background information was given for this request and it was not clear whether it was an emergency request to cease and smash a dangerously successful enemy armoured counter attack, or whether it was to take opportunity of exploiting a favourable situation. As a result of the Commander telephoning Chief of Staff, 21 Army Group, and further telephone calls to 83 Group, it transpired that the latter was the case. It was decided that on the information available there was no case

[53] Public Record Office AIR 37/574, diary of AVM S. C. Strafford CB, CBE, DFC.
[54] Public Record Office AIR 41/67.

> for calling on AEAF for heavy bomber assistance either that night or on the following morning. The medium bombers of the Ninth Air Force were already set up to attack one of the points named during the evening and arrangements had also already been made for 2 Group's night operations to be concentrated in that area. Although none of the points mentioned were particularly suitable for attack by mediums, in view of the strong request from the Second Army, and because of the chance of killing Germans passing through these points, the three best suited to medium bomber attack were selected for attack by the Ninth Air Force as early as possible on the following morning and for repeat attacks throughout the day. The remainder of the targets were allotted the fighter/bombers of both Tactical Air Forces and the Commanding General IXth Tactical Air Command was particularly instructed to put all his available resources (other than minimum required on his quiet front) at the disposal of AOC 83 Group.[55]

19 Squadron had played its part in Epsom. On 27 June Basil was out on an early morning recce in the Caen – Bernay – Dreux – Argentan area, with little seen. That evening the pilots took an opportunity to relax: 'a few sorties were made in Bayeux, and the town was clobbered in suitable "19" style.' The next day Basil didn't take part in a dive bombing of bridges south-west of Caen, but he would come into contact with the enemy later in the day when the airfield was strafed by eight FW 190s, fortunately without causing any harm.

On 29 June the squadron, including Basil Collyns, was sent again to bomb the bridges and although the result, amidst concentrated but inaccurate flak, was reported as excellent, with bursts visible all around the bridge, it wasn't breached. The next day pilots of 19 Squadron, without Basil, took off in the evening to dive bomb crossroads in the Villers-Bocage area, the bombing reported as good. One pilot was lost, killed when his Mustang span into the ground. A second sortie was carried out, the bombing hampered by cloud.

Overall, on 30 June, in view of the panzer build-up Epsom was abandoned and Caen remained in enemy hands. With respect to the air battle, on 30 June poor weather again troubled air operations, but by the end of the day 2nd TAF had flown 1,040 sorties, IXth AF 1,375.

> *30 June AVM Strafford's diary:* Medium bomber attempts on Second Army front abortive owing to cloud down to 2,000 feet. Fighter/bomber activity at full intensity under cloud cover. Main effort for today must be centred on Second Army front. Heavy bomber support requested for Villers-Bocage. Intention of Second Army for next day to hold line and had requested enemy movement be stopped through a number of selected points. F/Bs, mediums and heavies (BC) called on.

> *1 July AVM Strafford's diary:* It was noted that the German counter attack SW of the Second Army bulge had petered out at 0945 hours this morning. Bad weather was again impeding air operations by mediums and the bulk of the work for the day would thus again fall on the

[55] Public Record Office AIR 37/574, diary of AVM S. C. Strafford CB, CBE, DFC.

fighter/bombers both immediately on the Battle front and in attacks on communications further afield, in particular in the Paris Gap.

AVM Strafford's diary also noted on 1 July that a POW from 10 Panzer Division, on interrogation, had reported that out of 25 tanks used in the counter attack at Carpiquet (west of Caen) only eight had advanced, the rest being knocked out by RPs. 'The Germans confirmed that they are terrified by the Rocket fighter/bombers. Which are proving our best close tactical weapon. 9 and 10 Panzer are affected as they have not seen them before.'[56]

The battle in the east had ground to a halt and opposing the British front, and defending any offensives to take Caen, was a considerable German force. But a stalemate was not an option, somehow the Allies had to break the front.

Out of the Frying Pan...

Harry Pattison, 182 Squadron: One time coming out at very low level near Caen, I was hit by ground fire, light stuff, about five times, you could sort of count the individual thumps. And quickly looking at the instruments, as one did if anything happened like that, the oil pressure needle just fell completely to zero, and the engine, which comprised 24 sleeve valves cylinders required a lot of oil and of course if you lost your oil pressure that was it, within seconds the propeller had just stopped dead. So I had no motor but fortunately we had carried out the attack and were coming out on the safety vector which headed us towards our own lines. And with the excess speed it was a toss up whether I kept going and force-landed or pulled up and baled out. Well I didn't fancy baling out because the Typhoon wasn't the easiest aircraft to bale out from. So I kept it going at low level looking for a spot to land and ahead there did appear, as the speed was dropping off, a clearing in amongst a wood. It was the only clearing within sight so I pulled up, opened the hood – there were no hydraulics at all because they had been shot – and stuffed it down on this ploughed field rather hard. I ended up with clods of earth flying all around, and came to a shuddering halt safely fortunately. But it was in the middle of a tank battle, Germans one side, Brits the other and they were firing over the top so I cowered like a coward under one wing tip for about half an hour while this tank battle was going on. Eventually this Canadian captain in a jeep drove out to me when the tanks had stopped firing and picked me up and took me back in. An experience not to be repeated if one could help it.[57]

On 16 June 1944, 403 Squadron carried out two convoy patrols. In addition the squadron moved across the Channel to B.2 Bazenville, the ORB recording, 'We spent the night five and six to a tent, with just a small visit from the Hun.'

Hart Finley: It was the greatest feeling to us that we didn't have to always cross that Channel to get into action. It was a constructed field and we did land on one or two occasions before we actually moved over there to

[56] *Ibid.*
[57] Interview with Harry Glendining Pattison, 1996, Imperial War Museum Sound Archive 16598.

refuel, go back in the air, do a further patrol and then back to Tangmere for the night. The dust was indescribable. It was very difficult to try and stay clean or free of the stuff. I recall the first night that we were actually in Normandy. Andy Mackenzie was a flight commander and I was a flight commander and with our squadron commander, the three of us were to share a tent. We pitched it and then everybody was told to dig a hole, just like digging your grave. We spent a good part of the day throwing the dirt out digging this hole about the size of a regular grave and down about three feet. Then we put our little cots down there, and across the top of our heads a couple of pieces of two by four. We had a steel parachute trunk, in which we carried a lot of our possessions. We put that on top of the two by fours to act as a cover for our heads. That first night we were lying there joking and laughing, and all of sudden there was a most nerve-wracking clatter and booming and banging. Right behind the hedge, where our tent was, was an anti-aircraft battery. We knew nothing about it. Suddenly there was a German aircraft coming in and this thing let loose with all its fury. I tell you we all practically knocked ourselves out hitting our heads on the two by fours, sitting bolt upright.

Excerpts from the 403 Squadron ORB describe further attempts for self-preservation and encounters with unwanted guests.

18 June: Sunday – a day of rest. That was the way most of our day went, that is, as far as flying was concerned. Some say the reason was due to the fact we had no bombs, so soon we shall be doing close support to the army. Much was done for self defence as sleeves were rolled up and the pick and shovel were the tools for making trenches. One short sweep later in day.
19 June:... early in the morning, on the way to dispersal an FW 190 came out of the low cloud and rain to drop parachute anti-personnel bombs. No one was injured.
20 June: Last night Jerry came over again and disturbed our peace... [later that evening the pilots] returned to our tents had a snack and went to bed to await Jerry's visit.

On 21 June there was no flying owing to the poor weather. The next day 403 Squadron carried out two operations, the first to cover 412 Squadron on a dive-bombing mission, the second to bomb woods in which an ammunition dump was believed to be located. 'We had hits in the target area but little happened.' On the way back a staff car was claimed shot-up.

The squadron ORB again:

The exciting feature of the day was watching the crew of a Fortress baling out after their kite had been hit by flak over Caen. Their aircraft flew for a while making a large spiral then suddenly a wing broke and the aircraft went into a couple of rolls and crashed with plenty of flame and smoke NE of us. One of the crew arrived safely at our airfield. Another sight was that of the Marauders bombing some target near Caen. They had all hell thrown up at them and one was seen to go down in flames. Another was smoking but the crew managed OK. Yes we are sure getting nearer to real war.

Over the next few days the squadron took part in a patrol during which FW 190s were engaged and claims were made, dive bombing on 24 June, and on 25 June an uneventful long fighter sweep in the morning and an escort to Mustangs around Paris. Then bombing again, with the army marking the targets with smoke.

403 Squadron now prepared to assist with Epsom. On 26 June an early morning armed recce was carried out. After shooting up a truck Hart Finley spotted a gaggle of Me 109s, 'We got into them and would have done the squadron proud had not cloud conditions favoured the enemy', although claims for three destroyed and two damaged were still made. Later in the morning the Luftwaffe was engaged again, this time a claim of an Me 109 damaged, the ORB recording, 'The afternoon was spent on readiness which meant doing beach patrols as the ADGB boys were grounded by the weather.' On 27 June 403 carried out a bombing attack and 'pranged with very excellent results some enemy gun positions enabling the army to advance west of Caen without great difficulty.' The next day the squadron would lose the author of the ORB, Flying Officer Rhodes, on an early morning patrol. He was last seen chasing an enemy aircraft, but out of petrol he force-landed south of Caen, and became a prisoner. Flight Lieutenant MacKenzie claimed his fourth enemy aircraft on the same patrol over Évreux. On the second patrol of the day 403 Squadron lost one pilot west of Falaise, who said he was 'baling out but cloud obscured any confirmation of this statement.' In fact Flying Officer Lanfranchi lost his life. On 29 June, 403 Squadron pilots would again engage the enemy, one claimed destroyed for the loss of one Spitfire and pilot, who evaded capture.

On 30 June it was more armed recces and patrols, still in the area south of Caen, 403 Squadron adding its firepower to oppose the German build-up for a counter attack against the Odon bridgehead. Early in the morning on an armed recce, between Falaise and Lisieux, Hart Finley would sight an enemy aircraft.

> *Hart Finley's combat report:* We were flying west at 8,000 feet when we observed an Me 109 flying towards us from nearly head on. We chased him into cloud. As we came down below cloud I saw another Me 109 in a break in the cloud layer below us flying in a northerly direction. I went up after him. He broke port and headed south. Three of us went down after him and all fired but were out of range. I followed him down to 1,000 feet below cloud layer and he disappeared up into cloud again. As he disappeared another Me 109 was spotted flying in an easterly direction. I pulled up behind him. As he spotted me he broke and I broke with him. I gave him about a 5 second burst from 600-500 yards from nearly dead astern. I saw strikes on the cockpit and wing roots as he pulled up into cloud. I claim this Me 109 as damaged.

And this would actually be Hart's last encounter with the enemy over Normandy. He was deemed to have completed his tour of ops and was sent back to England. But he would return to the air battle over Western Europe at a later date.

197 Squadron's Typhoon pilot Derek Lovell describes a typical operational sortie from Needs Oar Point in support of the Normandy campaign.

> You would be woken up at some ungodly hour. We had double summer time in those days so you could be woken up at 3 o'clock in the morning,

by the squadron batman. 'Briefing in half an hour.' You would get your gear on, battle dress, flying boots and your gun belt, silk scarf. Buckle on your revolver, which you didn't wear high up on your waist as you were supposed to because it would cut into your thighs. You used to sling the ammunition pouch below the gun belt and the gun below that. It was halfway down your thigh like a good cowboy. This meant you could strap it onto your leg with your parachute harness.

At briefing, details of the target, the flak, the way we were going to attack. It would be two sections of four, generally, with the CO leading Green section, with the flight commander leading Yellow section. And with a spare man taking off in case someone dropped out. Then out to dispersal, get your gear on, into the cockpit. You were given a start time, effectively known as press tit time, because there were two buttons you pressed to start a Typhoon. One to fire a cartridge and one to liven up the magnetos. You would sit and listen for the first Typhoon to start, which was the CO. Once you heard his start, you'd fire up and taxi out. You would now be too busy to worry about being frightened although you may have been beforehand. Take off in pairs, climb out over the Isle of Wight and towards Normandy. In line astern initially and then halfway across the Channel into battle formation, finger fours. On arrival in the target area, echelon port or starboard depending on which way we were going to dive. You wanted 20 degrees past the target, and then turn back towards the target, which gave you a 60 degree dive down to the target. Drop your bombs at about two, two and a half thousand feet, clonk, clonk as they came off, and then pull up and open full throttle and get the hell out of it as fast as you could to the rendezvous point, back at 8,000 feet. Reform and then halfway across the Channel line astern and then a stream landing. A four would go down line astern, the CO would peel off, count three and then the next one and so on, by which time the other flight would come round, so you could get the whole squadron down very quickly. Then debriefing and then sit down awaiting the next show.

This tells of a typical operation from England but what the Allied air commanders were keen to do was establish their squadrons on the continent. Lovell gives an example of some of the problems of operating at considerable range.

On one occasion we came back having been on a fighter sweep. We came across the Channel in a thunderstorm and there was St Elmo's fire all round the propeller and dancing up and down the aerial. And we were very short of fuel and people were dropping out of the skies to the airfields along the south coast. Two I know landed at Hurn and they got to the end of the runway and the engine stopped, as they had run out of petrol.

On 26 June AVM Strafford recorded in his diary:

Although 13 airfields were technically now available on the continent, it must be remembered that some of the British airfields were under shell fire and some of the US airfields were going unserviceable owing to heavy use of these fields by heavily loaded transport aircraft.

Now that we had 30 fighter squadrons based on the continent it was

> interesting to note that the total number of aircraft we had based in the tactical area was almost equal to German fighter strength in the tactical area.[58]

More fighter squadrons based in Normandy were nevertheless needed. The air commanders still pushed for expansion of territory around and beyond Caen to obtain more airfield space, deploy more of their squadrons and shorten their operational range.

On 16 and 17 June, 197 Squadron's Derek Lovell made his contribution to delaying enemy troop movements, his logbook recording: '16 June – Bombing bridges at Cabourg les Bains. Uneventful – bridge damaged, gasometer strafed. 17 June – Bombing bridges at Thury Harcourt. Uneventful – bridges damaged.' Derek's two sorties on 18 June were frustrated owing to poor weather. 197 Squadron's ORB frequently mentions the poor weather, but a special operation was set up to raise morale, the ORB recording, '19 June Liberty run in the evening Operation Bournemouth . . . which proved most successful.' On 20 June Derek missed out on two attacks on Noball targets, a response to the call on 2nd TAF to help in the flying bomb counter offensive. On the evening of 16 June AVM Strafford had recorded in his diary:

> AVM discussed with Commander points raised at CinC's meeting in the morning. The Air CinC had ruled that fighter/bombers of the Second TAF must assist in attacking the new NOBALL sites which were now in operation and which, owing to their size, were difficult to locate by heavy or medium bombers . . . D/SASO Second TAF was instructed accordingly.[59]

Derek Lovell was back in action on 22 June, his logbook recording, 'Went to S.W. Paris area. Attacked a train at Rambouillet, damaged.' 197 Squadron sent its pilots on Ramrods and Rangers on the next two days. On 26 June the ORB would record no flying, 'Weather today was completely duff.'

On 27 June Derek was detailed to act as escort to a rocket and bomb attack by other Typhoons on a German HQ south of Carentan. Owing to low cloud the squadron was forced to turn back. On their return they learnt of the loss of one of their colleagues.

> *Derek Lovell:* Dumbo Taylor took off from Needs Oar Point, you're taking straight off towards the Isle of Wight. This time we were flying with a bomb under one wing and a long-range tank under the other. And to even out the bombing area, one flight had the bomb on the left and the long-range tank on the right, and the other flight had it the other way round. Dumbo, as far as we can make out, switched from main tanks to long-range tanks, to use that. He switched the wrong way, and of course the engine cut. He tried to get back, but went into the Solent.

---

58 PRO AIR 37/574.
59 *Ibid.*

On 28 June the weather again kept the 197 Squadron pilots grounded, but they were back in action the next day, Derek's logbook recording, '29 June – Rail – road junction S.E. Lisieux – yards + rail pranged. 29 June – Attacked a viaduct – one hit on railroad. Fair amount of flak.' On 1 July 197 Squadron began preparing for the move to France. Two days later aircraft were flown from Needs Oar Point to Hurn, from where they carried out an evening Ramrod. Derek Lovell recalled, 'There must have been three or four Typhoon wings there at the time waiting for their ground crew to get across to France.' He went on:

> When at Hurn we had thick fog at one point. A number of us disappeared into Bournemouth. About half past twelve the fog had cleared and it was a bright blue, clear sky day. Meanwhile the squadron had come from stand down to report to ops room immediately and the CO was running around trying to find eight people. Some were in the mess writing letters, some had been celebrating someone's promotion in the mess. Anyway he got eight together and set across the Channel. Halfway across the Channel, the chilly atmosphere, the beer and the nervous tension, placed a demand on bladders. In British fighters there is no pee tube, and people were getting quite anxious to relieve themselves. The CO said, 'Nobody is turning back because they want a pee. Manage as best you can in the cockpit, but mind you don't hit anything electrical.' Well the formation broke up a bit while people undid their parachute harness, Mae West harness, fly buttons and managed as best they could. For some it happened two or three times, there and back. Anyway when they landed back at Hurn and parked their aircraft, the groundcrews came over to check for any flak damage; the armourer came to see if there were any blockages with the cannons and the mechanic wanted to know if the engine was working alright. The main check was that there wasn't any flak damage to the big radiator. A small piece of shrapnel in there would cause the glycol to leak and the engine to seize up in no time. When you cut the engine on the Typhoon, the carburettor would empty down the back of the radiator and this was streamed out the back. Now it could be petrol, it might be glycol and there was only one way to check it. The mechanic would dip his finger in and taste it. And they were saying, 'Excuse me sir, you appear to have a glycol leak but it doesn't taste like glycol.' The reply was, 'Well don't bother – forget it!'

'Unkempt Ruffians'

Flight Lieutenant G. Millington served as a Mosquito navigator with 125 Squadron, based at Hurn, at the time of the invasion and recalled how fighter squadrons moved through on their way to Normandy.

> These squadrons would fly into Hurn and remain there until airfields had been captured when they would leave Hurn and fly to Normandy. Consequently the Officers' Mess at Hurn was always crowded with fighter pilots awaiting instructions to fly to Normandy. These chaps only had what they stood up in, so after a few days at Hurn they began

to acquire a rather unshaven and disreputable appearance. Also they were all well armed with pistols and knives.

As may be imagined, the Officers' Mess at Hurn was a memorable sight. Hundreds of whiskery unkempt ruffians, festooned with pistols, sitting round small tables drinking beer and playing cards. It reminded one irresistibly of a scene from some Wild West film, except for one very strange and incongruous detail. From this barbarous and wild-looking mob there arose a babble of conversation, but all in the purest accents of the English Public School.[60]

On the morning of 4 July a 197 Squadron operation was aborted owing to the weather again, but two sweeps were carried out later. The next day there was only one operation, the pilots having to return owing to the bad weather. One pilot did not come back, however. At the time his fate was not known, but he had lost his life. On 6 and 7 July there were Ramrods and armed recces and on 8 July Squadron Leader Taylor led some of the 197 Squadron pilots, including Derek Lovell, to B.15 with a view to operating from there, but as the weather was again poor they returned to Hurn, and were able to report on the conditions of the airfield. 'Our temporary airfield in France is very rough. It consists of one strip NE – SW and is merely a clearing through corn fields. It has a large dip in the middle of the strip which makes taking off with bombs tricky. The pilots spent their first day in France taking stock of our newly won territory and acquiring souvenirs.'

But of course not all squadron personnel could move to their new base by air. An intelligence clerk with 146 Wing recorded the move of the ground party to Normandy.

> On 2 July, 1944, our small convoy of about 20 vehicles and 50 men (known as the 'Sea Recce' party) left Needs Oar Point, Hants. In pouring rain the five-hour journey to the 'Sausage Machine' was anything but pleasant. A hot meal and accommodation, under canvas, were soon provided and everyone settled down to a couple of pleasantly lazy days spent reading, drinking tea, or visiting the cinema and ENSA shows on camp. Most people took the opportunity of enjoying a hot bath – a welcome luxury. 'Old Sarum' will always be vividly remembered for its camp broadcasting system which, with amazing regularity, announced its messages day and night.
>
> Very early on 5 July our party moved off to an army transit camp at Farnham, Hants. Here the food, and accommodation in wooden huts were excellent. We started 'collecting' various items of equipment for our sea voyage – life jackets, rations etc.
>
> The following day we left the transit camp and journeyed to Gosport marshalling area. Our stay here will I am sure be remembered for the generous hospitality of the local residents who provided everyone with tea, cigarettes and matches and allowed us the use of their bathrooms for

60 Papers of Flight Lieutenant G. Millington IWM 92/29/1.

a final wash and brush up before embarking.

Finally at 1600 hours on Thursday 6 July our turn came to go on board the LCT that was to convey us to the beachhead. Two 'craft' were allocated to our unit and here I must pay tribute to the personnel of the army and navy responsible for the excellent organisation in 'shepherding' all vehicles and personnel safely aboard.

It had been arranged that we should sail at midnight, but 'Met' had other ideas and a heavy thunderstorm accompanied vivid lightning, which destroyed a number of barrage balloons protecting our convoy, forcing us to spend a night in the Solent in sight of Needs Oar Point, our late 'home'.

At 0600 hours the following day we set sail for the beachhead. It was a beautiful day and everyone took advantage of the warm sunshine. The crew of the LCT were very helpful and most of us learned something more of life in the navy. The journey was uneventful, but we had the pleasure of seeing many RAF squadrons heading for the continent.

At 2000 hours we anchored off 'Green beach' at Graye-sur-Mer, to await landing instructions. In the next few hours many of us witnessed some never-to-be forgotten scenes. The 'first' battle for Caen was raging, and to our left, about half-a-mile away a destroyer was shelling some unseen target in the battle area, whilst 800 Halifaxes and Lancasters added to the devastation. Many times have we read in the press that our bombers 'queued up' in the air to bomb the target, and it was a most awe-inspiring sight to us in reality.

At 2300 hours we went ashore almost 'dryshod', and without any interference from the Hun. We were conducted to the RAF marshalling area at Tierceville, where from high ground we had an excellent view of the battle in the valley below. Persistent enemy bombing and strafing of the area apparently in our immediate vicinity, gave us a wakeful night, and everyone was relieved to see, from under the vehicles, the dawn break, happy to know that we had suffered no casualties. At 0900 hours we set out for our first airfield on the continent – B.15 at Ryes and here amid pleasant surroundings we were ready to operate within 90 minutes of securing our site and on the arrival of our aircraft from England our portion of the Battle for France was on!

On 9 July 197 Squadron pilots returned to Normandy. Weather put paid to any operations and the airmen stayed overnight. On 10 July Derek Lovell took part in a Ramrod, attacking a village near Évrecy, recording in his logbook, 'My dear the flak!!!' On 11 July the squadron ORB recorded, 'The weather, our greatest enemy since D-Day, again hampered operations and the squadron only attempted one operation.' Railyards were bombed the next day and on 13 July 197 Squadron detailed pilots for an armed recce, one of whom was Ken Trott. Ken would not be returning.

On the day I came down I reported an armoured personnel carrier to Wing Commander Johnny Baldwin [who had taken over from Reg Baker] and he said, 'OK you can go down with your No. 2 and attack.' We saw two people get out as soon as they saw us coming down and race out to the left. We shot the thing up, and it was obviously damaged in some way and wasn't going anywhere. I reported it and asked if we should go around again, suggesting it would be a good thing to set it on fire. Wing Commander Baldwin replied, 'No, for goodness sake, get back up here quickly. We are being attacked by 30 Me 109s.'

On reaching the aerial mêlée Ken soon found himself head to head with an enemy aircraft.

He was coming towards me and I was going towards him. I went to break and as I did so we collided. I felt my head hit the cockpit and the cockpit cover came away, and I went out. I'd lost my helmet, my oxygen, I'd had a revolver. I'd lost everything really except my parachute and once I pulled the cord I became unconscious. I ended up in a field with Germans all round me.

Ken would see out the rest of the war as a POW.

In the ensuing combats, which also involved aircraft from 257 Squadron, claims would be made of two destroyed and two damaged. In addition to the loss of Ken Trott, 257 Squadron would also lose one pilot, who managed to evade capture. That evening the pilots got back to Hurn and 'enjoyed the luxury of baths'. Derek Lovell returned with his colleagues to France on 14 July, in the evening, but again the weather prevented any ops. Then another move, on 15 July, as Squadron Leader Taylor took B Flight to France and a Ramrod was attempted. The Typhoons were then set down at B.3 near St. Croix-sur-Mer, 'an excellent strip. The camp site is also very good, but the dust proves to be very trying and damaging to the aircraft.'

Flight Lieutenant H. Neville Thomas: After a week at B.15 we moved to B.3, St Croix-sur-Mer, north of Caen, where 'tracking' made take-off and landing with heavy bombs less hazardous.

Normandy dust – greyish brown in colour – inches deep on the roads – covering the hedges, houses and trees, in your hair and eyes, in your tea, on your food, between your teeth and in your blankets. Dust of shell-shattered roads, dust of thunderous transport day and night, dust storms by aircraft taking off and landing, dust obscuring the sun and darkening the moon – a veritable pall over all the beachhead.

Derek Lovell: The enemy knew we were taking off as these big clouds of dust would appear. They knew where our strips were of course. There was this fine Normandy dust and once we had got down the runway, there were clouds of it, you couldn't see the one in front at first. If we were taking off in pairs you had to wait until they got down the runway a bit, until you could see them, and then you could take off.

Job Done

On 10 July 83 Group commander Harry Broadhurst wrote to his superior Air Marshal Coningham:

> My dear Air Marshal
>
> Now that the whole of 83 Group is safely and firmly established on the Continent I feel I must write and thank you and your staff for the wonderful way in which the various 'situations' and variations in plan have been handled.
>
> To transfer a complete Air Force Group from the U.K. to the Continent over beaches could never be termed an easy task even were everything to go according to plan. But when the plan is varied from minute to minute due to a somewhat 'gluey' Army situation the repercussions on your operational and administrative staff must have been tremendous.
>
> Nevertheless our proposals and counter-proposals have always been met in the most kindly and helpful way by your Staff and my own chaps have done nothing but sing their praise.
>
> As you know, it takes a good deal to urge me into letter writing but I would like to convey my great appreciation for all that you have done for us and particularly to Victor Groom and Tommy Elmhirst for the way in which they have helped us over our many stiles.[61]

Of course whilst the Allies exercised air superiority in the daylight over Normandy, there was still a role for the night fighters of the RAF, protecting shipping and the beachheads. Norman Crookes and Bill Jameson would play their part. In January 1944 Norman and Bill joined 488 Squadron, a New Zealand night fighter squadron based at Bradwell Bay in Essex.

> *Norman Crookes:* 488 Squadron was equipped with Mosquitoes. In contrast to the sturdy Beaufighter, the 'Mossie' was much lighter and more manoeuvrable – the pilot and navigator sat side by side. By this time we had a more sophisticated radar, Mark VIII. Instead of two scopes there was one, which had a circular time base, and was easier for the navigator to interpret as a clock face.

At the time the squadron's main function was to try and combat enemy aircraft flying high at 30,000 feet and dropping bombs on London . . .

> *Norman Crookes:* . . . and then getting the hell out of it as quick as they possibly could. The squadron had quite a lot of success at the time but much to our disgust we didn't seem to have any. We had one or two contacts with searchlights but not with enemy aircraft.

Then in April they were assigned to 85 Group in 2nd TAF and training began for operations in France.

---

[61] Public Record Office AIR 37 1237.

Norman Crookes:... in other words we were to sleep in tents on the airfield and eat in our tents, meals provided by cooks who did not have the normal facilities. That time was frustrating when we couldn't enjoy the amenities of the officers' mess. In May 1944 we were then moved to a little place called Zeals, a grass area in Wiltshire, near Wincanton. This is where we were actively focusing on the invasion. We did patrols out in the Channel but we didn't have any contact that was enemy activity, we didn't seem to be able to get near to any combat.

The invasion was bound to happen in the early part of June and for three or four days we didn't leave the camp for anything. We were 'obliged' to stay on camp although it was difficult because the sleeping quarters were away from the dispersal hut but we did keep ourselves to ourselves.

Bill and Norman's first flight over Normandy after the invasion was on 8 June, a three-hour patrol landing at Hurn. Further patrols were carried out on 11, 12 and 23 June without any trade. Other crews were seeing some action however.

A Good-Natured Comrade

On 22 June the 488 Squadron partnership of Pilot Officer 'Stan' McCabe and Warrant Officer Terry Riley managed its first kill, despatching a Ju 188 with three bursts, the enemy aircraft falling to the beaches east of Bayeux. Flight Lieutenant Leslie Hunt of 488 Squadron recalled Stan McCabe's character.

Stan was one of the most popular of aircrew with his quiet demeanour, and was often caught for 'lines' which we knew were purely unintentional, but which caused much amusement. For example, one day in dispersal, all was still when Stan burst out with, 'I have a friend' and was not allowed to finish his statement until the entry had been made in the book as a funny contribution. Another time he announced, 'I have a kind face' and that was added to his collection. His best effort was when someone rang for the flight commander. Stan answered the call and exclaimed, 'Flight commander is out but I'm a potential flight commander!!!' He was also connected with a laughable incident when he was heard to ask one of the English chaps to his room for a piece of cake... all available members of the flight arrived at the time appointed and, following the guest into the room, demanded their share of Stan's cake – it must have seemed like a never-ending procession to our good natured comrade who came in for much leg-pulling.[62]

On the night of 24/25 June Bill Jameson and Norman Crookes had their first contact since the start of the invasion. But of course the key to obtaining a successful contact with an enemy aircraft was communication with the ground controllers. One such controller was A. J. May, who was operating in the western sector of the invasion area.

We had come to take part and now was our chance for we were very willing and able. We had a wonderful set-up in our mobile station and were itching to use it.

---

[62] *Defence Until Dawn – The Story of 488 NZ Squadron*, compiled by Flight Lieutenant Leslie Hunt, February 1949.

We controllers were waiting to see what kind of a picture we were going to get as the mechanics were setting it up and we were not disappointed. We could see the whole of the peninsula and way out across the sea to the east from where we assumed that any night attack would come. We took note of the daytime traffic, which showed up beautifully but this was not our responsibility. The more independent day fighters took care of that.

We had no means of identifying aircraft over here prior to intercepting them. Every blip was a Hun unless we could prove differently. We had no system as in England of the CH chain and sector ops, to refer to, not to mention MLOs. We would have to investigate every blip and we might find a German – we hoped so.

We were still mystified by the absence of the German Air Force. The fact that they didn't try to bomb the seventeen LSTs when we landed and nothing since was very puzzling. The mighty Luftwaffe of 1940 seemed to seriously have declined, was busy elsewhere, or was short of petrol. All these possibilities went through my and my companions' thoughts.

We had two night fighters call us during the evening of our first night, at different times. They came from Hurn near Bournemouth and stayed about an hour each. They belonged to 604 Squadron. We investigated quite a few aircraft but they all turned out to be friendly. We controllers were very keen to talk to an aircraft again and all had a spell. Unfortunately none of us picked a winner, better luck tomorrow night we thought.

So keen were we controllers that we wanted to be on duty all the time. Secretly I think we all wanted to be the first one to make a score, but this wouldn't do at all. Two would share the night on alternate nights to enable two to go to bed. This was very necessary if we were to be the smartest, most alert and ready for anything GCI station in the RAF and that applied to the crews as well as the controllers.

The Luftwaffe did show up at night in ones and twos, but they were very elusive and I think that too many did get home because we had to investigate everything showing up on the tube, owing to having no prior knowledge of our own aircraft movements. We did have nights when we were successful and our night fighters didn't all go back to England empty-handed. Our problem was always which to choose. We could be investigating one which turned out to be friendly when five miles away was another which could be a Hun, we could only do our best. Sometimes we made the right choice.

Jack Meadows DFC, AFC, AE flew Mosquito night fighters and describes the relationship between the controller and the night fighter crew over Normandy.

The procedure was basically the same before the invasion, operating from UK bases under UK GCI control, or on and after D-Day when first there were also three shipborne GCIs [the FDTs] and soon afterwards mobile GCIs landed which began operating on the continent. They moved up with the army and the same procedure applied right the way through until the end of the war.

Generally what we did was the same routine. We knew what we had to do, it was pretty simple. Whether it was just a routine patrol (usually) or a scramble to meet an attack for which there was no available fighter in position to be used, or a reinforcement needed, the procedure was the same and well known.

Immediately after clearing the airfield, airfield control told us to change over to another frequency. That would be sector control who would direct us, height, course, to our patrol area, or the scene of activity, and as soon as we were picked up on the GCI screen tell us, 'Call Marchbank on D Dog', or whatever.

'Marchbank', the GCI, would then give us instructions, height and heading. Assuming we would just be patrolling, we would then fly to and fro aimlessly as directed by it, waiting for something to happen. More often than not nothing happened and after a very boring, say two hours, they would say, 'Thank you Natty 27, steer xyz for home and call Woodrush on B Baker', which meant a replacement had arrived.

If we were lucky GCI would say, 'I have some trade for you' or, 'I have a bogey for you', 'Steer zero niner zero make angels fifteen', or whatever, 'target ten miles crossing starboard to port'. They would then continue to direct us, heading and speed and height, the aim being, ideally, to put us so that the target crossed ahead of us, and a few hundred feet above.

Or we might have a tail chase in which case we were told to use maximum speed to catch up. Woe betide the controller who put us in front of the target! A head-on interception was always, obviously, avoided. He bent us out and around onto a crossing position.

Meanwhile the R/O was looking frantically in his set to try and find a blip. He might pick it up as far away as five miles but, while telling his pilot of this, he would not take over until he was absolutely sure, from what he saw, and from what GCI control were saying, that he had got it properly and knew what it was doing. Then he would tell his pilot something like, 'OK I've got it' or, 'OK I'm taking over', 'it's four miles crossing now turn left, steady…'. The pilot would then say to GCI, 'Marchbank from Natty 27, Contact' and shut off radio reception so that no noise or other transmission would interfere with, or distract from, his R/O directing him. The R/O would then direct the pilot, perhaps continuing the curve of pursuit from a crossing target until astern, directing him into position a few hundred feet below dead astern. 'Left, left. Steady now. Left a bit. OK two miles. You aren't closing, more throttle, steady now, closing fast, too fast, one mile, left a bit that's it, now 60 degrees above dead ahead, closing slowly, half a mile, four hundred yards, right slightly, straight now, dead ahead three hundred yards 60 degrees above, slow down a bit', and so on until scanning the sky ahead, flying almost entirely by feel with occasional glances at the flying instruments, the pilot would see, exactly where he had been told to look by the R/O, perhaps a pair of pinpricks of light, exhausts, or even a dim silhouette against the stars, or against a cloud cover in which case it would be quite close before he saw the shape.

Once he had got it firmly fixed, and was sure he would not lose it, he would tell the R/O who would also look up to help identification, perhaps using night binoculars. On a dark night this was very difficult; all that there was to go on was a silhouette and the pilot would swing about a bit from side to side, making sure not to lose the target, nor to get too close and be seen by a nasty tail gunner who would not worry about identification, trying to get a bit of profile as well as the plan silhouette, until he was sure. On a dark night he would be so close he would then have to draw back to about 150 yards behind before opening fire.

Assuming he was then successful he would switch the radio back on:- 'Marchbank from Natty 27, Murder.' 'Well done Natty 27, make angels fifteen again, steer 270 back on patrol' or whatever.

So there it was, great teamwork. GCI controller to get us in the right place and height and speed for the R/O to pick up the blip, then between R/O and pilot to come in a little below and behind and complete the interception, then the identification.

On the morning of 25 June 1944, at 0225 hours, Bill Jameson, with his navigator/radar operator Norman Crookes lifted his Mosquito XIII from the runway at RAF Zeals. They flew on to Pool 2 and at 0305 hours 15081 GCI took them over, instructing them to patrol south of Bayeux. One interception was attempted on a target flying south but no contact was made.

Bill Jameson's combat report: At approximately 0400 hrs we were vectored onto another target which was flying due west, height given as 7,000 ft. Contact was gained at 3 miles range, 1 o'clock, 10 degs above, on target flying straight. We closed very slowly climbing gradually, using full throttle. IAS 270. While closing, small white flares were observed on our own level. Visual was obtained on two very bright exhausts, silver/white, which, on closing, was seen to be exhausts on each engine in approximately the same position as a Mosquito exhaust.

We closed in to about 300 yards and attempted to identify. At this time the enemy aircraft fired off another flare. The enemy aircraft was flying away from the dawn and looking through night glasses [the specially adapted binocular, making shapes more distinctive in the dark] my navigator thought it was probably a Mosquito; no resin lights [small dim lights on the wingtips of Mosquitoes], IFF or type 'F' were showing. We closed and coming underneath from the beam, at 100 yds range identified it as an Me 410 with L/R tanks outboard of the engines. We dropped back again to 150 yds, dead astern, where I opened fire with 3/4 second burst. I was at 6,000 ft altitude. Strikes were seen on the centre of the fuselage, and pieces fell away. The enemy aircraft continued straight and level. Two more half-second bursts from dead astern and more strikes were seen, with more pieces falling away. The enemy aircraft then dived steeply downwards, hitting the ground about 10 seconds later, with a vivid flash. It continued to burn on the ground. I landed at base 0523 hours.

Four nights later, 28/29 June, Bill and Norman would again engage the enemy. Taking off from Zeals at 2235 hours they arrived over Pool 2 at 2300 hours. They were then informed there were bogies due east.

Bill Jameson's combat report: I flew due east in the direction of flak which appeared to be coming from shipping just off the beach. Losing

> height to 5,000 ft I then patrolled as a free lance north and south and while again flying towards the flak, contact was obtained, range 3 miles starboard, at 2 o'clock, on the same level. I turned starboard, losing height slightly and then turned port, following bogey who was flying due east and weaving gently. A visual was obtained at 2,000 feet. 12 o'clock. No resin, no type 'F' and cockerel [IFF]. I closed in, to starboard to obtain the best silhouette.
>
> The enemy aircraft then appeared to see us. He throttled back and closed in rapidly to 75 yds directly below. Assisted by my navigator, who used his glasses, I identified the enemy aircraft as a Ju 88. It climbed steeply, at a low speed and I throttled back, pulling in to 100 yds astern and below. The enemy aircraft appeared to flatten out or stall and began to peel off. His nose dropped and he came into my sights. I gave him a one-second burst and observed strikes on the centre of the fuselage. He blew up and went into a spin, rolling over on his back and then going down vertically in flames. From the light of the flames no black and white markings were seen, but I did observe a yellowish colouring which may have been camouflage. Throughout the chase we were followed by flak from friendly shipping which caused a small hole in the fin of my aircraft.

This claim would bring Bill's total to five destroyed and one damaged. He could now be classed as a night fighter ace, but he wasn't finished yet. There would be plenty more action coming his way.

FDT 13

Flight Lieutenant R. J. Unstead, a controller in FDT 13, recorded in a diary his unit's role in the co-ordination with the Mosquito squadrons.

> *Sunday 18 June:* 2330 our Night Fighters (now supplied by 125 Squadron, Middle Wallop Section) arrived on patrol Goodwill 23 (CO controlling) destroyed 2 Junkers 88s, one at 2340, 25 miles north of ship, the second at 0005, a few miles away was seen to go down.
>
> *June 22:* During the night (22/23) activity started before midnight and we destroyed several enemy aircraft before it was fully dark. Night results: Fighters controlled 8. Contacts 29 Friendlies 14, enemy destroyed 5 Junkers 88, enemy damaged 1 Junkers 88 (shared by CO and Flying Officer Brown).
>
> At 2340 we were attacked by a Ju 88, which came in low from port side and dropped its torpedo which passed some 20-50 feet astern, due to the Captain putting us hard to port. All our guns opened fire. Attacking aircraft appeared to drop flares round us but is thought to have been destroyed a few minutes later by one of our own Mosquitoes.
>
> *June 24:* Night effort 24/25 Hun 10+, window to SE 2 Ju 88s destroyed (CO).
>
> *June 25:* Night effort Hun 10-15, 1 Ju 88 destroyed (Flight Sergeant Griffin).

Our night score 12 destroyed 1 damaged.

On 27 June FDT 13 sailed back to England, and the chance arose to meet up with some of the airmen they had been directing in the night aerial battle.

July 2 At Cowes: 3 members of 125 Squadron entertained on board including Flying Officer Grey who shot down 3 enemy under 13's control and a FAA crew attached to 125 who obtained 2 successes.[63]

---

[63] The papers of Flight Lieutenant R. J. Unstead held at the Imperial War Museum file p270.

CHAPTER 8

'THE UNEQUAL COMBAT IS NEARING ITS END'

At the American sector in Normandy, once Cherbourg was taken, the focus became to seize the line St Lô – Périers, prior to an advance south. This the Allies achieved ably supported by air power, mainly from American tactical squadrons, but calls were made on 2nd TAF when necessary.

The next major effort was to take Caen, in the British sector, which took place at the end of the first week of July, with the Allied ground element to advance at dawn on 8 July, preceded by bombing the night before. 2nd TAF weighed in; from 0455 hours until 2255 hours on 8 July, 83 Group conducted 766 sorties from France, with 116 sorties from 2nd TAF squadrons in England. On the second day of the offensive 170 sorties were flown from England, 490 from within Normandy. By the evening the whole of Caen on the north-west bank of the Orne was held by the Allies, but still the town was not completely in Allied hands. The expansion on the east flank of the Allied operations had faltered again and Montgomery would come under further pressure. Caen had to be taken.

Escorting the Heavies

One further important duty for the Allied fighter squadrons over Normandy was to fly escort to the daylight heavy-bomber attacks. A sight many would never forget. Major General Count du Monceau de Bergendal DFC and Bar took part in the escort of RAF Bomber Command heavy bombers to Caen and entered in his logbook: '2,000 tons on target or Air Power without tears.'[64] But despite the general absence of the Luftwaffe against the heavy-bomber attacks, there was still flak. Frank Mares DFM took part in a heavy-bomber escort on July 10 to Normandy, 'There was no fighter opposition but the flak became mercilessly accurate and very soon there was evidence that acts of war inevitably cost lives. On returning to base our hearts were heavily laden with deep sorrow.'[65]

By the middle of July plans were made for two major Allied offensive operations, Goodwood and Cobra, to try and break the German defences. Time was rapidly running out for Rommel's forces.

> Rommel's summing up of the situation on 15 July together with reports from lower levels and a covering letter addressed to the Führer by [Field-Marshal Günther] Von Kluge [who had replaced Von Rundstedt as C-in-C West], have fortunately survived from the wreckage of the German collapse in Normandy. Rommel begins, 'The situation at the front in

---

[64] Papers of Major General Count du Monceau de Bergendal DFC and Bar, IWM Con Shelf and 02/35/1.

[65] Papers of Frank Mares DFM held at RAF Museum Hendon.

> Normandy is daily becoming more difficult and is rapidly approaching a crisis.' 'Fighting strength was quickly being worn away and reinforcements were inadequate and slow in arriving,' he continued. The disruption of the railway system and the continued attacks on all road transport by Allied aircraft had paralysed the supply organisation. This was becoming worse as more airfields were constructed in the beachhead. The strength of the Allies was steadily growing; in these circumstances it was inevitable that the Allies would break through the German line – probably on the Seventh Army front – and thrust deep into France. No mobile reserve was available to the Seventh Army to prevent this. 'The unequal combat is nearing its end... I feel it my duty to express this clearly.'[66]

The Allied plans at this stage required the Second British Army to secure a bridgehead across the Orne at Vaucelles (Caen), but only if it was possible without undue loss. The British in addition were to press south towards Thury Harcourt – Mont Pinçon – Le Beny Bocage. But a reserve was also ordered of three armoured divisions to drive east of the Orne towards Falaise. The First US Army was tasked to drive south and east on the line Le Beny Bocage – Vire – Mortain – Fougères and on reaching Avranches, one corps to advance into Brittany, the rest of the force to sweep south towards Laval and Mayerne and onto Le Mans – Alençon. The Third US Army would then prepare to take the west flank, with airborne troops also to be prepared for a deployment in Brittany.

These plans caused great disappointment amongst air commanders, still clamouring for space in the east to build airfields and deploy squadrons, notably from 84 Group. Montgomery was under considerable pressure and planned operation Goodwood, which was designed to push through beyond Caen and gain territory south of there in the direction of Falaise. Eisenhower backed the proposal.

> We are enthusiastic about your plan. I think that Coningham has already given you the assurance you desire concerning air. All senior airmen are in full accord because this operation will be a brilliant stroke which will knock loose our present shackles. Every plane available will be ready for such a purpose.[67]

Montgomery called on the air forces in three main ways. To delay enemy reinforcement towards the lodgement area, to study the problem so that air could play its fullest part whatever the weather, and to provide the full weight of air power when called for. When the first part of this was translated through 2nd TAF to 83 and 84 Group operational orders the task was to hinder enemy movement across the Seine as well as the railways. On 17 July 83 and 84 Group was ordered to carry out armed recces over the area Le Beny Bocage – Domfront – Alençon – Dreux – Mantes Gassicourt – Quillebeuf. One of these paid particular dividends when Rommel was caught in a staff car by the RAF and seriously injured. He would no longer take any part in the direction of the land battle.

---

[66] Public Record Office AIR 41/67.
[67] *Ibid.*

The following table, which covers the period 1 to 18 July, gives a clear indication of the disproportionate contributions from the opposing air forces in the battle over Normandy.

July 1944	German Air Force aircraft Sorties	Actual Losses	Claimed Destroyed By Allies	Allied aircraft Sorties (Luftflotte 3 area)	Actual Losses	Claimed Destroyed By GAF
1	572	14	23	1,967	23	20
2	396	25	14	1,636	8	9
3	129	5	10	1,185	4	1
4	617	34	26	4,205	20	15
5	795	58	45	3,397	45	58
6	491	39	32	5,037	29	13
7	491	27	11	2,636	17	16
8	497	35	26	4,426	23	68
9	281	16	10	3,062	11	5
10	331	4	1	2,393	8	1
11	509	9	3	2,049	11	2
12	618	28	12	4,653	8	16
13	585	7	7	1,270	9	16
14	428	12	35	2,918	14	23
15	578	7	9	2,341	20	10
16	536	8	9	2,083	6	9
17	546	7	15	3,772	18	10
18	440	20	41	6,717	38	22
Total	**8,840**	**355**	**329**	**55,747**	**312**	**314**[68]

(From 1 to 11 July Fliegerkorps III also claimed to have destroyed 17 aircraft)

From the beginning of July until the middle of the month, Basil Collyns took part in six of the numerous armed recces carried out by 19 Squadron behind the front lines. The weather still hampered operations, but at every available opportunity 19 Squadron sent its airmen into battle. On 2 July Basil, whilst attacking bridges over the Orne, had had a near escape with light flak. He wouldn't take part in operations on 7 and 8 July, 19 Squadron had been released for maintenance on 7 July. On 8 July 19 Squadron carried out armed recces strafing a goods train, attacking buses loaded with enemy troops, as well as strafing lorries and a truck. Basil also missed out on the dive bombing of a German HQ south-west of Caen on 10 July. There was the occasional contact with the Luftwaffe, however, with two Me 109s being claimed on 8 July, and on 12 July Basil would enter in his logbook, 'Good fight with 16 Me 109s S of Cabourg.' On landing he would not be making any claims but other 19 Squadron pilots would claim two Me 109s destroyed and three Me 109s and an FW 190 damaged. All this without loss, although one pilot suffered slight head injuries.

On 15 July the Wing moved to B.12, Ellon, from which an armed recce was carried out that evening. That night would prove eventful.

68 *Ibid.*

> *19 Squadron ORB:* In the early hours of the morning (0300 hrs) the Hun artillery opened up with extremely accurate shell fire. This continued intermittently until 0400 hrs, by which time everyone was considerably shaken, especially as nobody had had time to dig slit trenches. Several of our tents were damaged by shrapnel but fortunately no pilots were damaged (not physically anyway), although three of our ground crew were killed and several others injured. When dawn came we discovered that we had only four serviceable aircraft left. The squadron was released for the day to enable maintenance to start repairing the damage and enable the boys to catch up on their sleep. Needless to say we changed our sleeping site to a much more pleasant and healthy spot some three miles from the drome.

On 17 July there was no flying and, in case of another bombardment that evening, the four Mustangs that were still serviceable were flown to B.6 Colombs, led by Basil Collyns. The Mustangs were flown back the next morning in time for him to take part in Goodwood.

The main requirement from the air in direct support of the army was for heavy bombing of positions on the flanks of the advance and fragmentation bombing in the path of the advance. Attacks on gun positions out of artillery range were also needed. Tactical support came from 83 and 84 Group squadrons in Normandy, to attack prescribed positions and operate a 'cab rank', patrolling fighter-bombers in radio contact with a controller on the ground, ready to respond to army calls.

Allied heavy and medium bombers attacked their prescribed targets, fighters gave their support and fighter-bombers attacked their targets. At 0930 hours on 18 July Basil, and his fellow 19 Squadron pilots, lifted their Mustangs from B.12 to give their support to the army, bombing the village of Garcelles to the south-west of Caen. The target was claimed as 'duly pranged'. And early in the afternoon 19 Squadron pilots (not including Basil) would operate again over the Goodwood battle area.

The main effort of 2nd TAF came from the Typhoons, flying 468 sorties in support of VIII Corps, 306 aircraft flying to prescribed targets and 162 aircraft on specially requested attacks. Other 2nd TAF squadrons sent pilots on armed recces behind the battle. 2nd TAF would record 833 and 1,943 sorties, ADGB 448 and 914 sorties on 17 and 18 July respectively. On the second day the fighter bombers kept up their support but on 20 July the advance was halted, much to the frustration of some of those in the Allied senior command.

> *AVM Strafford's diary, 20 July:* It appears therefore that the phasing over of further elements of 84 Group (and of elements of 85 Group and the Headquarters of the two Tactical Air Forces) will need to be phased-back as a firm date for a major enlargement of the bridgehead is not yet in sight.

Eisenhower wrote to Montgomery on 20 July:

> When the armoured divisions of Second Army, assisted by tremendous air attacks, broke through the enemy's forward lines, I was extremely hopeful and optimistic. I thought that at last we had him and were going to roll him up. That did not come about.... The recent advances near Caen have

> eliminated the necessity for a defensive attitude, so I feel that you should insist that Dempsey keep up the strength of his attack. Right now we have the ground and air strength and the stores to support major assaults by both armies simultaneously... Eventually the American ground strength will necessarily be much greater than the British. But while we have equality in size we must go forward shoulder to shoulder, with honours and sacrifices equally shared...

Tedder would be less diplomatic when he wrote to Eisenhower:

> It is clear that in the recent operation to the south of Caen there was no intention to make that operation the decisive one which you so clearly indicated as necessary in your letters and signals to General Montgomery. An overwhelming bombardment opened the door, but there was no immediate determined deep penetration while the door remained open and we are now little beyond the furthest bomb craters.

But attention on the ground would now shift to the American sector and the western flank, as they prepared their offensive, one which would finally break open the front in Normandy.

For the remainder of July, Basil Collyns would complete nine further operational sorties, fighter sweeps, armed recces and escorts. Weather would still hinder the number of operations 19 Squadron could carry out and their effectiveness. There was the occasional engagement with the Luftwaffe, however, and claims were made. On 25 July whilst on an armed recce two FW 190s were sighted in the Évreux area and bombs were jettisoned, but the 'Huns got away above cloud'. Then a further four FW 190s were sighted, having a height advantage of 2,000 feet, but the Mustangs climbed to attack. The extra fuel tanks were seen to fall from the German aircraft, but then it appeared to Collyns that two enemy pilots baled out and Basil would later report, 'They quit from sheer fright. They showed no fight at all.' But apart from the odd incident, the 19 Squadron pilots were unmolested as they bombed and strafed rail targets and enemy MT. Meanwhile there were significant developments on the Allied western flank.

A heavy-bomber bombardment and fighter-bomber attacks on the German positions opposing the Americans, on the morning of 25 July, launched operation Cobra. Then the American land forces began to advance. Little ground was gained initially but steadily the thin German crust was broken and the Americans poured on, supported by their fighter-bombers. In support of the advance Coningham ordered 2nd TAF squadrons to hinder movement from the British to the US sector. On 28 July American units reached Coutances and by 30 July Avranches.

Plans were also underway to go on the offensive again to the east, the 2nd British Army and 1st Canadian Army (now on the far eastern flank), to seize the Caen – Avranches road and the high land of which Mont Pinçon was the main feature. Again air power was called on when the offensive was launched on 30 July. Altogether 83 Group flew just short of 1,000 sorties, with some support from 84 Group. The next day 83 repeated a similar scale of sorties. 19 Squadron and Basil Collyns had played their part. Basil conducted his penultimate sortie of the month midday on 30 July attacking Coulvain, north-west of Mont Pinçon and some crossroads with 1,000 lb bombs. Basil would later be recorded in the ORB as saying the 'crossroads were well and truly plastered'. Then Basil's last sortie, a 1 hour 30 minute sweep, acting as top cover to 65 Squadron, of the Chartres – Dreux – Alençon area, the ORB recording, '19's part of the show was completely uneventful.' The next day 19 Squadron pilots would twice penetrate the airspace over enemy territory, without any sign of the Luftwaffe. Then at the start of August the squadron would initiate a series of attacks on a new kind of target, during which the chance for combat would arise, and Basil Collyns would be right in the midst of it.

Attacking German Transport

One of the major air contributions to the success of the Normandy campaign came from aerial attacks on the enemy transportation networks. The Allied heavy bombers carried out a very successful campaign against rail yards. In addition fighter-bombers fought to delay enemy reinforcement as it travelled towards the battle area.

On 18 July a message was sent to 151 Squadron, from the Headquarters of 10 Group.

> Operational Role of No. 151 Squadron: With effect from today, July 18 1944, the Night Fighter defensive role of No. 151 Squadron is to cease until further notice. No. 151 Squadron, which will be equipped with Mosquito VI Fighter Bombers will be employed in an offensive...

The next day George Kelsey and his pilot Barry Kneath found themselves detailed to take the offensive. George recalls the briefing as, 'Go on and get it.' They took off at 1440 hours, accompanied by another aircraft and crew, (Flying Officer Cox and Flying Officer Poole) detailed to 'seek and stop' a German Panzer Division reported as being en route by rail northwards to reinforce German troops in Brittany. Intelligence had not pinpointed the enemy position, but the instructions were to proceed southwards down central France and when east of Bordeaux, turn westerly and pick up the railway line running north.

> *George Kelsey DFC:* We were at super low level. Tree-top height all the way there. It was that sort of operation. You were flaked up when you went over every gun that was on the run. That's why our losses were so heavy on these kinds of ops. You were just like a pheasant being shot at with a shoot on. It was just like a firing squad really. There's no evasive action. If you're hit you're bloody well hit.

Eventually the Panzer Division was located in the railway station of St. Jean D'Angeley.

> *George Kelsey DFC:* I know it was St. Jean D'Angeley because we were flying so bloody low I could read the station name. We had eight 20 lb anti-personnel bombs and our number 2 had got some 250 lb heavies. These anti-personnel bombs, as soon as they touched the ground they would give a sideways blast and mow down personnel. Vicious blooming things.

After identifying the target by flying over it, the Mosquitoes went in to the attack. Barry Kneath went in first with cannon fire and when over the target released the anti-personnel bombs amongst the troops around the train. Cox did likewise with the heavy bombs. The Mosquitoes ran the gauntlet of intense medium and light anti-aircraft fire.

> *George Kelsey DFC:* We went in as number one and Barry was firing the guns and I let the bombs go. We were hit all over the place. We had shells through the main spar, both sides of the engine. We had one of the external wing tanks shot out. The starboard engine was hit and the cooling system. We daren't go back and have another look at it.

George recalled his feelings about attacking the ground troops.

> You are just doing your job and you might get killed. There's no hate in it at all. When you're hardened to it that's how you were. Young crews would come to the squadron and you would see them sit down writing their letters before their first trip. It used to make me shudder. And a lot of them didn't come back. It was bitter fighting this was. You had got to be experienced really to get round it. I knew where a lot of flak positions were and I could get my pilot underneath. You would fly under power cables and crazy things like that, look out of your window and see the tops of trees.

On 22 July 1944 George and his pilot would again have an unpleasant encounter with flak. George and Barry (accompanied by another aircraft) were detailed to attack railway targets in the Tours area of central France. They located a target at Château-Renault, but the guns failed. George sorted out the problem and they came in for a second attack. There had been no anti-aircraft fire on the first pass. That was to change.

Their aircraft was hit, the starboard engine set on fire by a direct hit from what appeared to be a large-calibre shell. At the same time the starboard wing was struck and twelve square feet of wing surface just disappeared. The electric compass was hit, and so was the instrument panel and the magnetic compass.

> *George Kelsey DFC:* Having been subjected to intense and accurate anti-aircraft fire on the 19th, just a few days previously, this second exposure to such severe conditions was of some concern. After we had been set on fire, and being at such a low level with part of the wing missing, and with the aircraft not being under proper control, the next few seconds were a nightmare. To realise that disaster had been averted, and that we were still alive is an experience difficult to describe. When we had climbed to about 1,000 ft, Barry said, 'Get your chute on, we may have to jump for it.' I clipped on my parachute, but after assessing the situation, I knew that if I jumped, Barry could not possibly get out because of the drag from the dead engine and damaged wing.

Fortunately the fire petered out, and just trailed smoke. To try and reduce the drag an attempt was made, without success, to feather the starboard airscrew. The full drag of the free-turning airscrew and the loss of part of a wing was placing considerable strain on Barry Kneath. So George took the knife from his flying boot, cut off his Mae West tapes, tied the rudder pedal and relieved some of the strain of flying the badly damaged aircraft.

They set course on what they thought to be a northerly direction for an emergency landing at the beachhead. However, without any compass they passed over St. Malo, receiving an unpleasant welcome from friendly fire. Having managed to reach 2,000 feet they decided to head across the sea for home, crossing the English coast in the vicinity of St. Austell.

> Barry Kneath again pleaded with me to 'jump for it'. Again I declined, since it was obvious that he could not possibly get the plane down on his own. I felt that if I stayed in the aircraft there was at least a fifty percent chance of survival for both of us.
>
> We arrived over base after a journey of 390 miles with our plane in this condition. Hydraulics had been shot-up, but operation of the hand pump enabled me to get the undercarriage down. We could only assume it was safely locked down. We could not get the flaps down so it was a high speed landing. We ran off the end of the runway into soft ground which stopped us fairly quickly, and after switching off and getting out of the aircraft, the starboard engine kept rotating for a long time on its own bearings. On the lighter side, the event was covered in the national press and brought in some interesting fan-mail.

197 Squadron carried out its fair share of operational duties in the last two weeks of July, although it didn't escape from the limitations of the poor weather. Derek Lovell took part in two close-support Ramrods on 16 and 17 July, 'N of Valognes. Bombed an orchard. Successful', and, 'W of Évrecy. Successful.'

> *Derek Lovell:* With regard dive bombing, you would fire your guns on the way down. You might hit something and it was a great morale booster (provided you didn't hit your number one in front). You would sight the target so that it was in your gunsight, and then lift up so the target was just at the bottom of the gunsight. At about 2,500, having armed your bombs, you press the button and feel clonk, clonk, as the bombs go off, and then heave back on the stick, you'd come down on about a third throttle. Full power and full rudder in one direction so that you skidded up. The theory being that any gunner aiming at you was aiming along the line of the aircraft and you weren't going that way you were going sideways. It worked for me anyway.

Although detailed to take part Derek missed out on armed recces in support of Goodwood on 18 and 19 July, 'aircraft u/s'. 'Hood u/s.' Morale was boosted when Winston Churchill paid 146 Wing a visit on 23 July, the airmen gathering round him as he gave an update on the war. 'Everyone was cheered by what he had to say', recorded Derek.

> *Flight Lieutenant H. Neville Thomas:* 'Winny' spoke well and wittily, though as usual he promised us 'only tears and toil', heartened everybody by his presence, as witnessed by the tremendous cheers given by the 'immaculate' assembly of RAF personnel.

The next day there was a change of CO for 197 Squadron, Squadron Leader Allan Smith arriving from 486 Squadron.

> *Allan Smith DFC and Bar:* When I arrived at B.3 in France to take command of the squadron they had a hard core of very experienced pilots. Some of the foundation members – Ted Jolleys, Jimmy Kyle, Len Richardson, and Gubby Allen – were reaching the end of their first tour. The bulk of the others had learnt operational flying under two very skilful wing leaders – Des Scott and Denys Gillam – as part of the Tangmere Typhoon Wing. They participated in the six months build-up to the Invasion where they daily attacked heavily defended targets in France, particularly radar stations, and gave active support to the D-Day landings. The end result was a highly professional group of ground-attack pilots with whom it was a pleasure to fly. I had previously only flown with New Zealand pilots and thought they were something special but my experience with 197 Squadron convinced me that high calibre pilots are international. 197 Squadron comprised Canadians (Plamondon, Wakeman, Hall, Reid, Jones), Australians (James, Welsh), English (Gilbert, Jolleys, Allan, Vance, Rook, Richardson, Lovell, Curwen, Harding, Rumbold, James, Matthews, Oury, Farmiloe, Bowman), Scotsmen (Kyle, Ellis), Irishmen (Byrne, Kilpatrick, Mahaffy), a Welshman (Price) and a New Zealander (Necklen). When I became better acquainted with them and their flying ability it amazed me that so many of these high-class pilots were NCOs, so after a short conference with 'ADJ' Whitear I put 10 of them up for commissions. Everybody told me I couldn't do this and would have to dribble them through two or three at a time but my argument was that they had earned their commissions a long time ago and I was going to fight to the death to get them approved. I must have convinced somebody because they were all approved.

Allan Smith was quickly into action with his new squadron, leading a Ramrod to an ammunition dump near Argentan. And for the rest of the month 197 Squadron sought out and attacked its designated targets.

> *Derek Lovell's logbook:*
> 24 July – Armed Recce. Successful bombing of a quarry.
> 26 July – Armed Recce. McFee led. Ted Jolleys forced down with engine trouble, own area.
> 27 July – Close support Ramrod. Cloud over target – prang not so good. Fontenay-le-Marmion [few miles south of Caen].
> 27 July – Close support Ramrod. Clear patch over target – wizard prang. Same target as above.
> 27 July – Close support Ramrod. Abortive. Weather u/s.
> 29 July – Close support Ramrod. Spare (Abortive, weather u/s).
> 30 July – to Tangmere. Home for '48'.

Derek returned home for two days leave; by this point he had notched up 34.10 hours on Typhoons. Flight Lieutenant Neville Thomas summed up the nature of 146 operations during July and the early part of August 1944.

> Strong points, S.P. Guns, Mortars, Tanks in woods, Observation posts,

Headquarters, Troop concentrations, Dumps and M/T – so ran the Army demands and all within our power fulfilled – day after day – in rising crescendo – but always accompanied by the hellish crackling cacophony of flak!

Yes, 'twas not always burning vehicles and running Huns but often burning planes, shattered planes, missing planes, weary pilots flying from dawn to dusk, weary groundcrews servicing aircraft before dawn and after dusk – planning, plotting, computing – 'hard tack' – little sleep – dust – dirt and flies – until – FALAISE!

August would be the decisive month in Normandy, with fierce fighting both on the ground and in the air, with our selected airmen in the thick of the action.

Capturing Enemy Soldiers

On 3 August 1944, 193 Squadron's Flying Officer Kilpatrick was shot down by flak near Vire. 146 Wing's Flight Lieutenant Neville Thomas would later recall his return to the squadron.

16 August 1944: Good news this evening. Flying Officer Kilpatrick of No. 193 Squadron returned after nine days on the 'wrong side of the line'... with a week's growth of beard and an even broader grin than usual. He had a great story to tell, which briefly is as follows:

His aircraft was hit by flak near Vire, and he force-landed half a mile on the wrong side of the line. By the time German patrols reached the point, he was hiding beneath one of their own tanks. He could hear the scraping of feet as the tank crew moved about inside it, but before he could move to a safer spot he was seen by other Germans coming along the road and taken prisoner. Each night for nearly a week he was taken further into enemy-occupied territory until on the sixth night, Allied aircraft dive-bombed the cluster of buildings where he was held.

The German guards were themselves in such a hurry to take cover that he had no trouble in gaining a ditch – where already five German soldiers were crouching. 'After a lot of argument I persuaded them that if, posing as my escort, they would see me through the German lines to our own, I would see that they were well treated,' he said. 'I was to take them over as soon as we reached our lines. During the night I managed to steal a German lorry, and we covered some distance towards Allied forward troops. The lorry let us down, so we set fire to it and started to walk.

'From some French people I discovered the exact position of our forward troops, and decided it was better to wait until they reached us rather than we should try to reach them. While we were waiting 22 more Germans located us and were persuaded to be "guards" on the same terms.

'I handed over my "escort" of 27 Huns to our advanced columns later the same evening and then hitch-hiked back to my own squadron. By that time I had covered about 250 miles and been away nine days.'

It's good to think that some of the Boys are getting away with it.

As the bridgehead expanded, the fighter control units were able to move inland, giving greater range at which patrolling aircraft could operate. Fighter controller A. J. May had been plying his trade from Quettehou on the east of the Cotentin peninsula. But with the whole area now in Allied hands a move to the western side, to Beaumont Hague, was made.

> *A. J. May, GCI fighter controller:* We were on the road very early and the trip went without a hitch. We were at our destination well within the time we had allowed ourselves to be set up ready for the night. Moving gave us a sense of freedom, and to me personally a sense of exhilaration. I liked being on the move and on such a fine morning as this it was good to be alive. Living out of doors in a tent gave a feeling of health and physical strength – sometimes the work set the heart beating faster too.
>
> As expected our new site, with the expertise of the radio mechanics, gave us a splendid picture of the PPI and we settled down hoping that the first night in the new location would be a lively one. We were very disappointed. Mosquitoes came over from Hurn and stayed an hour. One succeeded another and accomplished nothing. The part of the PPI looking out to sea was completely blank except for our night fighters who we could pick up many miles out to sea.
>
> We took the fighters over land and intercepted quite a few blips but they all turned out to be friendly. We were here to guard Cherbourg at night and who knows, perhaps Jerry would have a go at the docks tomorrow night. After all it was the only major port the Allies had.
>
> After a week or so in our new position we were very concerned that we were no longer participants in the war for liberation but only onlookers. We hadn't intercepted one German aircraft. We were stagnating in this far-away corner beside a road leading to nowhere. In addition to seeing no enemy activity we saw no American soldiers either, they had all been moved to areas likely to see action. It wouldn't have mattered our being isolated if our nights were busy but the German Air Force was not providing the expected opposition. They were infrequent visitors to the area around Caen and along the front line, which now extended to the west coast south of Barneville. The hope that enemy aircraft would be coming up to the top of the peninsula and out to sea was a forlorn one. Our CO requested a meeting with the Commanding Officer of 21 Sector and after putting our case it was decided that we should move to a more likely site.
>
> The day after the decision was made to move we were on our way and the destination this time was Barneville. No recce this time, we just upped and went. This small town is on the west coast of the peninsula on approximately the same line of latitude as St Mère Eglise and Utah beach, only a short trip which didn't interfere with our nightly readiness. We were wishing very much that this would be a more profitable site. Jersey was fifteen miles out to sea and at times quite visible. Still occupied of course but perhaps these brave people could soon be free.
>
> A road a quarter of a mile from the beach and running parallel to the sea was the main artery and the land on the sea side, just fields, sloped gently down to the beach. It was in one of these fields that we set up our

operational equipment and our camp was erected in an apple orchard on the opposite side of the road.

This site was going to suit us better than the last one and hopefully be more productive. Our field of vision was fifty miles in all directions and we hoped that the Germans would make a few sorties in our area during the night. 'Perhaps the Germans will evacuate Jersey by air at night,' suggested one of our officers. More in hope and jesting I think but what a prospect that would be . . . A few at a time and lasting all night. A dream of course for the enemy still had the sea routes should they wish to evacuate.

Business did pick up a little, we had a few successes but not enough. If we completed more than one successful interception in one night it was a cause for celebration. We worked very hard for our successes and scores amongst the controllers were about even. The CO would come into the operations wagon and even if it wasn't his watch would itch to take over if there was any possibility of enemy activity.

He was a first class controller as we all were. He could get the fighter in the right proximity to the bomber but he was impatient. With no 'contact' coming back from the fighter he would be asking, too soon I felt, 'Have you any joy?' meaning have you anything on your AI and he would persist with his any joy request so much that among the men his nickname was 'Any Joy'.

Our business at night could not be called brisk. Each evening we were ready, before dusk was upon us, to find the set working perfectly, the R/T OK and the men keen to make this a memorable night if given the chance, but most nights it was not to be. The Germans came only in singles and infrequently. They seemed to have no specific targets and were quite elusive. However our scoreboard was filling up and our morale was maintained. At night we practised with two Mosquitoes while waiting for enemy action, and sometimes in the afternoon when the squadron requested it.

Much of July had proved to be a fruitless month for Bill Jameson and Norman Crookes, but that changed on 29/30 July, the two men carrying out one of the most successful night sorties in the history of RAF night fighting. But it didn't start well.

Norman Crookes: We took off on 30 July at 0255 in the morning having learnt that the flight commander and my best navigator friend had been shot down that night over France [both men killed]. We were sent out to patrol initially over the Channel Islands. We knew this was a pretty duff patrol and strangely enough our contact with ground control was not at all a good one at that time so they transferred us to patrol over Normandy in the Coutances – St Lô area and . . .

Squadron combat report: . . . they then patrolled east to west. At approximately 0500 hours they were informed that there appeared to be trade approaching them and a vector of 100 degrees at full throttle Angels 5 was given.

Bill Jameson's combat report: I proceeded on the vector of 100 degrees at Angels 5 and the controller asked me to make my Turkey Gobble [IFF] and told me that he could not give me much assistance. I saw light anti-aircraft fire two miles ahead and almost immediately a contact was obtained, 0502 hours, range two miles, 10 o'clock height, 5,000 ft head on. I obtained a visual on a Ju 88 range one mile against the dawn, still approaching head on and at the same height. My navigator using Ross night glasses confirmed the identification. Meanwhile I turned hard to port after the enemy aircraft, following it by means of AI as the enemy aircraft skimmed through the cloud tops. I closed in to 300 yards range at full throttle as the enemy aircraft was then doing 260 ASI.

Meanwhile I saw a series of explosions on the ground caused I believe by the enemy aircraft dropping its bombs. Visual was regained in a clear spot (with no cloud) and I closed in and gave the enemy aircraft two short bursts from dead astern. Strikes were seen on the fuselage causing a fire there and in the port engine. The enemy aircraft went down through the clouds vertically and well alight and about 20 seconds later hit the ground with a terrific explosion. I reported the kill to Tailcoat and gave him a fix. The enemy aircraft was destroyed 5 to 6 miles S of Caen at 0505.

Norman Crookes: The enemy often took advantage of cloud but we could follow them on radar through it and it was a bit disconcerting for them to find us still behind them when they came out.

They had 'window', strips of aluminium foil that were meant to mess up the radar reception, but we could establish the difference between an aircraft echo and these strips of window and after a time you got to be able to distinguish quite easily. There would be lots of blips on the screen but there would be one blip that you could pretty well make out as an aircraft as opposed to the window.

Bill Jameson's combat report: When I was doing a port orbit over the scene of the kill much window was seen and a contact was almost immediately obtained, 0506, range 2 miles, 11 o'clock, height 5,000 ft. A visual was obtained very quickly on an enemy aircraft flying slightly above cloud. This aircraft was also skimming the cloud tops. I gave chase at full throttle to overtake. His speed was approximately 280 ASI. While giving chase another Ju 88 came up through the cloud dead ahead one mile range and flying in the same direction as the former aircraft. I closed in rapidly to 400 yards range and confirmed the identity of the aircraft as that of a Ju 88. The enemy appeared to see me and turned very hard port, diving towards a thick cloud layer. I followed on the turn and closed in to 350-400 yards when I opened fire from dead astern. Strikes were observed which caused a large fire in the starboard engine. The enemy aircraft now well alight disappeared vertically through the cloud. At this moment I saw two aircraft approaching me through cloud and as I was satisfied that the former combat had ended in a kill and that the Ju 88 would inevitably hit the ground, I did not follow but turned towards the two enemy aircraft whom I suspected to be customers. I closed in on both of them and identified them as Mosquitoes. Sub/Lt Richardson [a number of Fleet Air Arm aircrew were allocated to night fighting at the time] a navigator of 410 Squadron Jungle 33 confirms my first kill, having seen the enemy aircraft well alight and hit the ground, and he saw the second enemy aircraft well alight. I reported the second combat to Tailcoat. The combat took place 5/6 miles south of Caen.

Almost immediately after identifying the Mosquitoes referred to above I obtained a freelance visual on an aircraft 4,000 ft range, same height 5,000 ft crossing starboard to port. I closed to 2,000 ft dead astern and identified the aircraft as a Ju 88, the identity of which was confirmed by my navigator. When I was about 300 yards behind the enemy aircraft it dived steeply to port towards cloud. I followed and gave two short bursts and observed strikes from one of the bursts on the fuselage. The enemy aircraft took advantage of cloud cover and I followed with the use of AI, though it was taking violent evasive action and dropping large quantities of window. When we were almost at treetop height visual was regained range 4,000 ft dead astern. The enemy had ceased evasive action. I closed in to 250 yards dead astern and gave it a short burst from which strikes were observed. The enemy aircraft pulled up almost vertically and turned to port with debris falling and sparks issuing from it. The enemy stalled and then nose-dived into a four-acre field and exploded. The kill took place 5 miles S of Lisieux. I climbed to 5,000 ft, called Tailcoat, reported the kill and at my request was given a north westerly vector back to the scene of enemy activity. I once again saw AA fire ahead above cloud and I went towards it and at 0522 hours contact was obtained on two aircraft and much window a) at a range of 4 miles 10 o'clock b) 2 miles 10 o'clock. I decided to intercept the nearer of the two and obtained a visual dead astern at a range of 4,000 ft on a Do 217. The enemy aircraft must have seen me for almost immediately it dived into cloud and took very intensive evasive action and threw out large quantities of window for several minutes in cloud. I followed through cloud using AI and the enemy aircraft eventually straightened out at cloud base. Visual was regained at a range of 2,000 ft dead astern and below. I closed to 300 yards and fired a short burst. Strikes were seen on the fuselage, which began to burn furiously. The enemy aircraft turned gently starboard, pulled his nose up and the dorsal gunner opened fire, a wild burst which headed in the wrong direction. The enemy aircraft dived into the ground in flames.

Norman Crookes: We landed back when most of the others were asleep. But when we got up there was a celebration. We had claimed three and a probable but the probable was confirmed two or three days later.

But then tragic news would reach Bill Jameson, the death of his father. Having already lost a brother, the decision was made, following a request from his mother, for Bill to return to New Zealand to run the family farm. Bill had another brother serving with the RNZAF, 20-year-old Flight Sergeant Leslie Jameson. He would lose his life in a flying accident in October 1944.

Norman Crookes: The loss of his brother and death of his father had brought to an end a period in his life in which he felt he was doing something positive. I wouldn't use the term enjoying it because one didn't enjoy combat. One had to do it because it was part of the job and there was satisfaction in doing the job properly. Bill's intention was to stay in this country after the war and train to be a doctor, instead of which he was sent back. It was suggested that Bill should not do any more operational flying but he insisted on doing two patrols in early August.

And he was going to do all he could to make them successful. At 2325 hours on 3 August Bill and Norman took off from Colerne heading for Normandy. They reported to Pool 2 and were given a vector of 100 degs to a patrol line north of the beachhead area, and passed to another control.

Bill Jameson's combat report: When I was taken over by Yardley I was told to patrol north and south off shore of the peninsula. Yardley control then informed me that trade was approaching from the east and gave me two vectors of 140 and 200 degrees. Angels 7. Contact was obtained range 3 miles 10 o'clock, height 7,000 ft and the target was climbing. The target was also weaving and was dropping large quantities of window. I opened to full throttle and climbed steeply. I closed to 3,000 feet positioning myself well above as the target was travelling towards the moon and visual was obtained at 3,000 feet range against a background of white haze. I identified the aircraft as a Ju 88, which was confirmed by my navigator who was using night glasses for this purpose. I closed to 250 yards 10 degrees above when the enemy aircraft appeared to see me and began a turn to port. I opened fire at 20 degree angle off, giving a 1 second burst allowing deflection. Many strikes were seen on the cockpit and the enemy aircraft began to spin to port. I followed and fired another short burst but no strikes were observed. I pulled out of the ensuing dive and last saw the enemy aircraft spinning steeply down. Both my navigator and myself saw a large part if not the whole of the port wing break off and the wreckage burning below on the ground. I claim 1 Ju 88 destroyed.

On the night of 6/7 August Bill and Norman flew their last sortie together. The two men were airborne at 2150 hours again reporting to Pool 2. They were given a vector and handed over to Yardley control immediately on arrival, to be placed on patrol in the vicinity of Vire. Shortly after they were vectored south-east and turned to investigate a bogey flying north.

Bill Jameson's combat report: After several vectors contact was obtained range 3 miles 2 o'clock, crossing starboard to port. At the time of contact I was flying at Angels 7 and I opened up full throttle to give chase to bogey who appeared to be doing 280 ASI and was at this time taking no evasive action. I closed in very slowly to 1 mile range when bogey began to weave just as AA gunfire was seen. The bogey then began to drop quantities of window and on closing in further a visual was obtained on a Ju 88 flying directly towards the moon. Range 2,000 feet slightly below 6 o'clock. My navigator confirmed his identification. The enemy aircraft then started weaving violently. I closed in to 200 yards dead astern and fired a short burst seeing several strikes on the fuselage of the enemy aircraft. The aircraft then peeled off to port and dived very steeply jinking violently. I followed firing three short bursts and seeing many strikes from one of these bursts. The enemy aircraft continued to dive very steeply and turn hard to port disappearing under me. As I pulled up to avoid hitting the ground the visual was lost. We were unable to pick up further contact. I called control who told me that they could give me no further help.

Norman Crookes: This was a particularly tense flight. I knew that Bill was going back to New Zealand in two days time and he was determined that we should not let one get away if we came across it. So when we realised we wouldn't be able to claim the first Ju 88 as destroyed I knew that when we came across a second one, Bill would be determined that we should not let that one get away. It was quite an exciting chase I can tell you.

Bill Jameson's combat report: We returned to the Vire area and obtained contacts on two friendly aircraft. Later a freelance contact was obtained on an aircraft in window range 1½ miles crossing starboard to port.

I closed rapidly and obtained a visual on a Ju 88 with very bright exhausts well above. Enemy aircraft climbed very steeply and appeared to know that we were in the vicinity as he then dropped large quantities of window and commenced violent evasive action. I closed in to 200 yards range and opened fire with a short burst from which a few strikes were seen on the fuselage of the enemy aircraft. I received inaccurate return fire. Enemy aircraft then did a half roll. I followed down to 4,000 feet and gave it another burst from astern and below. Strikes were seen on the cockpit and starboard wing root and debris fell away as the enemy aircraft dived fairly steeply at a low speed straight into the ground. As he was going down I closed rapidly and flew alongside the enemy aircraft which appeared to be painted grey underneath. When the aircraft hit the ground it exploded and burnt fiercely. I claim 1 Ju 88 damaged, 1 Ju 88 destroyed.

The Bill Jameson/Norman Crookes partnership had ended. Flight Lieutenant Leslie Hunt would recall:

On the 15th the squadron said 'Goodbye' to Jamie [i.e. Bill Jameson] wishing him the best of luck and thanking him in their own way for his contribution to the success of 488. His stay had been all too short, due to the tragic circumstances which called for his return to New Zealand, but no-one will ever forget his charming unassuming manner and his desire to help the new crews.[69]

Bill would be New Zealand's top-scoring night fighter of the war, with eleven destroyed, two damaged. He was awarded a DSO. Norman received a bar to his DFC, but his operational experiences were not over. He would see more action, within days.

---

69 *Defence Until Dawn – The Story of 488 NZ Squadron*, compiled by Flight Lieutenant Leslie Hunt, February 1949.

CHAPTER 9

LOSS OF AN ACE

Operation Cobra broke open the western sector of the Normandy battle at the end of July 1944. American forces thrust forward and reinforcement came in to exploit the break out. Fighter controller A. J. May witnessed the drive south.

> Those nights not spent on duty were of course spent in bed and it was pleasant, reassuring and exciting to hear tanks rumbling south. Night after night it went on and we speculated as to how many there must now be in the assembly area. It was not long before we knew the answer.
>
> I was standing and waiting to cross the road to our camp when a young American soldier pulled up his Harley Davidson motor cycle and said to us, 'The General's in.' 'Which General?' we enquired. He said, 'Patton, and he spoke to us last night in Cherbourg and said in nineteen days I will be in Paris.' Having delivered his message and why to us I don't know, he was probably telling everyone, he shot off on his bike.
>
> Two days later Patton's Third Army broke out. It fought its way down the western side of the peninsula through Coutances, Granville and Avranches, where it turned left towards Paris and right into Brittany.

The Fighter Control Unit

A. J. May's fighter control unit followed behind the American advance to Avranches and beyond.

> We were instructed to follow and set up in Granville. We were good at this and delighted to be keeping up and took our gear to pieces as soon as dawn came up and were on our way by six a.m. Fifty miles we had to cover, find a site and be operational the same evening. All went well and we had no mishaps. Once or twice we were held up in traffic jams as there was great activity on this road...

Soon the unit arrived on the outskirts of Granville and moved to high ground to the south of town.

> We had chosen a good site for the GCI and the mechanics produced an excellent picture. On the first night here the Germans were much more curious than before, there had been bomb explosions and much Ack Ack fire and we in our ops room were very busy and successful. We intercepted and destroyed two of the raiders. I was not on watch but was happy for the controllers that were. The second night was not so successful. There was still a great deal of noise going on but we could only report 'contacts' and no kills.
>
> The third night war really broke out. The noise around us was intense and it was fortunate for me that I was on duty that evening and had two Mosquitoes under my control.

Quite unexpectedly, coming from inland, were a stream of aircraft and I tingled with anticipation at the thought of it being a strong German raid. The watch were on their toes as I directed one of the fighters towards a likely blip. We were all working very hard on speed, height and course to convey to the pilot and finally the turn in behind the bomber. The pilot came back very quickly with 'contact' and I turned to the second fighter who was ideally placed to join in and, following the same procedure, he too was soon in contact. The first fighter came back to me saying, 'I got that one, any more?' There were more and I selected another one for him and he, now very keen, was soon in contact with his second one of the night. The second fighter came back saying, 'That was good any more customers?' I chose another bomber for him. This time with an enemy aircraft in the latter part of the stream and he too scored again.

The invaders who had not been intercepted went out to sea a few miles, turned to port, lost height and disappeared from our screen. The raid died down as fast as it had started. Four successful interceptions in half an hour. This was the best night we had had in France. It was also the first night that the Germans had come into our area in strength and on a raid which appeared to have a specific target. They were we thought attacking the Third Army supply lines in preparation for what was to happen tomorrow.

On the morning after our most successful night, and after the coming of dawn, heavy field gun firing and exploding bombs were coming from a few miles inland, accompanied by much activity from our air forces.

With Avranches taken the way was now open to Brittany and its Atlantic ports, which Patton's Third Army exploited. But the American General also looked east, with a view to enveloping the German forces in Normandy. With the approval of his superiors, at the start of August, the envelopment that would seal the fate of the German forces in Normandy began. This move would be greatly assisted by a strategic direction from Hitler, who had decided to try and cut off the American units in Brittany by thrusting panzer divisions to take Avranches. C-in-C West Field Marshal Günther von Kluge, who now also commanded Army Group B, was extremely reluctant. Nevertheless on the night of 6/7 August XLVII Panzer Corps engaged the Americans to the east of Mortain.

During the first week of August the Allied fighter-bombers were deployed restricting enemy movement and barge traffic on the Seine, thereby hindering enemy troop movement to the battle front. Also 84 Group finally moved across to Normandy, and on 6 August the HQ was set up at Amblie. Some squadrons still had to remain behind, but by 7 August 41 squadrons of the 2nd TAF were deployed on 11 airfields.

When Derek Lovell returned to 197 Squadron from leave he no doubt picked up the latest gen on operations in recent days, notably those supporting the British Army push. On 2 August Derek witnessed this at first hand as 197 Squadron supported a 266 Squadron rocket attack which, according to the squadron ORB, 'had quite a field day with tanks'. 197 Squadron continued the aerial offensive against enemy troop positions over the next few days, and there was no mention in the ORB of any aerial opposition. Derek Lovell played his part, '3 August – Close support Ramrod. Attacked an ammo dump SE of Caen – good prang.' On 5 August two pilots returning from England were bringing a most precious cargo, beer in long-range tanks, the squadron ORB recording, 'but unfortunately one dropped off in the sea much to our disgust.'

On 7 August with the panzer counter offensive underway around Mortain, calls were made to 2nd TAF to support the IXth AF. 174 and 181 Squadrons were first into action shortly before 1300 hours and within an hour a shuttle service was pounding the German ground units. The Typhoons took full advantage of the Allied air superiority.

> Early in the afternoon the Seventh Army Headquarters had urgently requested General Bulowius to provide the XLVIIth Panzer Corps with the air support planned as the latter was being subjected to heavy fighter-bomber attacks. Bulowius replied that fighters of Jagdkorps II were over the battle at that very moment with instructions to hold off the Typhoons. Later that evening the Luftwaffe admitted that they had been so hard pressed by Allied fighters on taking off from their bases that the German fighters were unable to reach the Mortain area. Thus the arrangement made between the British and American Tactical Air Forces whereby the British aircraft attacked the tanks and the US squadrons held back the enemy fighters proved highly successful. The nearest point to the battle reached by the Luftwaffe appears to have been Couterne well to the east of Mortain and over 40 fighters were intercepted by the IXth Air Force that evening. Credit is also due to the VIIIth Fighter Command whose fighters were out in great strength during the day over German advanced airfields, around Chartres and east of the Seine.[70]

At 1940 hours the Chief of Staff of the German Seventh Army called the Chief of Staff of the Supreme Command West stating that the armoured attack had been at a standstill since 1300 hours due to the 'employment of fighter-bombers by the enemy and the absence of our own air support.' 197 Squadron and Derek Lovell continued to see action in the area, Derek recording in his logbook, '7 August – Close support Ramrod. Bombed a wood S of Vire. Strafed 4 M.T. 1 Flamer.'

Following the clashes of 7 August around Mortain, the situation eased over the next few days. In the meantime the US Third Army, sweeping east, were shifting the line of advance north to Alençon, and the British and Canadian armies were ordered to press on towards Falaise.

The Canadians were tasked to reach Falaise as soon as was possible and with this in mind operations Totalize on 8 August and Tractable on 14 August were initiated. In support of Totalize heavy bombers were once more called in on the night of 7/8 August, and the next day the ground troops moved off, with 2nd TAF in the morning attacking targets on both sides of the road to Falaise, and in the evening attacking gun positions and enemy reserves forming for a counter attack. 83 and 84 Group completed 200 sorties with only a few casualties. Yet still the

---

[70] Public Record Office AIR 41/67.

Germans resisted and on 14 August heavy bombers again bombarded their defences and again 2nd TAF flung its squadrons in to support. Finally on 16 August the Canadians entered Falaise.

On 8 August 146 Wing had thrown its pilots into the offensive, the Wing setting a record of 158 sorties flown. Derek Lovell took part, as his logbook testifies:

> 8 August – Close support Ramrod. Bombed at Chateau nr Gouvix – good prang.
> 8 August – Close support Ramrod. Bombed at Poussey – very good prang.

On 9 August 146 Wing (which, with the addition of 263 Squadron, then comprised five squadrons) maintained the offensive. The 146 Wing diary records the scale of effort.

Part One	**Statistics**		
Date	9.8.1944		
Missions	10		
Sorties	122		
Ops hours	96 hours 22 min		
Bombs dropped	110 x 500 lb = 55,000 lbs		
	485 x 60 lb = 29,100 lbs R/P		
Casualties	a) Aircraft		2 Typhoons
	b) Pilots		Flight Sergeant Green, 266 Sqdn [evaded capture]
Claims	a) Aircraft		
		Destroyed	Nil
		Probable	Nil
		Damaged	Nil
	b) Ground Targets		
		Flamers	10 M/T, 1 Tank, 3 AFV, 1 Excavator
		Smokers	5 M/T, 2 Tanks
		Damaged	14 M/T, 1 Tank, 2 Guns

Part Two Narrative

266 Squadron were airborne at the 'crack of dawn' looking for trouble on the roads, near Falaise. They found only scattered M/T and tanks and claim one tank damaged and one M/T destroyed.

263 Squadron followed them and claim two tanks 'smokers' and four damaged.

Eight aircraft of 257 Squadron were given two pin points 880430 and 883421 which were said to cover tanks and M/T. Though no movement was seen they claim all bombs 'hit the pin point'.

Reported tanks at 854414 were next for attention by 197 Squadron. No tanks were seen but the pin point was bombed. Pilots were rewarded by the sight of a very large explosion.

'Thirty plus tanks' moving into Falaise were attacked by Wing Commander Baldwin and 266 Squadron. They claim one tank destroyed and two 'smokers', one AFV and three M/T destroyed, two M/T 'smokers' and one damaged. To this they added a mechanical excavator and infantry and 20 M/T well strafed with cannon.

An armed recce near Falaise by 263 Squadron produced two M/T destroyed and two damaged. Another by 266 Squadron in the same area, scored two AFV and three M/T destroyed, one M/T smoking and three damaged and two HD Guns also damaged.

Thirty-one aircraft from 193, 197, 257 and 263 Squadrons, including Group Captain Gillam, dropped 52 x 500 lb bombs and fired 64 x 60 lb R/P into a village in which tanks were said to be concentrating (163481). One M/T was seen to be destroyed and a large fire started in the village from which dark brown smoke billowed, accompanied by a large explosion.

A 'Nebelwefer' position at 981479 was attacked by 15 aircraft from 263 and 266 Squadrons. The area was blasted by 112 x 60 lb Rockets, but nothing was seen of the NBWs.

Sixteen aircraft of 193 and 257 Squadrons, led by Wing Commander Baldwin, attacked mortars (T.805423) with 32 x 500 lb bombs. A large column of black smoke rose from near the edge of a wood at 811420 and 815420.

Into the second week of August 197 Squadron maintained its attacks on the enemy whenever and wherever they could find it; they answered numerous calls by the army to bomb specific targets, marked by red smoke, attacked enemy tank concentrations and MT, and a radar station on 11 August. Falaise began to make regular appearances in the Squadron ORB.

Watching the Enemy

One key advantage the Allies had, which was derived from air superiority, was the ability of their reconnaissance aircraft to range across the battle zone, unhindered from the air. Danny Lambros flew Mustangs with 39 Reconnaissance Wing and recalls one incident on 2 August, an example of the contribution of the Allied fighter-reconnaissance pilots.

> [It happened] just before we arrived in the area where we were supposed to carry out our reconnaissance, which was down towards Falaise. It was on a road running south and a bit west of the Orne river. Flying along around 3-400 feet, we looked at the road and there seemed to be transport under every tree. At least 20. So I called back to ground control and gave them the pin point as to where I was at – 20+ MT. I didn't have my camera on, I had flown by too quickly, so I circled round to the right and climbed a little bit to see better, and I got into position to take pictures. And suddenly all hell broke loose, almost in the next field. Flak was coming up, these tennis balls flying out and coming up slowly and then whizzing by. Anyway it was tanks, so instead of taking a picture of the MT I took pictures of this particular couple of fields. When I got back they were able to identify at least 60 to 65 tanks. So it was quite a find. The Tiffees [Typhoons] came down right away, and I found out later that they had destroyed something like 37 tanks, and a number of MT. That night after I had

gone to bed they woke me up and said they wanted to see me at the mess. I went over and apparently General Dempsey had sent a telegram congratulating the Wing on the find that particular day so we had a couple of drinks celebrating.

A couple of days later it was almost déjà vu, except just a little further south, near the town of Vassy. I saw MT first and thought well I'd better take a look around, which I did and they gave themselves away, firing. Again the Tiffees did very well.

During the first week of August 19 Squadron had spent most of its time acting as escorts to bombers and operating against barges and tugs on the Seine, hindering the movement of enemy reinforcement from the north. They experienced little opposition from the Luftwaffe until 8 August when, following an attack on barges, 12 Me 109s and 13 plus FW 190s were seen and 'immediately attacked and clobbered'. 19 Squadron would claim four Me 109s destroyed with no loss. Basil Collyns had not been on operations since 30 July, but on 9 August he would get back into the action on the third 19 Squadron sortie of the day, all three being to attack barges. Just off Caudebec the 19 Squadron pilots released twenty 500 lb bombs on 12 barges. The pilots then swept on to carry out an armed recce in the Chartres – Dreux area. At approximately 1800 hours, from 3,000 feet Flying Officer Plumridge sighted two enemy aircraft at two o'clock, heading east on the deck.

Basil Collyns' combat report: I dived down with my section and intercepted one FW 190 which had turned and was flying west. I attacked at ground level firing a burst from a range of 300 yds with 5 degrees deflection and the enemy aircraft pulled up and stall turned. I fired a burst whilst he was turning and saw strikes. Following him round and still firing, I saw more strikes. The FW 190 then pulled to stall turn a second time and I got in a good burst at 75 yards range seeing him turn on his back, hit the ground, and explode. My Commanding Officer and my No. 2 confirm this. I claim one FW 190 destroyed.

The squadron reformed and started for base and about three minutes later the CO reported two enemy aircraft passing underneath in the opposite direction i.e. on an easterly course at zero feet. We turned 180 degrees starboard and as I dived to attack I saw six FW 190s flying line abreast on an easterly course. I selected enemy aircraft No. 2 from the starboard side and fired a long burst from line astern at 300-100 yds range seeing numerous strikes. The hood together with other pieces of the enemy aircraft flew off and the machine commenced smoking. I flew abreast of the enemy aircraft and saw the pilot remove his helmet and undo his strap. My No. 2 Warrant Officer Larson fired from line astern, 150 yds range, the pilot baling out and the enemy aircraft crashing in flames near Chartres. I claim half of one FW 190 destroyed.

In addition to Basil's claims two further FW 190s were claimed destroyed. Flying Officer Plumridge had latched onto one:

Flying Officer Plumridge's combat report: Rapidly registering strikes

> with intermittent bursts. Coming into line astern I gave him a good burst from 300 yards and saw his hood fly off. Several other bits came away from the enemy aircraft and this moment my guns jammed. I pulled up level with the FW 190 and saw that the pilot had slumped sideways in his cockpit. The enemy aircraft then nose-dived and crashed in a wood where it burst into flames. This is confirmed by Flight Lieutenant Collyns. I claim 1 FW 190 destroyed.

Flying Officer Clayton would be credited with the fourth FW 190 destroyed.

On 10 August Basil would again take part in one of three bombing missions against barges on the Seine. Over the next four days he would complete five sorties as 19 Squadron maintained their attacks on the Seine, and carried out armed recces. There were losses; on the 11 August morning mission one Mustang was downed by flak, the pilot evading capture, and in the afternoon one Mustang was seen to blow up in mid-air prior to the bombing, the pilot fortunately surviving. On one mission the next day the squadron was attacked by Lightnings, fortunately with no one hit. On 13 August following the one mission of the day the squadron was released for maintenance until the afternoon of the following day. Some of the pilots took the opportunity and 'mounted jeeps and scudded to Agy where welcome coolth [sic] was obtained in a very pleasant pool. Led by Flight Lieutenant Collyns a section swam upstream a way but Flying Officer Staples fouled a fishing line and the section returned to the pool.' A no doubt refreshed Basil took part in both missions the next day, and on the second, 'Once more the Yanks had a swipe at "19" with no ill results to the Sqdn. "Bigger and Better Roundels"!' The next day though it would be the Luftwaffe who would have a swipe at 19 Squadron, Basil Collyns entering in his logbook for 15 August, 'Terrific Battle.'

At 0743 hours that day, 19 Squadron pilots lifted their Mustangs from B.12 detailed for an armed recce in the Lisieux – Bernay – Dreux area. At 0815 hours in the vicinity of L'Aigle, at 4,500 feet, 80 to 100 FW 190s and Me 109s were reported approaching 500 feet above them.

> *Squadron Leader Loud's combat report:* I immediately climbed and got into the sun above the enemy aircraft and then dived to attack as they turned 180 degrees to starboard. As we engaged the 80/100 enemy aircraft I saw approximately a further 70 more 109s and 190s flying north-west at 10/15,000 feet. These enemy aircraft were carrying long-range tanks.
>
> My section attacked the first formation (i.e the 80/100 enemy aircraft). Green section engaged some of the lower aircraft of the second formation (i.e. the 70 enemy aircraft) and White section climbed to engage the top of the second formation. I got on the tail of an Me 109 and opened fire at about 500 yards closing to 200 yards – firing a three-second burst from dead astern. A lot of pieces fell off the tail of the Me 109 and a few seconds later it began to smoke and I saw flames coming from beneath the aircraft. By this time we were at zero feet and I turned to attack an FW 190, but unfortunately when I got onto his tail all my guns jammed. I broke off the engagement and set course for base.
>
> I claim 1 Me 109 destroyed.

Basil Collyns was flying White 1 and had climbed to engage the formation flying north-west.

Flight Lieutenant Collyns' combat report: In the general mêlée that followed I got my sights on to an FW 190 and fired a short burst from about 300 yards with about 20 degrees port deflection. I saw strikes on the port side of the enemy aircraft and observed smoke coming from it. As it pulled violently up I looked back and saw another firing at me and with my No. 2 I broke away.

Continuing to engage the enemy aircraft, with my No. 2, I flew straight through 10/15 plus FW 190s and milled around with these – rapidly losing height. I fired 2 two-second bursts at an FW 190 at deck level from 6/800 yards dead astern. I saw a few strikes but had to break to port with another Hun on my tail. I saw two fires burning in a wood west of Conches a/d about 600 yards apart on the area of the combat.
I claim 2 FW 190s damaged.

Pilot Officer Glanville, also of White section, would later make a claim too.

Pilot Officer Glanville's combat report: White section led by Flight Lieutenant Collyns, engaged eight out of a number of 109s. White leader dived on four and I singled out the other four. Going into the attack I fired a short burst at the 2nd Me 109 from the left at about 400 yards range with 20 degree deflection. I saw strikes on the port wing root, but was forced to break off the engagement as twelve 190s were diving on me from above. Making a full 360 degrees turn I got on the tail of a long-nosed FW 190 but again had to break off the attack as six enemy aircraft were uniting to come down on me. I claim 1 Me 109 damaged.

And 19 Squadron would make one further claim.

Pilot Officer Sima's combat report: After I heard the CO say that his guns were jammed he told me to join White 1 and 2 who were circling above a gaggle of 190s. I saw three 190s diving towards the deck at 10 o'clock, going east, and I chased them with my No. 4. One broke right, one left, and I followed the middle one chasing him flat out on the deck for about 5 minutes. I fired several short bursts at him from about 400 yards dead astern and saw strikes on tail-end of fuselage. I saw black smoke coming from him and fired again, but this time saw no positive strikes. By this time I had expended all my ammo so was forced to come home. I claim 1 FW 190 damaged.

So with claims for one destroyed and four damaged 19 Squadron could feel fairly pleased with its pilots, but there was little time for self congratulation as the squadron prepared to send the pilots out again that morning on another armed recce and sweep, Dreux – Mantes Gassicourt – Bernay. At about 1240 hours, just north of Dreux, the message came through that 122 Squadron was engaging 109s over Dreux aerodrome. Basil Collyns would for the second time that day engage an enemy pilot.

> *Flight Lieutenant Collyns' combat report:* My CO ordered 19 Sqn, to climb hard and turn to port. White section, on the inside of the turn, had turned about 180 degrees port when three Me 109s attacked from 1,500 feet above. A dogfight ensued and one Me 109 dived off in a south-easterly direction, at very high speed with emergency boost smoke pouring from his ports. I dived after this enemy aircraft but found I was not overtaking it so I fired a three-second burst at 800 yds from direct line astern. I saw an explosion that looked like the enemy aircraft blowing up and I then started to climb. My No. 2 saw this enemy aircraft going down vertically with black smoke pouring from it. I did not see this 109 strike the ground. I claim 1 Me 109 probably destroyed.

On the ground, with Americans to the south-east, south, and west, and British and Canadians to the north, what became known as the Falaise pocket was forming, and the gap for any German retreat to the Seine was steadily constricting. Now the Allies made every effort to close this gap. The Polish armoured division, part of the Canadian 1st Army, crossed the Dives and pushed south to join with US units in the Argentan area. With the situation apparently hopeless for the German forces in the pocket, Von Kluge ordered a retreat and as his forces streamed back in the direction of the Seine the Allied ground forces strived to shut as much of the enemy in as possible. On the evening of 17 August pilots of 2nd TAF sighted hundreds of vehicles on roads to Chambois and Trun and the Allied tactical air forces tore into them.

The flying weather for 18 August was excellent for fighter-bombers, and that morning small units of enemy transport were attacked on the roads to the Seine from the neck of the pocket. On the Seine itself 83 Group claimed ten barges sunk and two steamers, carrying retreating forces.

Then in the afternoon convoys of approximately 400 vehicles were seen heading for Vimoutiers. Allied artillery pounded away and with the gap narrowing the Germans had to keep on the roads during daylight, to try and escape before the trap snapped shut. By 1700 hours enemy tanks and transport were grouped outside Vimoutiers. 2nd TAF seized the chance.

> Never before had the pilots seen so many targets and they were able to attack them with comparative immunity. The photographs which they took were ample proof of the high claims they made. Road blocks were formed by blazing trucks and the drivers either abandoned their vehicles or drove off across country to find shelter in the woods; others turned back vainly endeavouring to discover a safer route. Some troops even spread out white flags on their vehicles. The area between Trun and Chambois where these attacks by fighter-bombers were made became known as the Shambles. Investigators, after the battle, counted over 3,000 motor vehicles and about 1,000 horse-drawn carts and wagons which were either destroyed by Allied air and ground attacks or else abandoned and set on fire by the enemy.[71]

At the end of the day 2nd TAF would claim 1,304 vehicles and 110 tanks destroyed (the majority attributable to 83 Group) but with such an intensity of

71 Public Record Office AIR 41/67.

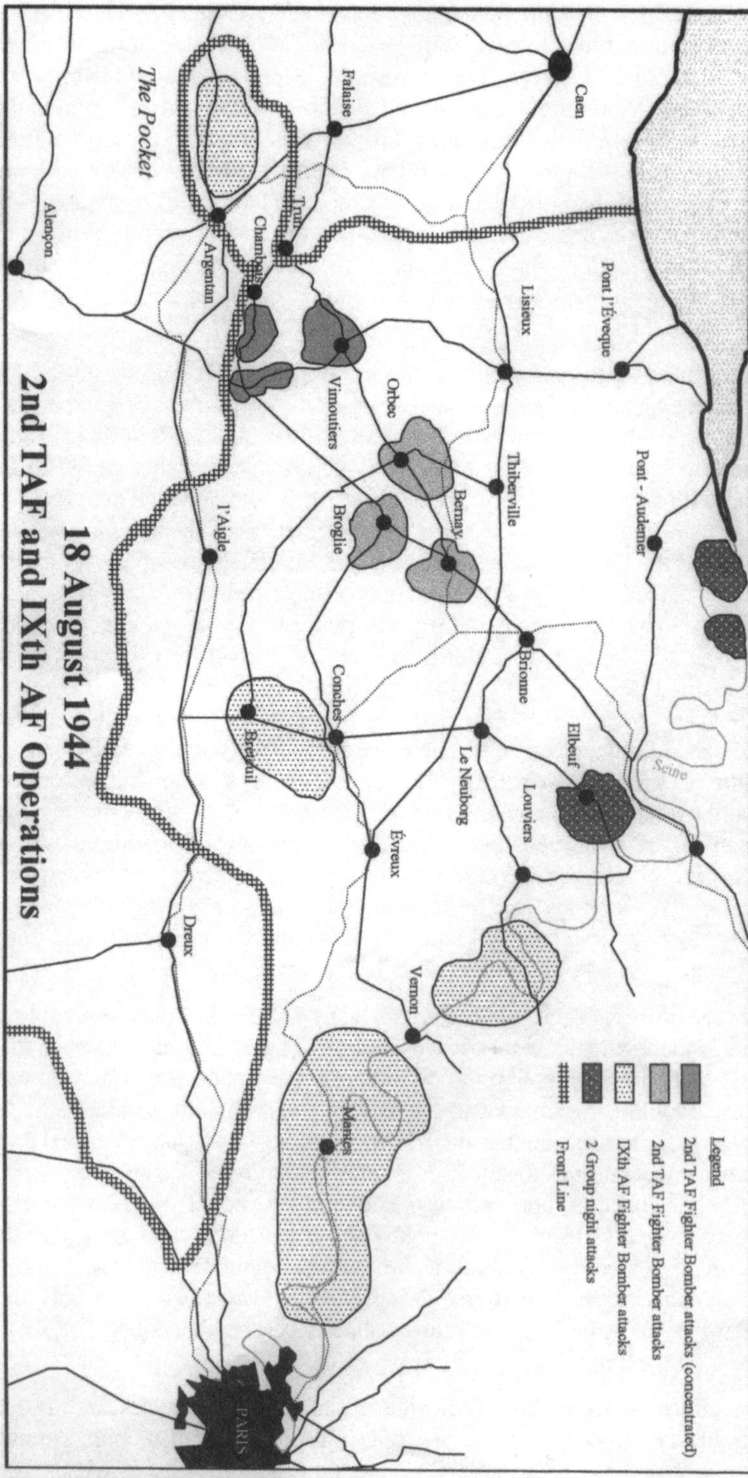
18 August 1944
2nd TAF and IXth AF Operations
Legend
2nd TAF Fighter Bomber attacks (concentrated)
2nd TAF Fighter Bomber attacks
IXth AF Fighter Bomber attacks
2 Group night attacks
Front Line
Caen
Falaise
The Pocket
Trun
Chambois
Argentan
Alençon
Pont l'Évêque
Lisieux
Vimoutiers
Orbec
Thiberville
Pont - Audemer
Bernay
Broglie
l'Aigle
Brionne
Conches
Breteuil
Elbeuf
Seine
Le Neubourg
Louviers
Évreux
Dreux
Vernon
Mantes
PARIS

low flying it came at a cost, 83 and 84 Group losing 17 and 8 aircraft respectively. That night 2 Group kept up the bombing and the next day 2nd TAF showed no mercy, with over 1,000 sorties flown, 649 vehicles and 51 tanks claimed destroyed, for a loss of 15 aircraft. The next day the gap was closed.

General Hans Eberbach, Commander Panzer Group West and Fifth Panzer Army, would later confirm to his post-war interrogators that:

> We [i.e. the Allies] had actual superiority, despite their [i.e. the Germans] plans and promises, as we were capable of air reconnaissance, therefore we had the weapon of surprise. We could also control our artillery from the air. Our aircraft inflicted terrific losses. The whole air situation had a depressing effect on the morale of the troops. We could stop or make very doubtful any concentration on their part for attack. They were confined to night movement and day movement only in bad weather. This meant they could carry out movement in only six to eight hours in summer and could move only one-third as fast as we could. Reinforcements were delayed and critically reduced.[72]

Two of our featured airmen, Derek Lovell and Basil Collyns had been part of the air action over the Falaise pocket. On 13 August 197 Squadron only conducted one operation, 'as the heavies were pounding the Huns who are now more or less caught in a sack.' But the next day 197 added its weight to the attack on the enemy concentrations near Falaise. On 15 August came a change of target as aircraft were despatched to attack barges on the Seine. Later in the day the squadron returned to the attack on enemy positions near Falaise.

> *Derek Lovell's logbook:*
> 14 August – Close support Ramrod. Bombed an orchard to clear way for Army attack.
> 15 August – Ramrod. Bombed + strafed barges in the Seine – 3 sunk.

On 17 August 197 Squadron continued the offensive, four Rhubarbs in the afternoon, then an armed recce during which one aircraft was hit by the explosion of a truck, the pilot seen to bale out but too low for his parachute to open. The Luftwaffe also engaged 197 Squadron, one Me 109 claimed damaged. That evening four Typhoons with 1,000 lb bombs, and four more Typhoons acting as cover, bombed a road at Vimoutiers 'important to the Hun retreat.' The next day 197 Squadron went on the search for enemy transport, with some success though one pilot was lost. The squadron also completed a successful attack on a railway tunnel near Beuzeville. In total 197 Squadron conducted 35 sorties and 146 Wing 160.

> *Derek Lovell's logbook:*
> 17 August – Rhubarb. With McFee as No. 1 – very little seen. I destroyed 1 car & 1 D.R. [Despatch Rider].
> 17 August – Close support Ramrod. Bombed a road into Vimoutiers (important). Good prang.
> 18 August – Armed Recce. Searching for transport in Vimoutiers area – no joy.

---

[72] German General interrogations, Public Record Office files WO 205/1020 to 1022.

But all this success was coming at a price.

Derek Lovell: There was a lot of flak when you got the other side. It was quite intense the whole time. After we got to Normandy and the village of Bretteville had been taken, at which we had had a lot of trouble, intense flak, we found these multiple 20mm guns just outside the town, abandoned. And very primitively we all stood round and peed on them. Very symbolic. We didn't lose as many as the rocket squadrons. Dive bombing you're coming in at 450/500 mph and you are in a steep dive, and you're pulling up at 550, so you are in and out bloody fast. You put up a sort of barrier against the losses. You had to.

This would be Derek's last action over Normandy, as he was now given seven days' leave, returning on a Dakota to England on 21 August. 146 Wing and 197 Squadron kept up the offensive, with numerous armed recces, fighter sweeps and attacks on barges. But late on in August the airmen had to put up with suffering of a different nature.

Derek Lovell: We were all having trouble with diarrhoea. They divided the wing up, not into squadrons, but into those who had bad diarrhoea and couldn't go anywhere. Those who weren't too bad and might last twenty minutes and those who didn't have it would do the longer shows.

But during August 1944 as the German Army was routed from Normandy, 146 Wing could claim considerable success.

146 Wing's claims for the month of August

	Destroyed or Burning	**Damaged**
Aircraft	0	3 x FW 190
Tanks	40	36
AFVs	13	21
M/T	223	242
Barges	16	36
Guns	3	0
Railway trucks	12	0

Rain put paid to any 19 Squadron operations from B.12 on 16 August, but the next day Basil Collyns participated in one of the two 19 Squadron armed recces that left enemy transport smoking and one motor cyclist chased off his bike. On 18 August he went on one of the two dive-bombing missions attacking barges on the Seine. Then that afternoon Basil and his squadron colleagues took part in 19 Squadron's 'greatest MET strafing expedition – the long awaited chance had arrived'.

19 Squadron ORB: German transport was pulling out of the Vimoutiers area, and 19, like all other squadrons in Normandy, sailed in and dealt Von Kluge's elements a mortal blow. A total of 21 MET destroyed and 17 damaged was obtained on this one sortie. It is with great regret that we record that Flying Officer Glanville and Flying Officer Connor did not return from this mission. Flying Officer Connor was thought to have been

> hit – he lost height and crashed into a house [being killed]. Flying Officer Glanville went off into cloud on his own and we have no idea as to his mishap – we hope he is OK [hit by flak and survived].
>
> From 1710 hrs until dusk the Sqdn went out in pairs & fours to bash the retreating Hun and ended the day with 38 MET destroyed, 11 smoking, and 42 damaged. Great show '19'.

Basil would recall his feelings on the carnage he and his squadron colleagues were inflicting upon the enemy, 'It was just slaughter. I have never been so near being sick in my life.' There appear to be mixed feelings from those who took part in fighter-bomber ground attacks. Some like Basil found it disturbing. Others revelled in the chance to see and attack their enemy.

> *Rod Davidge, 193 Squadron:* I delighted in it. They were Germans and it was a feather in my cap. I was beating up a tank one day, of course they didn't see me coming. The German had his girlfriend on the back and on the other side of the tank was a cow. I felt for the cow.

Many pilots would not forget the sights around Falaise in the second half of August 1944. Rod Davidge was one of those able to witness the aftermath of the carnage on the ground.

> Bill Switzer got shot down [by flak on 15 August 1944 near Argentan], and I knew where he'd landed or close to where he had been shot down, which at the time was behind enemy lines. So when we liberated Falaise I took a Jeep and went looking for him. When we got to Falaise, well, there were horses all bloated, dead Germans all bloated. The guys on the bulldozers had gas masks on and they were digging holes and shoving these horses and Germans in.

On 19 August 19 Squadron continued to harass the retreating Germans with Basil flying in two of the missions. By the end of the day the squadron would claim 27 – 3 flamers, 12 smokers and 12 damaged. Two Mustangs were lost to flak, one pilot baled out and landed on friendly soil and returned to the squadron later that day. Flight Lieutenant Wood lost his life, although it was initially reported that he had landed safely.

On 20 August 19 Squadron once more threw its pilots into action although the number of available aircraft was diminishing owing to the high sortie rate of previous days. Late that evening 19 Squadron took off to conduct what the ORB would describe as the 'most successful fighter sweep to date.'

> *Wing Commander Johnston's combat report:* I was leading the wing on a fighter sweep of the Paris area, when NW of Meux, Huns were sighted almost at deck level flying NE. The whole wing attacked simultaneously and I led my section in pursuit of four FW 190s flying NE at zero feet. Opening fire on the left-hand Hun to slow him up at 700 yards range I saw one strike and the Huns pulled up and entered a small cloud at 5,000 feet. An amusing but rather ineffective hunt started in and out of cloud, which I had to terminate when I heard Sifta leader in trouble. He was found near the scene of the original sighting engaged in a turning match with two FW 190s. This was split up and I saw one FW 190 destroyed. I then ordered

all pilots to return to base. I claim 1 FW 190 damaged.

Flight Lieutenant Taylor's combat report: I was flying Jamjar 4. When the dogfight started Jamjar section led by W/Cdr Johnston attacked two FW 190s at zero feet. They climbed into cumulus cloud at 5,000 feet. The section orbited the cloud waiting for the enemy aircraft to reappear and attacked each time they reappeared. I selected a 190 when it appeared and closed to 300 yards opening fire from dead astern. As I closed to 50 yards the enemy aircraft went into cloud again but, continuing to fire until I lost sight of it, I saw strikes on the starboard wing. I broke upward into cloud and as I came into clear sky I saw the enemy aircraft breaking cloud about 500 feet below me. I went down on him as he started a gentle turn back into cloud opening fire again at approx 300 yds. I fired a steady burst and closed the range rapidly, and observed pieces fly off him as he went into cloud. I followed right through the cloud emerging about 40 yards from the enemy aircraft which was now on my port side. He entered a large bank of cloud almost immediately and I lost him completely. However in this short space of time I could see that something approx 4 feet long was hanging beneath the fuselage of the FW 190.

I claim one FW 190 damaged.

Warrant Officer Carson's combat report: I was flying Jamjar 3 and we were flying south when near Meux, FW 190s were reported heading NE on the deck. I broke round and followed the starboard two of four FW 190s. I opened fire at long range on one of them to make him turn but observed no strikes. One of the two FW 190s broke to port and the other climbed towards some clouds. I chased this latter 190 into cloud, firing intermittent bursts from approx 500-300 yards range and saw strikes on the starboard side of the fuselage. I had to finish the engagement because the wing was ordered to reform.

I claim one FW 190 damaged.

Meanwhile White section, led by Basil Collyns, was also in action. Basil sighted four FW 190s low down and took his section into the attack.

Flight Sergeant Abbot's combat report: I was flying White 4. We were just north of Paris and flying at 6,000 feet, beneath 65 Sqn, when No. 1 informed us that there were some FW 190s flying deck level at 9 o'clock. We were instructed to go down and make individual attacks. I selected an FW 190 and approached him from dead astern. He came within my sights at about 800 yds but I held fire until I was within 4/500 yds. At this distance I opened fire and held the burst until I was within 200-250 yds of the enemy aircraft. The FW 190 turned port during the attacks and whilst allowing between a half and three quarter deflection I noticed numerous strikes on the fuselage of the 190 from the engine to the tailplane.

At this moment our section were instructed to break as more FW 190s were coming in behind us. I pulled up immediately into a 90 degree bank to port and whilst making this bank the FW 190 must have crashed and hit the deck because I saw the burning scattered remains immediately beneath me. I did not see the 190's actual impact on the ground.

I claim one FW 190 destroyed.

Flight Sergeant Wells' combat report: I was flying White 3 . . . whilst at 6,000 ft, Huns were reported flying on the deck at 10 o'clock. White section immediately turned port and I saw four 190s. We bounced them from behind and I saw two FW 190s crash and burst into flames.

At this moment I looked behind and saw an FW 190 coming at me from a height of 2,000 ft. I broke and in one and a half turns got on to his tail. The enemy aircraft dived to ground. As he was doing so I got in a burst at 300 yds range with just over a ring's deflection and saw strikes just behind and below the cockpit with further strikes at the wing root. I claim this enemy aircraft as damaged.

Another FW 190 was coming up behind me so I had to break [off] this engagement and lost sight of the enemy aircraft I had hit. I then sighted another FW 190 which was diving down from a height of 1,000 feet and heading away from the scene of the combat in a south-easterly direction. I followed and gave him a four-second burst from extreme range with about 1 ring deflection. I could not observe any strikes because my incendiary ammo had stopped but I saw the FW 190 go through some trees along a road and then crash in flames in a field.

I claim this FW 190 destroyed.

Total claims 1 destroyed and 1 damaged.

Flying Officer Staples' combat report: We were flying at approx 6,000 ft and White 1 instructed us each to select an enemy aircraft. I took the starboard one of the four flying at 500 ft, which accelerated and went down to zero feet . . . White Leader (F/L Collyns) selected the enemy aircraft next to my target . . . I fired a short burst from extreme range, approx 1,000 yds and the 190 commenced to weave. I closed the range steadily and fired several short bursts from 400 yds dead astern and saw strikes on the ground below the enemy aircraft. He then made a climbing turn to port and I got in a short burst at 350 yds with 30 degree deflection. I saw no strikes but the FW 190 jettisoned his hood and the pilot baled out. I followed the enemy aircraft taking photographs until it hit the ground and burst into flames . . . whilst flying after him I looked back and up to port and saw White Leader engaging an FW 190 from line astern. This 190 was fairly close behind and above me so to protect myself I not only kept my own target in view but kept a close watch on the other 190 that White Leader was engaging. I saw this 190 do a steep dive behind me to starboard and go straight into the ground and explode. Seeing this I continued attacking my target. Subsequent to my combat I called White Leader on the R/T and he replied, 'Good show, I have got one too.'

At this point whilst still flying at zero feet I was bounced by another FW 190 – his bullets hitting the ground in front of me. I broke starboard towards him and we started a turning match at about 500 ft. I was able to turn slightly better than the FW 190 and after five complete turns he broke away. I gave chase – the Hun taking violent evasive action. I fired several bursts at ranges varying from 500-300 yds, some at dead line astern and others with deflection up to 20 degrees. Once again I saw no strikes but

> the pilot baled out. As no other Mustang was near me at the time I took photographs for confirmation of the enemy pilot hanging from his parachute.
>
> I claim two FW 190s destroyed.

The 19 Squadron pilots certainly had cause to celebrate but they had not all returned. The squadron ORB recorded, 'It is with deep and sincere regret that we record that F/Lt "Buck" Collyns did not return from the trip. He was seen by his No. 2 F/O Staples to engage and destroy an FW 190, and it is thought that he was bounced subsequent to this. As a flight commander his place will be difficult to fill.'

Basil's Mustang crashed to earth near a railway crossing, about one kilometre from Rouvres and he was killed instantly, his body being thrown about 20 metres from the aircraft. When the Germans arrived they ordered the mayor of Rouvres to carry the body to his house and here the local people prepared it for burial. At ten o' clock the next morning Basil Collyns was buried, the entire population of the village turning out to pay their respects. There were so many flowers, the Germans protested. Basil's wife, Ann Collyns quickly learnt of her husband's fate.

> I knew quite quickly that he had been shot down. The pilot he was in the air with at the time reported it immediately. It sounded fatal. We then received a message from the French Resistance, who had collected his body and arranged a military funeral. They sent a report through and photographs.

When the war finished, within months Ann was able to go to France to visit Basil's grave.

> Everything was very chaotic and they were still very short of food. I stayed in a small hotel in the centre of Paris. I was able to buy a box of peaches in the market, which I had for breakfast one morning and then somebody managed to find a car with petrol and take me to the village. I met the mayor and members of the Resistance and I gave them presents and coffee and candles and soap, which we could get in England but they were still short of. We had a little lunch in the Mairie and somebody produced some eggs and we had an omelette and somebody produced some peaches, it was that time of year.

Ann would be repatriated later in the year, part of a group of 24 widows sent back to New Zealand.

> I found it very difficult to settle because strangely enough although New Zealand had an enormous amount of casualties in the war nearly all my friends still had their husbands, whereas in England I knew so many who had lost their husbands, and also lots of other old air force friends. I came back after about a year, via South Africa and Kenya where I joined a lot of air force chums who had gone out there after the war, and went to an air force wedding. Then I came to England and stayed for many years.

New Zealand fighter ace Flight Lieutenant Basil Collyns DFC (gazetted 16 October 1944), five and two shared destroyed, one probable, three damaged, one and one shared damaged on the ground, now rests at Villeneuve-St-George Old Communal Cemetery.

CHAPTER 10

JETS, V2s AND AIRBORNE ASSAULTS

As the Allied forces ground away at the Germans in Normandy, and the RAF utilised air supremacy to the full, there was still a battle of a defensive nature going on over south-east England, as the V1s continued to come over daily.

The intensity of anti-diver operations continued into July for Bob Cole and 3 Squadron, but it wouldn't be until 12 July that Bob increased his score, his logbook recording: 'Patrol. Destroy one diver 7 mls N of Hastings + one 15 mls N of Bexhill.' Then a further fallow period of ten patrols with 'No joy'. On 19 July though he managed to 'Destroy a diver in Appledore area. Blew up in a corn field.' Then another two fruitless patrols. On 22 July Bob moved his score on from 14 to 17 V1s destroyed (13 individually, 4 shared). On his first patrol that day he recorded: 'Patrol. Destroy a diver S of Ashford in open country.' And on his second patrol, 'Destroy one diver 6 mls N of Pevensey + one in Sandhurst area. Both explode in open country.'

The next eight patrols resulted in a 'No trade' entry in Bob's logbook. But on 29 July he managed to get behind another V1 and prematurely send it to ground: 'Patrol. Destroy a diver E of Mayfield in open country.' Three further patrols saw 'No trade' until the end of July, a month in which Bob had flown 34 anti-diver patrols, and a total flying time of 46 hours 45 minutes.

During this period, and despite the best efforts of the defences, V1s were still getting through, and in numbers. In mid July, however, Air Marshal Hill had redeployed his defences giving each component more exclusivity, fighters to operate over the Channel, with the guns placed on the coastline beneath the V1 flight path. Behind this more fighters would patrol and behind them a balloon barrage protected London. In addition RAF Bomber Command was now attacking the V1 storage depots, notably the underground caves at St Leu d'Esserent. Consequently the V1 launch rates were falling, thus preventing the defences being swamped, in turn meaning that the number of V1s reaching London fell. But the menace was still there and it was still costing lives. Up to 31 July 4,640 people were killed, with 13,571 injured. Bob Cole and pilots like him still had a tremendous responsibility to shoot down the flying bombs and save lives.

However because V1 launch rates were diminishing, it's hardly surprising that the first two weeks of August resulted in ten 'No trade' entries in Bob Cole's logbook. Then on 15 August: 'Patrol, Destroy a diver between Sgts + Offs mess at West Malling. No one hurt.'

> *Bob Cole:* I chased this one and I couldn't hit the blasted thing for some reason. I got up to West Malling aerodrome. Then I fired and I hit it and I saw it go down, and it was spinning right over the aerodrome. I thought bloody hell what a place to shoot it down. It went in between the sergeant and officers' mess. It didn't kill anybody.

Of course there was always the risk of a V1 being shot down over Kent and falling on a built-up area. However, overall the chances of killing anyone in Kent were small, and of course a lot less than if the V1 fell in London. It was therefore a necessary risk to take.

> *Bob Cole:* One V1 was shot down by one of our people, and hit Shorecliffe barracks. And another one that I could have shot down was got by someone else and went down in the main street in Bexhill, right in the middle of the street. But one I shot down one morning, went down about 30 yards from a house. I went down and had a look. It had blown all the tiles off. I didn't see any movement.

On 15 August Bob carried out another fruitless anti-diver patrol. The next day however, a break from the usual, a sweep N of Paris, although no action was seen. Later in the day it was back to countering the divers and he would add to his score: 'Patrol. Destroy a diver N of Tenterden. Exploded in field.' And the next day it was number 21: 'Patrol. Destroy a diver 4 mls NW of Rye. Blew up in the air.' It was 'No trade' on 18 August and then the next day: 'Patrol. Destroy a diver 4 mls SW of Maidstone. Exploded in a field.' Bob's next ten patrols are mostly recorded as 'No joy', or 'No trade', although a diver was seen on 21 August but Bob records, 'Flak got the only one.'

On 28 August Bob was to shoot down his last V1s: 'Patrol. Destroy two divers one 5 mls N of Rye + one 4 mls NW of Rye. Both explode in open country.' Bob's logbook had now recorded the destruction of 24 V1s (20 individually and 4 shared). On Bob's second patrol on 28 August, 'Flak got all that came in.' There were then a further four fruitless anti-diver patrols for the remainder of August, a month in which Bob had conducted 33 patrols and spent 41 hours 20 minutes flying in a Tempest V. He had played a full part in seeing off the main V1 offensive. With Allied land forces now overrunning the launch sites up through the Pas de Calais, and with the Germans in full retreat, the defensive measures over England could be relaxed. So with its anti-diver duties curtailed, 3 Squadron began to give direct support to the land forces in the push from France through Belgium and into Holland.

On 20 August the main battle in the Falaise pocket had effectively been won. Against the Germans who had escaped in full retreat Montgomery began to re-align his armies for the drive to the Seine and beyond and 2nd TAF continued to harass the retreating enemy whenever and wherever possible. In particular they inflicted further loss and suffering as the Germans attempted to cross the Seine. However many German units would escape and Coningham would vent his anger at this, writing to Air Vice-Marshal Robb at Supreme Headquarters Allied Expeditionary Force on 29 August.

> The attachment to the enclosure will interest the Chief as it provides further confirmatory evidence of the poor performance we may expect from our infantry.
>
> In that connection I think I should tell you how disappointed I have been at the air effort against German retirement over the Seine at Rouen. Apart from some weather difficulties this has been principally due to the attitude of the Canadian army. They had taken over from the Americans at Elbeuf and optimistically reported that they expected to be opposite

> Rouen on Sunday 27th. They therefore exerted pressure to stop us bombing the railway bridge from 1300 hours on that day. We know from various sources that since that time very considerable forces of the enemy have crossed over both night and day to the eastern bank. On the morning of the 28th they were still six miles away, and this morning they are still three miles away. The bridge has therefore been in free use by the Germans for steady retirement for 48 hours.
>
> I have made a big row about this incident here and find that De Guingand and his staff fully agree with my view. This is not the first time that optimism and ridiculous bomb lines have let the Germans escape.
>
> I have now instructed the groups, and am informing the IXth Air Force for like action, that they will continue the attack on such special targets or focal points in future until they see our land forces within reach to take on the target adequately by gunfire. At a guess I have said the distance should be something like two miles, and when the air sees our advancing forces making their smoke and plainly marked within that distance, they can then leave off their bombardment. On the army side 21 Army Group are issuing instructions that spearhead formations should be lavishly provided with smoke and special markings so that they can be clearly identified.[73]

Once the Seine had been crossed by the Allies in the wake of the retreating Germans, Eisenhower planned to 'push forward on a broad front with priority on the left' to open the Channel ports and Antwerp (and hence shorten supply lines), overrun the V-weapon launch sites and pose a threat to the Ruhr. In the middle of August a further Allied seaborne assault had been made in the south of France, operation Anvil. Little German resistance was met and French and American forces pushed west and north. With the success of Anvil Eisenhower intended on his right to join with the advancing Anvil forces and establish the broad front, then take the west bank of the Rhine before driving into Germany. 'We wanted to bring all our strength against the enemy, all of it mobile and all of it contributing directly to the complete annihilation of his field forces.'[74]

Unfortunately his subordinate land commanders, Montgomery and Bradley, held differing views. On 1 August 1944 the Allied land forces in Normandy had divided into two army groups; Montgomery led the British and Canadian 21st Army Group, Bradley commanded the American 12th Army Group, but until 1 September, when Eisenhower took over control of both army groups, Montgomery maintained operational command.

But as it became clear that the battle for Normandy was shortly to be won, Montgomery and Bradley's focus began to shift beyond the battlefield and their roles in the advance towards Germany. Unfortunately they were not looking in the same direction. Montgomery was seeking a main advance north to Antwerp and Aachen, with the Ardennes on the right flank. Bradley was looking eastward to advance to the Rhine south of Frankfurt. Both commanders made their case to Eisenhower. Montgomery wanted his northward thrust to have first call on supplies, most which were still coming ashore in Normandy and would be for the foreseeable short term. Such a requirement would halt Patton's (3rd

---

[73] Public Record Office AIR 37/1.

[74] Eisenhower, D., *Crusade in Europe*, (William Heinemann Ltd, 1948).

Army, part of Bradley's 12th Army Group) eastward advance. Eisenhower feared political consequences, and he sought and found compromise. He allowed Montgomery's drive north with the American First Army on his right (similarly advancing north), to give flank cover. All this at the expense of Patton's supplies. But once Antwerp had been secured the Allied armies would look to advance to the Rhine on a broad front. Patton felt slighted and still pushed his army on, but was limited by lack of supply. On 4 September the 21st Army Group's 11th Armoured Division entered and captured Antwerp and Patton, now promised his quota of supplies, looked to continue east, but a stronger enemy now stood in his way and the Third Army's advance faltered at the Moselle river.

On the same day von Rundstedt took up position as Commander-in-Chief West again, with von Kluge relieved of command on 17 August and subsequently taking his life. According to Field Marshal Walter Model, who had temporarily acted as C-in-C West, then commanding Army Group B, the Germany army from the North Sea to the Swiss border amounted to a fighting strength of no more than 25 divisions. At the end of August it was apparent that the Siegfried Line fortifications, protecting the German border, were not in a fit condition to block a concerted Allied push, and a fresh supply of German manpower was desperately required for the retreating broken divisions. So on 4 September Model assessed a requirement of 25 fresh divisions with a reserve of five to six panzer divisions.[75] The Reich was scoured and men were found that could hopefully strengthen the defensive line, but von Rundstedt still viewed them as 'totally inadequate'. There was hope when Goering found 20,000 men available from parachute regiments, and a further 10,000 Luftwaffe personnel who could be withdrawn from participating in the aerial battle owing to the shortage of fuel. Thus was the First Parachute Army formed on 4 September, this being the only significant reinforcement von Rundstedt had with which 'to fight for time so that the West Wall [the Siegfried Line] can be prepared for defence'.[76]

Meantime the Allies pressed forward, crossing the Meuse and the Albert Canal. It was certainly looking bleak for the German forces, as von Rundstedt strove to stabilise the front. But the Allied advance did result in one problem, the lengthening of supply lines. On the evening of 4 September Montgomery pressed Eisenhower to allow 'one powerful and full-blooded thrust towards Berlin', Montgomery favouring a northern push, capturing the Ruhr on the way. Eisenhower saw value in the idea but did not wish to compromise other operations. He still believed in an advance primarily on a broad front to cross the Rhine, but he did prioritise the advance north. Montgomery felt his superior officer lacked the understanding of the realities at the front. He believed there was an opportunity to strike at the Ruhr, but did not have the forces and supplies at his disposal at that time. The Canadian army was still sieging the Channel ports, Hitler ordering the defenders there to hold to the last man, and of the three corps of the 2nd British Army only XXX Corps was placed to strike into Holland. This push managed to cross the Albert Canal and Dempsey looked forwards to the Meuse-Escaut Canal, which his troops crossed on the evening of 10 September. But Montgomery was already looking beyond into Holland and to

---

[75] C. Wilmot, *The Struggle for Europe*, (Collins, 1952) p478.
[76] *Ibid*, p480.

the Rhine. On the afternoon of the 10th he had met Eisenhower in Brussels discussing operation Market Garden.

In August Lieutenant General Lewis H. Brereton had taken command of the newly formed Allied Airborne Army and numerous deployments had been devised to exploit the German retreat, but each time scrubbed owing to the speed of the advance. But now Montgomery planned to use the airborne troops to facilitate a deep thrust by the 2nd British Army to the Rhine and beyond, the idea being to use the airborne troops to secure river and canal crossings over which the 2nd Army would advance to the Rhine. Two possible routes were investigated, north-east crossing the Maas at Venlo and the Rhine at Wesel, or north crossing the Maas at Grave, Waal at Nijmegen and Lower Rhine at Arnhem. The whole operation of course, whichever route was chosen, would require assistance from the air.

The rapid advance of the ground forces proved problematic for the tactical air forces. 83 Group, supporting 2nd British Army, leapfrogged as and when airfields became available. Early in September the main HQ and squadrons of 83 Group were around Brussels. 84 Group, mainly supporting the 1st Canadian Army, was around Merville and Lille Vandeville, but would shortly move to Ypres. With all the movements going on (and with some bad weather) 2nd TAF operations in the first week of September were unsurprisingly few in number. Attacks were made on ferries and barges, though, transporting retreating Germans across the Scheldt. On 12 September 83 and 84 Groups flew 428 sorties on armed recces over the Dutch Islands. However another German secret weapon threat would now become a reality, and place demands on the Allied air forces.

On 8 September the first V2 rocket was launched against London, assumed by Allied Intelligence to have been fired from Holland. Pressure came to steer strategy towards overrunning the area or at least to cut the V2 supply lines to Germany. With respect to Market Garden the advance to Arnhem met such demands. In addition, it was decided to adopt a similar air deployment to that used to counter the V1, in that ADGB would predominantly deal with the menace, 2nd TAF being still heavily involved in the land advances. However, 2nd TAF would give support whenever possible with armed recces in the supposed launch areas. To the airmen of the Allied air forces there was nothing they could do once the rocket was launched. The best thing to do was try and get them on the ground, by attacking the launch sites themselves. In the week leading up to operation Market Garden 3 Squadron would conduct armed recces, act as escort to Bomber Command, undertake Jim Crows (patrols over the Channel) and in particular carry out attacks to counter the V2 threat – known as Big Ben sorties. On 11 September Bob Cole attacked the transportation system which was feeding the V2 launch sites and moving German troops.

> *Bob Cole's logbook:* 11 September: Recco. Shoot up two trains. One between Rotterdam + The Hague + one on Ceeflakee. Both destroyed. 7 attack first. 8 second. Lots of L.A.A. [Light Ack Ack] Inaccurate.

The next day there were further Jim Crow patrols and Big Ben sorties. On 13 September one patrol over Holland was to cost the life of 3 Squadron's CO. Bob Cole didn't take part, he had been given another job to do.

> *Bob Cole:* When we were on patrol we would see the V2s go up regularly,

> then the vapour trail as they disappeared. Beamont's aircraft had Ack-Ack damage, a hole through the wing. And I took it up to Hawkers at Slough. I rang Wigglesworth [Squadron Leader K. A. Wigglesworth DFC], I had just been commissioned, and asked if I could go into London and get a uniform the next day. He said that would be OK. That's the last time I spoke to him. Potty [Ron Pottinger] was doing a patrol in south Holland and he saw this rocket fire from a wood. So eight of them went out, and went line abreast and strafed the wood. And something blew up and Wigglesworth went into it.

On 16 September the pilots would carry out an armed recce, during which V2 trails were visible. The next day 3 Squadron supported Market Garden.

Eisenhower, although still of the broad front mind set, had given his approval to Montgomery for this operation. He saw it not as his main strategic emphasis but as an 'extension of our eastward rush to the line we needed for temporary security'. On 15 September Eisenhower ordered that:

> All possible resources of the Central Group of Armies must be thrown in to support the drive of the First US Army to seize bridgeheads near Cologne and Bonn in preparation for assisting in the capture of the Ruhr. After the Northern Group of Armies and First Army have seized bridgeheads over the Rhine, Third Army will advance through the Saar and establish bridgeheads across the Rhine . . . Operations on our left will, until the Rhine bridgeheads are won, take priority in all forms of logistical support.[77]

Patton, however, kept his army focused on the drive east and was still drawing resources to do so. The outcome was that Market Garden, scheduled to be launched on 17 September, would be under-resourced. Montgomery was unable to bring the divisions of VIII Corps into the advance in time, and hence could not go into the offensive alongside XXX Corps. On the right of the planned advance First US Army, supposed to protect that flank, was now involved in operations around Aachen and could not carry out offensive operations in support of XXX Corps' drive. The historian Chester Wilmot assessed the situation thus.

> In these circumstances there was no likelihood of First Army being able to conduct any offensive operations in support of Market Garden. By losing flexibility, First Army had lost the initiative, but this was not altogether the fault of Hodges [commanding First US Army]. It was the direct result of Eisenhower's determination to move on a broad front, of his inability to restrain Patton and especially of his anxiety to bring about an early link up with the Anvil Forces. By his advance from the Marne to the Meuse and then from the Meuse to the Moselle, Patton had distorted the Allied Front and dragged it too far to the south. Third Army had become a magnet drawing forces and supplies away from what Eisenhower had declared should be the main drive.[78]

---

[77] C. Wilmot, *The Struggle for Europe*, p493.
[78] *Ibid*, p495.

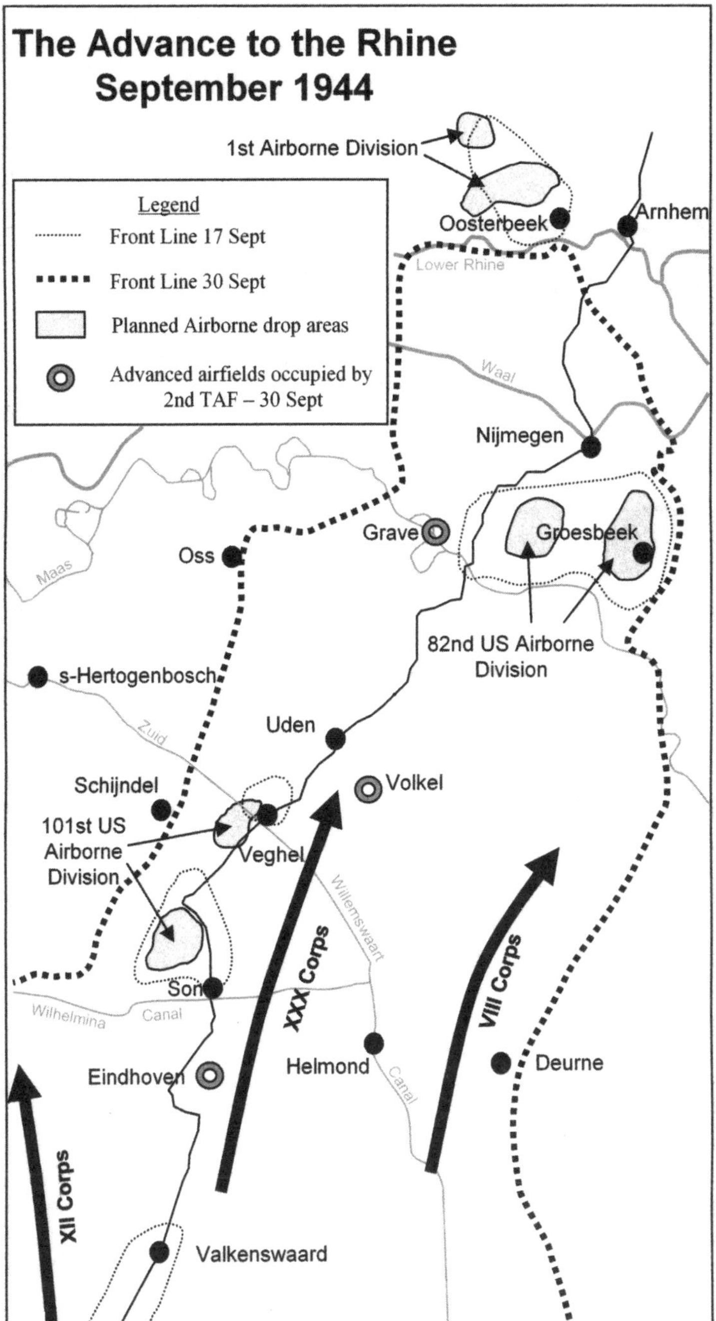

On 16 September Bradley received instruction from Eisenhower to give priority in supply to First Army. But Patton had not been held and had maintained his push, although it soon stalled against the congealing German front around the Moselle. Indeed this was happening to the whole German front. It appeared the

opportunity for continuing the mobile warfare the Allies had pursued since breaking out of Normandy was passing. Perhaps Market Garden could restore some of that mobility. And with supplies still having to come from Normandy, opening up the port of Antwerp and the Scheldt estuary was a key objective.

Montgomery's thrust required the British 1st Airborne to take the bridge spanning the Neder Rijn at Arnhem, and hold the bridgehead until reinforcement could arrive. The US 101st Airborne were tasked with taking bridges over the Wilhelmina Canal, Dommel and Willems Canal. The US 82nd Airborne were to seize the Grave bridge, across the Maas, and the bridge over the Waal at Nijmegen. Then through this corridor held by the airborne troops Horrocks' XXX Corps (Guards Armoured Division, 50th Division and 43rd Division) were to advance, to be in Arnhem in two days. There were not enough aircraft available to transport all the airborne troops in one go, so a deployment in three waves was planned.

With regard to fighter support, aircraft were detailed to attack flak positions on the approach and retirement routes, provide aerial cover to the airborne transports, and protect the skies over the battle area by day and by night and send squadrons on armed recces. One unit acting in the anti-flak role was 80 Squadron. Hugh Ross flew Spitfires with the squadron over Normandy during the invasion, mainly on patrols and escort to heavy-bomber attacks. In September 1944, having switched aircraft to Tempests, the squadron started low level attack.

> *Hugh Ross:* When we were on Spits it was all fairly high level stuff, but when we changed on to Tempests we did a bit of normal Spit work but then went over more and more into attacking ground targets of all kinds. The Spitfire IX was a beautiful aircraft, but when it came down to being an aircraft for warfare, the Tempest carried the heavier punch, it could climb faster, it could dive faster. When you were doing air-to-ground shooting it was rock steady. So it was a very, very good aircraft.

On 14 September 1944 Hugh took part in operations over Holland.

> It was quite early in the morning and I was told I would be flying No. 2 to the CO Bob Spurdle. I was just sitting around waiting and later on the phone rang and I had to go to dispersal and was told it would be Johnny Heap who would be leading the trip. My aircraft was u/s so I had to have somebody else's. It turned out that I had to have the A Flight commander's aircraft. His groundcrew had just polished it pretty well from head to toe in beeswax, a fantastic job. I went to collect it and one said, 'Don't bother coming back if you scratch it.' I said, 'Ah don't worry.'
>
> Johnny Heap led off. We were supposed to be looking for army concentrations anywhere near Arnhem. We had a good look around for some time, but couldn't find any real evidence of anything. We then attacked a big white barge, and as I pulled away I noticed my oil pressure was dropping off a little more than it should. When we levelled up at a reasonable height I called up Johnny and told him. He said, 'You lead the way, and I'll keep an eye open.' We were over Holland at the time. It was obvious I was going to have to force land or bale out. If I had done that I would have become a POW which I had no wish to be. So I thought I would take a chance on the sea. We set course to get us as near home as we could. It took us a bit of time to get over the water and then, after a

little bit longer, the engine just cut. The huge prop just stopped dead. So I thought I'd better get out. I opted to fly straight and level and jump out over the side. I had got all my straps undone and everything, but when I jumped the cord on my R/T caught on something and I was half in and half out for a while being buffeted about by the wind. I managed to get back in and undo the helmet and then jump out and pull the parachute. I had my dinghy attached to the Mae West. I inflated it, got in, and sat in it. Johnny Heap stayed there quite some time. I always wondered how he got back with any petrol left at all in his tank. He was a great bloke. Everybody looked out for everybody else, quite prepared to take pretty fair risks to see that the other chap was alright. He stayed on until a couple of aircraft came out to take over and then shortly afterwards a Walrus came out and landed more or less alongside, got a boat hook into the dinghy, yanked me in close and dragged me in through the hatch. They got me to Martlesham Heath, an American station. The doctors there were very particular and they had me there for ages. I was dying to get something to eat. But they were sticking discs all over, all the latest equipment and it wouldn't work but they were persevering. I was gagging for a good drink and bite to eat. Anyway about a day or so later I was picked up and taken back. When I got back I met the groundcrew of the aircraft, and this lad came over, tears welling in his eyes. He said, 'I'm sorry, me and my big mouth.' I said, 'Don't worry it's not you that brought me down, forget about it.'

On his return Hugh would learn of the loss of a number of his colleagues on low level attacks in the preceding days, sustained as they fought to support Market Garden.

80 Squadron ORB
16 September: The squadron was airborne at 1030 hours on an armed recce in the Hague area. Germany was entered for the first time. A loco together with 45 wagons were attacked just west of Arnhem and strikes were seen on loco – black and white smoke soon appeared. The wagons were strafed well three times. Aussie P/O W. E. (Bill) Maloney was seen to crash land nearby – glycol was streaming from the engine.
17 September: The Allied invasion of Holland took place and 80 Squadron were detailed for anti-flak duties. The squadron took to the air and several guns were silenced within a short time in the Walcheren and Schouwen Islands. One armed barge was attacked and left burning whilst four others were damaged. Flak was plentiful and a Tempest piloted by W/O P. L. (Pete) Godfrey was hit. He was not seen to bale out and aircraft was seen to crash into sea. An armed recce of Hague – Wassenaar – Leiden – Katwyk was carried out. Three barges were hit, results not observed. One MT with gun was hit and one MT flamer. Strikes were also obtained on a car. Considerable L.A.A. fire was met. A flash of V2 was observed and contrails at angle of 60/70 degs. Observed when it reached 10/15,000 feet from E end of Walcheren. F/L Irish successfully baled out from his aircraft which had developed glycol trouble.
18 September: The invasion continued and we were again detailed to attack flak positions, this time around Flushing. Airborne troops were

being led in over us. Concentrations of light flak attacked. Several guns silenced and the place was generally strafed. F/O P. S. (Lofty) Haw was hit by flak. He attempted to ditch but eventually baled out at 1,200 feet, and is 'missing', believed killed [later confirmed]. F/O Haw and Tempest were seen to crash into sea, his parachute being only half opened. F/O R. H. (Rob) Hanney disappeared mysteriously and no facts are available about him [also killed]. As reported, it was a day of suicide flying.

Killed in Captivity

80 Squadron pilot Bill Maloney had been forced to land in enemy territory on 16 September 1944. He survived the landing but was soon captured. Shortly after he would lose his life, killed by the men who had arrested him. These men would be tried after the war; one was sentenced to death, the other three were given prison sentences. Below is a key statement of one witness, presented at their trial.

> I Johann Bosmann, born on 4 Jan 1896, and domiciled at the time in Grondstein, make the following declaration.
>
> In September 1944 an aircraft landed about 1,500 metres from my house in the meadow of Johann Franken's property. The aircraft turned over and I thought that no person could have survived in it. I thereupon went into my house, fetched my identification papers and proceeded to the aircraft. When I had gone about 100 metres, an auto came along and stopped in the road at Johann Franken's. Four or five men got out of it and went toward the aircraft. When I was still 200 metres away from it, the men came with an airman, who had hidden in the bushes, and they brought him to the aircraft. When they got near the aircraft a struggle ensued. I recognised one of these men as Pelgrim. Then I saw the airman beaten with rifle butts. The latter tried to ward off the blows, but it was to no avail. The beating was taking place mostly on the far side of the aircraft. Then they came around the aircraft where I could see everything very clearly. The airman was bleeding and his skull was smashed in. He was bleeding terribly. He was now bent over and four men were beating him; one man came and kicked him in the face with his boot. I shall never forget this scene. Then Renoth went up to them and told the men to go away. He took aim with his carbine and at that moment I turned away. When I had gone a few steps the first shot was fired. The airman uttered a cry. When I had gone a few more steps, the second shot was fired. Thereupon I went home. About an hour later, I went back to the aircraft with the intention of seeing what had actually taken place. I found the body near the aircraft and Renoth was standing guard. The other people had gone away. Renoth started to tell me what had occurred. I told him, however, that I myself had been present. He replied: 'In my excitement I did not see anyone.' Then I went home and did not see any more of the affair. I recognised the victim as a pilot because he was wearing a blue uniform and shoes and I could not understand his language. He was small in stature and had long black hair.
>
> I declare that all the above statements are true.
>
> Elten, 11 Jul 45.

Bob Cole and 3 Squadron were also detailed to attack flak positions in support of Market Garden, on 17 September.

> *Bob Cole:* We went in and shot-up three barges. We were halfway between Arnhem and the coast. That was our area to subdue any flak. If the guns had fired at us we would have strafed them. We were fired at on the way in but in our area there was nothing. When we came back out, over the Dutch Islands there were two great lines of aircraft, with gliders being towed. It was pretty impressive actually, and they were flying, one from north-west and one almost due west.

On 17 September Allied air forces flew 4,500 sorties (2nd TAF 550, ADGB 438), and the fighters attacked numerous gun positions and railway traffic in north-west Holland. Luftflotte 3 had 150 aircraft with which to oppose the airborne landings, only half of which were sent to the landing areas. The Allied fighter protection kept them at bay. The Luftwaffe was again kept at a distance on 18 September, but bad weather hampered the Allied operations. On 19 September poor weather again limited aerial operations for both sides, 2nd TAF flying only 102 sorties.

On the ground the 82nd Airborne captured the Grave bridge but progress at Nijmegen was slower. The 101st Airborne achieved partial success, but the bridge at the Wilhelmina Canal was blown up by the Germans. The British 1st Airborne landed in scrubland seven miles from the bridge at Arnhem, in a bid to keep the aircraft clear of anti-aircraft fire. But shortly after landing communication broke down, particularly by radio. That evening Lt Col John Frost's 2nd Battalion of the 1st Parachute Brigade had made their way through to the Arnhem bridge, but were meeting a stiff counter attack. Model's HQ was only a few miles from the British landings. He moved back and could bring in reinforcement from two panzer divisions, which were regrouping north of Arnhem. Crucially, the Allied plans were now in the possession of the Germans, having been taken from an American glider which had been shot down into German positions.

At the end of the first day the advancing ground attack column had reached Valkenswaard, and on the 19th the Guards Armoured Division advanced to, repaired and crossed the Son bridge over the Wilhelmina Canal. Later in the day units of XXX Corps had arrived at Nijmegen but met fierce resistance at the Waal crossing. But with all the delays the situation at Arnhem was getting very serious indeed. On 21 September 1st Airborne Division's Major General R. E. Urquhart pulled back his men from Arnhem to Oosterbeek. Frost was isolated at the bridge and that evening his resistance came to an end. The 1st Airborne was reinforced by the Polish 1st Parachute Brigade but too late. XXX Corps' Guards Armoured Division could not reach Arnhem and the shattered and seriously depleted British 1st Airborne pulled back over the Neder Rijn. Although considerable ground had been gained Market Garden had failed in its strategic objective, the Rhine remained a barrier and the Siegfried Line had not been flanked.

Whilst the Allied armies had been pushing through France and into Belgium, it was the job of the Canadians to open the Channel ports. To support the siege 84 Group would make its fighters available. Prior to this, however, 197 Squadron had moved, to fly from England, and therefore be closer to the operational areas.

Derek Lovell's logbook:
31 August – Armed Recce. Arras-Cambrai area. Attacked some barges. 1 Flamer 2 damaged.
1 September – Armed Recce. Attacked transport in St. Po area. Many damaged.
4 September – To Manston. B.3 out of range for us, so we operate from England.
6 September – Fighter cover. Covered rockets attacking ships, then we attacked. 3 damaged.
9 September – Armed Recce. Spare, all got off.
11 September – Returned to France. Flak as we crossed in nr Calais – poor show. Landed at Lille.

Flight Lieutenant H. Neville Thomas describes the move of 146 Wing's ground units to Lille:

> At 2230 hours on 5 September 1944, in pouring rain, the 'Penguin' began the long trek through France, in the wake of the army. 'The powers that be' had planned a strip at B.23 – Thiberville – but when we arrived there it was waterlogged and so up we pressed on to B.37 – Corroy – south-west of Abbeville. There conditions were found to be precisely the same.
>
> 'Forward' was again the watchword – this time to Lille, which was reached at 1500 hours on 10 September. The whole journey was a nightmare – rain – bad roads – little sleep – wet clothes and an overpowering stench of dead cows and petrol. Still 'we made it' and drew comfort from the thought that the Huns were having a much worse trip!

From Lille, Derek Lovell flew as part of 146 Wing's contribution to the attacks on the Channel ports and also to give support to the attempts to clear the enemy from the Dutch Islands. His logbook records:

15 September – Ramrod. Abortive weather u/s.
20 September – Close support Ramrod. Strong point nr Calais. Well pranged. V.G. bombing.
22 September – Ramrod. HQ in wood nr Middleburgh. Weather poor, fair result.
26 September – Close support Ramrod. Gun position N of Antwerp. Excellent prang.
26 September – Armed Recce. Dutch Islands – Groupie + self. Attacked 2 MT both destroyed. 1 for self.
27 September – Close support Ramrod. Strong point nr Dunkirk – excellent bombing.
27 September – Close support Ramrod. Power house Dunkirk – excellent bombing.
27 September – Armed Recce. Round the Dutch Islands with G/C – no joy – bags of cloud!!!
28 September – Ramrod, Spare.
1 October – Ramrod. Attacked barges in water round Dutch Islands. 2 dmgd.

But there now came about a change in the nature of their targets.

High Spirits over the Channel Ports

Max Collett's diary, 485 (NZ) Squadron: Saturday 16 September 1944: Did three wizard shows today, best day's flying I've had. Started off by dive bombing a strongpoint near Boulogne about 1/2 mile from the Front Line. They were all on the target except one and as there was very little flak we went in and strafed it for good measure. Second show we were briefed to attack a convoy last seen at Hulst in Holland. When we arrived there was no sign of the convoy so we careered around for about an hour beating up anything we could see – had a go at a couple of trucks but couldn't find very much. Third do, we had to dive bomb coastal batteries in the middle of Dunkirk harbour. Was one of the funniest trips I've done – went out in a gaggle and joined up OK. About halfway to target went over target, stepped up and all went down together; one gaggle of twelve Spits dodging each other's bombs and trying to find a hole through the Spits to bomb through. The results were excellent, ten direct hits on the guns and one miss due to faulty departure from plane. All the boys in very high spirits.[79]

Flight Lieutenant H. Neville Thomas: On 29 September, we received the first intimation of a type of operation which was destined fully to occupy the Wing during the winter months.

'INTERDICTION' – the purpose of which is to deny the enemy use of rail communications.

As the army overran the flying bomb and rocket sites in France, the Hun had been feverishly constructing others in eastern and western Holland, so to continue the offensive against London.

Our task was to 'out' the lines of communication between the factories in Germany and the firing sites in Holland and thus prevent the delivery of these infernal weapons.

Derek Lovell's logbook reflects the nature of 197 Squadron operations as part of 146 Wing's interdiction campaign.

2 October – Ramrod. Railway embankment nr Ede – excellent bombing.
5 October – Ramrod. Attacked above target again. Lost Wakeman [killed]. Strafed some barges. 1 flamer, 1 smoker, 2 dam.
5 October – Ramrod. Railway junction at Utrecht. Good prang – my dear the flak!!
6 October – Ramrod. Railway bridge S of Zwolls – bridge hit by 2 bombs.
6 October – Ramrod. Railway junction at Utrecht. Good prang. Flak not so bad this time.
7 October – Ramrod. Railway bridge at Deventer. 2 hits. My dear the flak!!!!

The next day, to the south-east Hodges' US First Army opened its attack on the Siegfried Line on a five-mile front near Maastricht. But with the Ruhr behind

[79] Courtesy of New Zealand Fighter Pilots Museum.

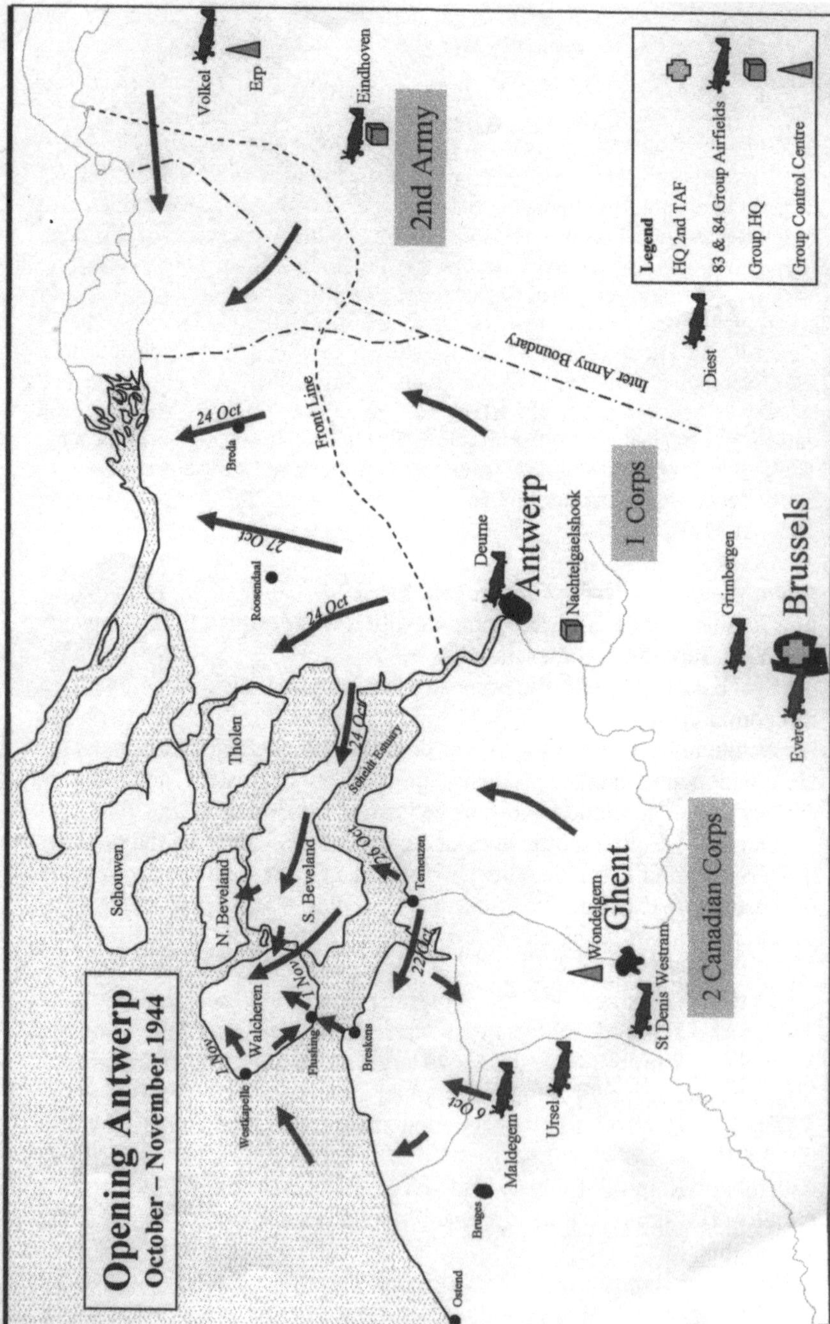

them the Germans defended in strength. The US XIX Corps advance was slow, five miles in five days. By 17 October Hodges had Aachen surrounded, the first German city to be taken by the Allies.

On the Allies' left flank, although Antwerp was taken on 4 September the Scheldt estuary, the route to the North Sea, remained hostile. Whilst Market Garden had run its course the German 15th Army had strengthened its hold on the north bank. For much of October the British I Corps and Canadian II Corps slowly advanced. Breskens was captured on 22 October, then up to 31 October a pincer movement resulted in the capitulation of the German 64th Division and Zuid-Beveland was taken. But there was still the need to overrun Walcheren Island. The centre was flooded but its perimeter was held by the German 70th Division. 197 Squadron would enter the affray around the Scheldt estuary, attacking communication lines to the islands and gun positions, in support of the army offensive.

> *Derek Lovell's logbook:*
> 11 October – Close support Ramrod. Village Oostburg [south of Breskens] to be wiped out. Excellent bombing.
> 11 October – Close support Ramrod. Same target more good bombing.
> 11 October – Close support Ramrod. Same target with 1,000 lbs low level then anti-flak.
> 11 October – Close support Ramrod. Same target low level, then anti-flak again.
> 12 October – Ramrod. Railyard at Valdenkirchen. Yard hit, bombing fair, redskins [red tracer].
> 13 October – Close support Ramrod. Strong point S of Bergen Op Zoom. Low level good bombing.
> 15 October – Ramrod. Rail cross over at Geldem. V good prang. Attacked a train, engine damg.
> 17 October – Ramrod. A bit more Oostburg written off – good prang.
> 19 October – Fighter cover + Ramrod. Cover to PRU Typhoons. Weather dull. No bombing, bit dicey!
> 20 October – Close support Ramrod. Bombed & strafed roadside N of Antwerp to assist Army attack.
> 20 October – Ramrod. Railway crossing nr Harderwijk. Good prang.
> 21 October – Ramrod. Rail junction N of Breda – 4 direct hits. Accurate flak!

On 24 October 146 Wing went after the 15th Army HQ.

> *Derek Lovell:* The Dutch had got, from the enemy side, a telephone line through to us. The enemy didn't know it still existed. So the Dutch underground would ring through targets, which would be passed down to us.

Denys Gillam led the attack, dropping two phosphorous bombs as guides. 146 Wing's Typhoons swept in, very low, dropping eight 1,000 lb and fifty 500 lb bombs. Derek Tapson of 197 Squadron would also take part in the operation:

> It was a wing operation and we were the first squadron to go in. It was one of those when we went down to about 25 feet. I released the bombs as we were going up the front garden. I always said that my bombs went in the windows either side of the front door.

Members of the Dutch Resistance watched and were able to report that one building was in ruins, many others damaged. The staff were about to sit down to lunch and several senior officers were killed.

> *Derek Lovell:* It got back to us about this devastation that we caused and it was reported that the staff officers were due to be given funerals with full military honours at 12 o'clock the next day. Gillam was restrained from a follow-up.

Towards the end of October 197 Squadron kept up the offensive in support of the army.

> *Derek Lovell's logbook:*
> 24 October – Close support Ramrod. Village of Bath, holding up troops. Good prang.
> 28 October – Close support Ramrod. Factory at Dunkirk. Good prang. Mahaffy forced down.
> 29 October – Close support Ramrod. Guns nr Flushing. Excellent prang, debris 3,000 feet, later attacked a barge – smoker.

On 1 November a brigade of Royal Marines came ashore at Westkapelle on Walcheren Island and the British 52nd Division crossed from Breskens. But it was not easy going, the battle raged, and it was not until 9 November that the island was finally secured.

> *Derek Lovell:* It was essential to get Walcheren. There was a heavy artillery battery, which we had to attack. I remember pulling out of the dive and passing what I thought was a big black piece of paper or something, until I saw the rivet holes in it. It was a sheet of metal that had come up from something we had hit below and I was formating on it.

'Bugger it'

257 Squadron's Brian Spragg took part in the attacks on enemy positions, on South Beveland, and on 4 November he would fall victim to the defences.

> I was just over the target, at about 8,000 feet, and about to roll in to the attack, when I was hit in the engine and it stopped, and a lot of oil came over the front. The propeller stopped. My first thoughts – bugger it! I dropped my bombs. We were fairly close to the bomb line, where the army were. I called up Jerry Eaton who was leading our four, and told him I had been hit. I said I was going to try and put it down. I daren't jump out because I thought I might come down the wrong side of the bomb line. So I drifted down, switched everything off, strapped myself in tightly and got the hood back. I managed to pump a bit of flap down, and started looking for a place to land. Very luckily I just managed to put it down on a strip just clear of one of the big dykes they had on these islands. I slithered to a halt in about 300 yards. My radio was still working so I called Jerry Eaton up and said, 'I'm OK, you can bugger off home now.' An army sergeant came running out to me, and asked if I was alright – I nodded. They took me into a farmhouse. They were Royal Artillery who had been attacking the same target as we had been attacking. They gave me a large cup of whisky and found a driver and drove me all the way back to Antwerp.

Although Market Garden had been a strategic failure, there was still a considerable bridgehead extending to Nijmegen, which needed protection. 2nd TAF aircraft would try and cut the rail lines through which the enemy intended to pass reinforcements. In addition the skies over Nijmegen needed defending. On the night of 26/27 September and on 27 September itself a large force of enemy aircraft were sent to try and destroy the bridges there. They met considerable opposition, notably from Spitfires of 2nd TAF, with 520 defensive sorties flown, and 46 enemy aircraft claimed destroyed. Towards the end of September seven Mustang and Spitfire squadrons from 83 Group were sent back to ADGB to act as escorts to daylight Bomber Command raids. Five squadrons of Tempests and three squadrons of Spitfire XIVs came in as replacements. This was also in part to meet a request made by Coningham on 9 September for two wings of Tempests, a squadron of Meteors, and a Mustang wing (lent to ADGB to counter the V1s) to oppose the enemy jet fighter, the Me 262, which had recently entered the affray, and the long-nosed FW 190s. Part of this redeployment involved 3 Squadron and Bob Cole. On 28 September he flew his Tempest V from Matlaske, Norfolk to Grimbergen, Belgium, 3 Squadron becoming part of 122 Wing. The next day Bob was on ops, as his logbook shows:

> 29 September: Patrol over Nijmegen. Some flak.
> 30 September: Patrol Arnhem area. Some flak.
> 30 September: Patrol Arnhem-Nijmegen area. Quite a bit of flak.
> 1 October: Grimbergen to Volkel. Lots of extremely accurate L.A.A. from Hun lines. Frank Reid in second lot shot down in flames [and killed].

When Bob arrived at Volkel, conditions were somewhat different to those previously experienced. The airfield had been detailed for a number of visits by the Allied bomber forces.

> We flew up and the army were there. But we were the first squadron in and our groundcrew came up the next day. Of course when we got there, there was nowhere to sleep and nothing to wash with. We spent the night in a disused house. No beds, virtually no mattress on hard boards. But it was better than actually sleeping on the floor.
>
> I carried a revolver. When I went to sleep I used to go to bed with a lanyard wrapped round my wrist and the revolver under the pillow. We knew the Germans had infiltrated south of us and killed some soldiers.
>
> [Owing to the Allied bombing] we had one runway and one perimeter track in use. If you skidded off the runway you'd go into a pothole. There was hardly anything left. We built our own dispersal out of rubble. The only place that was near us and useable was the air raid shelter. We put our parachutes down there.

Bob Cole and his squadron now endeavoured to keep the airspace above the Allied armies in Holland extremely hostile to enemy aircraft. Coningham had brought them in to counter the Me 262 threat, which became apparent very quickly when Cole was on patrol on 2 October, his logbook recording: 'Patrol Arnhem. Me 262 dived through formation + kept going. Couldn't do anything about it.'

> *Bob Cole:* There were four of us and he came in, none of us saw him it was a bright day, he fired and I saw smoke from his cannon. He made no

attempt to come back. He wasn't allowing any real deflection. You have to allow a lot of deflection at 90 degrees. He just kept going. I didn't turn behind him. I was tempted to but the trouble is if you turn behind when there are two of them, you are a sitting duck for the second one.

Poor weather would considerably constrain the number of sorties 3 Squadron could send its pilots on over the next few days. But when the opportunity arose the Tempest pilots were airborne.

Bob Cole's logbook:
7 Oct: Sweep Münster area. Marauder shot down by flak. No flak at us. No enemy aircraft seen. Some reported.
11 Oct: Patrol Nijmegen area. Engine cutting return early. No enemy aircraft or flak. Patrol at 16,000'.
12 Oct: Cover for Marauders. Cannon jammed. A little H. [Heavy] flak.
12 Oct: Armed recco. Sqdn attacked a troop train. Engine blew up. 5 coaches catch fire. I made 3 attacks using most of my ammo. Lots of troops strafed.

A devastating attack but at a cost. Wing Commander Beamont was forced to land in enemy territory. He would see the war out as a prisoner.

The next day Bob was on patrol over Grave.

Bob Cole's combat report: I was flying Green 1 on a defensive patrol... when Control reported an enemy aircraft believed jet in the area. Blue 1, who was patrolling over Volkel warned me that a 'bastard' was flying on 160 deg from his patrol area at 14,000 ft. I flew S.E. with my No. 2, climbing slightly, and soon sighted vapour trails approaching. An aircraft came rapidly towards me, slightly above. I decided it was an Me 262, pulled up, and fired two long bursts head on as it passed 100 ft over me. I was caught in the slip-stream, stuck my nose down, recovered, turned 180 deg and gave chase. I was doing 480 in a slight dive, and found the Hun was pulling away slightly. He continued the slight dive for some miles and then suddenly climbed vertically about 800 ft then levelled out again. This climb did not appear to affect his speed. I continued on a straight course and began turning right. Luckily the Hun also turned right and I closed a little.

Bob Cole: I reckoned at some time he had to turn back east. So I cut across, and went about due north. He had to go back towards Germany at some point. I had plenty of fuel, we hadn't been up long, I could have chased him indefinitely, I could have gone to his aerodrome.

Bob Cole's combat report: I went on with the pursuit, without my No. 2 and after some miles saw a fair quantity of dark grey smoke from both jets, and what may have been a stab of flame from the right-hand one. The smoke lasted about 5 seconds and then disappeared.

Bob Cole: I kept it going and kept just below him. I reckoned if he looked back and I was below him he wouldn't see me. I would be in his blind spot. After about 40 miles I caught him up.

Bob Cole's combat report: I was slightly below him (at 10,000 ft) and I believe he thought he had shaken me off. I closed in to about 500 yards, and fired one short burst, dead astern, which missed. I closed in to about 150 yards, still dead astern and fired another short burst. The enemy aircraft immediately exploded just as a doodlebug does, and many pieces flew off, including what looked like a plank 6 ft long. I broke to avoid this, and by the time I turned again the pilot was in his open parachute, and the aircraft was doing a gentle spin, still appearing to be nearly intact. This continued until the aircraft hit the ground, when there was another explosion, the aircraft burning out. At the same time as I first saw the pilot in his parachute I also noticed about 12 red balls, rather larger than cricket balls, in the air alongside the aircraft, floating down at about the same speed. They were a very vivid colour, much brighter than tracer. In any case there was no flak.

Bob Cole: I went down, we were well inside their lines, and took a picture of it crashing, then I took a picture of him. I didn't shoot at him. Logically I should have done.

Bob Cole had notched up the first Me 262 destroyed by his Wing.

Outwitting a Jet

80 Squadron Tempest pilot Hugh Ross recounts his contribution to countering the Me 262 threat on 4 November 1944.

The Me 262s were attacking here, there and everywhere. Not that they were a big threat really. But at any rate we couldn't get near them if they had set off. So we had a scheme whereby whenever Me 262s were airborne word would come in we would be sent off. We used to sit at the end of the runway and would go off in pairs to various aerodromes where they were likely to land. Rheine was the main one. We would try and get there as quickly as we could. Then it was a case of stooging around until one of them showed up. Just sort of orbiting the aerodrome at height. The Me 262s came up lanes and these great long lanes were bordered with ack-ack all the way along. So that if you came in behind them when they were in that lane, a mile or so away from the aerodrome even, they could have a good crack at you. On this occasion we were at about 8,000 feet and just waiting. When we did spot an Me 262, it was well along this lane, practically touching down when I picked it up and I went down straight away. I had never seen anything like it in my life. I think Rheine was the most heavily defended aerodrome. You would never reckon getting through the ack-ack. You couldn't see through it hardly. I opened fire on the Me 262 on the runway, there were quite a lot of strikes all over it. It was still moving on the runway. It sort of went straight off into some trees [later believed destroyed] and that was it. So we went back up again and as we were doing so another Me 262 came out on the end of the runway which seemed a bit suspicious. So I thought shall I or shan't I. I thought I would do a little dive and see what happened. I made a kind of attempt as if I was going in to attack again. The Me 262 seemed to disappear rather suddenly, so I thought, 'I'm not going back.'

For the first week of November Derek Lovell and 197 Squadron maintained their support of the Canadian army, clearing the area around the Dutch Islands and west of the Nijmegen bridgehead.

Derek Lovell's logbook:
3 November – Ramrod. Village N of Breda – not attacked because of white smoke.
4 November – Ramrod. NE of Breda. Good prang, lovely fire.
4 November – Ramrod. 1 man sub factory in Utrecht. Excellent bombing, only 2 misses.
5 November – Ramrod (commission through, back dated to 29/7/44) – Squadron split up. Attacked rail crossing at Hoef, direct hits.
6 November – Ramrod. Marshalling yard N of Gouda. Very good prang. Place left burning.
7 November – Ramrod. Bags of cloud. Cut railway N of Hoef. Split up on way back but reprieved.

Derek recounts a typical 197 Squadron operational sortie from Antwerp in November 1944. Derek's call sign was Nero 19.

'Mr. Lovell, Mr. Lovell, Mr. Lovell!'

Slowly I come out of deep sleep in a nice warm camp bed.

'What?'

'Mr. Lovell, it's half past five, briefing in three quarters of an hour.'

It was Taffy the batman and the call to action. Tumble out of bed, don shirt, thick white sweater, battledress top and trousers, sea boot socks, escape flying boots, gun belt, revolver and silk scarf. Out into the dark, cold, frosty morning and to the mess for early breakfast. Who wants breakfast at this hour in the morning? Stomach and nervous tension say a definite no to porridge, greasy egg and bacon and sawdust-tasting soya sausage. But a good mug of hot sweet tea – yes. In saying 'no' to food one is only too aware that one ought to eat in case one gets shot down, taken prisoner and, perhaps, has a long wait for the next meal. Look around the mess to see who else has been called for the first operation of the day. See I am in good company. The Squadron CO, B Flight commander and five of B Flight's old hands, plus me. Not much chatter. So down to the operations tent and briefing.

On the blackboard are our eight names under the heading of 'Nero', two sections of four. Green section led by the CO. Yellow section, the flight commander. I am yellow three with Paddy behind me as my number 2 and Jock in front, Yellow leader's number two. Next to the list is a map with the target marked on it – the railway marshalling yards at Utrecht, again. It is where the enemy brings the V2 rockets on their way to the launching sites directed at Antwerp or London. The CO briefs us after the intelligence officer explains where the rocket wagons are placed and, importantly, where the anti-aircraft guns (flak) are. It is to be a dive-bombing attack from 8,000 feet. Each aircraft carries two 1,000 lb bombs, one under each wing. We are to approach from the south avoiding the 88mm and 40mm flak sites across the Rhine as best we can.

'Check watches, press tit time (engine starting time) in 20 minutes.'

We all pile into and onto the CO's jeep which was designed to seat four not eight! So out to aircraft dispersal. We dismount at the 3-ton truck which acts as the flight sergeant's office. We each sign for our aircraft. I have 'OV-S' which I consider as mine. Into the next truck to collect parachute, life jacket (called a Mae West), flying helmet and fireproof gloves. So out to our aircraft. I hand my 'chute to one of my mechanics who puts it into my aircraft. Meanwhile I, like the rest, have a 'panic pee' near the tail wheel, taking care to avoid the tyre as urine tends to rot the rubber! Then check over the outside of the aircraft, making sure that the main wheel tyres are OK. A burst tyre on take-off can be lethal.

Tie up my Mae West, clamber up into the cockpit and with the help of the two mechanics, strap myself in, on with helmet and gloves, plug into the radio socket and oxygen. At this point my engine mechanic hands me a mug of hot sweet tea for a welcome swig to moisten a dry, anticipatory mouth. Up until now, nervous tension has been dominant. That is about to change as I begin the start-up procedure which keeps me busy. And busy I will be for the next hour or so.

Oxygen on, radio on and to the right channel. Check flying controls are moving freely and in the right way. Trim wheel set, propeller pitch fully fine, throttle slightly open, flaps 15 degrees, petrol tanks full and switched on to main tanks, engine primer pumps open and ready, harness tight, oxygen flowing OK, bomb switches off, gun button off, gun sight on. Check time, one minute to go before 'press tit' time. Prime engine, switches on, fingers on starter buttons (tits), ready. The seconds tick by. I hear the hiss and coughing roar as the CO starts. Then we all join in. The starter cartridge fires, the prop turns, hesitates, then continues. Flames and smoke belch out of the exhausts, the mighty Napier Sabre engine's 2,400 horse power bursts into life. Press home the primer pumps. Check all instruments are working; set the giro compass against the main compass, set the altimeter, oil pressure OK, brake pressure OK. Now ready to go. Wait for the CO to move. There he goes, followed by the rest of Green section. Wave the chocks away, thumbs up to the mechanics and I follow Yellow one and Yellow two.

We all zig-zag towards the runway – zig-zagging so as to see ahead round the massive sabre engine in front of the cockpit. At the end of the runway we all turn half left, heave back in the stick and open the throttle to test all is well by switching off and on the two magnetos one at a time. The revs don't drop so all is well. Set 15 degrees of flap, close the hood. We are ready.

'Nero Leader to Bradshaw (flying control) clear to take off?' 'Bradshaw to Nero Leader, clear to take off, wind 250 degrees, 15 knots over.' 'Roger Bradshaw.'

The CO lines up on the right of the runway with Green two on his left and slightly behind. The rest of us follow suit, Green three right, Green four left and so on.

There is a mighty roar as the CO opens up to full throttle and off he goes, with Green two close by, slowly at first but quickly gathering pace, halfway down the runway they are followed by Green three and four then the rest of us follow.

As it gathers speed the Typhoon, in its eagerness to get going, gives the pilot a mighty push from behind. The rumble of the wheels stops, we are airborne. Wheels up, follow Yellow one and two as they slowly turn left as we climb away, 200 feet, flaps up. Climbing on course for the target.

'Nero aircraft, channel 2' (change of radio frequency to group control). As we climb we move in to battle formation, two sections of four, Green on the right, Yellow down sun on the left and slightly above. Each section is in two pairs. The leader with his No. 2 on one side and three and four on the other. Each aircraft about 200 feet apart and slightly behind each other, like the fingers on a hand.

Eight thousand feet, level out and throttle back to cruising speed. Eyes on swivels, watching out for any enemy aircraft and for flak!

Check all instruments are saying what they should say. Check the map to see where we are. Check in right position on right of Yellow one, 100 yards away and slightly behind his tailplane.

There is the River Maas and there the enemy front line, and here comes the heavy 88mm flak. Big black puffs of smoke, in fours, just in front. There's another four, closer this time, too close for comfort!'

'Nero aircraft weave,' calls the CO.

We all start by varying our height by 2-300 feet, some go up some down, then change. All this to upset the enemy's radar and the next bursts show way behind and below. It does not always work, but it does this time. The 88mm flak stops and soon we stop weaving. There ahead is Utrecht and just outside the town the target, the marshalling yards.

'Nero aircraft, echelon starboard.'

We get to the right of our respective leaders. Yellow section moves to the right of Green. And here comes the medium flak, 40mm with red tracer bullets every sixth one hose-piping round the sky!

'Oh, oh, redskins,' calls an anonymous Nero pilot. (Don't worry we have all seen it!)

There is the target, to the left and just behind (at 7 o'clock). Check gunsight on, bomb switches on, finger on release button on the top of the throttle. Gun button on the control column, thumb at the ready. Up goes the starboard wing of the CO and over and down he goes in a 60 degree dive. Followed on the count of three by the rest of us in turn.

Flak is coming up thick and furious. Now 20mm flak has joined in, bursting grey puffs all around. The ground is coming up fast. Start firing my four cannons aiming to hit some flak sites. There is a big explosion in front of me. Someone is hit and has exploded. A ball of fire tumbles to the ground. 3,000 feet, target in gunsight, ease stick back a bit. 2,500 feet, bombs away, two clicks and a slight jump as 2,000 lb of bombs leave the aircraft. Now pull out of the dive good and hard, nearly black out; full throttle hard left rudder to skid the aircraft to make it a bit more difficult for the flak gunners to hit. I hope! 8,000 feet again, circling left with the rest of the squadron. A quick look below, lots of black smoke and explosions, target well hit. Reform in sections and make for home. Quick count, only seven. Who is missing, Green four?

Flak has stopped, but still need to keep our eyes open for enemy fighters (bandits). There is the Rhine and here comes that 88mm flak again, weave as before. No one hit thank goodness. We are now over friendly territory, so can relax a bit. I always started singing to myself, 'You are my sunshine, my only sunshine'... We slowly start to descend, 4,000 feet, there's flak bursting below us. What's going on?

We all look hard. There below us is a VI, on its way to Antwerp and our anti-aircraft is after it. Suddenly, big explosion, and it is gone and so has the flak. 'Nero aircraft, channel one.'

'Hello Bradshaw, Nero leader approaching from the north.'

'Roger Nero leader, clear to land. Runway 240, wind 20 knots.'

'Nero aircraft line astern, go.'

Each section gets behind its leader and Yellow section on the right. Down we come towards the runway, as we reach the beginning at 300 feet the CO pulls up, going left and on the count of three we each follow in what is called a stream landing. The idea being to get us all down as quickly as possible. Up to 1,000 feet parallel to the runway. Throttle back, radiator flap down, undercarriage down (clonk, clonk as the two main wheels lock), three green lights confirming all three wheels are locked. Propeller pitch fully fine, turning left again now down to 500 ft, left again lining up with the runway. In front the CO, on the left of the runway, Green two to the right and so on. Over the boundary, cut the throttle, touch down, keep straight, don't run into the one in front. Turn off at the end of the runway. Flaps up, taxi back to dispersal. Waved into position by mechanic. Stop, brakes on, switch off engine, switch off petrol, radio and oxygen.

All is suddenly very quiet. Mechanics on wing. 'All OK.' 'Engine?' 'Great.' 'Any jammed guns?' 'No.' 'Any flak holes?' 'Don't think so.' Undo seat harness, unplug radio, disconnect oxygen, release parachute harness, clamber out. Gather with the rest of the squadron in centre of a ring of aircraft. Light cigarette. All on a high having survived another op. Tough about Green four, direct hit, new bod too, only his third op, often happens that way. De-brief by intelligence officer.

'Target well hit, big explosions, lots of flak, no enemy aircraft sighted.'

Point out latest flak positions on his map.

Return flying gear to truck. Tell 'Chiefy' (Flight Sergeant) 'All well with aircraft thank you.' Wander back to the mess for a much needed breakfast of porridge, greasy egg, bacon and soya sausage – and more sweet tea!

It is still only half past eight. Time to wash and shave... There will probably be another briefing in an hour or so...

On 9 November Derek went to England for some leave. On 18 November he joined the squadron at Antwerp and would experience some of the unpleasantries of the German secret weapon campaign. With the Allies in possession of Antwerp, much of the German V1 and V2 campaign was directed at the essential port. As witnessed by the personnel of 197 Squadron:

197 Squadron ORB:
14.10.44 – The German V2s, which have been falling from time to time are getting too close to the aerodrome to be funny. In fact pilots feel safer when airborne.
16.10.44 – A few more V2s today, one near enough to make the 'ADJ's' knees tremble.
9.11.44 – After dusk there was a brisk run in the arrival of rockets. One landed at the eastern end of the runway thereby rendering the airport u/s until midday on the 10th, and adding yet another grey hair to our anxious adjutant's ever increasing crop.
17.11.44 – The arrival of rockets during the recent period of bad weather has increased considerably and today has been as lively as any. One landed on a nearby hospital.
20.11.44 – Several flying bombs were seen passing on their way to the town during the day, but the one of most interest to the airfield appeared from the S.E. corner at 1,500 feet travelling fast. The writer of this journal was standing outside the dispersal vans at the time and called attention to what he thought was yet another passing over. F/S Adcock eyed it fixedly for a second and then with an agonised expression on his face screeched, 'It's coming down', and bounded like a stricken deer for an adjacent shelter. Most of the groundcrew followed suit smartly. The V1 landed about 150 yards from the dispersal. After impact a surprisingly large ball of flame shot up to 150 feet followed by debris. Fortunately nobody was hurt and no damage done. The story that Flying Control was flashing reds in an attempt to send it round again is quite untrue.

On 21 November Derek took part in some interdiction, then as November drew to a close the squadron was sent back to the UK.

Derek Lovell: It was a rest really. We went down to Fairwood Common. On the way we landed at Tangmere to refuel and were met by customs. The CO said stay in your aircraft I will talk to them, because we had taken half the ammunition out of our gun bays and filled it up with liquor. When we arrived over Fairwood Common the CO went in first and yelled at us 'Be careful as you land, there's a big dip at the beginning of the runway. If you land there you'll drop like a stone and break all your bottles.'

We were told at practice camp that unless our dive bombing was at least as accurate as the rocket squadrons had been we would change over to rockets. We didn't want that, so we did some rather serious dive bombing. [It was good] so they said OK you stick with your bombs.

I remember talking to Denys Gillam after the war and I said, 'Why did you keep us on bombs.' He said, 'Because you were good at it!'

At Fairwood Common Derek was able to hone his dive-bombing skills further. On five practice dive-bombing flights his logbook records his improvement, 66 yards, 38 yards, 33 yards, 10 yards, 9 yards. On 11 December he returned to Antwerp, via Manston.

Changes in Command

In October the Command structure of the Allied air forces was reorganised and simplified. Leigh-Mallory was appointed Air Commander-in-Chief South-East Asia. The HQ of AEAF had been established at Versailles, with SHAEF by the end of September. However HQ AEAF was no longer needed was disbanded and Eisenhower took control of the air forces which had been under Leigh-Mallory's control. This responsibility he would delegate to his deputy Tedder, who was unwilling to relinquish his other duties as Deputy Supreme Commander. As such a Deputy Chief of Staff (Air) was appointed responsible for the day-to-day operations of the tactical air forces. This position was taken up by Air Marshal J. M. Robb. Beneath Robb were the Air Staff SHAEF (Main) situated at Versailles, concerned mainly with tactical air operations, but also to pass on requests for heavy bomber support, and Air Staff SHAEF (Rear) kept in the UK, owing mainly to the fact that the air transport groups were still UK-based. And heavy bomber requests were passed from SHAEF (Main) to SHAEF (Rear) who could then liaise with the strategic bomber commands based in the UK. ADGB reverted back to its old title, RAF Fighter Command, under Air Officer Commanding-in-Chief Air Marshal Hill. Coningham was also redesignated as Air Officer Commanding-in-Chief 2nd TAF.

Following the excitement of his Me 262 combat, and despite the fact he was awarded the DFC on 23 October, the months of October and November were to prove a frustrating time for Bob Cole, and 3 Squadron, as patrols were mostly limited to taking place around Nijmegen.

Bob Cole's logbook (operations only):
13 Oct: Armed recce. Nothing to attack. A little flak.
14 Oct: Armed recce. Weather rendered it u/s.
15 Oct: Patrol around base. Nothing doing.
24 Oct: Patrol Nijmegen – Arnhem. Nothing doing.
28 Oct: Patrol Helmond. Nothing doing. V2 trail to E.
28 Oct: Patrol Helmond. Some L.A.A. S/E of Venlo. No enemy aircraft.
29 Oct: Patrol Helmond. No enemy aircraft seen. Some reported.
29 Oct: Patrol Nijmegen – Arnhem. Nothing doing.
2 Nov: Scramble to Rheine. No interceptions. Some H. flak.
4 Nov: Patrol Nijmegen. Some H + L flak. No trade.
4 Nov: Patrol Nijmegen. Nothing doing.

From the 6th until 14 November Bob was out of the front line. The next day it was back to patrols, but trade remained elusive.

15 Nov: Patrol base. Weather rotten.
16 Nov: Patrol Deurne. 18,000′. Nothing doing. Some H.A.A. N of Venlo.
17 Nov: Patrol… Nothing doing.
18 Nov: Patrol Weert – base. 18,000′.
19 Nov: Patrol Grave – Weert. 18,000′.
19 Nov: Patrol Grave – Weert. Some H.A.A. from Venlo.
24 Nov: Squadron spare. Nijmegen patrol.

24 Nov: Patrol Nijmegen.

Bob Cole: We used to fly up and down, Grave to Nijmegen, and when you got to the end of it the Germans would open up with the 88s. You'd turn back and then when you went back you'd get the same again. The most exciting part was when you turned and your number 2 went underneath you.

It was quite clearly a wearisome time for Bob. But on 26 November, instead of waiting for the enemy to come to them, 3 Squadron sent some its pilots on a sweep to the Münster – Rheine area looking for trouble, which they found.

Bob Cole: There were eight of us. Harvey Sweetman was leading it, he was CO of the squadron. We went looking for anything actually. Fly east over Germany and see what you can see. We were initially over 10/10ths cloud but we came off the edge of it and a little further on was an aerodrome. I could see an aircraft on it and I called up and was told if you can see it then have a go at it. So I peeled off and 'had a go at it'. I shot it up and kept going over the aerodrome. There wasn't much flak first time in.

In addition to Bob, Pilot Officer Dryland also attacked and would later record in his combat report:

The enemy aircraft was stationary on the east end of the east-west runway and I saw no evidence of the units operating. The squadron leader detailed myself and Pilot Officer Cole to attack and after one orbit we dived from north of the A/Fd. Pilot Officer Cole was leading and fired one 3 second burst from 600 yards from which I saw strikes on the fuselage. I had followed approx 400 yards to the rear of Pilot Officer Cole's aircraft and fired one 4 second burst from the same range observing strikes on both wings and fuselage. As I pulled up at 0 ft and flew across the A/Fd to the south, the enemy aircraft was enveloped in smoke and a little later Green section on top cover reported that the aircraft was burning fiercely and ammo exploding.

The enemy aircraft was camouflaged grey/blue.

Bob Cole: I pulled up east and as I did so I saw a lorry going round the perimeter area, a big lorry. I thought well I can get that to. I was about a couple of miles away. I turned towards it. It was bright and sunny, and it was like a hornet's nest, there was flak everywhere, and like a bloody fool – I could have broken off – I threw away an aircraft for a lorry.

I had got the sun behind me. I rammed the throttle, I was doing 450 miles per hour. I thought I could hit it and probably get away with it. I was firing at the lorry when I got hit from both sides at the same time. I got one smack in the engine and one straight through the cockpit, it cut my clothes. I got a smack in the face although I don't know where that came from. The controls worked, but glycol was coming out. I pulled up and called up saying I was going to bale out. As soon as I dropped to 200 mph, I crouched up in the cockpit and put my foot up on the stick. I had got rid of the hood and side panel, my RT and oxygen mask. I booted the stick, as hard as hell, and went out like a pea out of a pod, I just catapulted out. It means you miss the tail if you are lucky. I was at a few thousand feet.

I didn't pull my parachute until I was nearly on the ground. I was in a bit of a panic. I was thinking that as I had been strafing them and was now stuck in a parachute, they would look to blow my brains out. So I hung on as long as possible. I pulled it but I thought I was going to hit the ground.

The parachute opened but I still hit the ground with quite a bang actually. I ran east away from some people working in a field. I went through a wood and then thought if I double back, they would look the other way. Apparently they did. I walked back, about a mile and a half, and into a village. It was broad daylight. I didn't want to be there, so I went into a wood. There was this damn great stream which I couldn't jump and I didn't fancy wading, it was freezing cold. I just stayed there and then three Volkssturm with rifles walked by. They weren't 20 yards from me and they were yapping away. They must have thought I was somewhere else and just walked by. Never even saw me.

I walked through the village, at night. I found an old swede, wiped it on my uniform and ate it. I came across what appeared to be a bar with a bike outside. I wondered whether I should pinch it. I thought that if I did it would commit me to the road. Anyway I walked up the road and a woman on a bike came past beside me and looked round. I was in army battle dress, which we wore in Holland. I thought hell she'll report me so I cut across up a lane and across fields. I walked all night and I tried wading a river, which was a mistake, so I got back out of that and walked round it. I went along a railway line until there was daylight. Then I found a barn. I entered and got on some straw, spending the rest of the day there. I had never been so cold in my life. I was soaking wet from trying to wade the river. I kept taking my socks off and warming them under my armpits and putting them back on my feet. There were some people working all day in the barn and when it went quiet I went into the house to try and pinch some food. Inside were two or three kids and two women and a Dutchman, working on the German farm. Instead of being anti they were extremely friendly. These women sat me by the fire. I had my feet on the oven drying my trousers and my boots, I was still wringing wet. The next thing a couple of Volkssturm came in. They took me over to their house about 60 yards away. They were in some ways overwhelmingly friendly. I thought that the day before I had been shooting at their people. That's the bloody stupidity of war.

One chap gave me a seat by the fire, then he gave me some food, something floating in milk. I had hurt my foot when I baled out, I couldn't walk very well and it had got worse in the night as I hadn't been using it. I thought I would wait until everything quietened down then disappear back to the railway and carry on. This must have been about 11 o'clock at night. I didn't think anyone was going to come now. Well they did, a couple of men obviously from the German air force. They were a bit more officious. They searched me and gave these people some cigarettes. They took me to an aerodrome and shoved me in the guardroom. It was hot there, like a furnace. I had a bed and all my clothes dried out. The next day, I don't think they knew what the hell to do with me. I said to one chap, 'It's terrible, can I go outside?' This guard took me out in the air. I didn't speak German and he didn't speak English, we made signs. A German sergeant came out and he was furious at this chap.

I was moved from there to another aerodrome and here I met up with a Polish-American guy. We had two guards. A German officer came up and asked one of them whether we'd had any food. He was quite furious when told we hadn't. We went to the officers' mess and had a bowl of cabbage-like leaves and bit of swede. They were terribly short of food as well. When we were walking back six Forts went over. The next thing there was a hell of a whistling noise. I shouted and we threw ourselves in a ditch on one side and the guards threw themselves in a ditch on the other. This damn bomb went in no more than twenty odd feet away, all the blast went up and you could smell the cordite. They only dropped two bombs but the Germans got all the people off the aerodrome. We were taken a mile away. They were very apprehensive.

Then we were moved by rail to Frankfurt, Oberursel. It took four days to get there, we had nothing to eat, neither did the guards. We went to Hamm which was flattened. We were outside the railway station and I thought we stood an even chance of being lynched. I was in RAF uniform with ordinary boots, the Yank had a flying jacket with flying boots. We were there a few hours but there was no train, so we went on a coal lorry, which took us to another station, which had trains. But still it took us four days to do a couple of hundred miles.

I was put in solitary, in rows of cells for interrogation. I was there for fifteen days. I was interrogated by this chap, he spoke much better English than me. He spoke flawless English, no accent whatsoever. I suggested, I was a pilot officer at the time, that if he took me to Allied lines there would be no chance of him ever being treated as a prisoner of war. But he didn't wear it. He said things had got beyond war. He lived in this small town which had never been touched. And then it was bombed. He was frightened for his wife and family. He was given time off to go and see if they were alright.

I was interrogated by somebody else in civvies, and he said I wasn't in uniform so how could I prove I wasn't a terrorist. He could have me shot. If I was shot, I said, he'd be shot as soon as our army got there. He wanted to know all sorts, about call signs, when the squadron moved over. I said I had no idea when they moved over, I wasn't with them. And the call signs, I didn't recollect them. What armament we had? I said well I wasn't an armourer I only fired the guns. I told him I had shot down a Me 262. He said, 'You couldn't have done.' He thought they would win the war with the Me 262. They were under that delusion at the time. One thing I didn't like in solitary was the bloody fleas. I was bitten to hell. I complained and was told that our people had brought them!

From Oberursel I went to Wetzlar. There they wanted us to join the German air force. They said we would only serve on the Eastern Front and how terrible it was that the red hordes were overwhelming Europe. They put us in a bed with fine sheets, but when we declined their offer they kicked us straight back to the other place.

From here I went to Barth and that took about eight days. We ran out of food after about four. We stopped at one place, went into a field and ripped up some potatoes. There were eighteen in a carriage with six guards, straw on the floor to sleep on. The six guards put a wire across and had half of it. Well we had a bloody row and then it was divided evenly.

We got to Barth just before Christmas. It was freezing cold, I never took my clothes off . For heat we had four brickets of coal, coal dust with cement in it. That's all we had. And lack of food was also a problem. We had two months with a cup of soup and about two pieces of bread a day.

Bob Cole would see out the rest of the war as a POW.

CHAPTER 11

THE ARDENNES AND THE LUFTWAFFE'S LAST SHOW

When Bill Jameson left 488 Squadron and went home there was some discussion as to who Norman Crookes should fly with. On the night of 29/30 July 1944, when Bill and Norman had met with considerable success, 488 Squadron had lost a pilot, Nigel Bunting, and his navigator, Ted Spedding, whose usual pilot was New Zealander Ray Jeffs. But he had been ill on this particular night and Bunting's navigator was away. Norman Crookes would now team up with Ray Jeffs, and the partnership was soon into action.

> *Norman Crookes:* On 18 August we took off at about 0915 from RAF Colerne and we were directed to fly south of Caen by the same ground control that had controlled Bill and I on our last trips. We were put onto a contact which turned out to be a Dornier 217, which was flying easterly away from the battle area. We had a fairly long chase and eventually brought it within range. Ray Jeffs was a bit more excited than Bill was, because this was one of the first enemy aircraft that he had seen. He opened fire at too long a range and I encouraged him to get closer, which he did. He opened fire again and destroyed it. He was quite excited at having done that. I was happy that at least we had made a successful attack and been able to work together so well so quickly.
>
> Ray was a completely different character to Bill. He was a good pilot but he had only had one contact with an enemy aircraft before I flew with him, and hadn't got the control that Bill Jameson had when he was flying. The relationship between us was vastly different to the one I had with Bill. Ray and I worked together very well, but he was more happy-go-lucky than Bill, and on our first operational sortie I had to encourage him to get much closer to the aircraft before opening fire. A thing I would never have done to Bill, because he knew how to attack.

The month of August 1944 had certainly been a remarkable period for Norman Crookes.

> On my four operational trips from 30 July I had been concerned in shooting down at least one enemy aircraft on each trip. After that life became a little more humdrum. We were still flying from Colerne, but at the end of August we were given instruction on a new radar – Mark X, which had been introduced to a number of night fighter squadrons. It was supposed to give a greater range, both horizontally and vertically, but I found it not as effective, initially at any rate, as the Mark VIII radar, which was more like pointing a torch in the direction of the target aircraft. We spent almost the whole of September in doing practice with this Mark X radar.

In October, 488 Squadron was sent to Hunsdon in Hertfordshire, prior to a move to France. From here operational duties involved flying over the Scheldt estuary, where most of the enemy aircraft appeared to be concentrating their efforts, notably in mine-laying. Ray and Norman chased a number of bogeys but never had any contact with an enemy aircraft.

> *Norman Crookes:* When we were flying over the Scheldt estuary the ground control in the main was based in the south-east of England, but there were some roving units with the ground forces that could give information to the controlling station which helped us in our contacts. But it was largely a long-range control. It was more hit or miss in that situation than we had had in Normandy. That was one reason why we went over to France.

In the middle of November the squadron moved over to Amiens/Glisy and on 19 November Ray and Norman flew their first sortie from there – a 2 hour 45 minute patrol north of Aachen.

> *Norman Crookes:* We were then able to make direct contact with the control units that were almost constantly on the move, in order to keep up with the pace of the army advance. We operated from Amiens from November, and all the time the ground forces were moving further away from us. Eventually in December we were able to be controlled by ground units near Ostend where we did a number of operational patrols.

On 24 November Ray and Norman flew a patrol south of Utrecht, on 11 December one off Ostend, 12 December one north-east of Nijmegen, and on 16 December off Ostend, during which they chased a balloon, which had come up on radar, and was thought to be an aircraft. It was certainly a quieter time for Norman, far removed from all the activity of August, but the situation was about to change. A major German counter offensive would result in them engaging in further combat.

On 18 October 1944 Eisenhower conferred with Bradley and Montgomery, the outcome being the decision to seek the capture of the Ruhr, thereby taking out the major industrial centre in Germany, and thus diminishing her ability to wage war. The next focus for offensive action was to breach the Siegfried Line, with the US Ninth and First Army then to advance to the Rhine through the Aachen gap. The US Third Army would drive on to Mannheim and Frankfurt. In support the 2nd British Army was to push on from Nijmegen to the Reichswald and thence south between the Rhine and the Maas.

The US Ninth Army offensive opened on 16 November, but the 5th Panzer Army offered stiff resistance. On 25 November it was just 25 miles to Cologne but the Roer dams needed capture. The US Third Army encircled Metz on 18 November and pushed on towards the Saar. The 90th Infantry Division reached the German border on 20 November. On 3 December XX Corps crossed the bridge over the Saar near Saarlouis and over the next two weeks the bridgehead was secured. Further south the French armies were applying pressure in Alsace, and the US Seventh Army were also attacking the Siegfried Line.

It appeared that the German army in the west was on the brink of collapse. If the Allies maintained the offensive, ensuring the necessary materiel was forthcoming, then victory by numbers would result. But the Germans were not yet defeated and perhaps their only chance lay in taking the initiative, by using surprise and daring. On 16 December 1944 Hitler did just that and launched his final gamble in the west.

With German rear lines now within their national territory, it afforded the opportunity to assemble and deploy forces without the scrutiny of hostile civilians, some of which would have undoubtedly sought to report such movements to the Allies. The place of opportunity for the German army in December 1944 was, as it had been in the Blitzkreig of 1940, to be the Ardennes forest. The Allied strategists failed to see the threat, undoubtedly compounded by a lack of intelligence, or perhaps a disbelief that the Germans had the capacity for a sustained counter offensive. But they did. Hitler had assembled 21 divisions, deployed through three armies; the 6th SS Panzer Army (Dietrich) and 5th Panzer Army (von Manteuffel) to strike out for the Meuse in two days, the 6th SS Panzer Army then to try and retake Antwerp and the 5th Panzer Army to advance on Namur and Brussels. The 7th Army (Brandenburger) was to cover the southern flank of the push. The plan threatened to sever the supply lines of the Allied northern forces. Over half the Allied forces would be cut off.

On 16 December fog and cloud negated the Allied air superiority and kept most of the aircraft on the ground. The ground attack opened against the front of the US First Army. The 6th SS Panzer Army, despite making ground, met stiff opposition and the Germans failed to obliterate the northern shoulder of the Bulge. The thrust on the northern sector of the 5th Panzer Army's advance met with quick success in the Schnee-Eifel area, and on 17 December the US 106th Division was surrounded and 7,000 men were forced to surrender. On the southern sector, by the night of 17 December, Houffalize and Bastogne were seriously threatened. The next day the US 7th Armored Division was deployed to oppose the German advances on St. Vith, but the road centre was being outflanked on either side. The 47th Panzer Corps' (5th Panzer Army) drive to Bastogne was slowed by elements of the US 9th Armored Division and on 19 December the US 101st Airborne arrived at Bastogne, but on the next day the town was encircled.

On 19 December Bradley ordered the 10th Armored Division (Third Army) north, the US 30th Division (First Army) was sent to Malmédy and then turned to assail Battle Group Peiper at Stavelot, which would become isolated from the 6th SS Panzer Army and by 24 December their fuel supplies would dry up, forcing them to abandon their armour and retreat east by foot.

Meanhile von Manteuffel's forces took St. Vith and continued the advance. With the situation looking serious for the Allies, Eisenhower responded by putting Montgomery in command of land forces north of the breach, Bradley to the south. Montgomery looked to Major General J. Lawton Collins to stop the German advance to the Meuse using the 2nd and 3rd Armoured Divisions, and the 75th and 84th Infantry Divisions, and to counter attack. Bradley looked to Patton to redeploy the III and XII Corps to counter attack and break the encirclement of Bastogne.

On 23 December the weather finally broke and Allied air power could now intervene. On 17 December Coningham had agreed that 2nd TAF aircraft could support the IXth AF the following day with just a small force left behind covering the British sector, although low clouds seriously hampered Typhoon ops that day. Heavy bombers did manage to attack rail targets on the approaches to the battle, though. From 20 to 22 December thick fog blanketed north Europe. On 22 December 2nd TAF did manage 316 sorties, but with little gain. On 23 December the weather improved sufficiently for both the opposing air forces to take to the air. At the end of the day 2nd TAF and IXth AF had flown 2,128 sorties with 96 enemy aircraft claimed, 220 motor vehicles and 17 armoured vehicles. The VIIIth AF claimed 80 enemy aircraft destroyed. Then came the chance of the night fighters. Under darkness the German bombers tried to penetrate and harass Allied movement towards the Bulge. In doing so they met the night fighters of 85 Group, in particular those of 488 Squadron.

The first three weeks of December had been a lean period for 488 Squadron. In between uneventful patrols and night flying tests, members of the squadron spent their time making toys for local children and planning a Christmas event. But on the night of 23/24 December 488 Squadron was once more back into action with a vengeance. One pilot and his navigator, Flight Lieutenant 'Chunky' Stewart and Flying Officer Bill Brumby, would have their first contact with the enemy.

> *Flight Lieutenant Stewart:* While on patrol near Roermond I noticed clusters of white flares and obtained permission to investigate. The Controller said there was no activity in that direction but my navigator succeeded in putting me on to an aircraft and after a short chase, with target taking mild evasive action, we both identified it as a Junkers 88, but for positive identification I closed to 100 feet, whereupon the enemy aircraft fired off a red flare which illuminated the black crosses on the fin, fuselage and mainplane. I dropped back to 150 yards and fired a short burst observing strikes between the port engine and fuselage. With a second burst the port engine caught fire and the Hun span down in flames, exploding before hitting the ground... The Controller told me to climb to 7,000 feet and whilst doing so I saw further flares and again requested permission to chase. After changing Controls my navigator seized upon an opportunity and after the enemy aircraft had throttled back, turned, climbed and straightened out, I obtained a visual at 2,000 feet, which my navigator confirmed with his glasses as another Junkers 88. At 300 yards this aircraft also dropped reddish flares and we plainly saw the black crosses and also the bomb racks. I closed in to 200/150 yards and gave two short bursts, which started a fire in the fuselage. The enemy aircraft did a diving turn to starboard and when I was down to 1,000 feet he hit the ground and exploded.

The CO, Wing Commander Watts, claimed a Ju 188. Flight Lieutenant John Hall would claim an Me 410, following his enemy in a twisting and turning dogfight. A fourth burst of gunfire from the Mosquito tore into the enemy aircraft's starboard engine, setting it alight and shortly afterwards the Me 410 dived and then exploded. The fifth combat of the night involved Ray Jeffs and Norman Crookes. Their combat report recorded:

Date – 23/24 December
Mosquito XXX A.I. Mk X
Time attack was delivered – 02.50 hours, near Malmédy
Clear visibility, dark

Took off from Amiens/Glisy at 0030 hours, and was taken over by Marmite control. Flight Lieutenant R. G. Jeffs continues:

I was given several vectors and had a long chase on bogey, which was identified by me as a Mosquito. During the chase our weapon became partially bent, i.e. scan became restricted. Immediately afterward I was vectored east to investigate another bogey flying east at 10,000 ft taking evasive action. A long chase ensued and contact was obtained at $3^1/_2$ miles range, 20 degrees off 2 o/c angels $10^1/_2$. Followed target through evasive action and obtained visual 40 degrees off at 2 o/c at a range of 1,500 ft. I closed in to about 1,000 ft and identified it as Ju 88, confirmed by my navigator using Ross night glasses. I followed enemy aircraft through fairly severe evasive action for about 4 mins. Finally I opened fire with one ring deflection at a range of 600/800 ft. I observed a strike on outboard of starboard engine. Enemy aircraft immediately peeled off to starboard and I gave another short burst with full deflection, no results being observed. Visual contact was lost and not regained though we orbited down to 4,000 ft. Ground control could not give any further assistance.

At the time Ray and Norman claimed the Ju 88 as damaged. But in recent years it was discovered that the aircraft had in fact failed to return to base, and the crew had baled out. As a result of the action the Americans subsequently awarded Norman the US DFC. 85 Group flew 59 sorties that night, claiming 12 aircraft destroyed or damaged.

On 24 December 2nd TAF aircraft attacked transport and engaged the German air force, with nine aircraft claimed destroyed by that evening. The American tactical air forces caused similar carnage, and the medium bombers were also out in force. The VIIIth AF attacked airfields, road and rail communications at the base of the Bulge. They would claim 75 aircraft destroyed. RAF Bomber Command attacked the airfields. By the end of the day Allied aircraft had flown 7,380 sorties in support of the battle. They continued to exercise their overwhelming air power over the next few days. The contribution of the Luftwaffe declined in the last days of December, but it was about to make another appearance in force.

Meanwhile the American land forces had redeployed for further pressure and subsequent advances on the southern flank of the Bulge. The defenders at Bastogne heroically held their position and on 26 December the US 4th Armored Division broke the siege. Nevertheless the situation was still serious, the 5th Panzer Army were still pushing for the Meuse and the 9th Panzer and 15th Panzergrenadier Division were released by Hitler to reinforce the advance. But Collins met the thrust and drove it back, recapturing Celles on Christmas Day. The German advance west was halted and turned, and there would be no recovery. The battle had been costly for both sides, but only one side could afford such cost.

During November 1944 146 Wing underwent some command changes, with Wing Commander Baldwin leaving on 3 November.

> *Flight Lieutenant H. Neville Thomas:* Though he strongly denied it, the 'powers that be' had ruled that he was operationally tired and must go on rest, and well he might be, for in four short months, in addition to carrying out the planning of numberless successful operations, he himself had led over 150 missions and under his brilliant leadership the Wing had built up a reputation second to none.
>
> His enthusiasm, determination, fine strategy and consideration for his pilots and all under him, had greatly endeared him to those with whom he came in contact, and made his loss, temporary though it may be, keenly felt by all.

On 19 November Wing Commander J. C. Wells, DFC and Bar, Croix de Guerre, joined 146. Thomas continues:

> Some of us had known him during the old Manston days when he 'shared' the Manston Typhoon Wing (Nos. 198 and 609 Squadrons) as Commanding Officer of 609 Squadron, with our [former] Wing Commander Flying – Wing Commander 'Johnny' Baldwin, as Commanding Officer of 198 Squadron.
>
> It may be said that we were extremely fortunate in keeping the Wing 'in the family', so to speak, which is a great factor in preserving the team spirit in a 'heterogeneous mob' of five squadrons.
>
> So under our new leader it was 'the mixture as before' and everyone was happy.

Whilst the Ardennes offensive ran its course, to the north the 1st Canadian Army became wary of facing their own potential German counter attack. As such about two thirds of 84 Group were held to the north in case any such attack should develop. Calls were made on 84 Group, including 197 Squadron, to assist in action against the enemy. Flight Lieutenant Thomas recalled the nature of 146 Wing operations.

> 'Interdiction' – poor weather – close support – bad weather – 'Interdiction' – impossible weather – so December slipped away.
>
> There were two 'bright intervals' in an otherwise dark and gloomy month, the announcements of the award of a second Bar to the DSO to Group Captain Gillam and a Bar to Wing Commander Baldwin. To these officers we offer our sincere congratulations. Needless to say both awards were duly 'christened' in the customary manner – with champagne!

Derek Lovell, with other 197 Squadron pilots, was sent up to try to find, and engage, Luftwaffe pilots, though with little joy, as his logbook testifies. Though on Christmas Eve, things changed:

> *197 Squadron ORB:* Ten aircraft were airborne at 1104 hours for a fighter sweep round Lingen – Osnabrück – Nijmegen. The intention was to

intercept Hun aircraft returning to their bases from the Ardennes area. The visibility was excellent and the formation was flying at 10,000 feet over Nijmegen when a formation of 195 Squadron reported that they had engaged 40-50 Hun fighters near Enschede. Our formation headed for Enschede and there picked up two of 195 but no Huns. These two returned to base as our aircraft set course for Lingen. At this stage a mixed dozen of FW 190s and Me 109s attacked F/L Curwen's section out of the sun and though they were reported when 300 yards away no order to break was given until it was too late. Accurate medium flak burst in the middle of the formation as the air attack commenced. All the Huns dived through and three returned for a second attack. The formation evaded this. One lone 190 climbed back into the sun and attacked for a third time. A running commentary was given on his position and the squadron broke to meet the attack. P/O Allan held him in a climbing turn but spun off it. P/O Lovell took a quick full deflection squirt at him and he then half rolled and dived away with three of our aircraft in pursuit. However he pulled away and was last seen heading east. P/O Matthews' section reformed and returned to base followed by F/L Curwen and P/O Mahaffy. W/O Read of B Flight and P/O McFee of A Flight are missing as a result of the operation. W/O Read is believed to have baled out, nothing is known about P/O McFee. P/O Allan's aircraft was damaged both by flak and fighters.

Warrant Officer Read lost his life; Pilot Officer McFee was captured.

At Christmas intelligence came through of reinforced German forces near the mouth of the Maas, preparing for an attack south. Reports also came in of a possible attack by paratroops. 84 Group's attention was switched to cutting rail links to the area.

Derek Lovell: Christmas Day we were stood to, expecting parachutists any minute. I remember a fellow pilot Paddy and I decided we were better as pilots than infantry and the first sign of any paratrooper we were going to get on a motorbike and go like a bat out of hell for Bruges, or some other airfield.

Derek Lovell's logbook:
25 December – Ramrod (Xmas day!!). Marshalling yards at Amesfoort. Good bombing used anti-personnel bombs.
26 December – Ramrod. Cut line W of Utrecht. Attacked some MT. Got 1 damaged.
29 December – Ramrod. Bombed and strafed assault boats on Schouwen Island [at the mouth of the Maas]. VG.
31 December – Ramrod. German Army HQ in Gameren. Low level. VG bombing.

Derek Lovell: [On 29 December] we understood there were enemy soldiers with rubber dinghies planning to counter attack, so we went strafing, spraying bullets all over the place. If there were any rubber dinghies there we were going to make a lot of holes in them.

On New Year's Eve Wing Commander Wells led in Typhoons of 197 and 257

Squadron to attack the German 88 Corps HQ. High explosives, incendiaries and cluster bombs, as displayed by subsequent photographs, destroyed the house and everything nearby. But the day didn't all go the way of the Typhoon pilots. The Typhoon of 197 Squadron's Squadron Leader Allan Smith was hit by flak on an operation attacking a bridge at Culemborg. Smith managed to force land his damaged aircraft and was seen running. But news would eventually come through of his capture.

The next day, early on, the attention of all the Allied air forces was diverted away from the land battle. The Luftwaffe attacked in force – operation Bodenplatte. The 146 Wing diary recorded New Year's Day 1945:

> 1945 started with a 'Bang'. Between 0900 and 1000 hours, three formations of Me 109s flew across the Airfield at nought feet! Only the first formation carried out an attack, during which eight aircraft in dispersals received superficial damage by cannon fire!

> *Derek Lovell:* We were in the briefing tent, about nine in the morning. We were delayed going to our aircraft as the runway had iced up, and they got three tonners out there with salt. We had these Hessian-surrounded loos and I thought I'd take advantage of the spare time. I remember sitting there minding my own business. I could suddenly hear b-b-b-b-boom. I peered over the hessian and could see fighters going over the far end of the airfield, which I have to tell you is the most magnificent way of relieving any constipation.
>
> We all stood around and there were all these 109s flying around at a few hundred feet, in a haphazard fashion. I remember we were yelling out, 'Weave you stupid sods, weave.' They were getting clobbered all over the place. They caught some of 193 Squadron at the far end of the airfield but didn't do much damage. We weren't touched but it was quite a hairy morning.
>
> We all wanted to scramble, but were told, 'Don't be bloody silly. They'll have you before you get off the deck.' Once we were moving down the runway we would have been very vulnerable. We then got off after they'd gone but we didn't see anything.

The Luftwaffe, having marshalled a considerable reserve, were attempting a knock-out blow against the Allied air forces, principally against British airfields around Brussels, Antwerp and Eindhoven, but also some in the US sector. Complete surprise was achieved by flying in at low level and with complete radio silence.

> Once over their targets the German pilots strafed aircraft on the runways, vehicles, dispersal huts with cannon and machine guns and after about twenty minutes made off independently for home. The Me 262s dropped a few bombs of a 500 and 1,000 pound calibre. On the ground everyone found what cover he could in waterlogged trenches, culverts and behind vehicles. At Eindhoven the dispersal hut of one squadron was demolished but fortunately it was unoccupied by any pilots at the time. In a few minutes airfields were covered with clouds of smoke from burning aircraft and petrol dumps and bombs loaded on aircraft exploded in the heat for

> about an hour afterwards. On the whole the attacks were pressed home with determination but one case of an aircraft colliding with another was reported and there was a good deal of poor shooting. Several allotted targets such as Le Culot airfield south of Brussels were missed altogether and the aircraft intended to attack them joined up with other formations. A few aircraft attacked Antwerp docks and machine-gunned roads in the vicinity but this was probably not intended in the original plan.[80]

Caught by surprise, Allied opposition in the air was limited, although some wings managed to engage the enemy. Many of the low flying Germans fell victims to Allied anti-aircraft fire. The Germans paid a heavy price, German records giving 193 aircraft destroyed, 18 damaged. But they had exacted their toll, with 138 2nd TAF and IXth AF aircraft destroyed, 111 damaged, 17 non-operational aircraft destroyed, 24 damaged. Losses to other RAF commands came to 12 operational and five non-operational aircraft. Forty RAF personnel were killed, 145 injured and six pilots killed in battle. It is interesting to note that there were air force claims of 92 destroyed, and anti-aircraft claims of 363 destroyed. Whilst losses to the Allies had been considerable, the attack did not have the effect hoped for by the Germans. Indeed 2nd TAF was still able to carry out 1,084 fighter-bomber sorties on 1 January itself. The Allies had the resource to recover. But for the Luftwaffe the cost was too high.

One Man's Citation

Flying Officer Stephen Butte flew with 403 Squadron and would be awarded the DFC for his actions on New Year's Day 1945, his citation reading:

> *One morning early in January 1945, Flying Officer Butte was detailed to fly the leading aircraft of a section on a sortie over the battle zone. Just as the formation became airborne a large force of enemy fighters attacked the airfield. Flying Officer Butte immediately engaged one of the enemy aircraft shooting it down. A second and yet a third attacker fell to his guns before his ammunition was expended. He was himself then attacked by two fighters but outmanoeuvred them. In this engagement against a vastly superior number of enemy aircraft Flying Officer Butte displayed great skill, bravery and tenacity.*
>
> *Stephen Butte:* At about 0920 on New Year's morning 1945, at the ripe old age of 21 years, plus two months, minus six days, I was taking off on a dawn patrol into a total 'overcast of aluminium' comprised of hordes of enemy Me 109s and FW 190s. Since we were 20 minutes from enemy territory, disbelief in what was before me was erased when I saw the unmistakable black crosses on the wings and fuselages and swastikas on the tails of the aircraft ahead of me. I saw my cannon strikes on some of them. There was no time to reflect or try to keep score against such tremendous odds. Avoiding collisions and dodging debris from some of my victims kept me fully occupied. I do not know how many of them I might have winged when I fired into this large

[80] Public Record Office AIR 41/67.

mass of planes. I estimated about 60 aircraft over a small aerodrome going in all directions with guns blazing, and I still wonder how many might have succumbed on the long way back to their bases.

According to the enemy versions of the attack, the attacking pilots had not seen me and my Number Two taking off. They were concentrating on trying to destroy other Spits that were taxiing to the runway for take-off, or those that were parked in neat rows at the various squadron dispersals. We were negligent in not anticipating an attack of this sort and magnitude, and the aircraft on the ground suffered severe losses. In the mêlée, my extra fuel tank refused to jettison and it probably impeded the performance of my aircraft, but on the plus side its refusal to jettison probably saved the lives of our Group Captain, 'Iron Bill' MacBrien, and our Wing Commander, Johnny Johnson, who were just leaving the officers' mess after breakfast. The mess was on the flight path of my aircraft and by not being hit by my fuel tank, they were able to record events as they transpired. Our Squadron Leader, Jim Collier, also observed the action from the ground and he reported that I had started shooting before my undercarriage had been retracted, usually the first operation after take-off.

I ran out of ammunition after I shot down three of them, but was then attacked by two Focke-Wulf 190 Doras, long-nosed versions of the 190s, who were determined to get themselves a Spitfire that day. But by some fancy footwork on my part, I was able to evade them. At one stage, I was within 20 or 30 feet of one of the 190s and contemplated breaking off his tail with my wing but decided against it when I remembered that a second aircraft was back there somewhere. More fancy footwork on my part, and when the two of them were ahead of me, I made my escape. The attack was all over in 10 minutes.

Despite the morning activity 197 Squadron managed to get its pilots airborne that day, and throughout the month of January interdiction sorties occupied Derek Lovell, as his logbook shows, although he was able to enjoy seven days' leave.

Derek Lovell's logbook:
1 January – Ramrod. Village of Aalburg. Only 6 aircraft, good bombing, no flak!!
5 January – Ramrod. Low level on Bruinisse, good bombing, good prang.
14 January – Air test. Prop over-revved. Landed smartish like!!
14 January – Ramrod. Good attempt to prang a rail road bridge at Amersfoort. 3 hits!
16 January – Ramrod. Rail fly over W of Ede. Excellent bombing probably dest.
18 January – To Northolt. Back home for 7 days leave. Very rough trip, weather very stiff.
27 January – To Antwerp.
29 January – Ramrod. Original target u/s. Attacked rail bridge nr Gorinchen.

Poor weather, especially mist and snow, had in fact restricted the number of operations the squadron could carry out. But 197 was kept busy:

> *197 Squadron ORB:* 26 January – Snow fell from time to time during the day, and this coupled with ground mist, prevented any operational flying. There was a short discussion in the afternoon about tactics and flying generally. After this the pilots went to the dispersal and picked up odd fin boxes, petrol and glycol tins half covered by snow which could be dangerous to taxying aircraft. Quite as much snow as tins was thrown on and at the lorry driven by hapless F/L Mahaffy who fondly imagined that the best place during the expedition was in the driver's cab.
> 27 January –. . . The Hun put out a big effort during the night and the most conscientious counters amongst us claim that 67 V1s were sent over. Small quantities of plaster from the various ceilings were removed as a result of their arrival.

> *Flight Lieutenant H. Neville Thomas:* For four months we had operated from Antwerp and for over three of these months we had been 'pestered' day and night, by flying bombs and rockets. I use the word 'pestered' because even at the height of this unpleasant offensive when over 80 per day were 'coming over', there was no relaxing of the Wing 'air' effort, though shortly after our arrival in Antwerp, a rocket landed very close to a Typhoon on which groundcrew were working and a number of them were killed or horribly mutilated. Throughout the period at Antwerp the spirit of the 'ground' boys was such, that they never even attempted to take shelter, but went quietly on with their work throughout the 'Blitz'.

For the first week of February 197 Squadron, when the weather permitted, continued interdiction and attacks on V2 launch sites. Two of the squadron personnel also witnessed one particular V2 attack . . .

> *197 Squadron ORB:* Rain fell almost continuously all day and there was no flying. F/O James and the Padre had a narrow escape from being V2'd in the town. This particular rocket fell, rather superfluously, in the cemetery.

Force Landing

On a low level bombing operation in Holland on 5 January 1945, 257 Squadron Brian Spragg's Typhoon was hit by flak.

> I was struggling back to base knowing the engine wasn't too good and I got within about 15 miles of Antwerp when it packed up. I was too low to jump out by then, only about 1,500 feet. And by the time I had looked around and checked there was only one thing to do, put it down somewhere. But there wasn't much around that was suitable. There were trees and dykes and ditches. I hit the first two trees at about 120 mph, and hit about 20 in total. I finished up in a ditch with just the engine and me. That's why I loved the Typhoon. I just caught my lip

on the gunsight and cricked my neck a bit. I hit the end bit at about 20 miles per hour or so, but I had left the rest of the aircraft strewn over about three or four hundred yards.

A young girl came up to me, she could speak a bit of English, and then people started to come around, so I said, 'Keep them well clear.' There was still fuel and ammunition about. Eventually an army major came up in a Jeep. I told him what had happened and he asked, 'Where are you from?' I said, 'Antwerp.' He said, 'I'll drive you back if you like.'

The war was soon to enter its final phase, although there was still a lot of fighting to be done. With the front in the Ardennes stabilised, Eisenhower and his generals had now planned the advance beyond the Siegfried Line to the Rhine, the subsequent crossing and the exploitation into Germany. All this, of course, under the continued protection of the Allied air umbrella, and supported by Allied aerial artillery.

CHAPTER 12

VICTORY

To seek the final defeat of the German forces in the west Eisenhower planned three stages for the ongoing offensive, codenamed operation Veritable:

Phase 1: Overrun all German positions west of the Rhine.
Phase 2: Cross the river and secure bridgeheads.
Phase 3: Two thrusts. The 21st Army Group north from Duisburg, around the Ruhr and to take the North German plain. The 12th Army Group to advance south of the Ruhr from the Mainz/Frankfurt area to Kassel. Thus completing the encirclement of the Ruhr.

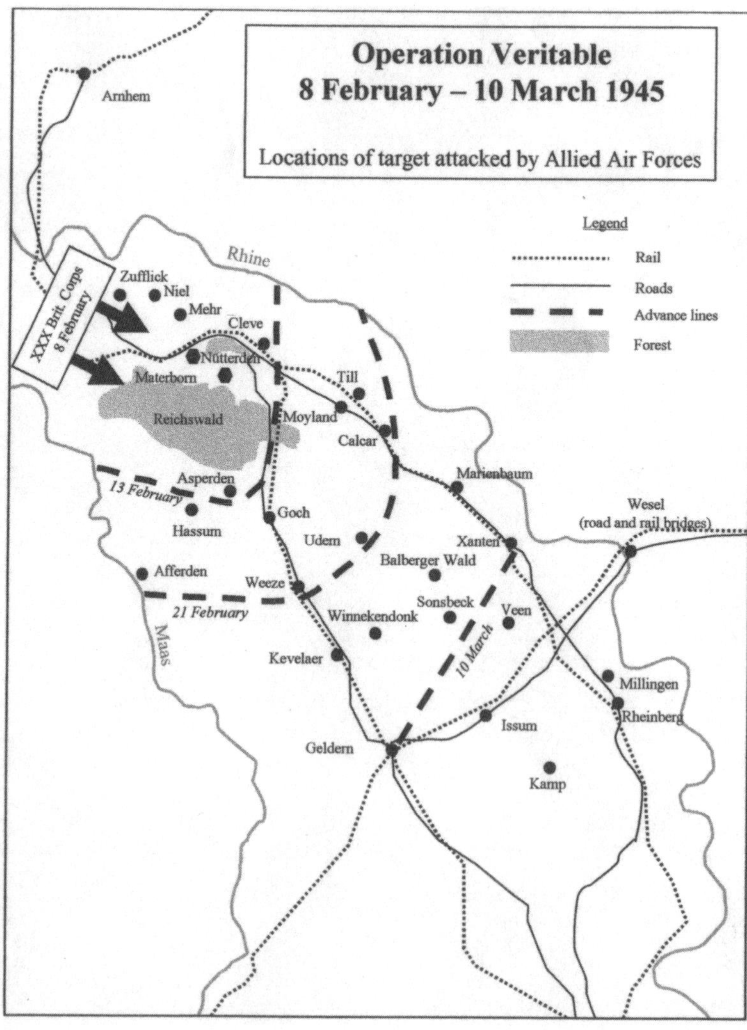

Meanwhile the southern Allied armies were to hold their positions on the Rhine. The 6th Army Group was battling against a German attempt to retake Strasbourg and the plain of Alsace. On New Year's Eve the Germans launched operation Nordwind, coming within eight miles of Strasbourg, and here the opposing troops struggled for the next fortnight. But towards the end of January the Germans began to withdraw back across the Rhine and the position in the south was stabilised by the Allies.

On 8 February 1945 the Canadian 1st Army opened the offensive in the north attacking south-west, with its left flank on the Rhine, and supported by Allied air power. The defences in front of the Canadian army were certainly deep, incorporating the northern edge of the Siegfried Line. Notably the advance had to push through the Reichswald forest where there was strongly fortified ground, known to the Allies as the Nütterden and Materborn features. The XXXth British Corps was to open the attack on 8 February preceded by a massive artillery bombardment. Following any breakthrough the IInd Canadian Corps was to take over the left side. The operation was planned in three phases.

> The first was the clearing of the Reichswald forest and an advance up to the line Gennap – Asperden – Cleve. Secondly the main German defensive line was to be breached east and south-east of the Reichswald. This included the capture of the towns of Weeze, Udem, Calcar and the ground on the south bank of the Rhine opposite Emmerich. Finally the Army was to break into the Hochwald 'layback' and advance to the line Geldern – Xanten.[81]

84 Group was to coordinate the air support. 83 Group was to carry out most of the fighter versus fighter operations, giving 84 Group the freedom to concentrate directly on the air needs of the ground battle. On 8 February the key operational focus was the blasting of the Nütterden and Materborn features. Medium bombers went to the latter, fighter-bombers to the former. Also notable is that immediate army support was to come from a Typhoon 'cab rank', each of the assaulting divisions having a contact car in which a tour-expired RAF pilot acted as controller.

At 1030 hours the advance began, following on from the artillery bombardment. There was considerable opposition, and minefields and floods also slowed progress. 2nd TAF aircraft played their part, although mist and low cloud would make operations problematic, with armed recces, tactical recces, village strong points bombed, and enemy telecommunications attacked. 146 Wing flew 156 sorties in the day and 197 Squadron would weigh in. One new aspect of the 8 February operations, was the use of blind bombing through cloud. This involved a controller on the ground, monitoring the position of the Typhoons at a set height, with radar, and then instructing the pilots to release the bombing when appropriate. Derek Lovell's logbook recorded his involvement on the opening day of the offensive:

> 8 February – Ramrod (blind bombing). Village of Mehr [between the Reichswald and the Rhine] thru 10/10 – never saw target. Coo!

---

[81] Public Record Office AIR 41/67.

> 8 February – Ramrod. Nütterden. Siegfried strong point bombed and strafed.

At the end of the first day 2nd TAF had flown 1,201 sorties, IXth AF 167 sorties. British troops had advanced, 1,200 prisoners had been taken, but the Materborn and Nütterden features were still in German hands. Low cloud and rain prevented 197 Squadron operating on 9 February, indeed all ops in the air were restricted. But on the ground the advance was maintained, the two features were overrun and the Canadians occupied Millingen and Mehr. Over the next three days 2nd TAF's main effort was to prevent enemy reinforcement of the area, and to attack German HQs. Derek Lovell flew on the first 197 Squadron operation on 10 February, his logbook recording, 'Ramrod. Original target under cloud, bombed wood containing M.T. & Ammo.' Lovell didn't take part in the second operation, but 197 Squadron's Derek Tapson did.

> *Derek Tapson:* We were after a German headquarters, a farmhouse being used by an army section. We were asked to take it out. It was on a crossroads. We got near the target and the CO said he couldn't identify it. My No. 1 was a flight commander, Toby Harding. He said he could and should we go down and mark it for him. So the CO said yes. We came down to make a low level attack on this building, but as we got to about 2,000 feet, the CO said, 'I've got it, return to formation.' So we pulled away from the target. Toby pulled up and I pulled up behind him and I thought, 'That's a bloody silly thing to do, if they shoot at him they'll hit me.' So I slid out to the left and I must have slipped across into a burst of flak. The beauty of it was that the engine protected me. The engine got it and I didn't, otherwise it could have come in the side of the aircraft. I kept on climbing, got up and thought to myself, 'Well the Rhine's over there, see if I can glide across, land the other side.' Then I realised that the Typhoon glides like a tank. Meanwhile the engine caught fire and flame was coming into the cockpit. I got burns to my wrist and my face and lost my eyebrows and eyelashes. I thought I'd better get out. I undid my straps, pulled a lever on the front, which meant the top flew off and a panel went down the side. The technique was to lean out the side, until you were level with the top surface of the wing, catch hold of the trailing edge of the wing, put your foot on the stick, push the stick, and the aircraft would go in one direction and you would go in the other and you wouldn't hit the tail. Anyway I got out and I was just catching hold, when I suddenly realised that I was looking at the sky and not the ground, so I must have been upside down. I got back in level with the aircraft and realised that I was climbing. I thought, 'Right it'll stall in a minute and if it does so and gets in a spin I'll never get out.' I pushed the stick forward, forgetting I had undone my straps. I went straight out, but did hit my head and shoulder, I had a great lump on my head eventually. But I was out cold. I was unconscious and falling through the air. I came to and got hold of the ring and pulled the ripcord. The parachute came out between my feet and I kicked it and flipped over. I went up, back, up and then hit the ground. It was reckoned I must have pulled the ripcord at about 1,000 feet. Another ten seconds and I wouldn't have made it.

I landed in a field and as I was sitting there, I got rid of my parachute, which blew away. Then I looked around and noticed a circle of German troops. Six feet away to one side was an anti-aircraft gun, 100 yards away in the next field was my aeroplane. The officer did say to me, 'You are a prisoner of Deutsch.' I misheard and wondered why the hell the Dutch wanted to take me prisoner. Then I realised what he had said. He asked for my revolver and I gave it to him. They took me back to a medical officer, who had a look at me, and gave me something to eat. I think it was lucky that the people I landed with were Luftwaffe. People that were picked up by the army were often shot – they hated the Typhoon.

They took me to a farmhouse that they were using as headquarters. I was taken up to trees at the top of a hill where they had their trucks, out of the way. I was put in the back and a corporal gave me his overcoat to keep me warm. They then took us into one of the towns. We went to the mayor's house I think. They had a guardroom there and I was put in until the next day. We were moved to part of the Siegfried Line, a cellar-like cell where I met a couple of chaps from Bomber Command. We were moved from there down to Dulag Luft, their interrogation centre. I was kept there for about 21 days, which was a long time, largely due I think, to the fact that they wanted to get rid of my bumps and bruises before they let me out for other people to see me. I only had about three or four interrogations while I was there. All we did was give number, rank and name. I was offered a cigarette the first time I went in, and then when he asked me a question I gave him my rank and he took the cigarette away.

Derek Tapson remained a POW for the rest of the war.

On 14 February the 1st Canadian Army embarked upon the second phase of Veritable, to assault the second defensive line in the area Goch – Udem – Calcar, the IInd Canadian Corps on the left, the XXXth British Corps on the right. On 14 February 2nd TAF aircraft were out in force, flying 1,822 sorties.

Derek Lovell's logbook:
14 February – Ramrod. Signals HQ West of Goch – completely destroyed.
14 February – Ramrod. Village of Asperden, [2 miles north-west of Goch] bombed from 2-1,000 because of cloud.
14 February – Ramrod. MT park in wood nr Marienbaum, bags of flak.

Then the weather intervened, preventing operations until the afternoon of 16 February. On this day support was given to the 51st Highland Division advancing on Goch.

Flight Lieutenant H. Neville Thomas: According to the army there is not going to be much left of the Siegfried Line to 'Hang out any washing', by the time we have both finished with it!

146 Wing then received a request to 'liberate' Asperden. Its pilots duly obliged and 66 Typhoons in seven waves dropped 80,000 lbs of high explosive on the village in a two-hour period. The Wing were no doubt pleased to receive a report from the army stating, 'As a result of your attacks on this "area of resistance", 170 "bomb-happy" Germans have walked out to meet us.'

A further army report would state:

> On 16 February the villages of Asperden and Hussum were focal points on the Western approaches to Goch, both were targets of our operations, the former by Typhoons, the latter by Spitfires. A statement received from army sources says that Asperden virtually surrendered when the ground troops attacked at dusk, prisoners stating that the constant attacks by Typhoons had prevented any defence being organised and incidentally killed any desire to fight on. Hussum was captured very easily though some sort of resistance was put up, but the prisoners' stories remained the same. The results achieved for the weight of attacks put in are extremely gratifying.

Poor weather again hampered operations between 17 and 20 February, meanwhile ground forces maintained the pressure. Goch was finally overrun on 21 February, but over the next four days progress was slow. The final phase of Veritable ran from 26 February to 10 March. On 26 February the IInd Canadian Corps began a drive to Xanten on the west bank of the Rhine opposite Wesel; the resistance was still strong. But to their west the XXXth British Corps benefited from the Canadian Corps' thrust, advancing beyond Geldern and joining with the US Ninth Army. On 3 March the battle became more mobile and by 9 March the IInd Canadian Corps had taken Xanten, and the XXXth British Corps had turned east toward Wesel.

German redeployment had tried to stall the 1st Canadian Army advance, drawing troops from the south and thus weakening the defensive line that would meet the launching, by the US Ninth Army, of operation Grenade. On 22 February there was a massive aerial bombardment against German communications and the next morning US artillery opened up. Simpson's US Ninth Army were able to bridge and cross the Roer. By 2 March they had reached the left bank of the Rhine, trapping the Germans with their only escape through Wesel.

Throughout this period 2nd TAF had played its part when the weather allowed, including 197 Squadron and Derek Lovell.

> *Derek Lovell's logbook:*
> 27 February – Ramrod (blind bombing) Winnekendonk again above 10/10 as usual.
> 28 February – Ramrod. Same place as above, saw it well plastered, little flak.
> 28 February – Ramrod. Troops in wood E of Weeze, well fixed up.
> 2 March – Ramrod. Twisterden liberated!, went back with Paddy, he had hang ups.
> 9 March – Ramrod. 10/10 most of way, cut rail nr Sogel, little flak R/T went u/s.

Throughout March 1945 German troops were steadily being pushed back to and even beyond the Rhine. On 7 March the US First Army was on the banks of the river at Cologne and 30 miles to the south the Ludendorff railway bridge was found intact and American units rushed across to open up a bridgehead. On 22 March Patton crossed the river itself. On the 23rd operation Plunder began, Allied ground forces crossing the Rhine either side of Wesel in assault craft and

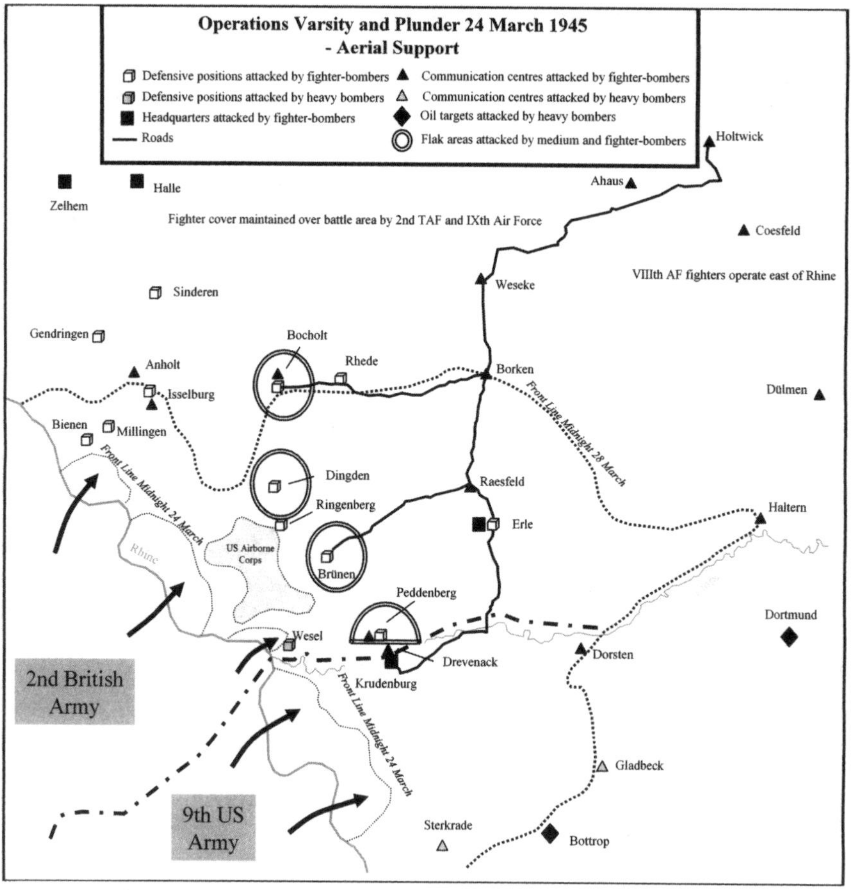

on the 24th the Allies launched operation Varsity, deploying 21,000 airborne troops, to come to ground north-east of Wesel, and secure the bridgehead over the Rhine. By the end of March and beginning of April the US Ninth and First Armies were encircling the Ruhr and 21st Army Group began a drive to the Baltic. The US First and Third Armies linked at Kassel, the US Seventh Army pushed for Heidelberg and the 1st French Army advanced to the south and Switzerland. It appeared that the defeat of Germany in the west was imminent.

Again, air power played a great part. To the north the Rhine crossing was supported by a concentrated effort against transportation targets leading to the proposed bridgeheads. In addition flak positions were attacked to try and neutralise the threat against the airborne landings, and armed recces carried out together with army support operations and interdiction. Moreover, prior to the northern crossing of the Rhine some special ops were laid on, utilising the experience of certain units which at that stage were becoming somewhat expert in their conduct.

During the second half of March a number of 'cloak and dagger' operations came 146 Wing's way. On 18 March 72 R/Ps, 48 x 1,000 lb and four x 500 lb of high explosive and two x 500 lb incendiary bombs were fired or dropped on the

HQ of General Johannes von Blaskowitz, commanding Army Group H. Reconnaissance later revealed that the house was completely destroyed, with other buildings severely damaged. The next day 146 Wing sent 36 aircraft against an M/T repair depot. Rockets, 1,000 lb and 500 lb bombs blasted the depot, reducing it to 'a burning mass of rubble'.

> *Flight Lieutenant H. Neville Thomas:* A recce pilot who photographed the target an hour and a half later needed no course for his flight. He was guided there by the volumes of smoke, which rose to a height of 3,000 feet from the flaming wreckage. The photographs when printed gave full proof of the claims made.

On 21 March the HQ of the German 25th Army was smashed, and on 23 March an enemy ammunition dump became a 'general conflagration'. Derek Lovell went on leave on 21 March and, to his chagrin, he would miss out on lending his support to the Rhine crossing.

> *197 Squadron ORB:* 24 March – The pilots were roused at the fantastic hour of 0430. F/L Jolleys DFC led the first show on the village of Zelhern. The bombing and strafing resulted in a heartening display of fires. F/L Jolleys led the first anti-flak patrol in the Wesel – Rees area. The squadron split into sections of four to bomb different gun positions. Three AMC were strafed with one written off and one damaged, both aircraft being hit in the process. The sky was full of tugs, gliders and parachute-dropping aircraft. Visibility was poor, due mainly to smoke from the ground. F/L Jolleys led the second anti-flak patrol and again the squadron split into sections to bomb different gun positions. F/O Welsh's aircraft was damaged by 40mm and a splinter hit his right arm.

But it was not just the tactical air forces which were exercising their power. The aerial support given to Plunder and Varsity was a staggering example of air supremacy. The Luftwaffe had tried to intervene, but 'its attempts to break into the ring made by the British and American fighters had been hopeless.'[82] The following table, covering the night of 23/24 March and 24 March, demonstrates the might of Allied air power in the west at this stage of the war.[83]

Air Force	**Effective sorties**	**Bomb tonnage**	**Losses**
RAF Bomber Command	719	3,429	4
US VIIIth AF Bombers	1,721	4,096	14
US VIIIth AF Fighters	1,404	–	9
US XVth AF Bombers	660	1,415	15
US XVth AF Fighters	394	–	–
2nd British TAF	2,223	511	17
US IXth AF	2,747	1,623	12
1st TAF	1,095	314	–
First French AF	263	94	–

[82] Public Record Office Air 41/67.
[83] *Ibid.*

Air Force	Effective sorties	Bomb tonnage	Losses
RAF Fighter Command	338	–	–
RAF Coastal Command	31	–	–
38 and 46 Group RAF	440	–	7
US IXth Troop Carrier Command	1,149		46
Total	**13,184**	**11,482**	**124**

Prisoner of Your Own Side

On 24 March Flight Lieutenant Harrison of 193 Squadron was shot down whilst attacking flak positions and baled out, coming down in the midst of the Rhine bridgehead ground battle. Americans took him prisoner.

> *Flight Lieutenant Harrison:* I tried to convince them that I was an Australian. I used all the American epithets I knew in the process, but I am tall and fair, and I was wearing a German belt and they were just not having any of it.

The Americans then made Harrison unload ammunition and supplies, but he eventually managed to persuade a lieutenant who he was. Harrison was given an American armband and a rifle and he dug himself a foxhole.

> *Flight Lieutenant Harrison:* I spent the time helping to pick off snipers, and taking a crack at any other Germans I could see.

Eventually British troops reached the area and Harrison was able to hitch-hike back to his squadron.

One other of our featured pilots would re-enter the fray in March 1945 and take part in the Allied air support to the Rhine crossings.

> *Hart Finley:* My posting [at the beginning of July 1944] was back to 53 OTU, and I was there as a flight commander in the training school for only about two weeks, when I suddenly had a phone call from Hendon, the main HQ of Fighter Command. I was asked to get down there very quickly, it was urgent. I was given permission to fly a Spitfire to Hendon. When I got there I was told by an officer that they wanted me to go over to Northern Ireland, to give instruction to two Fleet Air Arm squadrons in dive-bombing tactics and strafing. These were to go out to the Far East.
>
> I had about three to four weeks with these two squadrons flying Seafires. When I first saw the Seafires with their wings folded my first thought was I was going to have to take these fellows up to 17,000 feet, and dive bomb at a very steep angle and pull out at the bottom, and my fear was whether the wings would hold together. They assured me they were very secure when locked in and they showed me the size of the bolt, so I lost my concern and began the instruction.
>
> After that assignment I had another and this time it was to Boscombe Down, to do some intensive development flying on the Spit XXI, the latest

breed, with a five-bladed propeller and a Griffon engine, and much faster than the other aircraft in the series. It had an incredible performance. I must have put roughly 100 hours of flying in on this aeroplane to see how it would stand up to operational conditions. I had to take up a sort of checklist with me and run through a whole series of tests with the aircraft, everything from steep turns to aerobatics, to high power climbs, to dives and all the rest.

I flew down to Bournemouth and went low over the water in order to impress a few of the would-be fighter pilots, Canadians, who were likely to be at Bournemouth at the time. It was always one of my biggest thrills on arriving at Bournemouth when one of the first things we saw was a couple of Spitfires fly by and I'd thought, 'Oh man, that's for me.' This particular day I thought I was going to give somebody else that thrill and so I flew down low and did a pass and then I climbed up very rapidly to about 20,000 feet to start into my exercise of tests. I hadn't been in level flight for more than about a minute when suddenly there was an explosion and flames came out of the right side of the engine. I immediately had a dead engine, so I started to glide down. I thought about my options; I could bale out and forget about the aeroplane or I could try and get it down in one piece and hopefully they'd be able to find out what the reason for the explosion was. I elected for the second. I managed to get the fire out right away by side-slipping the aircraft, and then as I got lower and lower and got over the field and circled it a few times and gave a radio transmission that I was in trouble, they had all the fire-fighting equipment out on the field. I made my final approach and was able to get my wheels down and flaps down manually, and I put the aircraft down pretty much in the centre of the field and rolled to a nice easy stop. All the crash equipment came out and I got out and explained what had happened. To me the strangest aspect of this whole incident was that after doing what I did, I wasn't looking for any great pat on the back, I wasn't looking for any recognition, although I thought at least somebody might say, 'Jolly fine show old buddy.' Nobody said that, including the flight commander who I was working for there. He came out and looked at the aeroplane and they towed it away and that's the last I heard of it.

On completion of his work at Boscombe Down Hart was posted home to Canada, for some leave over the winter of 1944/45. Then in the New Year he learnt of his posting back to the battle over Western Europe to 403 Squadron. The squadron by then had moved, on 2 March to B.90 Petit Brogel, near Bourg Léopold, and it was from here that Hart would take part in 403 Squadron's support to the crossing of the Rhine.

403 Squadron ORB:
23 March – A beautiful clear day. Three operational trips completed. Uneventful. Rather a quiet day around the dispersal, everyone keyed up and wondering what day the 'big push' at the front will be coming off, which is rumoured very soon. All the boys are keen to chalk up a few Jerrys to their credit, and see some real action.
24 March – The big push is on. Boys were all up very early in the dawn

in readiness to take their part when called upon. A glorious day for all especially the pilots, who have been waiting so long to see a little real action. No victories scored by us, very little of the enemy seen in the air, which was a bit disappointing to most. Ten operational trips made – weather recce, dive bombing and armed recce.
25 March – Another heavy day of flying, and not much slack time now amongst the squadron. Five operational trips, all patrols completed, uneventful. Flying Officer Gillis force-landed amongst the paratroopers and gliders across the Rhine, and was seen to land safely. Word came through that he was safe, and would be returning to the unit.
26 March – Flying operations began in the early dawn, and carried on steadily all day. Ten operational trips completed, all patrols. The pilots are really getting the hours packed in these days, with a few near completion of their tours.

Hart Finley was certainly packing in his hours. Taking off at 0550 on 24 March, on a weather recce, he was able to bring back valuable information, reporting ten ambulances, ten scattered MET and much activity in the Brünen area. The next day Hart took part in two patrols, the first, Worston – Winterswijk, in the morning (during which Flying Officer Gillis crash-landed), the second, Dorsten – Winterswijk, late afternoon. It was similar action on 26 March, an early morning patrol Ruurlo – Winterswijk, then another in the same area later that morning during which MET were attacked, one damaged, one destroyed, and a motorcycle and two soldiers strafed. Hart was again operational that afternoon.

28 March was again a very busy day for 403 Squadron, Hart saw action, but on one patrol Flying Officer Reeves was seen to go straight in, a victim of light flak. Flak was the only real threat at this time, as 403 Squadron encountered little opposition from the Luftwaffe, although the value of the patrols lay as much in being able to report enemy troop concentrations and movements, as in attacking troops and transports.

Throughout April as the Allied land forces pushed onwards, 403 Squadron kept up the aerial offensive.

Hart Finley: It was mostly ground support, a lot of strafing, anything that was moving on the roads, trains, boats, ships. We attacked anything that we thought was of any value to the enemy.

Early on the morning of 23 April the object of Hart's attentions happened to be an aircraft.

Hart Finley's combat report: I was leading a section of four aircraft on a routine patrol between Bremen and Hamburg along the autobahn at 0615 hours. Flying west along the patrol line my No. 4 reported four aircraft at twelve o'clock. I looked ahead and saw two aircraft above my section flying in the same direction. I recognised them as long-nosed FW 190s. We climbed up under them and were closing rapidly when they spotted us. They started to pour black smoke but we closed easily even with jet tanks on. They climbed from 5,000 feet to 7,000 feet where we caught up to them. They broke one to port and one to starboard. I went after the leader who broke port and told my No. 2 to get the other. I let a squirt go at 500

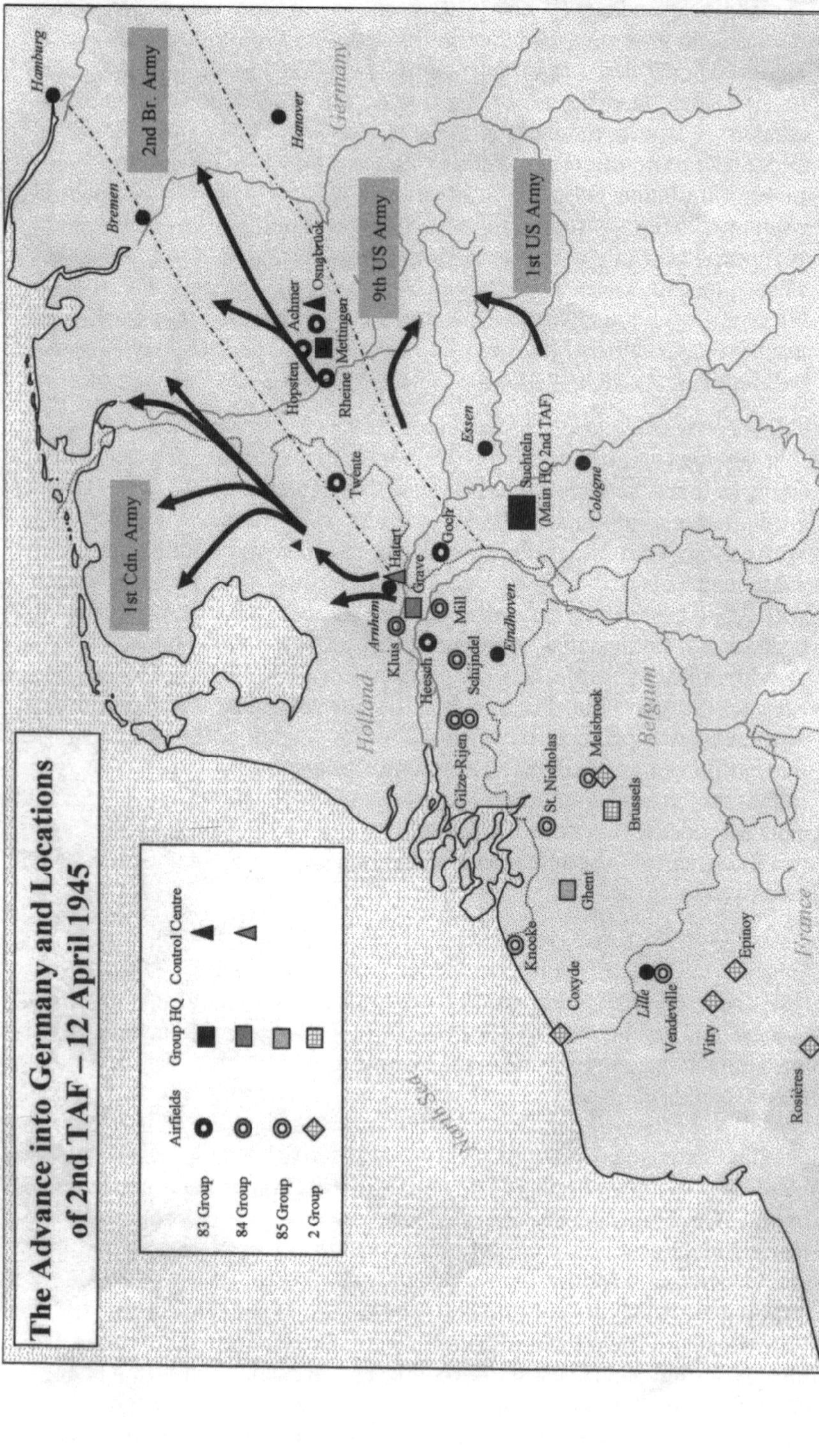

The Advance into Germany and Locations of 2nd TAF – 12 April 1945

yards (4-5 second burst with MG and cannon) and saw a couple of strikes on the enemy aircraft, one near the starboard wing root and one which appeared to hit the cockpit. The aircraft slowed down and I rapidly closed to 100 yards where I again opened fire (3-4 seconds with MG and cannon). I saw several more strikes near the cockpit and the enemy aircraft went out of control and started flicking down. There was no sign of the pilot baling out as I broke off the attack. I pulled up and saw it continue flicking down into the ground. It burst into flames and burnt up. As I opened fire the first time the FW started firing his guns off into space. I believe the pilot was wounded or killed on the first attack as he made no effort at evasive action after I saw strikes. Gyro sight and camera gun used. After the aircraft hit the deck I dived down and took pictures of it burning. I claim one FW 190 destroyed.

Flight Lieutenant Dove's combat report: I was flying No. 2 in a section of four aircraft... Four aircraft were reported by No. 4 in our formation flying in the same direction. My leader recognised them as FW 190s and we started to climb rapidly. We climbed up under them and were closing very quickly when the two enemy aircraft broke and my leader instructed me to take the No. 2. I closed quickly and gave him a short burst (1-2 secs with MG and cannon) but the deflection was too great. He was coming head on and disappeared beneath me. I immediately did a very tight turn to port and came out nearly on his tail. He was taking violent evasive action. I then gave him a long burst (4-5 secs with MG and cannon) from about 50 yards and about 60 degrees deflection. I saw many strikes on the port wing root and cockpit. The enemy aircraft immediately burst into flames and started into a dive. I flew alongside it and saw that he was carrying a bomb. I watched him go straight down in flames and crash on the road. No. 4 in our formation saw it crash. I claim one FW 190 destroyed.

The next day Hart was transferred to 443 Squadron to take up a flight commander position, the squadron ORB recording him on 25 April as, 'one of the old school' and that, 'he should be an asset'. The asset would immediately be into action, and making returns. On the squadron's third operation of the day, that afternoon, Hart was one of eight pilots who took part in a strafing attack on Schwerin aerodrome, packed with enemy aircraft. One aircraft was claimed destroyed and twelve damaged, Hart's contribution two Ju 87s and one unidentified damaged. On the next enemy aerodrome 'beat up' of the day, three FW 190s were claimed destroyed and two damaged, Hart claiming one FW 190 destroyed. On both operations a considerable amount of transport was also destroyed or damaged, along with gun positions. One pilot was lost on the operation, seen to crash on the aerodrome. On 26 April Hart took part in an uneventful patrol, but his No. 2, in the failing light, misjudged and swerved from the runway onto soft ground and crashed, the pilot fortunately only suffering minor injuries and scratches. For Hart, for the remainder of April, it was to be mainly uneventful patrols.

The situation on the ground could now be clearly seen by the Allied airmen, flying unmolested as they were above the confusion of the enemy. The 443

Squadron ORB recorded on 1 May, 'The boys think the Germans are really on their last legs now', on 2 May, 'Everything is mixed up now. Pilots don't know whether they are in Russian, German or British territory. The Germans are starting to blow up their aircraft and aerodromes.' Regularly the ORB records operations as uneventful. However, on 2 May Hart was airborne at 1520 hours on a fighter sweep in the Lübeck area, one of a group of six 443 Squadron pilots. It was certainly not uneventful. Enemy aircraft were found on the ground and claims would later be made for one Fiesler Storch destroyed, one He 111 destroyed and two He 111s damaged. Hart recalls this action:

> We were not aware that we were that close to the end of the war. We were just going about our business of strafing anything that moved and looking for German aircraft on the ground and in the air. We had made a series of raids on some of the German airfields up around Lübeck, north of Hamburg, Kiel. We had a lot of success as there were a lot of German aircraft on the ground, and we were able to go down and strafe them. It was an extremely dangerous operation. The anti-aircraft fire was absolutely intense, it was nerve-wracking to say the least. But we pressed home our attacks and made the most of it. We did lose people but we felt it was worth the risk to hasten the end of the war. On 2 May we were doing a reconnaissance and had shot-up an airfield. We all got strikes on a number of the aircraft, blew some of them up and damaged them or destroyed them. My method of operating under these conditions was always to break off our attack maintaining a certain amount of ammunition, so that if on the way back to base we got involved with some German aircraft, we wouldn't be out of firepower. So I called a halt to the raid after we had made two or three passes. Sure enough on the way back I spotted a Ju 88 above us. We were very low at the time, probably just about tree-top height, flying as a section of six. I immediately said, 'Come on boys, let's go get him.' I was first on the scene and as I pulled up behind this Ju 88, he was at about 3,000 feet, I noticed that he suddenly pitched into a very steep dive. So I pitched over and started closing on him and I started firing. As he dived and his speed built up I thought, 'Hey this guy's going to commit suicide or something. He's going to fly right into the ground.' I couldn't believe that such a large aeroplane as that would go into such a steep dive, almost vertical. I was having difficulty, even in a Spitfire, keeping in that same depth of dive. I started to get strikes on him and at this point he was getting so close to the ground that I thought I'd better pull out. Just as I was about to, he pulled out into a very steep turn starboard. I immediately went into a turn and cut inside so that I could get some deflection on him and I started to fire again, and got all sorts of strikes. He then straightened out, and by this time we were just over the tree tops. He was going into the ground and I was going to fly over the top of him. As soon as I did, and he was underneath going into the ground to explode and blow up, I started to pull up into a steep climb. And suddenly my cockpit burst into flames. I had been hit and I wasn't aware of it until this happened. With the cockpit on fire I realised that Mrs Finley's little boy had to get out in a hurry. I didn't have any time to plan anything. I was simply in a climb, with speed falling off of course, and the engine was

starting to act up. I opened the coop top, got rid of my harness and bunted. But I only got halfway out. One of my flying boots jammed in between the pilot seat and the fuselage of the aircraft. All I can remember was being buffeted about in the slipstream, the aircraft was probably about 110 mph at this point. I suddenly said to myself, 'My God, I can't die this way.' That is etched in my mind for ever. At this point adrenalin or something took over as I must have fought and the next thing I knew, boom, I was free of the aeroplane, just broke free. As it turned out I just came right out of my flying boot. Once I was free I immediately grabbed the ripcord, pulled it, the 'chute opened and I hit the ground at practically the same time.

I was very fortunate. I didn't break my ankle, I didn't break my leg, I didn't break my neck. I simply landed heavily. I got up and started to grab the parachute in, to take it away to hide it. Suddenly I heard voices shouting and dogs barking and I looked over to my right and there was a horde of people coming my way. I thought, 'This is no place for me.' I dropped the 'chute and took off, minus one flying boot. I ran up a hill, very exposed, in the open. It wasn't too steep and I ran and I think I broke every track record that was ever set because these fellows started firing at me, bullets literally zinging around my head and into the dirt. I did all the zig-zagging I could. I got over the crest of the hill, which was fortunate as I was now out of the line of fire. I went down the other side, then there was a fence and I literally flew over it into some woods. I must have dived. I ran along a track as far as I could, until I couldn't go any further, I felt I was going to be sick from exhaustion. At this time I just turned and bashed my way into the wood, as far as I could and then just flopped. I had khaki battle dress on so it was a good bit of camouflage. I pulled a bunch of leaves around me trying to cover up as best I could and I just lay there, it was about 4 o'clock in the afternoon. I heard people's voices, shouting, and the dogs barking and I thought, 'Oh those bloody dogs, they'll get me for sure.' They couldn't have been trained as trackers because they didn't sniff me out. But there was one point when one of them came awfully close because the ground was trembling with each footstep, and my heart was pounding. I was facing down and I had got my revolver ready. Would you believe though, I had a revolver which normally carried six bullets, but I had fired off two or three at a target somewhere, and I only had three bullets left in the chamber. I thought to myself, 'Well at least I'll get a couple of them if I have to.' Anyway the footsteps started to recede, and I relaxed a bit, and at 9 o'clock that night, with the dogs and voices gone, I was able to take stock of things. I had a pack of cigarettes. I had one match and fifteen cigarettes. I lit one and chain-smoked about six, after that I couldn't smoke another.

When it got dark I decided I'd better move, so I took my scarf and wrapped it around the bootless foot. I wanted to get as far from that wood as I could, thinking that maybe next day they'd come back and have another look. I must have walked about 20 miles that night, it was difficult going because of my foot, plus the fact that I had a few shrapnel wounds, one in my leg and one in my arm. Nothing serious though. A few minor burns. I just walked through fields and along roads and hedges and every now and then a dog would bark and I would get scared. I would come across a field with some cows and I would walk across past the cows and they would come herding around me and jam me in, and I would have a terrible time. I met several horses and they kept walking every time I'd walk. If I stopped they'd stop. It was an unusual experience. Fortunately I had some guidance in that I could see flashes of light off in the distance, so I knew the direction I should be heading to get to the Allied line. The next day I was trying to stay well hidden, I was afraid I would be too obvious if somebody saw me. I came across some German equipment, little slit trenches, and bits and pieces, great coats.

Suddenly, around noon, when I was on the crest of a hill hiding, the next thing I heard was a great burst of machine-gun fire down in this little valley. I looked down and there was a small town and a whole cavalcade of German vehicles, half tracks, personnel carriers. They took off in a north-easterly direction, going out of the town. I thought, 'There must be Allied forces there.' So I decided the best thing to do would be to work round to the south-west side of the town, so anybody coming into the town I would meet up with and they would probably be Allies. It took me about three hours, and about mid afternoon I got into a thicket by the road leading into the town. There was a tank coming out of the town heading south-west. I couldn't identify it. I should have been able to as we had training in that, but for some reason I couldn't, it just didn't look like anything I was aware of, until it got beside me and rumbled by at which point I realised it was a Sherman. I wasn't quite sure what to do, I didn't want to jump out in the road for fear they would think I was going to attack it with a grenade or something. Fortunately behind was a little staff car and there were two officers. They jammed on their brakes, I went over with my hands up, pointed at my shoulder flashes, 'Canada'. They rolled down the window and asked, 'Who are you?' I replied, 'I'm a pilot that got shot down.' They radioed to the tank, told it to stop and then told me to run and get on the back, which I did. We rumbled down the road about five miles and pulled into a farmyard. There were tanks there, about half a dozen coming from every direction. They all got out and they were laughing and joking and said, 'Hey you must be kind of hungry.' I said, 'I sure am.' They got their little teapots out and made up some tea for me, and gave me some cookies. Then they suddenly got orders to carry on so they just folded everything up, got into their tanks and told me to go out and stand on the road, I would be perfectly safe, and wait there and somebody would come by and I could flag a ride. They rumbled off north-easterly, back to work. Meantime I was able to get a lift to another base where they put me in an ambulance and took me to Löwenburg, where they had taken over a hospital, and I stayed overnight. The next morning they were going to fly me back to England. I didn't have any intentions to do that, I wanted to go back to my unit. I managed to commandeer a jeep and a driver, and I said take me to the nearest airport, which he did. We made contact with our base and they sent an Auster over, flew me back and I got back about four o'clock on the afternoon of 4 May. That night we had a great party and the next morning the CO came in and announced that the war was ending. Great timing.

Although, as Hart experienced, there could still be moments of intensity in the daylight air battle, the night fighter combat activity was certainly diminishing, with 488 Squadron no exception to the norm. There were the occasional combats but sometimes weeks would go by without successes.

Norman Crookes: We were somewhat anxious to return to the activity of August 1944, but that renewal of activity didn't come, not for myself and Ray, although the squadron did have some considerable success in January and February, flying from Amiens/Glisy. There was competition, but there was great friendship. There were five of us who shared a tent in Colerne and then a hut at Amiens/Glisy. We were on the same flight, and of those five we all had at least one successful combat with the enemy. There was certainly a great deal of rivalry between flights. The competition was such that we tried to emulate each other, but it was a matter of luck. If you were able to be in the right place at the right time and you could use your navigation skills and piloting skills and particularly your shooting skills, you were successful. It wasn't rivalry that had any malice in it at all. It was quite friendly but very determined. It was essential of course that each flight should be as well prepared as the other, as we were constantly one flight on for two days and nights followed by the other flight. It wasn't very often that we had to augment each other.

Norman and Ray did have one close encounter with an enemy aircraft in the last few months of the war.

Norman Crookes: We were not assigned to any V1 patrols but we did see the V1s. In fact one almost took our tail off one day when we were flying from Amiens to Gilze-Rijen in Holland where we used to do a detachment until we were eventually (the squadron) posted to Gilze-Rijen. We were to do a night fighter patrol because most of the action was in that area and we were skimming across the cloud top at about 5,000 feet when this V1 appeared going at 90 degrees to us and it kept very close to our tail. By this time they were launching the V1s against Antwerp.

In April 1945 Norman and Ray began operating permanently from Gilze-Rijen airfield in Holland.

Norman Crookes: We had had some very pleasant times in Amiens, where we had established quite good relations with some French families. To go into Holland where there was not quite such a pleasant atmosphere was a bit forbidding. We did spend time in Breda where there was an officers' club. We had problems with the town major, which some commando units sorted out for us but I'll not go into detail. We had an intelligence officer called Les Hunt who used to delight in taking out the aircrews on their nights off into Breda, using a radar truck, and we had one particular excursion where there was a circus in town, and we paraded with Les playing his trumpet at the head, in single file, giving a Nazi salute round the circus ring as the audience departed looking rather bewildered at the strange antics of these RAF flyers. But that was the sort of winding down that we sought from this rather tiresome flying that we had in the early part of 1945.

In fact Ray and Norman would not contact the enemy again. Some squadron aircrews scored successes, but they were few and far between. Not that flying at that time wasn't still dangerous. 488 Squadron did suffer losses, predominantly in accidents, with two crews killed in 1945.

Norman Crookes: We had one occasion flying from Gilze-Rijen, when we took off and one of the engines packed up on take-off. This had happened successively with this aircraft on four occasions and on each occasion Ray Jeffs had shown his piloting skills by taking the aircraft round on one engine and landing back, but on this fifth occasion he throttled back and we ran off the end of the runway and found ourselves in a bomb crater that hadn't been filled in. Someone sent a signal to the effect that we had been injured when in fact we had both climbed out of the aircraft. I had a bloody nose and Ray was completely unharmed. So much so that he was about to leave station sick quarters, to which we were taken by the ambulance, and go back to the sight of the crash and take the clock out of it, which was at that time purported to be a prize. The aircraft was a write-off.

Just before the end of the war 488 Squadron was disbanded. Norman Crookes' passage back to the UK was on a navy vessel.

Much to our disgust we were going back by sea instead of flying back to this country. We were in Ostend harbour when news came through that the Germans had conceded defeat. The only initial excitement was that everybody threw up their hats, the lieutenant commander in charge of the navy boat threw his hat in the air forgetting that we were under way, so it fell over board and he launched a boat to get it. After that RN opened up the liquor store and we don't remember a lot until we got back to England.

Norman Crookes DFC and 2 Bars, US (DFC), ended the war with twelve enemy aircraft destroyed and two damaged, although one of those credited as damaged has recently been confirmed as a destroyed. Norman took his place as the highest-scoring night fighter navigator of 85 Group.

Subsequent to the crossing of the Rhine the 1st Canadian Army had two responsibilities, to open and maintain a supply route through Arnhem and to clear north-east and western Holland. These tasks would all be rapidly achieved, ably supported by 84 Group. Derek Lovell had enjoyed the last week of March 1945 on leave, but he would be back at the start of April, to be part of 197 Squadron's support to the push on the far left flank of the Allied advance. It was armed recces again as the tactical fighters tried to destroy the retreating enemy. As the front line edged north the tactical squadrons came up behind. Derek Lovell's logbook gives a good example of the nature of operations:

2 April – Ramrod. Telephone exchange near Utrecht. Good bombing.

7 April – Armed Recce. Returned as whole area was 10/10 cloud.
7 April – Armed Recce. No joy at all. No MT or anything.
8 April – Armed Recce. Found some odd MT. 2 dest & 2 damaged.
9 April – Armed Recce. No joy at all. Weather duff on way out.
11 April – Armed Recce. Found a V1 store. Large explosion. Destroyed 1 MT self.
11 April – Armed Recce. No joy, too hazy & rather late, a little flak.
12 April – Armed Recce. No joy. No. 2 engine cut, sent him home with No. 3.
13 April – Armed Recce. No joy, only saw 1 civilian bus, did not attack.
14 April – Ramrod. All returned weather u/s.
16 April – Nickel raid. Private raid on Edewecht, very nice & quiet. Landed in Germany.
16 April – From B.105 to B.89. Landed at B.105 from above op. Not enough gas for home.
16 April – To B.105 from B.89. Unit move to Germany. Bullshit formation.

Flight Lieutenant H. Neville Thomas recorded the Wing's move to Germany.

In Germany at last! Today, 16 April 1945, the Wing moved to Drope, a few miles north-east of Lingen. From this airfield our major commitment was changed to shipping 'strikes' in and around the north Dutch Islands, though time was still found to carry out Wing attacks on special targets in Oldenburg district.[84]

Derek Lovell recorded in his logbook his contribution to these operations.

17 April – Ramrod. Army stores in Oldenburg – wizard prang.
17 April – Ramrod. Para Regt HQ in Brickyard – wizard prang.
23 April – Ramrod. Convoy nr Wangerooge. Very near misses, fair amount of flak.
25 April – Ramrod. Attacked two large ships in convoy off Cuxhaven, hits. My dear the flak!

Derek Lovell: Cuxhaven was very heavily defended. It was a Ramrod with the new CO, he was leading Green section and I was leading the other section. I saw him going down and he said, 'The flak's too bad don't come down.' By the time he peeled over I'd caught up with him and I went down and by God it wasn't half coming up from half a dozen flak ships, but none of us got hit.

28 April – Shipping & Weather Recce. Round Dutch Islands (Frisian). Not much seen.
29 April – Ramrod. HQ in Leer. Good bombing – no flak, very quiet.

On 18 April the US Third Army had entered Czechoslovakia, and the next day the US Ninth Army seized Leipzig and the British 2nd Army was at the Elbe. On 20 April the French 1st Army captured Stuttgart. Allied and Russian forces

---

84 *The Odyssey of No. 146 Wing* compiled by Senior Intelligence Officer Flight Lieutenant H. Neville Thomas. September 1945.

linked at the Elbe on the 25th and in the last week of April Berlin was under siege and the ring collapsed. Bremen was surrendered on 26 April. On 30 April the Reichstag was taken. On 2 May the German forces in Berlin surrendered to the Russians and on the same day British troops took Lübeck and Wismar and Canadian forces arrived in Oldenburg. On 7 May at Reims the unconditional surrender was signed. But even though German resistance was collapsing rapidly, the land, sea and air forces stayed on the offensive right to the end of the war.

On 30 April 146 Wing made its last move to Ahlhorn, south-west of Bremen. Weather put paid to operations at the start of May but on the 3rd the Wing was ordered to fly to B.150, Hustedt, a few miles north of Celle, to act under 83 Group control against shipping in the Baltic, attempting to hinder any enemy escape to Norway. In the first few days of May it appeared to Allied intelligence that German forces were attempting to make a retreat across the Baltic to Norway, with various types of ships assembling in the bays of Lübeck and Kiel. On the 3rd, therefore, a concentrated attack was made from the air.

> The ships were concentrated in an area about 40 miles north of Kiel to Fehrman Island, situated off the northern tip of Lübeck Bay. Other ships were still waiting to leave Lübeck, Schwerin Bay and Kiel. In all there were about 500 craft of all descriptions. At SHAEF it was believed that important Nazis who had escaped from Berlin to Flensburg were on board and were fleeing to Norway or neutral countries.
>
> As the Navy were unable to reach the area because of the minefields in the Kattegat an all out air effort was planned to block this last escape hole. RAF Coastal and Fighter Commands and the Ninth Air Force were called upon to assist 2nd TAF.[85]

2nd TAF squadrons carried out 840 sorties on 3 May. 146 Wing and 197 Squadron took part in the action.

> *Derek Lovell:* We were told to go up to the Baltic and attack shipping. On our way up we passed another Typhoon squadron coming back, they'd set the *Cap Arcona* on fire. It was red hot head to stern. There was this other one, I was flying number 3 to the CO and I saw his bombs go down the aft hatch. When we pulled off his number 2, Pilot Officer Brookes, was streaming glycol. He had been hit by flak, so they were firing at us. I warned him and directed him over land in the direction of Denmark. He belly-landed in a field. He called me up, he was alright, and said, 'Which way should I run?' I said, 'Wait a minute and I'll have a look.' I said run to the right, away from the railway line, because I suddenly realised I was flying over a flak train which wasn't firing at me thanks be to God. I left him on the deck, there was nothing more I could do, then full throttle to catch the squadron up, which I did before we got home.

Brookes returned to the squadron the next day. The liners *Deutschland* (21,046 tons) and *Cap Arcona* (27,561 tons) were hit and sunk. Tragically the *Cap Arcona* had in fact been acting as a prison ship for concentration camp victims;

---

[85] Public Record Office AIR 41/67.

the *Deutschland* as a hospital ship. None of this was known to Allied intelligence when selected for attack. There was considerable loss of life.

On 4 May further attacks would be carried out on shipping, involving 197 Squadron. Derek Lovell would record the attack in his logbook and then go on to record the last few days of the war.

4 May – to B.150. Back once again for more ships.
4 May – Ramrod – Left 3 smoking. Last op for 84 Group in Germany.
4 May – Return to B.111. Low flying most of the way – good fun.
5 May – Air test. Holland, NW Germany surrender. My birthday.
7 May – Squadron Balbo. Showing the 'Flag' around Wilhelmshaven.
MAY 8TH V-E DAY

Derek Lovell: For about a week after 4 May, each squadron in turn stood to at dawn, in case there was any revival. We got up and they wanted us to go to Wilhelmshaven, 'The commander refuses to surrender, so go and show him who's in charge.' Around Wilhelmshaven there is an inland sea. The CO said we were not going to go over Wilhelmshaven at 500 feet because they may well decide to fire at us, so we came to this bay and gradually crept towards it turning, waiting to see if they would fire at us. As we were doing this they called up and said, 'It's alright he's surrendered. Just show him the flag.' So we flew up and down the main streets of Wilhelmshaven, as low as we dared making as much noise as we could.

On VE-Day the sergeants' mess took on the officers' mess. It was a German airfield but we were in these, like, country houses. The officers' mess was one side of the lawn, the sergeants' the other. So we had a battle with Verey pistols, firing at each other. One went through our CO's bedroom window. We all tore upstairs, put out the fire and chucked everything out of the window, in case it caught fire again. I recall one chap on the squadron lugging a railway sleeper onto a bonfire. There was rifle fire going on all over the place. We did go to the sergeants' mess for a party and that got a bit out of control.

In the week after VE-Day the Wing practiced for a victory parade, which took place on 15 May. Derek recalled, 'I remember we were in sections line astern, and on looking up and as far as you could see ahead of you were aircraft. It was an amazing sight.' After the victory celebrations had died down a little, thoughts went elsewhere.

Derek Lovell: We were all talking about when we were going to go to Japan. Then a bit later when the atom bomb dropped we all started to say things like, 'You know it's going to be a bit dodgy next time with atomic flak.'

On 8 May 1945, Prime Minister Winston Churchill addressed crowds in London.

My dear friends, this is your hour. This is not victory of a party or of any class. It's a victory of the great British nation as a whole. We were the first, in this ancient island, to draw the sword against tyranny. After a while we were left all alone against the most tremendous military power that has

> been seen. We were all alone for a whole year.

Churchill called to the crowd, 'Did anyone want to give in?' He received a resounding, 'No!' 'Were we downhearted?' Again the crowd responded, 'No!'

> The lights went out and the bombs came down. But every man, woman and child in the country had no thought of quitting the struggle. London can take it. So we came back after long months from the jaws of death, out of the mouth of hell, while all the world wondered. When shall the reputation and faith of this generation of English men and women fail? I say that in the long years to come not only will the people of this island but of the world, wherever the bird of freedom chirps in human hearts, look back to what we've done and they will say, 'Do not despair, do not yield to violence and tyranny, march straight forward and die if need be – unconquered.' . . . a terrible foe has been cast on the ground and awaits our judgement and our mercy.

Basil Collyns, Reg Baker, Hart Finley, Bill Jameson, Norman Crookes, Derek Lovell, Bob Cole and countless other RAF Fighter Command airmen, of all nationalities, had been part of the aerial victory over Western Europe. Two of the featured airmen in this book lost their lives. Long years have indeed passed since these particular men, indeed all the men of the RAF, fought the air battle. But their story is still worth recording and remembering, because they secured the freedom of the society in which their deeds could be told.

APPENDIX 1

Below is the chain of command to the main airmen featured in this book, June 1944.

Supreme Headquarters Allied Expeditionary Force (SHAEF)
Supreme Commander – General Dwight D. Eisenhower
Deputy Supreme Commander – Air Chief Marshal Sir Arthur W. Tedder

Headquarters Allied Expeditionary Air Forces (AEAF)
Air Officer Commander-in-Chief –
Air Chief Marshal Sir Trafford Leigh-Mallory

2nd Tactical Air Force
Air Officer Commanding – Air Marshal Sir Arthur Coningham

83 Group		
122 Wing	19 and 65 Squadron	Flight Lieutenant Basil Collyns
127 Wing	403 Squadron	Flight Lieutenant Hart Finley
84 Group		
146 Wing		Wing Commander Reg Baker
146 Wing	197 Squadron	Warrant Officer Derek Lovell
85 Group		
150 Wing	3 Squadron	Flight Sergeant Bob Cole
	488 (NZ) Squadron	Flight Lieutenant Bill Jameson
		Flying Officer Norman Crookes

APPENDIX 2

146 Wing's Record

	Tanks AFVs and M/T	Aircraft				
		In the air		On the ground		
Squadrons	**Dest.**	**Dam.**	**Dest.**	**Dam.**	**Dest.**	**Dam.**
193	111	189	6½	6	–	–
197	147	244	–	1	9	3
257	46	91	1½	5	–	–
263	90	94	1	–	–	–
266	285	276	2	2	3	4
Total	**679**	**894**	**14***	**15***	**12**	**7**

* Including 3 aircraft destroyed and 1 damaged by Group Captain Baldwin DSO, DFC, when Wing Commander Flying.

In addition 146 Wing made the following shipping claims.
Cat. I 35,000 tons
Cat. II 32,000 tons, plus a dredger, two ferries and a number of small boats.
Cat. III 22,000 tons, plus a dredger, four ferries, two sailing vessels and an M/L.
35 Barges and Tugs have been destroyed and 156 damaged.

Bombs, R/P, and 20mm cannon shells expended

From date of formation 1 February 1944 to D-Day

	Missions	Sorties	1,000 lb	500 lb	R/P	20mm
	130	1,986	–	3,547	–	229,795

D-Day to 4 May 1945

	Missions	Sorties	1,000 lb	500 lb	R/P	20mm
	1,755	14,840	2,118	13,791	22,407	1,173,862
Total	**1,885**	**16,826**	**2,118**	**17,338**	**22,407**	**1,403,657**

PRIMARY SOURCES

Much of the first-hand information has come from interviews and correspondence with numerous RAF veterans, and their family members. I have also consulted the personal papers of RAF veterans held at the Imperial War Museum, London and at RAF Museum, Hendon. At all times I have sought to cross reference their recollections with official documents. With regard the papers of Flight Lieutenant G. Millington and Flight Lieutenant R. J. Unstead, these collections are held in the Department of Documents at the Imperial War Museum. Every effort has been made to contact the copyright holders but this has not always been possible.

The main source of official documents has been the files kept at the Public Record Office, London (detailed as notes in the main narrative of the book).

BIBLIOGRAPHY

The publication dates are the editions consulted, rather than the first year of publication.

Darlow, S. *Lancaster Down!* (Grub Street, 2000).

Darlow, S. *Sledgehammers for Tintacks* (Grub Street, 2002).

Darlow, S. *D-Day Bombers – The Veterans' Story* (Grub Street, 2004).

Delve, K. *D-Day, The Air Battle* (Arms and Armour Press, 1994).

D'Este, C. *Decision in Normandy* (Penguin, 2001).

Eisenhower, D. *D-Day to VE-Day: General Eisenhower's Report 1944-45.* (London: The Stationery Office, 2000).

Eisenhower, D. *Crusade in Europe* (William Heinemann Ltd, 1948).

Foreman, J. *Fighter Command War Diaries July 1943 to June 1944* (Air Research Publications, 2002).

Forty, G. *The Armies of Rommel* (Arms and Armour, 1999).

Franks, N. *Search Find and Kill, Coastal Command's U-boat Successes* (Grub Street, 1995).

Franks, N. *Typhoon Attack* (Grub Street, 2003).

Franks, N. *Royal Air Force Fighter Command Losses of the Second World War: Vol. 3* (Midland Publishing, 2000).

Golley, J. *The Day of the Typhoon* (Patrick Stephens Ltd, 1986)

Hastings, M. *Overlord: D-Day & The Battle for Normandy* (Simon & Schuster, 1985).

Hunt, L. *Defence Until Dawn – The Story of 488 NZ Squadron* (1949).

Liddell Hart, B. H. *The Other Side of the Hill* (Pan Books, 1999).

Murray, W. *The Luftwaffe 1933-45, Strategy for Defeat* (Brasseys, 1996).

Oliver, D. *Fighter Command 1939-45* (Harper Collins, 2000).

Price, Dr A. *The Luftwaffe Data Book* (Greenhill Books, 1997).

Rawnsley, C. F. & Wright, R. *Night Fighter* (Crécy, 1998).

Shores, C. & Thomas, C. *The Typhoon & Tempest Story* (Arms and Armour Press, 1988).

Shores, C. & Williams, C. *Aces High* (Grub Street, 1994).

Shores, C. *Aces High Volume 2* (Grub Street, 1999).

Shores, C. *Those Other Eagles* (Grub Street, 2004).

Terraine, J. *The Right of the Line* (Hodder and Stoughton, 1985).

Tedder, Lord, *With Prejudice, The War Memoirs of Marshal of the Royal Air Force Lord Tedder G. C. B.* (Cassell and Company Ltd, 1966).

Various authors, *The Battle of Britain* (Salamander Books, 1997).

Wilmot, C., *The Struggle for Europe* (Collins, 1952).

INDEX

Asterisks (*) indicate a Bar to an award.